ZAGATSURVEY®
25TH ANNIVERSARY

2004

MIAMI SO. FLORIDA RESTAURANTS

Local Editors: Victoria Pesce Elliott, Rochelle Koff and Jan Norris

Local Coordinators: Victoria Pesce Elliott and Deirdre Sykes Shapiro

Editor: Laura Mitchell

Published and distributed by
ZAGAT SURVEY, LLC
4 Columbus Circle
New York, New York 10019
Tel: 212 977 6000
E-mail: miami@zagat.com
Web site: www.zagat.com

Acknowledgments

In Dade and Monroe counties, our sincere thanks to: Elizabeth Adams, Zoyla I. Córdoba, Sabylizst Diaz, Edith Edwards, Eric R. Elliott, Sophia and Rose Elliott, Pilar Haro, Sharon Ives of In the Biz, Susan Kochan, Carole Kotkin, Kathy Martin and all Les Dames d'Escoffier, Helen Morales, The School of Hospitality at Florida International University, Paul and Eleanor Pesce, Dr. Lenny Sakrais of La Chaine des Rotisseurs, Lee Brian Schrager, Kathy Sinnes and Elizabeth Smith of *Wine News,* The South Florida Chapter of the American Institute of Wine & Food, Zoraya Suarez, Susi Westfall and the City Theater, and all the Women on the Verge.

In Broward and Palm Beach Counties, we thank: Jimmy Barron, Joe Bonikowski, Ilene Fetsch of the Kravis Center for the Performing Arts, Lou Ann Frala, Lee Gordon, Rand Hoch, Katrin Hussman, Bonnie Kaye, Michael Kenny, Taylor Morgan, Jason and Jennifer Norris, Joyce Reingold of the *Palm Beach Daily News,* Bill Selmier, Fred Shapiro, Scott Simmons, Mark Spivak, Nancy Stewart, Katie and Davis Ward, and Philip Ward.

This guide would not have been possible without the hard work of our staff, especially Caren Campbell, Reni Chin, Carol Diuguid, Schuyler Frazier, Michael Gitter, Katherine Harris, Natalie Lebert, Mike Liao, Dave Makulec, Jennifer Napuli, Emily Parsons, Rob Poole, Robert Seixas, Daniel Simmons, Yoji Yamaguchi and Sharon Yates.

The reviews published in this guide are based on public opinion surveys, with numerical ratings reflecting the average scores given by all survey participants who voted on each establishment and text based on direct quotes from, or fair paraphrasings of, participants' comments. Phone numbers, addresses and other factual information were correct to the best of our knowledge when published in this guide; any subsequent changes may not be reflected.

© 2003 Zagat Survey, LLC
ISBN 1-57006-555-1
Printed in the United States of America

Contents

About This Survey	5
What's New	6
Ratings & Symbols	7
MIAMI/DADE COUNTY	
Most Popular Places	9
Top Ratings	
• Food; Cuisines, Features, Locations	10
• Decor; Outdoors, Romance, Rooms, Views	13
• Service	14
• Best Buys	15
Restaurant Directory	
Names, Addresses, Phone Numbers, Web Sites, Ratings and Reviews	17
THE KEYS/MONROE COUNTY	
Top Ratings	
• Most Popular, Food, Decor and Service	90
Restaurant Directory	
Names, Addresses, Phone Numbers, Web Sites, Ratings and Reviews	90
FT. LAUDERDALE/BROWARD COUNTY	
Most Popular Places	113
Top Ratings	
• Food; Cuisines, Features, Locations	114
• Decor; Outdoors, Romance, Rooms, Views	116
• Service	117
• Best Buys	118
Restaurant Directory	
Names, Addresses, Phone Numbers, Web Sites, Ratings and Reviews	119
PALM BEACH/PALM BEACH COUNTY	
Most Popular Places	157
Top Ratings	
• Food; Cuisines, Features, Locations	158
• Decor; Outdoors, Romance, Rooms, Views	160
• Service	161
• Best Buys	162
Restaurant Directory	
Names, Addresses, Phone Numbers, Web Sites, Ratings and Reviews	163
INDEXES	
Cuisines	208
Locations	221
Special Features	
Boat Docking Facilities	233
Breakfast	233
Brunch	234
Buffet Served	235

Business Dining	235
Catering	236
Celebrity Chefs	238
Child-Friendly	239
Dancing	243
Delivery	243
Dessert	244
Dining Alone	245
Early-Bird Menus	246
Entertainment	247
Historic Places	248
Hotel Dining	249
"In" Places	250
Late Dining	251
Meet for a Drink	252
Microbreweries	253
Noteworthy Newcomers	253
Offbeat	254
Outdoor Dining	255
People-Watching	258
Power Scenes	260
Private Rooms	261
Prix Fixe Menus	263
Quiet Conversation	263
Raw Bars	264
Reserve Ahead	265
Romantic Places	266
Singles Scenes	267
Sleepers	268
Teen Appeal	269
Theme Restaurants	269
Views	270
Visitors on Expense Account	271
Waterside	272
Winning Wine Lists	273
Alphabetical Page Index	275
Wine Chart	284

About This Survey

Here are the results of our *2004 Miami/So. Florida Restaurant Survey*, covering 1,042 restaurants as tested, and tasted, by over 4,600 avid local restaurant-goers. This marks the 25th year that Zagat Survey has reported on the shared experiences of diners like you.

What started in 1979 in New York as a hobby involving 200 friends rating local restaurants has come a long way: Today we have over 250,000 surveyors and have branched out to cover entertaining, golf, hotels, movies, music, nightlife, resorts, shopping, spas and theater. Most of these guides are also available by subscription at **zagat.com**, where you can vote and shop as well.

By regularly surveying large numbers of avid customers, we hope to have achieved a uniquely current and reliable guide. A quarter-century of experience has verified this. This year's participants dined out an average of 3.6 times per week, meaning this *Survey* is based on roughly 870,000 meals. Of these surveyors, 46% are women, 54% men; the breakdown by age is 13% in their 20s; 23%, 30s; 21%, 40s; 24%, 50s; and 19%, 60s or above. Our editors have synopsized our surveyors' opinions, with their comments shown in quotation marks. We sincerely thank each of these surveyors; this book is really "theirs."

Of course, we are especially grateful to our editors and coordinators, Victoria Pesce Elliott, a freelance food and travel writer with the *Miami Herald*; Rochelle Koff, a restaurant critic, also with the *Miami Herald*; Jan Norris, food editor of *The Palm Beach Post*; and Deirdre Sykes Shapiro, a marketing and PR consultant in Palm Beach.

To help guide our readers to Southern Florida's best meals and best buys, we have prepared a number of lists. See top lists for Miami/Dade County (pages 9–16), Monroe County (page 90), Broward County (pages 113–118) and Palm Beach County (pages 157–162). In addition, we have provided 42 handy indexes and have tried to be concise. Also, for the first time, we have included Web addresses.

To join any of our upcoming *Surveys*, just register at zagat.com. Each participant will receive a free copy of the resulting guide when published. Your comments and even criticisms of this guide are also solicited. There is always room for improvement with your help. You can contact us at miami@zagat.com. We look forward to hearing from you.

New York, NY
November 27, 2003

Nina and Tim Zagat

What's New

Despite a downturn in tourism, South Florida restaurateurs are offering lots to celebrate.

Miami Rhapsody: Coral Gables is experiencing a Nuevo Latino moment with the debuts of Cacao 1737, Carmen The Restaurant from chef Carmen Gonzalez and Robbin Haas' Chispa. Meanwhile, Miami Beach is benefiting from the union of chefs Andrea Curto and Frank Randazzo at the New American Talula. In South Beach, the gorgeous Italian Casa Tua is wowing all comers, and the Upper East Side continues to flourish with Citronelle, a Caribbean, and the return of Douglas Rodriguez at year's end with OLA.

Broward Springs Forward: Among Lauderdale newcomers making a splash are Bungalow 9, serving New American cuisine, Red Coral offering Pan-Asian on Las Olas and the high-end Sublime giving vegetarians a victory. Cohiba Brasserie brings Eclectic fare to Pembroke Pines, while Josef's is introducing locals to Austrian-influenced Northern Italian in Plantation.

Palm Beach Story: Daniel Boulud's long-awaited Café Boulud debuted in Palm Beach's newly renovated Brazilian Court Hotel, while chic Tsunami rolled into CityPlace with upscale Asian fare. John Spoto presented West Palm Beach with a branch of his popular Oyster Bar, and the Painted Horse Café offers Downtowners a cozy dining choice featuring New American dishes.

Farewell and Hail: Notable closings include La Broche in Miami and Baraboo in Miami Beach. Looking ahead, though, the city will see the openings of an Emeril Lagasse destination in the Loews Hotel. New American Harrison's on Fifth will debut in South Beach, and Norman Van Aken will branch out in the Gables with Mundo.

(No) Smokin': The hottest news affecting restaurants statewide is the smoking ban, though a loophole permits puffing inside eateries that get only 10% of their profits from food (read: bars). Our surveyors suggest the law is a breath of fresh air, with 30% indicating they'll eat out more and only 3% saying less.

Numbers Game: A positive side of the slow economy is that the average cost of a meal out has actually decreased in Broward County (-.1%) to $30.89 and Palm Beach (-1.2%) to $34.28, while increasing only incrementally in Miami (3.5%) to $30.93 and the Keys (3%) to $29.68. It's no wonder that 39% of our respondents report they're dining out more than they were two years ago.

Miami, FL
Ft. Lauderdale, FL
Palm Beach, FL
November 27, 2003

Victoria Pesce Elliott
Rochelle Koff
Jan Norris

Ratings & Symbols

Name, Address, Phone Number & Web Site

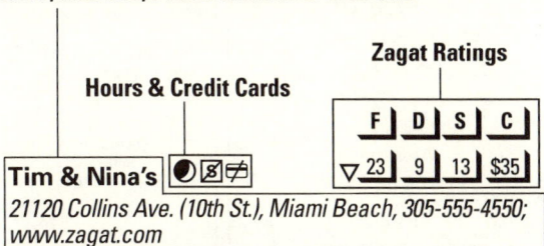

Zagat Ratings

Hours & Credit Cards

F	D	S	C
▽ 23	9	13	$35

Tim & Nina's ◐ ☒ ⌿

21120 Collins Ave. (10th St.), Miami Beach, 305-555-4550; www.zagat.com

☒ Reeling in fish fiends with its "all-around originality", this "trendy" South Beach seafooder in a "wacky setting" (watch out for the "enormous, talking stuffed marlin" by the door) features "fabulous" fare like lobster-and-roasted-octopus bruschetta; you may need to "shout your order" above this ocean's roar, but the "cheerful mates" steer the course straight every time; P.S. "be careful or they'll hook your wallet at meal's end."

Review, with surveyors' comments in quotes

Restaurants with the highest overall ratings and greatest popularity and importance are printed in CAPITAL LETTERS.

Before reviews a symbol indicates whether responses were uniform ■ or mixed ☒.

Hours: ◐ serves after 11 PM
☒ closed on Sunday

Credit Cards: ⌿ no credit cards accepted

Ratings: Food, Decor and Service are rated on a scale of **0** to **30**. The Cost (C) column reflects our surveyors' estimate of the price of dinner including one drink and tip.

F	Food	D	Decor	S	Service	C	Cost
23		9		13		$35	

0–9   poor to fair
10–15 fair to good
16–19 good to very good

20–25 very good to excellent
26–30 extraordinary to perfection
▽ low response/less reliable

For places listed without ratings or a numerical cost estimate, such as an important newcomer or a popular write-in, the price range is indicated by the following symbols.

I	$15 and below	**E**	$31 to $50
M	$16 to $30	**VE**	$51 or more

vote at zagat.com

Miami/Dade County's Most Popular

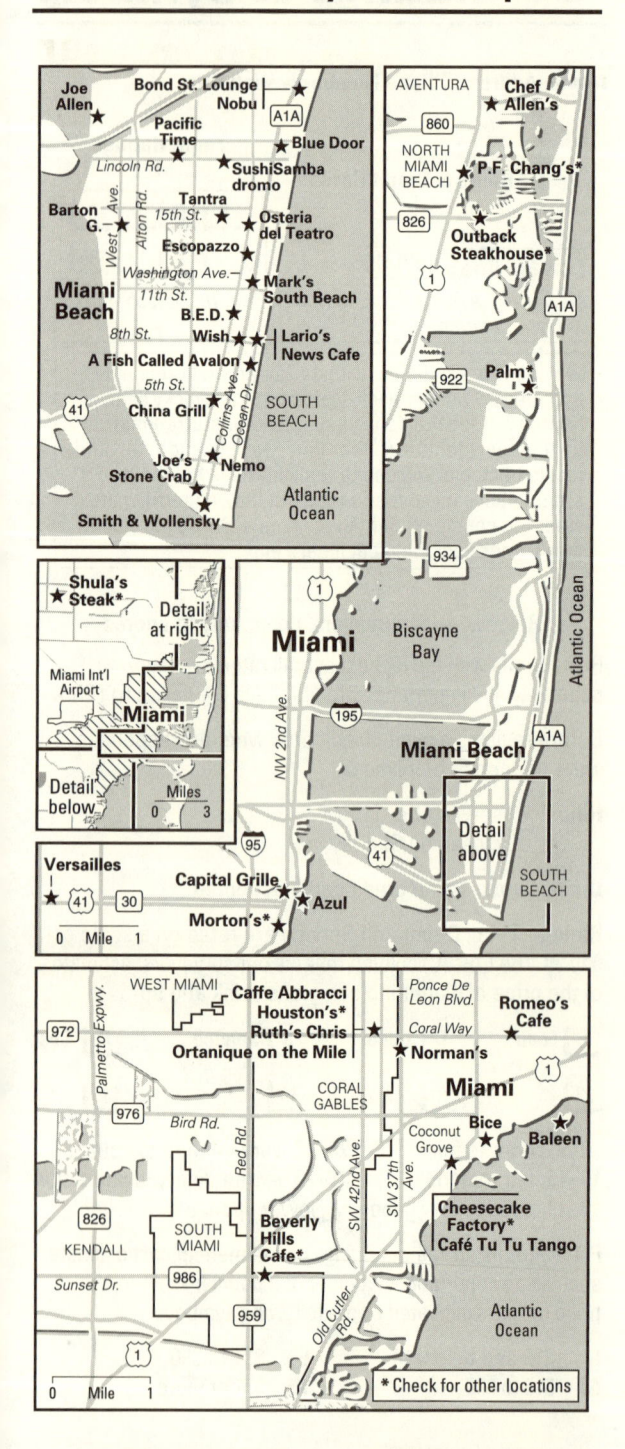

Miami/Dade County's Most Popular

1. Joe's Stone Crab
2. Cheesecake Factory
3. Norman's
4. Chef Allen's
5. Blue Door
6. Pacific Time
7. Nobu Miami Beach
8. Azul
9. News Cafe
10. Ruth's Chris*
11. Houston's
12. Morton's
13. Outback Steakhse.
14. China Grill
15. Ortanique on the Mile
16. P.F. Chang's
17. Baleen
18. Palm
19. Tantra
20. Nemo
21. Smith & Wollensky
22. Mark's South Beach
23. Caffe Abbracci
24. Osteria del Teatro
25. Bice Rist.
26. Capital Grille
27. Barton G.
28. Wish
29. Beverly Hills Cafe
30. SushiSamba dromo
31. Escopazzo
32. Bond St. Lounge
33. Café Tu Tu Tango
34. Joe Allen
35. Shula's Steak
36. Versailles*
37. B.E.D.
38. Romeo's Cafe*
39. Lario's on the Beach
40. A Fish Called Avalon

It's obvious that many of the restaurants on the above list are among South Florida's most expensive, but if popularity were calibrated to price, we suspect that a number of other restaurants would join the above ranks. Given the fact that both our surveyors and readers love to discover dining bargains, we have added a list of nearly 80 Best Buys on page 15. These are restaurants that give real quality at extremely reasonable prices.

---

* Indicates a tie with restaurant above

vote at zagat.com

Top Ratings

Top lists exclude restaurants with low voting.

Top 40 Food

- **28** Chef Allen's
  - Shibui
  - Nobu Miami Beach
- **27** Norman's
  - Tropical Chinese
- **26** Joe's Stone Crab
  - Cacao 1737
  - Osteria del Teatro
  - Ortanique on the Mile
  - Romeo's Cafe
  - Mark's South Beach
  - Azul
  - Capital Grille
  - Pascal's on Ponce
  - Francesco
  - Pit Bar-B-Q
- **25** Matsuri
  - Toni's Sushi Bar
  - Café Ragazzi
  - Miss Saigon Bistro
  - Palm
  - Tuscan Steak
  - Bangkok Bangkok
  - Fish Joynt
  - Nemo
  - Escopazzo
  - Tony Chan's
  - Pacific Time
  - Grazie Cafe
  - Bond St. Lounge
  - Shoji
  - Caffe Abbracci
  - Carmen
  - Caffe Vialetto
  - Ruth's Chris
- **24** Blue Sea
  - Baleen
  - Wish
  - Su Shin
  - Café Pastis

By Cuisine

American (New)
- **27** Norman's
- **25** Nemo
- **24** 1220 at the Tides
  - Icebox Café
- **23** Pelican Café

American (Traditional)
- **22** Christine Lee's
- **21** Joe Allen
  - Front Porch Cafe
  - Houston's
- **20** Cheesecake Factory

Caribbean
- **26** Ortanique on the Mile
  - Azul
- **25** Caffe Vialetto
- **23** TapTap Haitian
- **21** Versailles

Chinese
- **27** Tropical Chinese
- **25** Tony Chan's
- **22** Christine Lee's
- **21** P.F. Chang's
- **20** Two Dragons

Continental
- **24** Crystal Cafe
  - Bizcaya Grill
- **23** Fleming - Taste of Denmark
- **22** Piccadilly Garden
- **20** La Paloma

Cuban
- **24** Las Culebrinas
- **21** Versailles
- **20** Yuca
  - Latin American
  - Puerto Sagua

Delis/Sandwich Shops
- **24** La Sandwicherie
- **20** Perricone's
  - Paninoteca
- **18** Bagels & Co.
- **17** Arnie & Richie's

Floribbean/New World
- **28** Chef Allen's
- **27** Norman's
- **26** Mark's South Beach
- **24** Baleen

10   subscribe to zagat.com

Top Food

French
- **26** Azul
  Pascal's on Ponce
- **24** Wish
  Forge, The
  Blue Door

French (Bistro)
- **24** Café Pastis
- **23** Le Bouchon du Grove
- **21** Le Provençal
- **19** Provence Grill
- **18** L'Entrecôte de Paris

Hamburgers
- **17** Big Pink
  Beverly Hills Cafe
- **16** Gables Diner
  Tobacco Road
  Roadhouse Grill

Italian
- **26** Osteria del Teatro
  Romeo's Cafe
- **25** Café Ragazzi
  Escopazzo
  Grazie Cafe

Japanese
- **28** Shibui
  Nobu Miami Beach
- **25** Matsuri
  Toni's Sushi Bar
  Bond St. Lounge

Latin American
- **26** Cacao 1737
  Francesco
- **25** Carmen
- **24** Graziano's
  Porcão

Pan-Asian
- **25** Pacific Time
- **24** Cafe Sambal
- **23** China Grill
- **22** Lan

Pizza
- **23** La Gastronomia
  Pizza Rustica
  Andiamo!
  Spris
  Piola

Seafood
- **26** Joe's Stone Crab
  Francesco
- **25** Fish Joynt
- **24** Baleen
- **23** AltaMar

Steakhouses
- **26** Capital Grille
- **25** Palm
  Tuscan Steak
  Ruth's Chris
- **24** Morton's

By Special Feature

Breakfast
- **24** La Sandwicherie
  El Toro Taco
- **23** Abbey Dining Rm.
  Le Bouchon du Grove
- **22** Garcia's

Brunch
- **27** Tropical Chinese
- **25** Nemo
- **24** Baleen
  SushiSamba dromo
  1220 at the Tides

Hotel Dining
- **26** Mark's South Beach
  Nash Hotel
  Azul
  Mandarin Oriental
- **25** Tony Chan's
  Doubletree Grand
  Bond St. Lounge
  Townhouse Hotel
  Carmen
  David William Hotel

vote at zagat.com

Top Food

Newcomers/Unrated
Chispa
Pilar
River Oyster Bar
Talula
Tambo

People-Watching
28 Nobu Miami Beach
26 Joe's Stone Crab
   Mark's South Beach
25 Toni's Sushi Bar
   Palm

Waterside Dining
26 Pit Bar-B-Q
25 Tony Chan's
24 Baleen
   Cafe Sambal
23 Smith & Wollensky

Winning Wine Lists
28 Chef Allen's
27 Norman's
26 Joe's Stone Crab
   Cacao 1737
   Ortanique on the Mile

By Location

Brickell Area
26 Azul
24 Morton's
   Cafe Sambal
21 Sushi Siam
20 Perricone's

Coconut Grove
24 Baleen
   Bizcaya Grill
   Las Culebrinas*
23 Le Bouchon du Grove
22 Anokha

Coral Gables
27 Norman's
26 Cacao 1737
   Ortanique on the Mile
   Pascal's on Ponce
   Francesco

Downtown
26 Capital Grille
25 Tony Chan's
24 La Loggia
   Las Culebrinas
   Porcão

Kendall
28 Shibui
25 Bangkok Bangkok
24 Su Shin
23 Trattoria Luna
22 Lan

Little Havana
22 Casa Juancho
   Hy-Vong
21 Versailles
19 Islas Canarias
17 La Carreta

Miami Beach
24 Cafe Prima Pasta
   Forge, The
   Crystal Cafe
21 Las Vacas Gordas
   Shula's Steak

North Dade
28 Chef Allen's
25 Fish Joynt
24 Morton's
22 Bella Luna
   Kampai

South Beach
28 Nobu Miami Beach
26 Joe's Stone Crab
   Osteria del Teatro
   Mark's South Beach
25 Toni's Sushi Bar

South Miami
24 Café Pastis
23 Siam Palace
22 Two Chefs
   Grappa
   Blu la Pizzeria

subscribe to zagat.com

Top 40 Decor

29 Casa Tua
27 Pearl
  Barton G.
  Blue Door
  Azul
  Baleen
26 Nikki Beach
  Tantra
  Touch
  Cacao 1737
  Blue Sea
25 Red Fish Grill
  1200 at the Biltmore
  Cafe Sambal
  Capital Grille
  Wish
  Forge, The
  Pescado
  B.E.D.
  Norman's

24 Ristorante La Bussola
  Aria
  1220 at the Tides
  Bizcaya Grill
  Metro Kitchen + Bar
  SushiSamba dromo
  Don Quixote
23 Restaurant St. Michel
  Ortanique on the Mile
  Chef Allen's
  China Grill
  Abbey Dining Rm.
  La Loggia
  Rumi
  Red Thai Room
  La Palma
22 Rusty Pelican
  Two Dragons
  Nemo
  Smith & Wollensky

Outdoors

A La Folie
Baleen
Barton G.
Big Fish
Blue Door
Elia

Grass Lounge
Joe's Seafood
Nikki Beach
Nina Rest.
Red Fish Grill
Smith & Wollensky

Romance

A La Folie
Baleen
Escopazzo
La Palma
Melody Inn
Nina Rest.

Palme d'Or
Piccadilly Garden
Restaurant St. Michel
Ristorante La Bussola
Trattoria Sole
1200 at the Biltmore

Rooms

Barton G.
Blue Door
Casa Tua
Chispa

Palme d'Or
Pearl
River Oyster Bar
Timo

Views

A Fish Called Avalon
Aquatica
Baleen
Big Fish
Chart House
Garcia's

Red Fish Grill
Rusty Pelican
Smith & Wollensky
Tony Chan's
Torero
1220 at the Tides

vote at zagat.com

Top 40 Service

- *26* Chef Allen's
- Romeo's Cafe
- Norman's
- *25* Café Ragazzi
- Azul
- Capital Grille
- Bizcaya Grill
- Ristorante La Bussola
- Grazie Cafe
- *24* Blue Sea
- Crystal Cafe
- Escopazzo
- Cacao 1737
- Pascal's on Ponce
- Christy's
- Palm
- Osteria del Teatro
- Forge, The
- Cafe Sambal
- Shibui
- Caffe Abbracci
- *23* Ruth's Chris
- Peppy's in the Gables
- Fleming - Taste of Denmark
- Aria
- La Loggia
- Morton's
- Melody Inn
- Carmen
- Caffe Vialetto
- Miss Saigon Bistro
- Trattoria Luna
- Edelweiss
- Ortanique on the Mile
- Mark's South Beach
- AltaMar
- *22* La Dorada
- Nobu Miami Beach
- Tuscan Steak
- 1200 at the Biltmore

Best Buys

Top 40 Bangs for the Buck

1. Dogma
2. Bellante's Pizza
3. La Sandwicherie
4. Mrs. Mendoza's
5. Baja Fresh
6. San Loco
7. Pizza Rustica
8. Picnics at Allen's
9. Bagels & Co.
10. Cafe Demetrio
11. Daily Bread
12. Texas Taco Factory
13. Original Daily Bread
14. Pit Bar-B-Q
15. Andiamo! Pizza
16. Taco Rico Tex-Mex
17. El Toro Taco
18. Shorty's Barbecue
19. Siam Palace
20. Piola
21. Bar, The
22. Big Cheese
23. Latin American
24. Laurenzo's Cafe
25. Mario the Baker
26. Sergio's
27. Berries
28. Granny Feelgood's
29. Blu la Pizzeria
30. Bar-B-Q Barn
31. La Loggia
32. Paninoteca
33. Scotty's Landing
34. 11th St. Diner
35. Spris
36. Bamboo Garden
37. Puerto Sagua
38. Mama Jennie's
39. Flanigans
40. Here Comes the Sun

Other Good Values

Archie's Gourmet Pizza
Arnie & Richie's
Ayestaran
Bahamas Fish Market
Balans
Bella Luna
Big Cheese
Crab House
Crystal Cafe
Disco Fish
El Novillo
Fancy's
Garcia's
La Gastronomia
Las Culebrinas
Las Vacas Gordas
Lemon Twist
Lincoln Road Café
Maroosh
Miyako
Old Cutler Oyster
Piccadilly Cafeteria
Pilar
Piola
Red Lantern
Red Thai Room
S&S
Sushi Maki
Sushi Rock
Sushi Saigon
Trattoria Luna
Tuna's

vote at zagat.com

Miami/Dade County Restaurant Directory

Miami/Dade County F | D | S | C |

Abbey Dining Room 23 | 23 | 20 | $41
Abbey Hotel, 300 21st St. (Collins Ave.), Miami Beach, 305-531-0033
■ Oft-"overlooked because of its location" in the "beautifully restored" Abbey Hotel in South Beach across from the Bass Museum, this "treasure" treats intrepid types to "inventive" "Moroccan-inspired" Med dishes such as "delicious tagines" and "great chicken and fish"; the "serene" setting is "refreshingly free of design gimmickry", and the "friendly" service and "quiet" ambiance make it worth a pilgrimage.

A Fish Called Avalon 21 | 20 | 20 | $43
Avalon Majestic, 700 Ocean Dr. (7th St.), Miami Beach, 305-532-1727
■ A "favorite in the fun zone" that is SoBe, this seafooder in the "unpretentious" Avalon Majestic offers an "excellent experience" with "terrific" fin fare and "friendly" service; the "deco" decor's "cute" inside, but "people-watchers" opt for the "pleasant" patio overlooking "bustling Ocean Drive."

Ago ◐ 20 | 22 | 18 | $52
Shore Club Hotel, 1901 Collins Ave. (bet. 19th & 20th Sts.), Miami Beach, 305-695-3226
◪ With co-owner Bob De Niro's name on the marquee and a "majestic Shore Club setting", this SoBe sequel to the "famous LA" "hot spot" is bound to attract the "tragically hip" who prefer a "glamorous pool view" with their pizza; the Northern Italian fare's "straightforward and delicious", and if the service is a tad "disorganized" and offerings "overpriced", the "beautiful people" don't seem to mind.

A La Folie ◐ ▽ 19 | 18 | 17 | $17
516 Española Way (Drexel Ave.), Miami Beach, 305-538-4484
■ Champions cheer this Miami Beach "charming bistro where the French really do hang out" to dine on "cheap" but "amazing" crêpe-focused fare in a "lovely" setting that "transports you to your favorite Left Bank cafe"; the clientele's "beautiful" (as is the "eye-candy" staff), and the "new outdoor garden adds a nice, romantic touch."

Alcazar ▽ 16 | 19 | 19 | $33
7711 SW 40th St./Bird Rd. (SW 77th Ave.), Westchester, 305-261-7249
◪ This Westchester Spaniard boasts "elegant", "dark rooms with well-lit art on the walls" that make you "think you're in Madrid", as do impeccable" servers who don't always "speak English"; the food, however, wavers from "excellent" to "unexceptional", and some insist it's "overpriced."

AltaMar 23 | 15 | 23 | $36
1223 Lincoln Rd. (Alton Rd.), Miami Beach, 305-532-3061
■ "Gracious" chef-owner Claudio Giordano "keeps tabs on everything" at this SoBe "gem" tucked away from "the

Miami/Dade County   F | D | S | C

zoo that is Lincoln Road proper"; the Med-inspired seafood and pastas are "fresh" and "fantastic", the staff's "super" and the prices are quite "reasonable" according to the local "condo crew" and movie-going regulars; however, some say occasionally "rushed" service in the "small" setting mars the experience.

Amalfi   20 | 17 | 18 | $38
1930 Ponce de Leon Blvd. (bet. Majorca & Navarra Aves.), Coral Gables, 305-444-3083

☑ "High ceilings", an indoor waterfall and "beautiful" decor "take you to another world" at this Coral Gables standby for "fresh", "wonderful" Italian fare ("don't fill up on the delicious bread" before tackling "favorites like osso buco") at "reasonable prices"; the service can be "attentive", though some say the "slow staff" coasts a bit.

Anacapri   21 | 14 | 20 | $30
12669 S. Dixie Hwy. (SW 128th St.), Pinecrest, 305-232-8001

☑ Pinecrest paesani insist this "terrific family-owned" "neighborhood" Italian is "worth a try" for "excellent", "simple" pastas and other "standards" as well as "great wines at great prices"; the service is "knowledgeable" and "friendly", but detractors dis the "cramped" Pinecrest strip-mall setting, adding "it could use some sprucing up."

Andiamo! Brick Oven Pizza   23 | 14 | 17 | $15
5600 Biscayne Blvd. (56th St.), Miami, 305-762-5751

■ "A fun and funky place" to multitask, this "outstanding" brick-oven pizzeria in a "cool up-and-coming area" known as the Upper East Side "adjoins an efficient carwash" and offers a "surprisingly pleasant" alfresco environment "overlooking Biscayne Boulevard; the "fantastic pizzas" embroil regulars in "great internal struggles" as they try to choose among "gourmet" toppings that include "goat cheese, truffle oil and portobellos."

Anokha   22 | 13 | 17 | $27
3195 Commodore Plaza (Grand Ave.), Coconut Grove, 786-552-1030

☑ "Considering that good Indian food is rare in Miami", this "dependable" "family-run" eatery in Coconut Grove is a boon for boosters who admire its "eclectic approach" and "fantastic vegetarian" options as well as "reasonable prices" and "great ambiance"; however, a few are tikka-ed off over "slow service" and "small portions" that make it "hard to share."

Aquatica Beach Bar and Grill ◐   – | – | – | M
Eden Roc Hotel, 4525 Collins Ave., Miami Beach, 305-531-0000; www.edenrocresort.com

Outside you have "the best view" of the shore and from inside you can look through a window overseeing the pool at this newcomer in the Eden Roc Hotel in Miami Beach;

Miami/Dade County | F | D | S | C |

the "cocktail selection's great", and the American fare features "creative" appetizers and "basic but exceptionally well-done entrees", all at a "good value."

Archie's Gourmet Pizza | 19 | 15 | 14 | $18 |
166 Giralda Ave. (Ponce de Leon Blvd.), Coral Gables, 305-444-1557 ☽
Winn-Dixie Shopping Ctr., 600 Crandon Blvd. (Sunrise Dr.), Key Biscayne, 305-365-5911

☑ "Bring your children" and "your ear plugs" to these "lively", "noisy" "brick-oven pizza joints" where "terrific", "unusual" pies as well as "abundant salads" offered in a "casual" setting please partisans; though a few are arch about the "slow", even "spaced-out" service, parents can while away the waits with an "excellent wine selection" in the Key Biscayne branch and a full bar in Coral Gables.

Aria | 24 | 24 | 23 | $62 |
Ritz-Carlton, 455 Grand Bay Dr. (Crandon Blvd.), Key Biscayne, 305-365-4500; www.ritzcarlton.com

☑ "The Ritz never disappoints", and this Key Biscayne Mediterranean with its "exquisite" fare and "outstanding" fish and game, a "beautiful" interior and "unparalleled" patio with ocean views plus "superior", "sincere" service is no exception; though counterpointers proclaim it "overpriced" and "not up to" the luxury chain's "standards", more maintain it provides a "world-class" experience.

Arnie & Richie's Deli | 17 | 5 | 15 | $14 |
525 41st St. (bet. Prairie & Royal Palm Aves.), Miami Beach, 305-531-7691

☑ Snowbirds longing for a "typical NYC deli" experience complete with "wise-ass" staff should fly to this Miami Beach "monument" that's been serving "bargain-priced" "piled-high sandwiches", "great" smoked fish and "good bagels and knishes" for nearly 60 years; the digs are admittedly "grungy" and "noisy", but that doesn't deter a "roomful of regulars."

Artichoke's | ▽ 18 | 11 | 14 | $23 |
Arcade Plaza, 3055 NE 163rd St. (bet. 30th & 31st Aves.), North Miami Beach, 305-945-7576

■ "When vegetarians want to share a meal with carnivore friends", they strap on their Birkenstocks and head to this "great local" North Miami Beach health fooder; "unique salads and soups" and "homestyle entrees" are all "fresh", "good" and "inexpensive", and the strip-mall setting is a definite step up from your usual juice bar.

Aura ☽ | 20 | 20 | 16 | $34 |
613 Lincoln Rd. (Pennsylvania Ave.), Miami Beach, 305-695-1100

☑ "A real standout among the throng on Lincoln Road" is this South Beach bistro, thanks in part to its "fabulous" Morris Lapidus–designed decor but also to the "excellent"

Miami/Dade County | F | D | S | C |

Eclectic fare ("you can't go wrong" with the signature pistachio-crusted sea bass); though some say its "aura is all about the outside dining and watching scintillating characters stroll by", more maintain it's a "winner."

Ayestaran ◐ ▽ 18 | 7 | 14 | $17
706 SW 27th Ave. (SW 8th St.), Miami, 305-649-4982

☑ Though it's another "basic Cuban" joint in Little Havana, this *veterano* turns what some consider the "best plantain soup" and sandwiches in town; the "no-nonsense service" and adjacent piano bar for cocktails make it "a great find" despite a lack of decor.

AZUL ⊠ 26 | 27 | 25 | $63
Mandarin Oriental Hotel, 500 Brickell Key Dr. (8th St.), Miami, 305-913-8358; www.mandarinoriental.com

☑ "Chef Michelle Bernstein has raised the bar" with the "trailblazing" Asian-accented French-Caribbean cuisine served at the Mandarin Oriental Hotel on Brickell Key near Downtown; the "tremendous views", "sleek", "elegant room", "accomplished" service and "serious wine list" also reap raves, but the "haunting" dishes and "exquisite presentations" elicit "bravas"; however, those unimpressed cite "overrated" offerings and "sky-high prices."

Bagel Emporium 16 | 6 | 13 | $14
University Ctr., 1238 S. Dixie Hwy. (Mariposa Ct.), Coral Gables, 305-666-0074

☑ For a "good schmear on a nice bagel", "University of Miami students and other deli lovers flock" to this Coral Gables "staple"; the other "comforting" comestibles like the "best matzo ball soup" are certainly "affordable", but oysayers slam the "sloppy service" and "mediocre" offerings; P.S. a recent redo may outdate the Decor score and quell complaints of "unattractive" digs.

Bagels & Co. 18 | 9 | 17 | $11
11064 Biscayne Blvd. (NE 110th Terrace), North Miami, 305-892-2435

■ Perhaps there's "something in the water", but North Miamians maintain this "terrific neighborhood" deli's "bagels are better than those in NYC"; the other "nicely prepared" noshes served by a "pleasant" staff are just as "great", and the "best and hardest working busboys" keep you "drowning in coffee" during the busy breakfast crunch.

Bahama Breeze ◐ 19 | 22 | 19 | $25
12395 SW 88th St. (Kendall Dr.), Kendall, 305-598-4040; www.bahamabreeze.com

■ Offering "more variety" and "spice" than you would expect from a chain, this Kendall Caribbean with outposts in Broward satisfies with its "large portions" of "creative", "delicious" fare and "cheerful service"; "long waits" are forgotten "after a couple of monster drinks", and the "lively

vote at zagat.com

Miami/Dade County F | D | S | C |

atmosphere" is enhanced by "live band performances" on the patio.

Bahamas Fish Market ∇ 19 | 6 | 16 | $19 |
2851 W. 68th St. (W. 28th Ave.), Hialeah, 305-818-7220
7200 SW Eighth St. (SW 73rd Ave.), West Miami, 305-264-1448
13399 SW 40th St. (133rd Ave.), West Miami, 305-225-4932
◪ "The freshest fish simply prepared" and "delicious" Cuban specialties are the calling card of this trio of "good" seafooders in Southwest Dade and Hialeah; the "loud" atmosphere and Spanish-speaking staff do not deter gringos who manage to order their "perennially favorite" dishes like whole fried yellowtail and cheer the "cheap" offerings.

Baja Fresh Mexican Grill 19 | 12 | 15 | $11 |
20 Miracle Mile (S. Douglas Rd.), Coral Gables, 305-442-9596; www.bajafresh.com
■ "We need more fast food like this" boast baja-bitués of this "welcome" new Coral Gables chain link serving "fresh", "healthy", "delicious" Mexican fare at "great" prices; standouts include the "awesome burritos" and "excellent" shrimp tacos accompanied by "top-notch" salsas, and though it's a bit "cramped" inside, the "fabulous" fare's fitting for "takeout and a movie night."

Balans ◐ 19 | 18 | 17 | $28 |
1022 Lincoln Rd. (bet. Lennox & Michigan Aves.), Miami Beach, 305-534-9191; www.balans.co.uk
◪ "If the Village People and the Sex Pistols had toured together", this London import in South Beach "might be where they'd go after the show" say surveyors smitten by the "late-night happy hour", "interesting" Eclectic menu, "tasty" fare at "decent prices" and "delightful setting on Lincoln Road" that provides brilliant "people-watching"; it also serves "fab breakfasts", but the "snooty" staff has bashers crying 'bollocks'; P.S. "beware the translucent bathroom doors" upstairs.

BALEEN 24 | 27 | 22 | $58 |
Grove Isle Hotel, 4 Grove Isle Dr. (S. Bayshore Dr.), Coconut Grove, 305-858-8300; www.groveisle.com
◪ "It doesn't get more gorgeous" than this "magical" Grove Isle Hotel seafooder with a "magnificent view" overlooking Biscayne Bay and a "romantic" interior with "adorable" monkey motif; the menu features "fantastic" fin fare along with "excellent" meat dishes and "innovative desserts", and even if the service is "lackluster", it's still "the perfect place to propose" or "escape reality – until you get the check."

Bali Café ⌗ – | – | – | I |
111 NE 2nd Ave. (NE 1st St.), Miami, 305-358-5751
Though few surveyors have discovered this Downtown lunch-only yearling, boosters on a Bali high hail it as an

Miami/Dade County | F | D | S | C |

"unpretentious little winner" offering "good", "beautifully presented" Indonesian food; the staff's "helpful", and prices are comparable to a meal at a Cuban diner.

Bamboo Club, The | 19 | 22 | 18 | $27 |
Aventura Mall, 19501 Biscayne Blvd. (William Lehman Cswy.), Aventura, 305-466-7100; www.thebambooclub.com
See review in Palm Beach County Directory.

Bamboo Garden | 19 | 12 | 17 | $17 |
13195 Biscayne Blvd. (NE 130th St.), North Miami, 305-899-9902
1222 NE 163rd St. (NE 12th Ave.), North Miami, 305-945-1722
■ For "moderately priced", "good" Cantonese-Szechuan including "delicious vegetarian dishes", these "local favorites" in North Dade and Broward "are sure to please"; though some sneer at garden-variety "Americanized" fare, others reveal there are "hidden treasures" on the dim sum menu (in Pembroke Pines only).

Bangkok Bangkok | 20 | 16 | 19 | $24 |
157 Giralda Ave. (Ponce de Leon Blvd.), Coral Gables, 305-444-2397
◪ "A great place for a casual meal" or "pre-theater jaunt", this "solid veteran" in the Gables offers "affordable", "carefully prepared", "terrific" Thai served by a "friendly" staff; however, critics complain the "cramped" setting "makes you feel as though you're in the middle of Bangkok."

BANGKOK BANGKOK | 25 | 15 | 22 | $25 |
Shops of Kendall, 12584 N. Kendall Dr. (bet. SW 125th & 127th Aves.), Kendall, 305-595-5839
◪ Lesser known than the same-named Coral Gables eatery (no relation) but "popular" nonetheless, this "small" South Dade Siamese in the Shops of Kendall has supporters willing to endure "long waits" and "lame decor" to dine on "excellent", "authentic", "quality" Thai; its "consistency" and "low prices" make it "always a pleasure."

Bar, The ◐ | 14 | 13 | 18 | $16 |
172 Giralda Ave. (Ponce de Leon Blvd.), Coral Gables, 305-442-2730; www.thebargables.com
■ Coral Gables barflies have descended on this "friendly" "old-style pub" since 1946 to "guzzle" a "great variety of beers" (more than 50) and "gobble" "greasy but delicious burgers" and other "stout-hearted" fare; sure it's "dark" and "loud" with the sounds of "yelling college kids" and "live music on Saturday nights", but it's no longer "too smoky" since the recent ban.

Bar-B-Q Barn | 16 | 8 | 14 | $14 |
11705 NW Seventh Ave. (117th St.), North Miami, 305-681-2491
◪ "Bring a change of shirt" because the "great sauce" on the open pit–smoked ribs can get messy at this "old-school" "BBQ lovers' delight" in North Miami near Pro Player

Miami/Dade County | F | D | S | C |

Stadium; persnickety sorts sniff at the "poor atmosphere", but more prefer its "laid-back", "no-nonsense" digs.

BARTON G., THE RESTAURANT | 23 | 27 | 22 | $54 |
1427 West Ave. (14th Terrace), Miami Beach, 305-672-8881; www.bartong.com

☑ "The 'G' must stand for 'genius'" say supporters of this "exciting" SoBe newcomer" owned by renowned caterer Weiss; the "gorgeous", "stylish" decor featuring a "lovely garden" sets the stage for "excellent" New American fare presented in a "spectacular" fashion ("don't miss the popcorn shrimp served in a popcorn box"), and the service has "personality" as well; a few party-poopers protest it's all "smoke and mirrors" with "food that falls short", but more thrill to the "pure entertainment."

Basilico | – | – | – | M |
5879 NW 36th St. (NW 57th Ave.), Miami, 305-871-3585

Though under the radar of most surveyors, it may be worth seeking out this "true gem" in a West Dade strip mall serving "excellent" Northern Italian including "delicious" pastas at "bargain" prices; it's "busy at lunchtime", but lotharios laud it as a "great date place" come suppertime.

Bayside Seafood Restaurant | ▽ 14 | 17 | 12 | $21 |
3501 Rickenbacker Cswy. (½ mi. south of the bridge), Key Biscayne, 305-361-0808

☑ Key Biscayners and other salty locals have been coming to this "funky", "pleasant", "little" seafood shack for nearly 20 years; though a devastating fire did not affect the "oh-so-good" fried fish sandwich and other "basic dishes" like conch fritters and Key lime pie served on plastic, some say the rebuilding did strip it of "all the ambiance."

B.E.D. | 19 | 25 | 17 | $57 |
929 Washington Ave. (bet. 9th & 10th Sts.), Miami Beach, 305-532-9070

☑ Yes, you actually "eat your dinner in a king-size bed" after slipping off your shoes at this "decadent", "naughty" nightclub/eatery in South Beach, and pillow talkers proclaim the New French fare "fantastic" and "creative"; insomniacs insist the food's "mediocre" ("make that B.A.D."), the service "lame" and the prices "not worth the romp in the sheets"; still, it's an "amusing way to pass an evening"; N.B. there are two 'sittings' at 8 and 11 PM.

Bella Luna | 22 | 17 | 22 | $32 |
Aventura Mall, 19575 Biscayne Blvd. (William Lehman Cswy.), Aventura, 305-792-9330

■ "A winner in Aventura Mall", this "excellent" Northern Italian "makes you forget" the location with its "amazing" "homemade pastas", "good brick-oven pizzas" and other "reasonably priced" specialties; savvy shoppers also laud the "lovely", "accommodating" staff and "pretty" decor.

Miami/Dade County F | D | S | C |

Bellante's Pizza & Pasta ⊭ 13 | 10 | 15 | $7 |
1684 NE Miami Gardens Dr. (18th Ave.), North Miami Beach, 305-940-2264
◪ This Italianish chain is cheered by parents for its "cheap, cheap, cheap" chow ($3.99 for an all-you-can-eat buffet of salad, pizza and pasta) and its camera-bugged game room for "antsy kids"; sure, the food's "not going to win any awards", but it's "good" and "filling", and weary moms and dads can "relax" over beer and wine.

Benihana/Samurai 18 | 19 | 20 | $34 |
8717 SW 136th St. (S. Dixie Hwy.), Kendall, 305-238-2131
8727 S. Dixie Hwy. (N. Kendall Dr.), Miami, 305-665-0044
1665 NE 79th St. Cswy. (E. Treasure Bay Dr.), North Bay Village, 305-866-2768
www.benihana.com
◪ "Others may try to imitate but none can duplicate" this "Japanese chop-chop house" teppanyaki chain and its slightly "cheaper" sidekick; the chefs "still put on the best show in town" and fans find the food "delicious", though cynics sneer at the same old "shtick" and deem it "pricey."

Berries 19 | 16 | 18 | $19 |
2884 SW 27th Ave. (Coconut Ave.), Coconut Grove, 305-448-2111
■ Since this onetime Coconut Grove juice stand has "grown to become a real restaurant, it's berry, berry good", serving Eclectic eats like "generous" wraps and pastas and "inventive" seafood dishes while remaining true to its health food roots with "wonderful smoothies"; though service is "sooo slow", last year's renovation yielded a "lovely courtyard" in which to "chill."

BEVERLY HILLS CAFE 17 | 12 | 16 | $18 |
Cypress Village Shopping Ctr., 7321 Miami Lakes Dr. (Miami Lakeway), Miami Lakes, 305-558-8201
1559 Sunset Dr. (56th Ave.), South Miami, 305-666-6618
◪ "Big portions" plus "moderate prices" equal "faithful customers" at this Traditional American chain; "spectacular salads", "fabulous rolls" and "good burgers" are standouts on the "diverse menu", and even if the "staff could be more attentive" and the decor's "dated", they're "reliable for a quick sit-down meal."

BICE RISTORANTE 22 | 22 | 21 | $53 |
Grand Bay Hotel, 2669 S. Bayshore Dr. (SW 27th Ave.), Coconut Grove, 305-860-0960; www.biceristorante.com
See review in Palm Beach County Directory.

Big Cheese 19 | 9 | 17 | $15 |
8080 SW 67th Ave. (US 1), South Miami, 305-662-6855; www.bigcheesemiami.com
■ There's "always a line" at this "grungy" Italian, a "college student favorite" that's also "crowded" with "children and

vote at zagat.com

Miami/Dade County | F | D | S | C |

parents" who can't get enough of the "huge" slices of "cheesy" pizza and rolls "drowning in chopped garlic and oil"; both the "noise" and the Hurricanes motif "remind you you're close to U.M."

Big Fish ◐ | 18 | 19 | 15 | $35 |
55 SW Miami Avenue Rd. (Brickell Ave.), Miami, 305-373-1770

☑ "Spectacular views of city lights and the Miami River" transform this hard-to-find" "open-air" Italian seafooder into a "beautiful people" hangout, especially during Friday happy hour; the fin fare's "fresh" and "delectable", and though surveyors split on the tabs ("cheap" vs. "high") and service ("good" vs. "poor"), there's no arguing about the "incredible location."

Big Pink ◐ | 17 | 14 | 14 | $21 |
157 Collins Ave. (2nd St.), Miami Beach, 305-532-4700; www.bigpinkrestaurant.com

☑ "No one goes hungry" at this "upscale" SoBe American "diner with an edge" known for its "mammoth portions" of "inexpensive", "damn good" "comfort food" and "great desserts" served by a "goofy" staff; "clubbers", "kids" and "babes" "who look like they never eat" converge in the "cool", "futuristic" setting that's open till 5 AM on weekends.

Biscayne Wine Merchants Bistro ⑤ | 19 | 13 | 18 | $29 |
738 NE 125th St. (7th Ct.), North Miami, 305-899-1997

■ This "neighborhood" "favorite" might just be "the best-kept secret" in North Miami opine oenophiles who frequent this "offbeat but comfortable" wine store that doubles as a "great" Continental restaurant where you "pick your own bottle" from more than 700 "modestly priced" choices on the shelves; a "friendly" staff helps regulars "wind down after the work week."

Bistro Zinc | 19 | 16 | 18 | $33 |
Aventura Plaza, 17901 Biscayne Blvd. (NE 178th St.), Aventura, 305-935-2202; www.bistrozincmiami.com

☑ The Aventura crowd finds the "European flavor" of this strip-mall Italian-American "enjoyable" for its "consistently good" food, including one of "the best chopped salads in town", "delicious" fish as well as "yummy" "garlic rolls you can eat all night"; the "fall-all-over-you service" also soothes supporters, but some find the fare "disappointing" and wish they'd "lose the karaoke night."

Bizcaya Grill | 24 | 24 | 25 | $51 |
Ritz-Carlton Coconut Grove, 3300 SW 27th Ave. (bet. Bayshore Dr. & Tigertail Trail), Coconut Grove, 305-644-4675; www.ritzcarlton.com

☑ "A credit to the Ritz-Carlton chain", this "stylish" Med-Continental has the Coconut Grove bunch basking in the

Miami/Dade County   F | D | S | C |

"beautiful", "peaceful" setting as they dine on "excellent", "innovative" fare; the service is typically "impeccable", and though penny-pinchers cry "ouch!" over big prices for "little portions", others are "willing to pay more for a special evening"; P.S. its "Sunday brunch is the new see-and-be-seen" scene.

BLUE DOOR ◐   24 | 27 | 21 | $62
Delano Hotel, 1685 Collins Ave. (17th St.), Miami Beach, 305-674-6400; www.ianschragerhotels.com
■ "Ian Schrager's Philippe Starck–designed" "fantasy island" in the "amazing" Delano Hotel epitomizes the "South Beach mystique", with its "Cocteau-like surreal setting" and terrace "overlooking a pool that melts into the turquoise ocean"; "beautiful people" and "movie stars" "love" the "sublime" New French *mer*-focused fare from chef Claude Troisgres, but lament that the "prices are as jaw-dropping as the decor."

Blue Sea ◐   24 | 26 | 24 | $52
Delano Hotel, 1685 Collins Ave. (17th St.), Miami Beach, 305-674-6400; www.ianschragerhotels.com
■ Even aloof hipsters think it's "cool" to sit at the 18-seat communal table at this "trendy" "top spot", a "scene" in South Beach's Delano Hotel where the sushi's as "fabulous" and "delicious" as the Philippe Starck–designed setting; there's also a "great wine list" and "excellent service", and though it's admittedly "pricey", the "meal's worth it."

Blu la Pizzeria del Sole ◐   22 | 19 | 19 | $21
7201 SW 59th Ave. (Sunset Dr.), South Miami, 305-666-9285
■ "It doesn't get much better than" this South Miami "upscale pizza joint" ("Trattoria Sole's little brother") specializing in "unique", "gourmet" toppings on "delicious" pies as well as offering "excellent" salads and a "creative wine list"; service is "friendly", the setting's "romantic" and prices are "reasonable."

Bond St. Lounge ◐   25 | 21 | 19 | $43
Townhouse Hotel, 150 20th St. (Collins Ave.), Miami Beach, 305-398-1806; www.townhousehotel.com
■ "Much like its NYC cousin", this "dark", "sleek", "über-sexy" Japanese in SoBe's "trendy" Townhouse Hotel lures a "mod squad" that's "out-of-this-world beautiful" with "excellent" sushi as well as "less-common delicacies"; even though the "squish" factor created by "kindergarten-size chairs" and tables doesn't appeal to everyone, it's still considered "one of the best first-date places" around.

Bongos Cuban Café   14 | 22 | 14 | $31
American Airlines Arena, 601 Biscayne Blvd. (NE 8th St.), Miami, 786-777-2100; www.bongoscubancafe.com
■ An "eye-catching setting" makes this "lively" Downtown Miami "hot spot" owned by Gloria and Emilio Estefan a

Miami/Dade County — F | D | S | C

"must-go" for "tourists" and "party" people; although the "overpriced" Cuban cuisine's a bit humdrum ("if you want authentic" "eat in Little Havana"), there's "great music and dancing" on weekends; N.B. closed Mondays and Tuesdays.

Botticelli — 20 | 17 | 18 | $26
7382 SW 56th Ave. (SW 74th St.), South Miami, 305-665-8550
◪ "If you're not alert, you'll drive by" this "quintessential neighborhood" Italian "hidden behind a South Miami gas station", but you'd be missing out on some "delicious" "homestyle" food and a "pleasant", angel-adorned setting; a few devils, however, protest "poor service" and claim the food's "nothing to write home about."

Bugatti, The Art of Pasta — 22 | 15 | 19 | $25
2504 Ponce de Leon Blvd. (Andalusia Ave.), Coral Gables, 305-441-2545
◪ Champions of this Coral Gables Italian "workhorse" can't get enough of its "perfectly cooked", "terrific", "unique" pastas and "one heckuva lasagna" (available on the first Wednesday of every month); surveyors are split on the service, however, which can be "wonderful" or "downright nasty", but all agree the "prices are excellent."

CACAO 1737 ⌧ — 26 | 26 | 24 | $44
141 Giralda Ave. (bet. Galiano St. & Ponce de Leon Blvd.), Coral Gables, 305-445-1001
■ A "chocoholic's wonderland", this "impressive", "must-try" Nuevo Latino newcomer in the Gables offers "original", "spectacular" and "delectable" dishes, many using cacao, from "creative chef" Edgar Leal, as well as "exemplary" desserts and "outstanding wines"; the "fantastic" interior and "excellent" service help make this "one of the best places" on Restaurant Row.

Cafe Avanti — 20 | 16 | 21 | $30
732 41st St. (bet. Chase & Prairie Aves.), Miami Beach, 305-538-4400
■ A "home away from home" for many Miami Beach locals craving "quality Italian food without the crowds of SoBe", this "great neighborhood hangout" delivers with "diverse", "authentic" pastas and "noteworthy" chicken and fish dishes as well as "accommodating" service; N.B. a recent renovation may outdate the Decor score.

Café Cardozo ● — 17 | 17 | 17 | $29
1300 Ocean Dr. (13th St.), Miami Beach, 305-695-2822
◪ Located in the same-named hotel owned by Gloria and Emilio Estefan, this "lovely" SoBe eatery offers views from the "huge veranda" of the "models, paparazzi and pretty people" who populate Ocean Drive; the Cuban-Eclectic fare is "good", and though the service can be "confused", the "friendly staff allows you to enjoy a leisurely meal."

Miami/Dade County F | D | S | C |

Cafe Demetrio ☒ 15 | 19 | 14 | $12
300 Alhambra Circle (Salzedo St.), Coral Gables, 305-448-4949;
www.cafedemetrio.com
■ This "cute" "European-style coffee shop" on a prime Coral Gables corner is "wonderful for coffee and dessert" as well as simple sandwiches and quiches for a "casual lunch" in a "cozy" interior or "under the trees in the courtyard"; on Fridays it stays open late (past 6) and offers live music.

Café Ibiza ▽ 16 | 19 | 20 | $27
Village of Merrick Park, 370 San Lorenzo Ave. (S. Le Jeune Rd.), Coral Gables, 305-443-8888
◪ "A good place to share a few creative dishes", this Coral Gables Mediterranean in the Village of Merrick Park entices shoppers with "tapas with a twist" served in larger than expected portions (at prices some call "higher than appropriate"); "pleasant, efficient" service as well as "live music" on weekends in the mostly outdoor area make it especially popular with a European (read: smoking) crowd.

Cafe Med ❶ 15 | 16 | 15 | $27
CocoWalk, 3015 Grand Ave. (bet. McFarlane Rd. & Virginia Ave.), Coconut Grove, 305-443-1770; www.cocowalk.com
◪ A "dependable" destination "before or after a movie", this CocoWalk Mediterranean-Italian offers "great" "alfresco" seating "in the heart of Coconut Grove"; the "good", "simple" pizzas and pastas please partisans, but more meditative sorts slam the "disoriented service" and prices geared to the "hapless tourist crowds", warning "walk on by."

Café Pastis ☒ 24 | 15 | 19 | $32
7310 S. Red Rd. (bet. 72nd & 73rd Sts.), South Miami, 305-665-3322; www.cafepastis.com
◪ "Don't let the strip-mall setting turn you off" *parce que* this "teeny, tiny" "authentic French bistro" is a "hidden" neighborhood "treasure" in South Miami serving "hearty", "super" dishes including "favorites" like bouillabaisse at "reasonable prices"; even though the interior's "always crowded", the "rustic decor" is "charming", and locals are willing to endure "attitude" from the staff to dine on that "wonderful" food.

Cafe Prima Pasta ❶ 24 | 16 | 19 | $30
414 71st St. (Collins Ave.), Miami Beach, 305-867-0106;
www.primapasta.com
■ For "excellent" Northern Italian food at "great prices", this Miami Beach "locals' favorite" is "definitely prima" proclaim pastaficionados who praise the "to-die-for gnocchi" and other "well-prepared" specialties; "walls covered in memorabilia" create "hospitable surroundings", and the "owners make you feel like a VIP" – now if only they could do something about the "long waits."

vote at zagat.com

Miami/Dade County | F | D | S | C |

CAFÉ RAGAZZI | 25 | 14 | 25 | $33 |
9500 Harding Ave. (95th St.), Surfside, 305-866-4495
■ Cafe society swarms this "adorable", "teeny" family-owned Surfside Italian, where the inevitable "long waits" "on the sidewalk" for a table are "eased by a complimentary glass of wine"; it's "worth a trip" for the "exceptional", "authentic" cuisine, especially grandma's homemade pasta, and it doesn't hurt that the "charming" owner and "flirty" waiters make everyone "feel gorgeous."

Cafe Sambal | 24 | 25 | 24 | $41 |
Mandarin Oriental Hotel, 500 Brickell Key Dr. (SE 8th St.), Miami, 305-913-8251; www.mandarinoriental.com
■ Azul's "less formal" and "less expensive" "little brother" in the Mandarin Oriental has added a "great new sushi bar" in addition to the "incredible" Pan-Asian fare served in a "beautiful" interior that features a waterfall or on the patio with a "wonderful view of the Brickell skyline"; the "extra-polite" staff helps make you "feel relaxed and a million miles away from the Downtown Miami bustle."

Café Tu Tu Tango ● | 19 | 20 | 18 | $25 |
CocoWalk, 3015 Grand Ave. (Main Hwy.), Coconut Grove, 305-529-2222; www.cafetututango.com
■ "Try something new" urge tu-tutors of this CocoWalk chain link with a "wonderful setting" featuring the work of "local talent" in the form of "funky" art, "scintillating" belly dancing and tarot card reading, all attracting "a great singles crowd"; the "delicious" Eclectic appetizers and "novel" tapas are washed down by the "best sangria", and even if it gets "noisy", there's a patio for "people-watching."

CAFFE ABBRACCI ● | 25 | 21 | 24 | $42 |
318 Aragon Ave. (bet. Le Jeune Rd. & Ponce de Leon Blvd.), Coral Gables, 305-441-0700
☑ Host-owner Nino Pernetti "hugs" and "pampers" his "regulars", making them "feel like stars" at this "clubby" Coral Gables "hangout"; the "reasonably priced" Northern Italian cuisine is "delicious", the service is "impeccable" and the room's "romantic", but its "popularity" also means it's "crowded" and often "so noisy you can't hear" the conversation at your table.

Caffe Da Vinci | 21 | 20 | 21 | $32 |
1009 Kane Concourse (96th St.), Bay Harbor Island, 305-861-8166; www.caffedavinci.com
■ "You feel like you're in someone's gracious home" gush groupies of this "quaint" Bay Harbor Island "hideaway" where the "reliable", "delicious homestyle Italian food" is "top-notch" and "reasonably priced"; "reservations are a must", as it's "always crowded with regulars who love it", but the "warm owner" and "excellent" staff ensure an "outstanding" experience.

Miami/Dade County | F | D | S | C |

Caffe Milano ◐ | 20 | 20 | 18 | $37 |
850 Ocean Dr. (bet. 8th & 9th Sts.), Miami Beach, 305-532-0707; www.caffemilano.com

■ "It's worth battling the Ocean Drive crowds" to get to one of the "most consistent Italian kitchens" in South Beach offering "out-of-this-world" pasta Bolognese and other "excellent", "authentic" specialties, all "beautifully served"; a table on the veranda provides "views of pretty people" and sea "breezes."

Caffe Vialetto | 25 | 19 | 23 | $41 |
4019 Le Jeune Rd. (Bird Rd.), Coral Gables, 305-446-5659

■ Pastafarians proclaim the "offbeat menu" at this Coral Gables "jewel" that fuses Italian and Caribbean flavors to create "mind-blowingly" scrumptious" fare such as sweet potato tortellini or "excellent" black bean and pork ravioli served by a "capable", "exceptional" staff; though reservations aren't taken on "busy weekends", a "recent renovation provides more room" in the "romantic" interior.

CALIFORNIA PIZZA KITCHEN | 19 | 14 | 18 | $19 |
Miami Int'l Airport, concourse east, 2nd level, Miami, 305-876-7238; www.cpk.com

See review in Ft. Lauderdale/Broward County Directory.

CAPITAL GRILLE | 26 | 25 | 25 | $54 |
444 Brickell Ave. (SE 5th St.), Miami, 305-374-4500; www.thecapitalgrille.com

■ "An 'in' place for Miami power brokers", this "solid" Downtown steakhouse chain link is "the best place to close the deal" proclaim potentates who praise "wonderful", "CEO"-worthy service and the "beautiful" "wood, brass and glass"–filled decor; starting with the house cocktail ("great pineapple-infused vodka") and proceeding to "top-quality" beef and seafood accompanied by "terrific sides", it provides a "marvelous" experience; the only lament: "I wish my banker would let me eat here every day."

Captain's Tavern | 23 | 14 | 20 | $29 |
9621 S. Dixie Hwy. (bet. 98th St. & US 1), Pinecrest, 305-666-5979

■ "Before Miami was chic", this "seafood joint" near Pinecrest was serving "fresh", "fantastic", "affordable" fish dishes and it still does according to old salts who also savor the "great wine values"; aye, the digs are "dark" and "dated, with "de rigueur salt-water aquarium"/"pirate" decor, but once you "weathered the long waits", the seating is "comfortable" and the service "excellent."

Carmen The Restaurant | 25 | 22 | 23 | $42 |
David William Hotel, 700 Biltmore Way (Cardena St.), Coral Gables, 305-913-1944; www.davidwilliamhotel.com

■ "Carmen Gonzalez is back and better than ever" at her new Nuevo Latino "surprise" in Coral Gables' David William

vote at zagat.com

Miami/Dade County | **F** | **D** | **S** | **C** |

Hotel; the "diminutive chef" "delivers big flavors" with "excellent" cuisine that's "creative but not wild", and the setting's "elegant"; the service is "impeccable", and wallet-watchers sing arias about the "reasonable prices"; P.S. it's also become a "great neighborhood bar" scene.

Carnevale ◐ | 19 | 17 | 16 | $34 |
607 Lincoln Rd. (Pennsylvania Ave.), Miami Beach, 305-672-3333
☑ "A nice choice before hitting the clubs", this "busy" sister to Carpaccio "right on Lincoln Road" offers "terrific" pastas and other "dependable" Italian fare and a "pleasant atmosphere"; though a few barkers besmirch "unoriginal" food and "hurried" service, all agree the patio is a "great setting" from which to observe the "parade of passersby."

Carpaccio | 21 | 19 | 20 | $35 |
Shops of Bal Harbour, 9700 Collins Ave. (96th St.), Bal Harbour, 305-867-7777
☑ "Ladies who lunch" and other "upper-crust clientele" who deign to "wait for a table" for a prime spot at this Bal Harbor Italian are rewarded with "a great experience", which includes "bend-over-backwards service", "modestly priced", "authentic" pastas and carpaccio, *naturalmente*, as well as "people-watching" at the "most beautiful mall in the world"; claustrophobics cry it's "cramped and hectic" indoors, making "dining outside a must."

Casa Juancho ◐ | 22 | 22 | 20 | $38 |
2436 SW Eighth St. (bet. SW 24th & 25th Sts.), Miami, 305-642-2452; www.casajuancho.com
■ You'll "forget about Calle Ocho" once you walk into this chapter of "earthy Hemingwayesque Spain" with an "old Madrid" ambiance in Little Havana; "excellent tapas", "huge portions" of "delicious", Ernestly "authentic" entrees and an "extensive" Iberian wine list are prelude to a "party", with guitar-playing troubadours providing a "lively" evening.

Casa Larios | 18 | 17 | 15 | $23 |
5859 SW 73rd St. (bet. SW 58th & 59th Aves.), South Miami, 305-662-5656
7705 W. Flagler St. (SW 79th Ave.), West Miami, 305-266-5494
☑ Some say "the original on Flagler Street" is one of the "best" Cubans in the city, but the South Miami sibling is "a great addition" as well; in either case it's "fun to bring out-of-towners" over for "hearty portions" of "good", "reasonably priced" fare and "live Latin music" on weekends; however, service can be "slow" and it's helpful to know Spanish.

Casa Paco ◐ | ▽ 20 | 15 | 17 | $29 |
8868 SW 40th St./Bird Rd. (SW 88th Pl.), South Miami, 305-554-7633; www.casapacomiami.com
☑ Habitués hail this "old-school" Spaniard in a nondescript South Dade strip mall for its "great paella" and other "fabulous" fare at "reasonable prices" as well as a "great

subscribe to zagat.com

Miami/Dade County   F | D | S | C

wine list"; "families, young couples and grandparents" also appreciate "attentive service", but while some consider the cuisine "consistent", others maintain it's "hit or miss."

Casa Panza   ▽ 21 | 21 | 14 | $31
1620 SW Eighth St. (SW 16th Ave.), Miami, 305-643-5343
■ "After a few rounds of sangria you'll join the party" during the "lively", "fun" flamenco nights at this Spanish "hole-in-the-wall" "in the heart of Little Havana"; add to that "excellent" tapas at "good prices", and you'll put up with the "crowded" conditions for the "authentic" experience.

CASA TUA ⊠   22 | 29 | 21 | $70
Casa Tua, 1700 James Ave. (bet. Collins & Washington Aves.), Miami Beach, 305-673-1010
◪ "Savvy sophisticates and furtive celebrities" agree this "ravishing", "romantic" South Beach "newcomer" tucked into a "beautifully restored home" and its "enchanted garden" are "divine", and it nabs the No. 1 spot in Miami for Decor; the Italian fare is "sublime" and service can be "charming", but critics caution "you have to rob a bank to pay for it all"; P.S. loyalists laud the "large community table" next to the kitchen for a "little mingling while you eat."

Chalán/El Chalán   19 | 9 | 18 | $22
1580 Washington Ave. (16th St.), Miami Beach, 305-532-8880
7971 SW 40th St./Bird Rd. (SW 79th Ave.), Westchester, 305-266-0212
■ "Like a Lima neighborhood" eatery (but with "double the portion sizes"), these "authentic Peruvians" in South Beach and Westchester dish up "excellent", "affordable" soup and seviche; despite the "lack of decor", the "small tables covered in yellow mantles with rainbow stripes" make it cheerful, and "you won't leave hungry."

Chart House   19 | 20 | 18 | $39
51 Chart House Dr. (S. Bayshore Dr.), Coconut Grove, 305-856-9741; www.chart-house.com
◪ "If you can get a seat by the window" you're guaranteed "drop-dead views" at this "exquisitely located" Coconut Grove chain link with a much-loved "endless salad bar"; the American-seafood offerings fare less well, however, with some savoring the "good food" and others needling it "needs major help", adding it's become a "tourist trap."

CHEESECAKE FACTORY ●   20 | 19 | 18 | $25
Aventura Mall, 19501 Biscayne Blvd. (NE 195th St.), Aventura, 305-792-9696
CocoWalk, 3015 Grand Ave. (Virginia St.), Coconut Grove, 305-447-9898
Dadeland Mall, 7497 N. Kendall Dr. (88th St.), Kendall, 305-665-5400
www.thecheesecakefactory.com
See review in Ft. Lauderdale/Broward County Directory.

vote at zagat.com

Miami/Dade County F | D | S | C

CHEF ALLEN'S 28 | 23 | 26 | $60
19088 NE 29th Ave. (NE 191st St.), Aventura, 305-935-2900; www.chefallens.com

■ "Not just a meal, but an amazing experience", this "bastion of culinary excellence" in Aventura is once again Miami's No. 1 for Food (and now tops for Service as well), thanks to the "artistry" of chef-owner Allen Susser, whose New World cuisine is "extraordinary", "exciting" and "delicious", complemented by "excellent wines"; the staff is "impeccable" and "intelligent", and the "atmosphere's great", making it "worth a return trip"; P.S. "the tasting menus are a good way to sample lots of flavors."

CHINA GRILL ● 23 | 23 | 20 | $50
404 Washington Ave. (5th St.), Miami Beach, 305-534-2211

◪ "Fab, festive and fun" fawn fanatics of this "dazzling" "NYC import" whose "trendiness" may be "wearing off" a bit after nearly a decade but it "remains an easy favorite" thanks to "amazing", "expertly prepared" Pan-Asian fare including a new sushi bar; sure, there's "attitude" from the staff and the tabs are "outrageous", but diehards declare it's "worth the money to be part of the South Beach scene."

Chispa ● – | – | – | E
225 Altara Ave. (Ponce de Leon Blvd.), Coral Gables, 305-648-2600; www.chisparestaurant.com

One of the original Mango Kings, Robbin Haas (most recently of Baleen), has resurfaced at this stunning Nuevo Latino in Coral Gables with decor featuring orange beaded lamps, wood and leather accents and colorful floor tiles that lives up to its name (meaning "spark"); large portions of dishes such as imaginative seviches and roasted suckling pig are imminently shareable.

Christine Lee's 22 | 13 | 18 | $33
RK Shopping Ctr., 17082 Collins Ave. (Sunny Isles Blvd.), Sunny Isles, 305-947-1717

■ "If you can't decide between steak and Chinese", this "oldie but goodie" in a generic Sunny Isles strip mall offers "excellent" beef as well as "great" "traditional" Asian fare; the service is "good", "prices are reasonable" and there's a popular early-bird from 4 to 6 PM.

Christine's Roti Shop ⌦⊄ – | – | – | I
16721 NE Sixth Ave. (NE 167th St.), North Miami Beach, 305-770-0434

"Exotic" Caribbean fare meets "authentic" Indian and creates an "eclectic experience" at this take-out stand in an out-of-the-way NMB strip mall; rotis, curries, jerks and "filling vegetarian" options are all a "great value" and make for an "interesting meal", and converts claim "Christine singlehandedly made my vacation memorable."

Miami/Dade County | F | D | S | C |

Christy's | 23 | 20 | 24 | $44 |
3101 Ponce de Leon Blvd. (Malaga Ave.), Coral Gables, 305-446-1400; www.christysrestaurant.com
■ Despite "stiff competition" from the "fancy national chains" that have opened in the Gables, this "old-school", "good-value" steakhouse remains "steady as she goes", still serving "wonderful Caesars", "the best" prime rib and "unbeatable" baked Alaska; the "professionalism of the staff is unmatched", and even if some deem the decor "dated", others prefer its "dark", "classic", "clubby" ambiance.

Citronelle | ∇ 24 | 19 | 22 | $40 |
7300 Biscayne Blvd. (73rd St.), Miami, 305-757-2555
■ Pioneers who've sampled the Caribbean fare at this "hip" Miami newcomer in the "funky emerging neighborhood" dubbed the Upper East Side call it "a winner" for "excellent", "spicy" fare in "generous portions" cooled down by "amazing sorbet" for dessert; "friendly", "efficient" service, "interesting background music" and a "short" list of "well-priced" wines are other reasons buffs "will be back."

Crab House, The | 15 | 14 | 15 | $28 |
1551 NE 79th St. Cswy. (bet. Biscayne Blvd. & Collins Ave., on North Bay Island), North Bay Village, 305-868-7085; www.landryseafood.com
■ Put on your bib and "bang" away at the "good garlic crabs" served at this "reliable" seafood franchise that's also known for its "great-value buffet" of fin fare and salads; its waterfront location on the causeway between Miami Beach and the mainland affords "awesome views", but the decor's "divey", the service "slow" and critics crab the cuisine "lacks pizzazz."

Crystal Cafe | 24 | 18 | 24 | $40 |
726 Arthur Godfrey Rd. (bet. Chase & Prairie Aves.), Miami Beach, 305-673-8266; www.crystalcafe.net
☑ "Outstanding Continental cuisine", "generous portions" and an "excellent prix fixe for early diners" attracts a "sophisticated" clientele who are "treated like family" by "personable" chef-owner Klime Kovaceski as well as his "courteous staff"; however, though partisans praise the "romantic" ambiance, complainers call the digs "cramped" and decor "depressing."

Dab Haus | 19 | 13 | 21 | $22 |
1040 Alton Rd. (bet. 10th & 11th Sts.), Miami Beach, 305-534-9557
☑ The "best Wiener schnitzel", "must-have garlic-honey baked Brie" and other German dishes and "good beers" are delivered by a "friendly" staff dressed in "traditional Deutsch garb" at this "local treasure" in South Beach; the setting's "charming" and "prices are good", but a few haus-breakers bash the food as "nothing special."

vote at zagat.com

Miami/Dade County　　　　　F | D | S | C

da Ermanno
▽ 19 | 19 | 21 | $28
6927 Biscayne Blvd. (69th St.), Miami, 305-759-2001
■ "Loyal locals" claim this "tiny" Southern Italian on Miami's Upper East Side is the "friendliest place around" and champion its "charmingly eccentric" decor; "traditional" fare produced with "quality ingredients" is "made to your liking", the wines are "moderately priced" and the service is "excellent."

Daily Bread
22 | 10 | 16 | $12
840 First St. (Alton Rd.), Miami Beach, 305-673-2252
12131 S. Dixie Hwy. (121st St.), Pinecrest, 305-253-6115
■ For a "solid taste of the Middle East", these South Beach and Pinecrest take-out spots offer "great falafel", "excellent hummus" and "heavenly sweets", all "fresh", "healthy" and "cheap"; in fall 2003, the SoBe branch will change its name to Oasis and become an upscale Moroccan-themed restaurant/nightclub open till 4 AM.

da Leo Trattoria
17 | 16 | 18 | $33
819 Lincoln Rd. (bet. Jefferson & Meridian Aves.), Miami Beach, 305-674-0350; www.daleotrattoria.com
◪ Its "lovely Lincoln Road" location transforms this "inexpensive" Italian South Beach "staple" into a "people-watching paradise", and fans also lionize the "charming", "cozy" interior and "hospitable" staff; the fare, however, veers from "good" and "reliable" to "disappointing", but to most, it's "all about the outdoor seating."

Dan Marino's Fine Food & Spirits
18 | 17 | 16 | $25
5701 Sunset Dr. (57th Ave.), South Miami, 305-665-1315; www.danmarinosrestaurant.com
See review in Ft. Lauderdale/Broward County Directory.

David's Cafe
16 | 10 | 16 | $18
1058 Collins Ave. (bet. 10th & 11th Sts.), Miami Beach, 305-534-8736 ●
1654 Meridian Ave. (Lincoln Ln.), Miami Beach, 305-672-8707
www.davidscafe.com
■ "The best cafecito this side of Little Havana" is served at these 24/7 South Beach "landmarks" along with other "good", "traditional" Cuban specialties and an all-you-can-eat lunch buffet at the Meridian Avenue location; peso-pinchers should note they provide "great value", and while they're "always busy", you're "always made welcome."

Deli Lane Cafe
17 | 11 | 15 | $17
1401 Brickell Ave. (14th St.), Miami, 305-377-8811
7230 SW 59th Ave. (Sunset Dr.), South Miami, 305-665-0606
■ "Good", "cheap" deli fare from a "diverse menu that will please everyone from baby Louie to Aunt Mildred" has had locals "making frequent stops" at these Brickell Avenue and South Miami "neighborhood" nosheries; both also

Miami/Dade County   F | D | S | C

offer "quick" service and "pleasant outdoor dining" ("I can bring my dog").

Diego's ◐   18 | 18 | 18 | $45
65 Alhambra Plaza (bet. Ponce de Leon Blvd. & S. Douglas Rd.), Coral Gables, 305-448-2498; www.diegorestaurant.com

☒ Appraisals of this Coral Gables Spaniard are divided, with defenders acclaiming "good", "authentic" fare like "wonderful paella", a "great wine list", a "pleasant" room and live piano that "adds a nice touch"; detractors, though, dis the dishes as "disappointing" and "overpriced."

Disco Fish   ∇ 16 | 6 | 14 | $18
9899 SW 40th St./Bird Rd. (SW 99th St.), Westchester, 305-229-8600
1540 SW 67th Ave. (SW 16th St.), West Miami, 305-266-7323

■ Though few surveyors have boogied down to these seafooders in Miami, those who have applaud "amazing" fish as well as "down-home" Cuban cooking at a "great value"; "you don't go for the ambiance", but despite a Decor rating lower than a breakdancer in a split, some still deem them "delightful."

Dogma ⌀   20 | 14 | 16 | $9
7030 Biscayne Blvd. (bet. NE 70th & 71st St.), Miami, 305-759-3433

■ "Hot dawg!" – it's about time Miami got its "first outdoor gourmet" wiener stand, and this "funky" newcomer's offering the "niftiest concoctions you'll ever have", along with "veggie" versions, "good" chili fries and "delicious" mint lemonade; one ruff spot: "with only outdoor seating" available, it's "just too" doggone "hot" for some to eat here in the summer; N.B. South Beach will go dogmatic when a second branch opens in late 2003.

Doraku ◐   19 | 20 | 18 | $34
1104 Lincoln Rd. (Alton Rd.), Miami Beach, 305-695-8383; www.sushidoraku.com

☒ This "cool" Benihana-owned sushi spot on South Beach's trendy Lincoln Road next to the multiplex is "a favorite with moviegoers" for "top-quality" fish, "delectable" Japanese dishes and an "excellent sake menu"; those who call it "overhyped" and "overpriced" are overruled by groupies of its "great happy hour" on Fridays when "they almost give the place away."

Edelweiss Bavarian Gasthaus   20 | 21 | 23 | $31
2655 Biscayne Blvd. (26th Terrace), Miami, 305-573-4421

■ "The hills are alive" at this Upper East Side German and even though your heart won't be blessed if you overindulge in the "big portions", boosters brag the "wurst is the best" and the other "reasonably priced", "homestyle" offerings are "delicious"; the "charming" garden and "cozy interior" are "especially beautiful during the holiday season", and the "excellent" staff makes you feel *wilkommen*.

vote at zagat.com

Miami/Dade County F | D | S | C

11th St. Diner ◐   16 | 15 | 15 | $17
1065 Washington Ave. (11th St.), Miami Beach, 305-534-6373
■ "Locals" as well as "24-hour party people" "escape the lunacy" at this "genuine" South Beach "'50s-style diner" offering "ample portions" of "bargain-priced" "classic American chow", a full bar, patio and "spunky but friendly" servers; grouches gripes it's a "grungy" "greasy spoon", but that doesn't stop the perpetual "floor show."

Elia   ▽ 20 | 21 | 18 | $40
Bal Harbour Shops, 9700 Collins Ave., #135 (Bal Harbour Blvd.), Bal Harbour, 305-866-2727
■ Though word has only just begun to get out about this "wonderful addition" to the Bal Harbour Shops, early reports suggest the Mediterranean fare is "bar none", the wine list "stellar" and the staff "great"; some say it "started out shaky", but assert that with the arrival of "new chef Kris Wessel" (ex Liaison) it has "quickly improved."

El Novillo   18 | 19 | 19 | $28
6830 SW 40th St./Bird Rd. (67th Ave.), Miami, 305-284-8417
15450 New Barn Rd. (Main St.), Miami Lakes, 305-819-2755
◪ "Delicious *bistecs*," "excellent" churrasco and other "well-prepared" Nicaraguan *carne* specialties are the stars at this steakhouse duo in Miami; though some snipe the fare's "forgettable", the service is "courteous" and it provides "good value all around."

El Rancho Grande   20 | 16 | 18 | $23
1626 Pennsylvania Ave. (Lincoln Ln.), Miami Beach, 305-673-0480
■ "Potent margaritas" ("go for the Cadillac") are defused by "enormous portions" of "excellent" Mexican eats at this "convenient" South Beach "staple off Lincoln Road"; ranch hands hail the "awesome chips", "great guac" and "authentic" entrees, and the "charming" decor, "service with a smile" and "decent prices" also garner *olés*.

El Toro Taco   24 | 12 | 17 | $16
1 S. Krome Ave. (NE 1st St.), Homestead, 305-245-8182
■ Tacognoscenti seeking "the best Mexican food north of the border" find it after a "drive to Homestead" at this "mom-and-pop operation" that's been slinging "simple", "tasty" fare for 30 years at "prices that are hard to beat"; "caring, personable" owners, an "excellent staff", a BYO policy and "great tacky decor" have bullheaded sorts saying "I hope it never changes" (though a planned move in 2004 to a nearby location may alter things a bit).

ESCOPAZZO   25 | 21 | 24 | $51
1311 Washington Ave. (bet. 13th & 14th Sts.), Miami Beach, 305-674-9450; www.escopazzo.com
■ "You'd be crazy not to eat" at this "delightful little corner of Italy hidden" in SoBe; the "superior" rotating offerings

Miami/Dade County | F | D | S | C |

are "memorable", including "excellent risottos" revved up by "outstanding wines", and the "incredibly romantic" room comes "complete with fountain"; "gracious" owners Pino and Giancarla Bodoni and their staff clearly "love what they do", and if it's "a bit pricey", it "never fails to impress."

Fancy's Real Italian Cuisine | 20 | 15 | 22 | $28 |
12313 S. Dixie Hwy. (Chapman Field Dr.), Pinecrest, 305-256-0056
■ Folks who fancy a "friendly" "neighborhood Italian" serving "excellent" "old-world favorites" from the classic "red-sauce" repertoire should discover this "standby" in Pinecrest; "bargain prices", a "good selection of wines", "super service" and a "lovely" (if "small") setting are just whipped cream on the tiramisu.

Fish 54 ◐ | 17 | 17 | 16 | $34 |
Loehmann's Fashion Island, 18841 Biscayne Blvd. (187th St.), Aventura, 305-932-5022
◪ This "popular" Italian seafooder in Aventura is host to a "singles" scene of "rich locals" trolling the "active bar" area; the fin fare ranges from "tasty" and "well prepared" to "needs help", but the "nice outdoor dining area's a plus", especially if you're fishing for a "quiet" meal.

FISH JOYNT | 25 | 16 | 21 | $39 |
2570 NE Miami Gardens Dr. (W. Dixie Hwy.), Aventura, 305-936-8333
■ "Don't be fooled by the seedy strip" locale or the kitschy name, because this "top-notch" Aventura seafooder offers "the freshest fish around" prepared by chef-owner David Bianco, a "guy who understands how to cook it"; "portions are huge", "free latkes come with dinner" and best of all, the fare's "as good as any in Miami without the cost"; cast in "wonderful" service and you'll see why "locals" are hooked.

Flamingo | ▽ 21 | 7 | 18 | $15 |
16701 S. Dixie Hwy. (168th St.), Palmetto Bay, 305-235-3051
◪ Regulars who've filled the seats of this South Dade coffee shop "for years" "love the food and the staff" but "hate the waits" for American fare "like mama used to make", including "always-fresh" roasted turkey and chocolate layer cake; even though doubters dismiss it as "mediocre", most agree it's "the best diner around."

Flanigans Laughing | 19 | 13 | 18 | $18 |
Loggerhead ◐
2721 Bird Ave. (27th Ave.), Coconut Grove, 305-446-1114; www.flanigans.net
■ This "quintessential sports bar" with a "shipwreck decor" in the Grove garners raves for its "simple", "great" American fare, including "giant burgers" and "succulent" babyback ribs "that fall off the bone and stick to yours" as well as, of course, "cold, inexpensive beer"; the "cheap"

vote at zagat.com 39

Miami/Dade County | F | D | S | C |

eats and "service with a smile" help make it a "landmark" with "families", "fishermen" and frat boys alike.

Fleming - A Taste of Denmark | 23 | 17 | 23 | $32 |
8511 SW 136th St. (S. Dixie Hwy.), Pinecrest, 305-232-6444
■ A "favorite for 20 years", this "unpretentious" Pinecrest Danish-Continental serves "huge portions" of "wonderful" fish, meat and duck preceded by "crudités, fresh buns, soup and salad" that leave you "so stuffed" it's hard to finish the "sumptuous" desserts; a "relaxing" (if somewhat "stuffy") setting, "great service" and "reasonable prices" are other reasons it "never fails"; P.S. "here's hoping new owners don't change a thing."

Forge, The | 24 | 25 | 24 | $61 |
432 Arthur Godfrey Rd. (Royal Palm Ave.), Miami Beach, 305-538-8533; www.theforge.com
☑ "Still a classic for a romantic evening" for the past four decades, this "charming" Miami Beach "institution" keeps forging ahead with its "outstanding" French-steakhouse fare, "excellent" wine list comprising 300,000 bottles, "top-notch service" and "opulent" (some say "bordello"-like) decor; protesters say the "prices will give you a heart attack before the beef does", however, and lament it's "lost its luster"; N.B. a new chef has updated the menu while retaining its signature dishes.

Fox's Sherron Inn ● | 16 | 12 | 18 | $21 |
6030 S. Dixie Hwy. (Sunset Dr.), South Miami, 305-666-2230
■ Smoking may have been outlawed in Miami's indoor spaces since July 1, but the ban can't eradicate near 60 years' worth of "stale smoke" from this "archetypal '50s liquor lounge", the "dark" destination for an "illicit" rendezvous over "reliably good" American fare such as prime rib; sure, it's "seedy", but with the "best martinis in South Florida" (and "one of the best happy hours in the city"), "you can't go wrong."

FRANCESCO | 26 | 15 | 22 | $36 |
325 Alcazar Ave. (bet. Le Jeune Rd. & Salzedo St.), Coral Gables, 305-446-1600
■ "As close to Lima as you'll get" in Coral Gables, this Peruvian seafooder offers a "unique" opportunity to sample "excellent", "inventive" dishes as well as "superb" seviche and other "well-priced" dishes; the service is "attentive" but not "obsequious", and though the tables are a bit "crowded, it's worth it to experience" the "excellent" fin fare.

French Bakery Cafe ⌧ | – | – | – | M |
1023 Kane Concourse (E. Bay Harbor Dr.), Bay Harbor Island, 305-868-5212; www.thefrenchbakerycafe.com
Much more than the name indicates, this tiny Argentine-owned French eatery serves elegant breakfasts, lunches and dinners to the tony Bal Harbour area crowd; get there

Miami/Dade County   F | D | S | C |

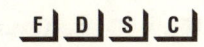

before its closing at 9 PM to sample soups, salads, crêpes, quiches and, of course, delectable baked goods, including an apricot tarte tatin with warm orange sauce.

Fritz & Franz Bierhaus   - | - | - | M |
(fka Da Capo)
60 Merrick Way (Aragon Ave.), Coral Gables, 305-774-1883; www.bierhaus.cc
Put on your lederhosen and clear the calendar in October, 'cause this onetime jazz club turned Continental has just been reborn as an Austrian-Bavarian sports bar; veteran restaurateur Harald Neuweg promises Wiener schnitzel, herring, stuffed cabbage and salads washed down by imported brews and delivered by dirndl-clad *bier*-maidens, along with lots of festivities.

Front Porch Cafe   21 | 15 | 17 | $21 |
Penguin Hotel, 1418 Ocean Dr. (14th St.), Miami Beach, 305-531-8300
■ "From sophisticated cuisine to comfort food", this "unpretentious" breakfast, lunch and dinner "hangout" in South Beach's Penguin Hotel "keeps getting better", serving "delicious", "affordable" American fare in an "ultra-casual" setting with "great views of the beach" and "lovely people-watching" as well; since it's been "discovered by tourists", the lines are "out of control", but the "friendly", "quick" staff keeps things moving.

Fujihana   21 | 14 | 22 | $24 |
Loehmann's Fashion Island, 18757 Biscayne Blvd. (NE 187th St.), Aventura, 305-932-8080
11768 SW 88th St. (SW 117th Ave.), Kendall, 305-275-9003
www.fujihanakendall.com
■ These "reliable" strip-mall Asians in Aventura and Kendall offer "vast Thai-Japanese menus" and feature "great, fresh" sushi including a "crunchy spicy tuna roll that's a must"; "pleasant" digs, "friendly" service and "good value" make them a "better choice" than some of the "overpriced" places in the area.

Gables Diner   16 | 14 | 16 | $19 |
2320 Galiano St. (Aragon Ave.), Coral Gables, 305-567-0330; www.gablesdiner.com
☒ "An all-American diner" "gone upscale", this "standby" in Coral Gables caters to a "yuppie crowd" serving "old classics with an edge" like the signature turkey meatloaf "that's a hit"; critics carp the service is "disorganized" and the prices are "higher than they should be", but admit the "various" offerings make it "great for families."

Garcia's   22 | 12 | 17 | $21 |
398 NW North River Dr. (NW 5th St. Bridge), Miami, 305-375-0765
■ It may be "tricky to find" and "hard to park" at this "funky" "local treasure" on the shores of the Miami River

Miami/Dade County   F | D | S | C |

skirting Downtown, but "it's worth it" to "feast" on the "best fish sandwiches in town" as well as "cheap" but "sophisticated" seafood; its "overcrowded" digs are affectionately deemed a "dump", but "natives" know there's a "nice patio" that's perfect for "long Friday lunches."

Gil Capa's Bistro   ▽ 23 | 14 | 22 | $26 |
Sabal Chase Shoppes, 10712 SW 113th Pl. (W. Perimeter Rd.), Kendall, 305-273-1102
◪ Even though few surveyors are familiar with this longtime mom-and-pop Italian in Kendall, partisans "pray that it remains undiscovered" so they can keep the "heavenly" garlic rolls, "to-die-for" pastas and "veal Française that can bring you to tears" all to themselves; it helps to be a "friend of Gil" and the menu may be "unvaried", but regulars have "loved it for more than 25 years."

Globe Cafe & Bar ⓢ   17 | 19 | 14 | $27 |
377 Alhambra Circle (Le Jeune Rd.), Coral Gables, 305-445-3555
■ The "young and the restless" find their way to this "hot" Gables Eclectic adjacent to a travel agency where the "sophisticated" setting with "drapes, sofa seating, dark wood and interesting paintings" makes it a "great place to socialize"; the food's "good" if "not exciting", but worldly types know it's the "drinks, the jazz and ladies at the bar" that are reasons to think globally.

Gordon Biersch Brewery   14 | 17 | 14 | $25 |
1201 Brickell Ave. (12th St.), Miami, 786-425-1130; www.gordonbiersch.com
◪ Its "happening location" Downtown makes this brewpub chain link a "great after-work happy hour" destination, and the "fine" housemade beers don't hurt either; its American menu featuring a "well-honed variety of vittles" elicits cheers (the "best burger") and jeers ("average bar food"), but it's still "where it's at on Friday nights."

Granny Feelgood's ⓢ   18 | 10 | 15 | $15 |
25 W. Flagler St. (Miami Ave.), Miami, 305-377-9600
◪ This Downtown breakfast and lunch health fooder is hailed by "on-the-go business types" who want "good", "light", "fast" fare featuring both "veg and non-veg options" like "great", "fresh salads" and fish dishes; time will tell if regulars feel good about the recent change of ownership.

Grappa ⓢ   22 | 21 | 21 | $37 |
5837 Sunset Dr. (bet. SW 58th Ave. & US 1), South Miami, 305-668-9119
◪ "A happening spot" in South Miami, this quite "classy" Northern Italian provides a "lively ambiance" for "getting together with friends" over "delicious", "well-executed" fare served by a "professional" staff in a "pretty" setting; grouches, however, have problems grappa-ling with the "noisy" environment and "high prices."

42   subscribe to zagat.com

Miami/Dade County F | D | S | C |

Grass Lounge ●◐☒   ▽ 19 | 27 | 15 | $44
28 NE 40th St. (N. Miami Ave.), Miami, 305-573-3355;
www.grasslounge.com

☒ "The beautiful people have migrated" to this "divine" newcomer in the Design District with "sexy" "all-outdoor" seating featuring a "Trader Vic's–meets–Prada" decor replete with "tiki huts"; the "creative" Pan-Asian–Caribbean cuisine as well as "gracious" service gratify its grassroots constituency, though a few lounge lizards taunt it's "trying too hard to be cool."

Graziano's Parrilla Argentina   24 | 19 | 20 | $41
9227 SW 40th St./Bird Rd. (92nd Ave.), Westchester,
305-225-0008; www.parrilla.com

■ What started as "a hole-in-the-wall" is now Miami's "best Argentinean", and this "impressive", "popular" Westchester *parillada* (grill) had to expand to accommodate the hungry carnivores who stampede for "excellent" steaks and "great" sweetbreads complemented by an "extensive" selection of "reasonably priced" wines; repentant regulars warn you'll have to "go to confession" if you indulge in the dulce de leche crêpes.

GRAZIE CAFE   25 | 16 | 25 | $39
Suniland Plaza, 11523 S. Dixie Hwy. (bet. SW 14th & 15th Sts.),
Pinecrest, 305-232-5533

■ Groupies are grateful for this "superb" "family-owned" trattoria tucked into a Pinecrest strip mall and hail the "huge portions" of "fabulous", "well-executed" Northern Italian dishes and "excellent wines" ferried by a "friendly", "knowledgeable" staff who've been known to "sing as they toss your pasta"; a few find it "pricey for a neighborhood place", but admit it provides a "wonderful experience."

Green Street Cafe   18 | 16 | 16 | $23
3110 Commodore Plaza (Main Hwy.), Coconut Grove,
305-567-0662

■ "For a good introduction to Grove culture", "an outside table" at this "French-Med" "mainstay" is "a must", especially on "weekend mornings" when you'll see the "SoBe hangover crowd, churchgoers, motorcycle" gangs – and lots of "dogs"; "brunch is best", followed by "great lunches and dinners" and there's a "terrific wine list" including some 107 by the glass, though, alas, "uneven" service disappoints doubters.

Grillfish   21 | 17 | 19 | $31
1444 Collins Ave. (Española Way), Miami Beach, 305-538-9908;
www.grillfish.com

☒ "The name says it all" at this South Beach branch of a seafood mini-chain known for "well-priced", "fresh", "delicious" fish prepared "over open flames" and paired with a choice of "exquisite sauces"; though the "snappy"

vote at zagat.com   43

Miami/Dade County | F | D | S | C |

staff sometimes displays an "attitude", overall it provides a "non-trendy", "casual" setting with a "fun ambiance" that's "good for getting together with friends."

Guayacan Restaurant | – | – | – | M |
1933 SW Eighth St. (bet. 19th & 21st Aves.), Miami, 305-649-2015
9857 SW 40th St./Bird Rd. (bet. 97th & 99th Aves.), Westchester, 305-559-6655
You can't beat the "fabulous appetizers" and the "excellent" steaks at these Little Havana and Westchester Nicaraguan "dives" where the "nice servers" do their best to ensure a "great" experience especially if you've got the family along; weekends usually find singing and piano music included in the already low tabs.

Hanna's Gourmet Diner | ▽ 25 | 13 | 20 | $27 |
13951 Biscayne Blvd. (135th St.), North Miami Beach, 305-947-2255
■ It looks like an old-fashioned diner, so the "authentic" French food served at this North Miami Beach bastion comes as a "delightful surprise" to the uninitiated; a "wide selection" of "delicious", "well-prepared" dishes including "great fish" are "reliable", and those who find it "pricey" should check out the prix fixe lunches and dinners.

Hard Rock Cafe | 12 | 21 | 14 | $24 |
Bayside Mktpl., 401 Biscayne Blvd. (NE 5th St.), Miami, 305-377-3110; www.hardrock.com
■ "Add another T-shirt to your collection" and peruse the "rock 'n' roll memorabilia" at these "fun" chain links that are "heaven" for "music mavens" but a bit hard on food lovers who lament the "generic" Traditional American fare; still, "open-air" seating at the Downtown and Key West editions makes dealing with the "dire service" a little easier.

Havana Harry's | 17 | 15 | 15 | $23 |
4612 Le Jeune Rd. (Ponce de Leon Blvd.), Coral Gables, 305-661-2622; www.havanaharrys.com
■ "Huge portions" of "better-than-average Cuban" *comida* in "slightly fancier" digs "than you'll find in Calle Ocho" please partisans at this Coral Gables "storefront"; however, a four-point drop in the Food score suggests the "quality of the fare has gone down", and snipers say the service at this "onetime favorite" "needs improvement."

Here Comes the Sun ⌀ | 19 | 6 | 16 | $16 |
2188 NE 123rd St. (east of Biscayne Blvd.), North Miami, 305-893-5711
■ Little darlings delight in the "delicious" health food served at this North Miami "landmark" that's been dispensing "delicious", "fresh", "consistent" "soups, salads and veggie dishes" along with vitamins since the '70s; a few feel a call to "*Trading Spaces*" is in order ("needs a redesign"), but more affirm it's "always a favorite."

Miami/Dade County | F | D | S | C |

Hiro Japanese ● | 17 | 10 | 13 | $29 |
3007 NE 163rd St. (Biscayne Blvd.), North Miami Beach, 305-948-3687

☑ You've "gotta love a sushi bar that's open until 3:30 in the morning" in otherwise sleepy North Miami Beach; some say that's the "only redeeming feature" of this Japanese, but others swear by the "mighty good", "imaginative" sushi and "efficient service" at this "high-volume crowd-pleaser."

Hosteria Romana ● | ▽ 27 | 21 | 27 | $36 |
429 Española Way (bet. Drexel & Washington Aves.), Miami Beach, 305-532-4299; www.hosteriaromana.com

☑ Though not many surveyors have stumbled across this "real deal" on "amazing Española Way", those who have declare it "looks and feels like a favorite neighborhood restaurant in Rome" with "cozy decor", "delightful alfresco" seating and "waiters yelling in Italian"; the cuisine's "awesome" and "authentic", from "great pastas" to "the best veal parm in town", all delivered by an "excellent" staff; N.B. check out its new wine and tapas bar.

House of India | 17 | 10 | 14 | $23 |
22 Merrick Way (Douglas Rd.), Coral Gables, 305-444-2348

☑ Supporters of this 30-year-old subcontinental in Coral Gables praise its "substantial", "well-prepared", "exotic" Indian fare and "good-value" lunch buffet; curry-mudgeons, however, critique the food as "mediocre", the digs as "dingy" and the service as "tortuously slow" ("put plenty of money in the parking meter").

HOUSTON'S | 21 | 20 | 20 | $29 |
201 Miracle Mile (Ponce de Leon Blvd.), Coral Gables, 305-529-0141
17355 Biscayne Blvd. (NE 172nd St.), North Miami Beach, 305-947-2000
www.houstons.com

See review in Ft. Lauderdale/Broward County Directory.

Hy-Vong | 22 | 5 | 11 | $24 |
3458 SW Eighth St. (SW 34th Ave.), Miami, 305-446-3674

☑ Miamians endure "long waits" in muggy weather, "extremely slow", even "rude service" and "cramped quarters" for what acolytes hail as "heavenly", "delicious", "authentic" French-accented Vietnamese classics at this Little Havana "hole-in-the-wall"; though a five-point drop in the Food rating gives credence to critics who claim it's been "vastly overated", the faithful insist it's "still a favorite."

Icebox Café | 24 | 13 | 16 | $23 |
1657 Michigan Ave. (Lincoln Rd.), Miami Beach, 305-538-8448; www.iceboxcafe.com

■ A "cute", "casual" and "smart" alternative in South Beach, this New American–Eclectic eatery just off Lincoln

Miami/Dade County F | D | S | C

Road offers an "interesting, daily changing menu" of "expertly prepared" dishes as well as "decadent desserts" at "fair prices"; "simple but good" Sunday brunch and "pretty decor" are pluses, and though a few would like to ice the "uncomfortable chairs, they take nothing away from the best food" around.

Il Fico ▽ 17 | 14 | 21 | $26
4770 Biscayne Blvd. (36th St.), Miami, 305-572-0400
◪ "Fig lovers" figure this "unpretentious" "great new spot" on Biscayne Boulevard's Upper East Side is "worth a drive" for "wonderful" Mediterranean fare with many dishes featuring the namesake fruit as well as pre-meal "tasty tapenade with bread" that's so addictive it may "kill your appetite"; it's also a "good value" for the area.

Il Sole ● 16 | 14 | 13 | $37
626 Lincoln Rd. (Pennsylvania Ave.), Miami Beach, 305-673-1858
◪ It's "worth going" to this South Beach Italian for the "people-watching" from the "patio seating alone" but the "good" pastas and "great wines" also have admirers; alas, as with "most Lincoln Road" eateries, the service is "spotty", and some sigh the food's "unmemorable."

Imlee 24 | 12 | 18 | $30
South Park Ctr., 12663 S. Dixie Hwy. (bet. 126th & 128th Sts.), Pinecrest, 786-293-2223; www.imleeindianbistro.com
■ "The best Indian food in the region" is served at this "excellent" Pinecrest storefront where "everything is made from scratch" ("go with a lot of time on your hands") yielding "superb", "exciting" dishes with "outstanding" vegetarian options; the "small", "spotless", "charming" setting and "gracious" service add to an "enjoyable" experience.

Islas Canarias 19 | 8 | 17 | $18
285 NW 27th Ave. (3rd St.), Miami, 305-649-0440
13697 SW 26th St. (SW 137th Ave.), Miami, 305-559-6666 ●
■ For some of the "best Cuban in town", fans flock to these "homes away from home" in Little Havana and West Dade for "classic" vaca frita, palomilla steak and ham hocks that are "as good as any *abuela*" can make at prices that can only be called cheep; it helps to know Spanish at this family-friendly duo.

Jake's Bar and Grill ●☒ 18 | 20 | 17 | $28
6901 Red Rd. (San Ignacio St.), Coral Gables, 305-662-8632
■ One of Coral Gable's "favorite places" to "have a great time" is this "beautiful" New American, a "hybrid of elegant restaurant and sports grill" with "low lighting" and live jazz on Tuesdays; a "spectacular New York strip" stands out on the "good" New American menu, the wine selection is "interesting" and the "unbeatable prices" are just jake.

46 subscribe to zagat.com

Miami/Dade County | F | D | S | C |

Joe Allen ◐   21 | 17 | 22 | $35
1787 Purdy Ave. (bet. 17th & 18th Sts.), Miami Beach, 305-531-7007; www.joeallenrestaurant.com

■ "I like it in New York, and I like it in Miami" laud "locals" of this "reliable" "jewel" that provides an "oasis from the South Beach madness", where the "straightforward", "reasonably priced" American "comfort food" meets the "highest standards" and the "friendly" bartenders mix drinks that'll put "hair on your chest"; an "eclectic crowd" also extols the "excellent" service and "sophisticated" but "low-key" setting.

Joe's Seafood   19 | 14 | 16 | $41
400 NW North River Dr. (NW 6th Ave.), Miami, 305-374-5637

◪ Often confused in name with the famous South Beach stone crab spot, this "grubby" Cuban seafooder on the Miami River has its own following that favors the "delicious" fin fare including "awesome fried shrimp" as well as the "great prices"; malcontents, however, maintain the chow's "mediocre" and "could do without the dancing waiters" when there's live salsa on weekends.

JOE'S STONE CRAB   26 | 19 | 22 | $54
11 Washington Ave. (1st St.), Miami Beach, 305-673-0365; www.joesstonecrab.com

◪ "Go early" to this 90-year-old South Beach "forever classic" because "getting seated is like winning the lottery" (and is once again voted Most Popular in Miami); once inside, however, you'll "devour" the "best" crustaceans "on the planet" (in season October–mid-May) and "heavenly" sides in an "old-school" setting; cognoscenti counsel "avoid the ridiculous waits" by getting takeout next door – either way, don't forget to "leave room for the Key lime pie"; N.B. now open for dinner in summer, although it is closed Mondays and Tuesdays.

John Martin's ◐   16 | 17 | 16 | $25
253 Miracle Mile (bet. Le Jeune Rd. & Ponce de Leon Blvd.), Coral Gables, 305-445-3777; www.johnmartins.com

■ Wayward Gaelics seeking a wee "bit of Ireland" in Coral Gables are gratified by this "welcoming" pub with its "attractive", "old-world" setting and "traditional" fare from "great potato soup" to corned beef and cabbage, all "cheap" and "consistent" and served by a "warm" staff.

Jumbo's ⊭   – | – | – | I
7501 NW Seventh Ave. (NW 75th St.), Miami, 305-751-1127

Even after 50 years, this old-time 24/7 Southerner still satisfies with the "best" fried chicken and shrimp costing mere peanuts as well as a staff that offers "traditional hospitality"; those hankering for a late-night grease job report it's "surprisingly safe to visit at 2 AM" despite its "dicey" Downtown neighborhood.

vote at zagat.com   **47**

Miami/Dade County F | D | S | C

Kampai
22 | 14 | 18 | $25
Waterways Shopping Ctr., 3575 NE 207th St. (NE 34th Ave.), Aventura, 305-931-6410
8745 Sunset Dr. (SW 87th Ave.), South Miami, 305-596-1551
www.kampaisunset.com

◪ "When you feel like Japanese without the theatrics", these "dependable" Aventura and South Miami siblings fill the bill with "fresh", "excellent" sushi and "good" Thai dishes as well; a "quiet", "relaxed atmosphere" and a staff that "tries hard to please" also pull in kampai-dres, though critics carp the digs are "nondescript."

Kebab Indian ⓈⓏ
– | – | – | M
514 NE 167th St. (NE 5th Ave.), North Miami Beach, 305-940-6309

"Tons of scrumptious Indian food" at the "great lunch buffet" and "spicy", "delicious" dinner entrees curry favor at this North Miami Beach storefront in the heart of Little Asia; though a few find the prices to be "high" for this cuisine, others insist it's worth it.

Khoury's
19 | 10 | 16 | $21
5887 SW 73rd St. (US 1), South Miami, 305-662-7707

◪ "Superlative salads", "good hummus" and "great kebabs" all made with "marvelous seasonings" as well as "heavenly pastries" are savored by South Miamians at this "family-owned" Lebanese "landmark"; though detractors could do without the "dreary" decor and sometimes "slow service", the Middle Eastern fare's "great for lunch on the run."

Kyung Ju
– | – | – | M
400 NE 167th St. (NE 4th Ave.), North Miami Beach, 305-947-3838

The few surveyors who've discovered the "only Korean restaurant" in town tout the fare at this NMB stalwart as "amazing", with "kimchi and mando" that are as "good as it gets" as well as "great barbecue"; the setting's "comfortable" and the staff's as "quick and helpful" as can be (despite a language gap).

La Carreta
17 | 11 | 14 | $19
5350 W. 16th Ave. (bet. 53rd & 54th Sts.), Hialeah, 305-823-5200 ◐
11740 N. Kendall Dr. (SW 117th Ave.), Kendall, 305-596-5973 ◐
12 Crandon Blvd. (Harbor Dr.), Key Biscayne, 305-365-1177 ◐
Miami Int'l Airport, concourse D, departure level, Miami, 305-871-3003
10633 NW 12th St. (NW 107th Ave.), Miami, 305-463-9778 ◐
3632 SW Eighth St. (36th Ave.), Miami, 305-444-7501 ◐
8650 SW 40th St./Bird Rd. (87th Ave.), Westchester, 305-553-8383 ◐

■ With locations throughout the city, including branches at the airport and on Calle Ocho, this "classic" Cuban

Miami/Dade County   F | D | S | C

chainlet guarantees "you won't go hungry" with "large portions" of "good", "rib-sticking", "cheap" chow; "not much English is spoken", but the staff's "friendly" and "fast", and if you're not "wowed by the atmosphere", you can always get it to go.

La Casita   19 | 13 | 18 | $21
112 Giralda Ave. (Ponce de Leon Blvd.), Coral Gables, 305-461-2729
3805 SW Eighth St. (bet. Galiano & 38th Aves.), Coral Gables, 305-448-8224
Plaza West Mall, 2660 SW 137th Ave. (Coral Way), Kendall, 305-553-0600
7931 NW Second St. (bet. Flagler & 79th Sts.), Miami, 305-267-4444

■ The "great", "traditional" Cuban fare served at this mini-chain is "so inexpensive you can hardly afford to eat at home", especially when you opt for the "extraordinary lunch specials"; the decor's "quaint", the service is "good" and prodigal kids claim the "flan's better than my mother's, but please don't tell her I said so."

La Dorada ●   24 | 19 | 22 | $53
177 Giralda Ave. (Ponce de Leon Blvd.), Coral Gables, 305-446-2002

◪ Afishionados affirm this "upscale" Coral Gables "Madrid-style" Mediterranean offers "one of the best experiences" around thanks to "excellent" seafood that's "flown in daily from Spain (in first class judging from the prices)" as well as the "delightful" "old-world" waiters; opponents object it's "overrated", but perhaps they haven't sampled the "amazing salt-baked fish."

La Gastronomia ⌧   23 | 13 | 18 | $22
127 Giralda Ave. (bet. Galiano St. & Ponce de Leon Blvd.), Coral Gables, 305-448-8599

◪ Coral Gables groupies "have fallen in love" with this "comfy", "cozy" Italian purveying practically "perfect" pizzas and pastas "prepared with flair and care" and "great" profiteroles, all "inexpensive"; others can't overlook the "cramped seating" and "disrespectful" service, but admit the owners are "gracious", and like the fact that "you can bring your own wine" (though some "excellent" choices are available).

La Loggia ⌧   24 | 23 | 23 | $25
68 W. Flagler St. (SW 1st Ave.), Miami, 305-373-4800; www.laloggiarestaurant.com

■ "Great for meeting friends before a show at Gusman or a "power lunch" between trials, this "busy" Northern Italian "across from the courthouse" Downtown serves "wonderful" food including "pumpkin ravioli that's better than sex"; the "Tuscany"-inspired setting is "beautiful",

Miami/Dade County   F | D | S | C |

and the equally "gorgeous" staff provides "fast" service for "movers and shakers" looking to move on.

La Lupa di Roma ◐   ▽ 19 | 15 | 19 | $32 |
610 Lincoln Rd. (Pennsylvania Ave.), Miami Beach, 305-532-6657

■ A "hidden treasure" in South Beach "tucked away in a storefront on the Lincoln Mall", this "great family-run" Italian cooks up "fresh", "good", "un-Americanized" fare and offers some "tasty", "uncommon" dishes among the "affordable" options; "nice outdoor dining" and an "excellent wine list" also give it a bit of "Roman" realness.

Lan   22 | 11 | 21 | $22 |
Dadeland Station, 8332 S. Dixie Hwy. (84th St.), Kendall, 305-661-8141

■ "Fabulous Pan-Asian cuisine" "never disappoints" at this "hidden gem" in a Dadeland "discount mall"; "impeccable sushi and noodles" as well as "super-creative specials" are all "delicious", "well presented" and a "terrific value" to boot, and the "congenial", "service-oriented" staff helps atone for a lack of "ambiance."

La Palma   19 | 23 | 20 | $38 |
116 Alhambra Circle (Galiano St.), Coral Gables, 305-445-8777; www.lapalmarestaurant.net

■ The "fabulous courtyard" with its "fountain and light-decorated trees" makes this "old-world" Coral Gables Northern Italian "one of the most romantic in town", made more so by "lovely" service and "great" entertainment; the food's "delicious", featuring "rich" pastas and "fantastic desserts", and the lunch buffet is "wonderful" (and may be the "greatest deal in town").

La Paloma   20 | 22 | 21 | $36 |
10999 Biscayne Blvd. (NE 110th St.), North Miami, 305-891-0505

◪ "A genteel dowager" in North Miami, this "old-world" Continental has been "enchanting" the "senior" set with its "glitzy", "elegantly baroque decor", "professional, formal service" and "consistently good" cuisine for more than a quarter of a century; perhaps it could use some "updating", but its faithful flock finds it "reliable" and enjoys an early-bird that's "one of the best deals in the city."

Lario's on the Beach ◐   20 | 20 | 18 | $33 |
820 Ocean Dr. (bet. 8th & 9th Sts.), Miami Beach, 305-532-9577

◪ Gloria Estefan's oceanfront "hot spot" is the perfect place to "bring out-of-towners" for their "first taste" of "*magnifico*", "mouthwatering Cuban cuisine" served in a "lively party atmosphere" in which most nights end with "everyone dancing"; the food may be "cheaper" and "more authentic in Little Havana", but it still provides "great value for South Beach."

Miami/Dade County   F | D | S | C

La Sandwicherie ⓞ   24 | 11 | 19 | $11
229 14th St. (bet. Collins & Washington Aves.), Miami Beach, 305-532-8934; www.lasandwicherie.com

■ "Don't be scared by the tattoo parlor next door" to this "teeny outdoor counter" in South Beach, because you'd be missing out on "possibly the best French bread sandwiches on the planet"; the "big", "zesty" creations come at "rock-bottom prices" and are assembled by "gorgeous" "food slingers" who also make "excellent" smoothies; N.B. open 10 AM to 6 AM.

Las Culebrinas   24 | 16 | 20 | $26
2890 SW 27th Ave. (Coconut Ave.), Coconut Grove, 305-448-4090
4700 W. Flagler St. (47th Ave.), Miami, 305-445-2337

■ These "family-oriented" *hermanas* in the Grove and Downtown serve "fantastic", "authentic" yet "imaginative" Cuban-Spanish fare in portions so "huge" that "four can share one appetizer"; the service is "good", the digs, if a bit "worn", are "civilized" and best of all, the "*muy bueno*" food's *muy* cheap too.

Las Vacas Gordas ⓞ   21 | 8 | 12 | $27
933 Normandy Dr. (Bay Drive E.), Miami Beach, 305-867-1717

◪ For a "trip to the pampas without leaving Miami", this "traditional Argentinean *parrilla*" with sidewalk seating in Normandy Isles offers "outstanding" steak and "awesome chimichurri sauce" that would be "worth it at twice the price"; "loud" music and "slow", "indifferent service reduces the dining experience" for groucho gauchos, but supporters still hope the "tourists don't discover" it.

Latin American   20 | 8 | 14 | $15
2740 SW 27th Ave. (US 1), Coconut Grove, 305-445-9339
2940 SW 22nd St./Coral Way (bet. 27th & 29th Aves.), Coral Gables, 305-448-6809 ⓞ
1750 W. 68th St. (bet. Palmetto Expwy. & 16th Ave.), Hialeah, 305-556-0641 ⓞ
9606 Sunset Dr. (SW 97th Ave.), Miami, 305-279-4353
9796 SW 24th St./Coral Way (97th Ave.), Westchester, 305-226-2393

◪ "A must-do for visitors and locals alike", this "excellent" quintet is known for its "superb Cuban sandwiches" and "huge portions" of "authentic comfort food" with "Latin flair"; the fare may "vary from location to location" and there's no decor to speak of, but the "cheap" chow and "unpretentious" atmosphere pleases partisans.

Laurenzo's Cafe ⌀   17 | 7 | 10 | $11
16385 W. Dixie Hwy. (NE 164th St.), North Miami Beach, 305-945-6381; www.laurenzos.com

■ This "help-yourself" counter "in the middle of a family-owned grocery store" is a "true gem" for NMB lovers of

Miami/Dade County　　　　　F | D | S | C

"mmm" Italian-American dishes like "good eggplant parmigiana"; there's "no atmosphere" and it's only open on weekdays till 7:30 PM, but the "big portions" and "bargain prices" have made it a must-stop for 40 years.

La Valentina ◐　　　　　▽ 18 | 22 | 18 | $34
Aventura Mall, 19501 Biscayne Blvd., Suite 783 (William Lehman Cswy.), Aventura, 305-705-1686

■ Providing "a great alternative" at the Aventura Mall, this yearling satisfies hungry muchachos with "upscale", "interesting" Mexican fare in a "surprisingly elegant setting"; moreover, the staff's "attentive", and weekend nights are a "blast" when there's a full-on 'Latin party' till 4 AM.

Le Bouchon du Grove　　　　　23 | 16 | 19 | $33
3430 Main Hwy. (Grand Ave.), Coconut Grove, 305-448-6060

■ The vibe "ranges from romantic to raucous depending on the night" at this "snappy French bistro" in the Grove; it gets "props for serving breakfast, lunch and dinner", all the dishes are "delicious" and "well prepared" ("amazing moules frites") and the "entertaining" owners and staff "make every meal a party"; though the "tiny" space gets "tight", it's still a "great neighborhood hangout."

Le Festival*Casa Vecchia　　　　　16 | 17 | 18 | $39
2120 Salzedo St. (bet. Alcazar & Minorca Aves.), Coral Gables, 305-442-8545

☒ Fans of the former "grande dame" of the Coral Gables dining scene aren't so sure its latest incarnation as a French-Italian hybrid "under one roof" works; some find the food "good" but others liken it to "cafeteria fare" and knock a nightly vocalist who is clearly "not Frank Sinatra"; despite a "beautiful interior", many lament it's "lost its glow."

Lemon Twist ◐　　　　　▽ 22 | 17 | 19 | $34
908 71st St. (Bay Dr. E.), Miami Beach, 305-868-2075

■ "One of the best-kept secrets" in Miami Beach, this "charming bistro" whisks you "out of the maelstrom" and into a "great all-around" experience that starts with "addictive" olives, moves on to "excellent", "honest" French fare and ends with a complimentary "lemon twist liquor" shot after your meal; the good-"value" prices ensure connoisseurs keep "returning."

L'Entrecôte de Paris　　　　　18 | 18 | 18 | $36
419 Washington Ave. (bet. 4th & 5th Sts.), Miami Beach, 305-673-1002

☒ Bring a "big gang, sit outside" and feast on "steak frites that's the bee's knees" at this South Beach Gallic bistro; though the menu is "very limited", the offerings provide "good value" and come with the "best french fries" around, though a few fulminate against "clueless service" and a "loud ambiance."

52　　　　　　　　　　　　subscribe to zagat.com

Miami/Dade County | F | D | S | C |

Le Provençal | 21 | 20 | 21 | $35 |
382 Miracle Mile (Le Jeune Rd.), Coral Gables, 305-448-8984

■ "There's a reason this bistro has been successful" – actually, there are several, starting with the "superb" French fare including a "wonderful wine and cheese selection" at "reasonable" prices; a "charming", "romantic" setting including a patio and "gracious" hosts and "impeccable service" are also acclaimed at this "Coral Gables standby"; P.S. the "lunch prix fixe is a bargain."

Les Deux Fontaines ◑ | 16 | 18 | 15 | $36 |
Hotel Ocean, 1230 Ocean Dr. (bet. 12th & 13th Sts.), Miami Beach, 305-672-7878; www.lesdeuxfontaines.com

◪ *Amis* gush over the "brilliant" "beachfront dining" on the "lovely" patio at this Hotel Ocean French seafooder as well as the "pleasant" live Dixieland jazz offered nightly; the "mediocre" fare, "overpriced specials" and "lackluster" service have cynics spewing it's a SoBe "tourist trap."

Les Halles ◑ | 18 | 17 | 16 | $33 |
2415 Ponce de Leon Blvd. (Miracle Mile), Coral Gables, 305-461-1099

◪ "Like its two NYC sisters", this "high-end bistro" is a "neighborhood favorite" in the Gables thanks to "terrific" French dishes like "to-die-for tartare" and the "best frites in town" along with a "relaxed" atmosphere and "authentic" decor replete with "wood-paneled walls and mirrors"; however, antagonists Halles-lege the food's "erratic" and the service can be "rude."

Lila's | ∇ 22 | 13 | 21 | $19 |
8518 SW 24th St./Coral Way (SW 84th Ave.), Miami, 305-553-6061

■ A visit to this "classic Cuban" is "like coming home" for those who crave the signature "Lila's steak with a mountain of fries" topped off by an "unparalleled flan" that make it "worth a drive" out to Westchester; it's also an "incredible bargain for that much food", making it easy to overlook the strip-mall setting.

Lincoln Road Café ◑ | 17 | 10 | 16 | $22 |
943 Lincoln Rd. (Michigan Ave.), Miami Beach, 305-538-8066

■ "There's nothing fancy about this" South Beach Cuban "relic" "except its location" on the "happening" Lincoln Road "where some of Florida's best people-watching takes place"; lots of "locals eat here", though, delighted by the "delicious", "traditional" and "so-cheap eats" like "scrumptious ropa vieja" served by a "friendly" staff.

Linda B. Steakhouse | 16 | 18 | 18 | $44 |
320 Crandon Blvd. (East Dr.), Key Biscayne, 305-361-1111

◪ This "pleasant" steakhouse is the place to go if "you're into power brokering" on Key Biscayne, with "great" rib-eye,

vote at zagat.com 53

Miami/Dade County | F | D | S | C |

"lovely", "old-fashioned" service" and a "relaxing" vibe; those who'd rather B elsewhere pout it's "past its prime" and pooh-pooh the "too-expensive", "unmemorable" fare.

Little Havana | 18 | 13 | 17 | $21 |
12727 Biscayne Blvd. (bet. NE 126th & 128th Sts.), North Miami, 305-899-9069

■ Providing a bit of "Calle Ocho in North Miami", this "small" "neighborhood restaurant" serves "flavorful", "fresh" and "truly authentic Cuban food"; sure, the "decor's nothing to write home about" (even with the recent redo), and it can get "loud" when "filled with children", but it also boasts "great prices" and there's something for everybody on the "extensive menu."

Little Saigon ◐≠ | – | – | – | I |
16752 N. Miami Ave. (bet. NE 167th & 168th Sts.), North Miami Beach, 305-653-3377

Sandwiched between a gas station and a Dairy Queen, this "friendly" North Miami Beach Vietnamese may have "no decor to speak of save a fish tank", but it still offers "superb" Vietnamese vittles; the "healthy", "fresh" fare features papaya salad, pho and lots of seafood.

Locanda Sibilla ◐ | – | – | – | M |
833 Lincoln Rd. (bet. Jefferson & Meridian Aves.), Miami Beach, 305-695-1654

A "good new addition" to "fabulous" Lincoln Road, this sidewalk Italian cafe owned by the Bice group impresses locals with its "outstanding pasta" and "delicious desserts", "fast", "friendly" service and, of course, prime people-watching opportunities; considering the South Beach location, the prices are surprisingly reasonable.

Lombardi's ◐ | ∇ 20 | 19 | 18 | $34 |
Bayside Mktpl., 401 Biscayne Blvd. (bet. NE 4th & 5th Sts.), Miami, 305-381-9580; www.lombardisrestaurants.com

■ "Even though it's located in the touristy" section of Downtown's Bayside Marketplace, the food's "excellent" and "consistent" at this "solid Italian eatery"; regulars recommend the "alfresco dining experience" on the patio to enjoy the "great view of Miami" and Latin music on weekends that creates a "lively" atmosphere.

Los Ranchos | 19 | 16 | 18 | $29 |
Cocowalk, 3015 Grand Ave. (Virginia St.), Coconut Grove, 305-461-8222
2728 Ponce de Leon Blvd. (bet. Almeria & Sevilla Aves.), Coral Gables, 305-446-0050
The Falls Shopping Ctr., 8888 SW 136th St. (SW 88th Pl.), Kendall, 305-238-6867
Bayside Mktpl., 401 Biscayne Blvd. (bet. NE 4th & 5th Sts.), Miami, 305-375-8188

(continued)

Miami/Dade County | F | D | S | C |

(continued)
Los Ranchos
Holiday Plaza, 125 SW 107th Ave. (Flagler St.), Miami, 305-221-9367
www.losranchossteakhouse.com

Ranch hands hankering for a "great cut of beef" go for the "delectable churrasco" with "outstanding" chimichurri followed by the "delicious" tres leches dessert at this Nicaraguan steakhouse chain; the "bargain prices" are also a plus, however, a few fume about the "indifferent" service and "noisy" atmosphere.

Macaluso's   22 | 17 | 20 | $40 |
1747 Alton Rd. (Dade Blvd.), Miami Beach, 305-604-1811

Direct from Staten Island, NY, "and proud of it", this "charming" Italian in South Beach ladles out "huge portions" of "incredible", "zesty" pastas made from chef-owner Michael Macaluso's "family recipes" in an "attractive", "intimate" space that makes you "forget its strip-mall" setting; nevertheless, dissenters dish it needs to "ease up on the prices and the attitude."

Magnum   ∇ 21 | 18 | 24 | $30 |
709 NE 79th St. (1 block east of Biscayne Blvd.), Miami, 305-757-3368

This Upper East Side "neighborhood joint in an area that desperately needed one" "feels like a speakeasy" with an entrance in the back and a "dark", "loungy atmosphere"; a mixed (gay/straight) clientele clamors for the "outstanding" American fare such as signature crab cakes and digs the "divine" talent on the piano every night.

Maiko ☻   23 | 11 | 20 | $28 |
1255 Washington Ave. (bet. 12th & 13th Sts.), Miami Beach, 305-531-6369

For more than a decade (forever in SoBe years), this "convenient", "not-trendy" sushi bar has delighted locals with "generous portions" of "excellent", "creative" raw fish and other Japanese specialties; a few feel the "basic decor" needs a maiko-ver, but the "good value" keeps it "popular."

Mama Jennie's   16 | 8 | 17 | $15 |
11720 NE Second Ave. (NE 119th St.), North Miami, 305-757-3627;
www.mamajennies.com

Loyalists of this 30-year-old North Miami "local landmark" laud the "large portions" of "good homestyle" Italian, "cute", "casual" setting and "friendly" service; it's also "cheap", but bashers boo the "bland", "Americanized" fare, saying "you get what you pay for."

Mama Vieja   – | – | – | M |
235 23rd St. (Collins Ave.), Miami Beach, 305-538-2400;
www.mamavieja.com

"Great, authentic Colombian cuisine" including "fantastic red snapper" is not the only attraction at this "down-

vote at zagat.com 55

Miami/Dade County | F | D | S | C |

home", "casual" hole-in-the-wall in Miami Beach; there's also an "attentive", "friendly" staff and a setting festooned floor-to-ceiling with hats – and if you donate your own bonnet, Mama will give you a meal on the house.

Mango's Tropical Cafe ● | 16 | 21 | 16 | $31 |
900 Ocean Dr. (bet. 9th & 10th Sts.), Miami Beach, 305-673-4422; www.mangostropicalcafe.com

☑ "Party all day" and "all night" too at this "ultimate SoBe experience" where "hotties dressed to kill" and "sexy servers" "dance on the bar"; even if "you're not here" for the Latin-accented Eclectic fare, it's "surprisingly good" if "overpriced", and though some sneer it's a "tourist trap", others prefer to have "pure, unadulterated fun."

Mario the Baker ⌀ | 20 | 7 | 16 | $15 |
13695 W. Dixie Hwy. (NE 137th St.), North Miami, 305-891-7641

■ "Two words: garlic rolls" pithily report patrons of this North Miami Southern Italian pizzeria, a "neighborhood haunt" (with a Lauderdale offshoot) for 35 years that also trades in "addictive", "wonderful" pies with "otherworldly crust" at "reasonable" prices; sure, it's "loud", "hectic" and not much on decor, but boosters brag this "treasure" only "gets better."

Mariposa | 22 | 22 | 22 | $29 |
Neiman Marcus/Village of Merrick Park, 390 San Lorenzo Ave., 3rd fl. (S. Le Jeune Rd.), Coral Gables, 786-999-1018

☑ "The ladies who shop" in Coral Gables agree that the comestibles at this New American yearling in Neiman Marcus are "wonderful", especially the "famous popovers with strawberry jam"; "beautiful" decor and a patio are pluses, though some pout it's a bit "pretentious" and warn "do lunch", but "eschew dinner."

MARK'S SOUTH BEACH | 26 | 21 | 23 | $58 |
Nash Hotel, 1120 Collins Ave. (11th St.), Miami Beach, 305-604-9050; www.chefmark.com

■ "When form meets substance, magic happens", most Mark-edly when "celebrity chef"-owner Militello is manning the stoves, and this "chic", "contemporary" SoBe "gem" in the Nash Hotel "never fails" to "amaze" with "refined yet robust" Floribbean fare that's certain to "satisfy the most discriminating palate"; the "penthouse"-caliber cuisine, "fantastic" service and an alternative alfresco space "by the pool" divert attention from the "dark, downstairs" digs.

Maroosh | 21 | 21 | 20 | $26 |
223 Valencia Ave. (Ponce de Leon Blvd.), Coral Gables, 305-476-9800; www.maroosh.com

■ "Awesome Middle Eastern" fare featuring the "best baba ghanoush in the world" and other "fresh", "reasonably priced" specialties lure "locals" to this "friendly" Coral Gables pita-ria; aesthetes applaud its recent move from

Miami/Dade County | F | D | S | C |

a strip mall to a "beautiful building" with a terrace, and weekend belly dancers add to the "enjoyable" experience.

MATSURI | 25 | 13 | 20 | $29 |
5759 SW 40th St./Bird Rd. (Red Rd.), Miami, 305-663-1615
■ Raw-fishionados swear by the "fresh, fresh, fresh" and "reasonably priced" fin fare at this West Miami "little dive" where a "loyal Japanese clientele" along with "Gloria Estefan" go for "the real thing"; despite the "crowded" digs that "could use an upgrade", partisans praise "great original dishes" as well as what may be the "best sushi in town."

Melody Inn | 23 | 18 | 23 | $33 |
83 Andalusia Ave. (1 block south of Miracle Mile), Coral Gables, 305-448-0022
■ The "antithesis of pretentiousness", this "old-world" Coral Gables "institution" offers "comfort" in the form of "wonderful", "straightforward" Swiss-Continental cuisine including "delicious" desserts, an "impressive wine list", "superb" service, a "dark", "romantic" setting and "roses for the ladies"; though the "fantastic specials aren't easy on the wallet", there's an "excellent" prix fixe option.

Melting Pot, The | 20 | 18 | 19 | $37 |
11520 Sunset Dr. (SW 117th Ave.), Miami, 305-279-8816
3143 NE 163rd St. (Biscayne Blvd.), North Miami Beach, 305-947-2228; www.meltingpot.com
See review in Palm Beach County Directory.

Metro Kitchen + Bar | 16 | 24 | 17 | $54 |
(fka Astor Place)
Hotel Astor, 956 Washington Ave. (10th St.), Miami Beach, 305-672-7217; www.hotelastor.com
■ Metropolitan sorts swarm this "sophisticated", "stunning SoBe scene" in the "dolled-up basement" of the Hotel Astor; assessments of the New American food range from "good" to "creative" to "standard", and the service can be "erratic", but the "beautiful people" don't seem to mind.

Mezzanotte | 20 | 19 | 19 | $37 |
Shops of Mayfair, 3390 Mary St. (Florida Ave.), Coconut Grove, 305-448-7677
■ "Party" people praise these "disco pasta" palaces in Coconut Grove and Lauderdale that "get pretty wild" late nights with "dancing on the tables", but the Italian food's "excellent" as well, along with some "beautiful wines" to match the "beautiful", "modern decor" and "good-looking staff"; a few fume they're "loud" and "overpriced", but more report a "wonderful time."

Miami Juice ⌧ | – | – | – | ⌐ |
16210 Collins Ave. (162nd St.), Sunny Isles Beach, 305-945-0444
"Nothing compares" to this "fantastic" Sunny Isles noshery serving "great health food" with a Middle Eastern twist,

vote at zagat.com

Miami/Dade County   F | D | S | C

including "killer juices", "super-fresh salads" and "superb sandwiches"; you may have to endure "impossible" service and long waits, but "if this place closed", some surveyors "would leave Miami"; N.B. it shutters at 8 PM.

MISS SAIGON BISTRO   25 | 14 | 23 | $25
148 Giralda Ave. (Ponce de Leon Blvd.), Coral Gables, 305-446-8006; www.misssaigonbistro.com

☑ "Vietnamese food is hard to come by in Miami", which makes pho-natics especially grateful for this "authentic", family-owned "little storefront" in the Gables; "outstanding" noodles and other "distinctive", "delicious" dishes at "reasonable prices" as well as "wonderful" service mean "long lines", but it's "worth the wait"; N.B. a new Dadeland branch is scheduled to open at press time.

Miyako ⓈI   ▽ 22 | 11 | 18 | $25
100 S. Miami Ave. (SW 3rd St.), Miami, 305-373-7745

☑ Though it's only open weekdays till 4 PM, finatics flock to this diminutive Downtown sushi stand (with five "little tables") for "excellent", "flopping-fresh" fish and Japanese combo deals that "give you a taste of everything"; the staff's "attentive" if overworked, and though some protest it's "on the pricey side", more consider it a "great value."

Molina's ●   – | – | – | I
4100 E. Eighth Ave. (E. 41st St.), Hialeah, 305-687-0008
11995 SW 26th St. (Florida Tpke.), Miami, 305-207-8600
www.molinasranchrestaurant.com

"You'll wish you had two stomachs" when you go for a "Cuban food fix" at these *dos* West Dade rice 'n' beaneries; the decor's "faux upscale", but the "good", "traditional" dishes are the real deal.

Monty's Stone Crab   18 | 16 | 17 | $39
Monty's Marina, 2550 S. Bayshore Dr. (Aviation Ave.), Coconut Grove, 305-858-1431
Miami Beach Marina, 300 Alton Rd. (5th St.), Miami Beach, 305-673-3444
www.montysstonecrab.com

☑ Part "bohemian" "tiki bar" with "fruity drinks", "great water views" and calypso music and part "upscale" seafooder, this South Florida mini-chain offers a "decent alternative to Joe's" serving "delicious" fin fare; however, crabby critics crack it's an "overpriced tourist destination" with "pedestrian" eats.

Moroccan Nights   ▽ 14 | 22 | 15 | $37
1630 Ponce de Leon Ave. (Douglas Road), Coral Gables, 305-569-0333 ⓈI
9555 Harding Ave. (Kane Concourse), Surfside, 305-865-5333 ●
www.moroccannights.com

☑ For an "interesting change of pace", Coral Gables and Surfside denizens shimmy over to these "surreal" Middle

58   subscribe to zagat.com

Miami/Dade County　　　　　　　F | D | S | C

Easterns replete with a "colorful", "desert tent" setting and "fab belly dancers"; the food's "good" (and kosher), but a few cynics say they're "ordinary" and express they're "not quite Marrakesh."

MORTON'S, THE STEAKHOUSE　24 | 21 | 23 | $56
1200 Brickell Ave. (Coral Way), Miami, 305-400-9990
17399 Biscayne Blvd. (NE 173rd St.), North Miami Beach, 305-945-3131
www.mortons.com
See review in Palm Beach County Directory.

Mrs. Mendoza's　22 | 7 | 15 | $9
Doral Plaza, 9739 NW 41st St. (97th Ave.), Miami, 305-477-5119
■ This "unpretentious", "little" West Dade destination serves the "best Mexican food" around including "fresh salsa", "amazing burritos" and "genuine tacos"; service is "friendly", and amigos ignore the "no-ambiance" ambiance in pursuit of "high quality at low prices."

Mykonos　18 | 7 | 17 | $19
1201 SW 22nd St./Coral Way (SW 12th Ave.), Miami, 305-856-3140
◪ A "friendly, family-run" "favorite" on Coral Way for over 30 years, this "homestyle" Greek offers "consistent", "great" "comfort food" like "huge portions of moussaka" at prices that aren't ex-zorbatant; the "divey" decor disappoints some, but most maintain it "never fails to satisfy."

NEMO ●　25 | 22 | 21 | $50
100 Collins Ave. (1st St.), Miami Beach, 305-532-4550;
www.nemorestaurant.com
■ Finding this "sophisticated" "favorite" "off the beaten path" in South Beach "is well worth the trip" say schools of supporters who swoon over the "superb raw bar", "inventive" New American fare, "heavenly Sunday brunch" and "orgasmic" desserts; the interior's "beautiful", the courtyard "in the winter months is especially divine" and the staff's "pleasantly professional"; though a few pout that "prices are creeping up", more maintain the "great people-watching" alone makes it a "must-go."

New Chinatown ●　18 | 10 | 18 | $20
5958 S. Dixie Hwy. (SW 73rd St.), South Miami, 305-662-5650
◪ Despite its "cafeterialike" feel, this "neighborhood" Chinese has been a "popular" "South Miami landmark for more than 20 years" thanks to its "reliable" roster of "tasty" "classics" and "reasonable prices"; detractors dis the dishes as "Americanized", but more affirm it's a "favorite."

NEWS CAFE ●　18 | 16 | 16 | $24
800 Ocean Dr. (8th St.), Miami Beach, 305-538-6397;
www.newscafe.com
◪ If "location is everything", then "it doesn't get much better than" Mark Soyka's "busy" "landmark" diner where all of

Miami/Dade County F | D | S | C |

SoBe turns out to watch the "Ocean Drive spectacle" on view 24/7; the food's "good" ("best for breakfast") and "reasonable" (for the area), and the service (though "slow") is "friendly"; a few sophisticates scoff it's "where tourist meets trap", but more "always have a great time."

Nexxt Cafe 18 | 17 | 12 | $25 |
700 Lincoln Rd. (Euclid Ave.), Miami Beach, 305-532-6643
☑ "Gigantic portions" of Eclectic eats from a "novel-size" menu are the hallmark of this "easy option" on the Lincoln Road in South Beach where "perfect people-watching" rules; "delicious" salads and sandwiches followed by "incredible desserts" attract "crowds" who don't mind sitting "cheek by jowl", especially on the patio, but the occasionally "rude" service has sticklers saying "next!"

NIKKI BEACH 18 | 26 | 16 | $45 |
Penrod's, 1 Ocean Dr. (1st St.), Miami Beach, 305-538-1231; www.penrods.com
■ Whether it evokes "Rio", the "South of France" or a "Pacific island fantasy", this SoBe "paradise" in the Penrod's complex is a "scene", with "models galore" dining "on the sand under the coconut trees" or in "lit-up tepees" and "raised cabanas"; even though "no one comes for the food", the Eclectic fare is surprisingly "good" and the "excellent" brunch "redefines a lazy Sunday."

Nina Restaurant ● – | – | – | M |
7330 Ocean Terrace (71st St.), Miami Beach, 305-861-5333
"Pick a nice night" when you visit this "lovely" all-alfresco newcomer in Miami Beach's Little Buenos Aires where the "peaceful oceanfront setting" complements Mediterranean fare like goat-cheese ravioli and seafood; it also offers a little-known bargain brunch on weekends.

NOBU MIAMI BEACH ● 28 | 22 | 22 | $68 |
The Shore Club, 1901 Collins Ave. (20th St.), Miami Beach, 305-695-3232; www.noburestaurants.com
■ "Celebrities" and "glam, skinny" types jam Nobu Matsuhisa's South Beach branch in the Shore Club and pronounce it "as good as the NYC" flagship, serving the "ultimate sushi and sashimi" and "exceptional" signature Japanese-Peruvian dishes like "excellent miso cod" (albeit at "outrageous" prices); the "swanky", "nouveau *Miami Vice*" digs set the stage for a "lively" scene, "service is superior" and though it only accepts reservations for parties of six or more, you can wait in the popular bar.

NORMAN'S ⌀ 27 | 25 | 26 | $63 |
21 Almeria Ave. (Douglas Rd.), Coral Gables, 305-446-6767; www.normans.com
■ "From start to finish", a meal at chef-owner Van Aken's "treasure" is "perfection incarnate" (and the Most Popular eatery in the area); the "wowed" avow "it's worth a drive

Miami/Dade County | F | D | S | C |

from anywhere" to this "grand" Coral Gables "gastronomic nirvana" for "amazing", "adventurous" New World cuisine (with a "recently introduced cheese cart"), as well as "suave", "attentive" service and a "romantic" setting; sure, it's "expensive", but "worth it" for "quintessential Florida fine dining"; N.B. Mundo, a more casual tropical offshoot, is scheduled to open fall 2003.

Novecento ◑ | 21 | 21 | 18 | $38 |
1080 Alton Rd. (11th St.), Miami Beach, 305-531-0900
■ Devotees who've discovered this "hip" "new kid on the block" in SoBe declare "don't cry for Argentina" after sampling that country's cuisine because it's "interesting" and "delicious"; a "fantastic" staff, "cheerful", "enjoyable ambiance", "good-looking crowd" and "great prices" are other reasons it's "definitely worth a visit."

Oasis Cafe | 19 | 14 | 15 | $22 |
976 41st St. (Alton Rd.), Miami Beach, 305-674-7676
■ "A hidden surprise" in Miami Beach, this "neighborhood" Mediterranean offers a "diverse menu" of "healthy, tasty", "well-priced" fare including "good veggie options"; though the "decor leaves a bit to be desired", the staff's "pleasant."

Oggi Caffe | 23 | 17 | 21 | $29 |
1740 79th St. Cswy. (Hispañola Ave.), North Bay Village, 305-866-1238
■ Perhaps the "ultimate neighborhood Italian" ristorante, this North Bay Village "sister to Caffe Da Vinci" offers "affordable" and "wonderful pasta, fish and veal" and "desserts worth the calories" in a "warm", "cozy" setting; the "top-notch" staff "remembers your favorite dishes", and even if it's "out of the way", it provides a "great experience."

Old Cutler Inn | 16 | 9 | 17 | $21 |
7271 SW 168th St. (Old Cutler Rd.), South Miami, 305-238-1514
◪ "Hop on the Harley, take the top off the T-Bird and cruise" to this "rustic", "old-fashioned roadhouse" in South Miami for a beer and some "good" Traditional American grub "like Caesar salad and prime rib"; its circa-1920s interior may be "grungy" but "locals like it" just as it is, and fresh-air freaks say the atmosphere "will be greatly improved with the recent no-smoking law."

Old Cutler Oyster Co. | ▽ 18 | 14 | 17 | $20 |
18415 S. Dixie Hwy. (Eureka Dr.), Cutler Ridge, 305-238-2051
◪ Known to locals as 'old C's', this South Dade seafooder also serves up country line dancing twice a week for those who like a little two-step with their "excellent bubba stew", she-crab soup and steamed clams at "reasonable prices"; the happy hour is the "place to test your pickup lines", but more reserved types find the scene too "active" to be "relaxing."

vote at zagat.com 61

Miami/Dade County | F | D | S | C |

Old Lisbon | 21 | 16 | 19 | $28 |
1698 SW 22nd St./Coral Way (17th Ave.), Miami, 305-854-0039
■ A spike in the Food score indicates that this "quaint", "cozy" Portuguese in Coral Way is doing lots of things right, and partisans praise "plentiful portions" of "tasty" "cod cooked in a multitude of ways", "out-of-this-world grilled sausage" and "awe"-inspiring desserts; a "friendly" staff and moderate prices help make it a "family favorite."

Old San Juan | – | – | – | M |
1200 SW 57th Ave. (12th St.), West Miami, 305-263-9911;
www.oldsanjuanrestaurant.com
Don't bother "carb counting" at this West Dade Puerto Rican where the food may be "authentic" but also "oh-so-heavy", compounded by the all-you-can-eat brunch and lunch buffets; though there used to be live bands on weekends, these days it's just the radio blaring salsa.

One Ninety ⓢ | ▽ 21 | 19 | 17 | $27 |
190 NE 46th St. (bet. 1st & 2nd Aves.), Miami, 305-576-9779
◪ "The closest Miami comes to being 'ouch' hip", this "East Village"–esque newcomer "on the border of Little Haiti and the Design District" attracts a "multicultural, bohemian mix of artists, musicians and other interesting" folks; the affordable, "inventive" Eclectic eats are "delicious" and "great for vegetarians", the "lovely" setting is "arty" yet "unpretentious" and if the service veers toward the "unprofessional", it's certainly "friendly"; N.B. open for brunch only on Sundays.

Original Daily Bread Marketplace | 22 | 10 | 15 | $13 |
2400 SW 27th St. (bet. SW 24th & 27th Aves.), Coconut Grove, 305-856-5893
■ No longer affiliated with The Daily Bread mini-chain, this "original" Middle Eastern market and cafe on the outskirts of Coconut Grove is a "great spot" for "authentic" fare including the "best" "fresh hummus" and "excellent pita"; though the service is cafeteria-style and the surroundings are "nothing fancy", the "quality's high" and the offerings are certainly "budget"-oriented.

ORTANIQUE ON THE MILE | 26 | 23 | 23 | $48 |
278 Miracle Mile (Le Jeune Rd.), Coral Gables, 305-446-7710;
www.ortaniqueontheweb.com
■ Caribbean cuisine "doesn't get any better" than at this "wonderful" "jewel of Miracle Mile" in Coral Gables, where chef-owner Cindy Hutson turns out "inspired", "exquisite" (if "a bit pricey") fare using island spices that "make your taste buds sing"; the majority maintains the "festive", tropical atmosphere with its "funky" decor and "enthusiastic" servers make for a "lively" evening, though a few fume the "tables are too close together" for "dinner conversation."

Miami/Dade County | F | D | S | C |

OSTERIA DEL TEATRO | 26 | 15 | 24 | $50 |
1443 Washington Ave. (Española Way), Miami Beach, 305-538-7850
■ "They know what they're doing" at this "top-of-the-line" SoBe "standby" that still does boffo box office thanks to its "creative", "habit-forming" handmade pastas and other "delicious" Northern Italian specials; owner/maitre d' Dino Perola provides a "warm welcome" and ensures the "quality never waivers", and though the setting's rather "so-so", "super service" and that "incredible" food keep it "popular."

OUTBACK STEAKHOUSE | 19 | 14 | 18 | $26 |
Town & Country Ctr., 11800 Sherry Ln. (N. Kendall Dr.), Kendall, 305-596-6771
Briar Bay Shopping Ctr., 13145 SW 89th Pl. (136th St.), Miami, 305-254-4456
Flagler Park Plaza, 8255 W. Flagler St. (82nd Ave.), Miami, 305-262-9766
2201 Collins Ave. (22nd St.), Miami Beach, 305-531-1338
15490 NW 77th Ct. (Miami Lakes Dr.), Miami Lakes, 305-558-6868
3161 NE 163rd St. (east of Biscayne Blvd.), North Miami Beach, 305-944-4329
www.outbacksteakhouse.com
See review in Keys/Monroe County Directory.

Ouzo's Greek Taverna & Bar | 20 | 16 | 18 | $28 |
940 71st St. (Bay Dr.), Miami Beach, 305-864-9848
■ "What a gem!" boast bacchanalian boosters of this new Miami Beach "neighborhood joint" where the "authentic", "terrific" and "affordable" Greek fare is matched by "great wines", "exceptional", "warm" service and "attractive" setting both "outside or in"; the weekend entertainment contributes to this "delightful surprise."

PACIFIC TIME | 25 | 20 | 22 | $54 |
915 Lincoln Rd. (bet. Jefferson & Michigan Aves.), Miami Beach, 305-534-5979; www.pacifictime.biz
☑ "This Pan-Asian trendsetter" is now firmly entrenched as a "classic" thanks to chef-owner Jonathan Eismann's "unusual" but "consistent" cuisine including "memorable seafood" and a "dizzying wine list" that lure both "locals" and imported "pretty people"; the SoBe setting's "beautiful" and staff "professional", and even though prices are "shocking" and clock-watchers warn "its time has come and gone", more retort "it gets better every year."

PALM | 25 | 19 | 24 | $57 |
9650 E. Bay Harbor Dr. (Kane Concourse), Bay Harbor Island, 305-868-7256
4425 Ponce de Leon Blvd. (Bird Rd.), Coral Gables, 786-552-7256
www.thepalm.com
☑ "Surf 'n' turf at its finest" are the currency at these "legendary" steakhouse chain links in Bay Harbor Island

vote at zagat.com

Miami/Dade County | F | D | S | C |

and the Gables that fans feel are "just as good as the NY parent"; along with "hefty cocktails", "excellent", "high-quality" fare and "great" (if "noisy") ambiance, the "accommodating" staff "creates a "feel-good" ambiance, and if a few fume they're "resting on their laurels", more consider them a "quintessential" experience.

Palme d'Or | – | – | – | E |

Biltmore Hotel, 1200 Anastasia Ave. (Granada Blvd.), Coral Gables, 305-445-1926; www.biltmorehotel.com

"The grande dame of Coral Gables" in the 1926 Biltmore Hotel has reopened its signature restaurant with a pared-down menu of French small plates at equally pared-down prices; after a summer renovation, the spruced-up interior should address complaints of "stuffy digs", and in any case the space affords views of the largest swimming pool in the country.

Paninoteca | 20 | 14 | 16 | $18 |

Aventura Mall, 19575 Biscayne Blvd. (Aventura Blvd.), Aventura, 305-937-4266
809 Lincoln Rd. (Meridian Ave.), Miami Beach, 305-538-0058

■ Though the name "sounds like an Italian University", the only lesson you'll learn at these Aventura and South Beach "Euro"-style sandwich shops is how to enjoy "terrific", "inexpensive" panini made with the "best bread around" as well as "delicious" salads; even if the service is "surprisingly slow" for "fast food", both locations offer "great people-watching" to while away the time.

Panya Thai | – | – | – | M |

520 NE 167th St. (NE 6th Ave.), North Miami Beach, 305-945-8566

Few surveyors have discovered this NMB newcomer, but fervent followers feel it offers "the most authentic Thai" fare in Miami including "amazing" duck and "super" noodles, all "fresh", "healthy" and "spicy"; firebrands warn "just be careful of ordering dishes hot, because they really mean it."

Pao ● | ∇ 17 | 22 | 15 | $39 |

Clinton Hotel, 825 Washington Ave. (8th St.), Miami Beach, 305-695-1957

◪ With "beautiful", "interesting" decor just made for pao-wows over "great" Cantonese cuisine, this "welcome" newcomer adjacent to the Clinton Hotel in South Beach has fashionistas affirming "finally, good Chinese in Miami"; foes, however, fume the fare's "so-so" and service "confused", but weekend DJs and a kitchen open till midnight are pao-werfully appealing.

Paquito's | 20 | 18 | 19 | $24 |

16265 Biscayne Blvd. (Sunny Isles Blvd.), North Miami Beach, 305-947-5027

■ "Located in the corner of a strip mall but worth looking for", this NMB Tex-Mex has a "dual identity" comprising

Miami/Dade County | F | D | S | C |

one-part "singles bar" with an "unbeatable happy hour" and one-part "family-oriented dining" serving "excellent", "high-quality", "authentic" food at "fair" prices.

PASCAL'S ON PONCE ⊠ | 26 | 19 | 24 | $47 |
2611 Ponce de Leon Blvd. (bet. Almeria & Valencia Aves.), Coral Gables, 305-444-2024
☑ "Exactly what a restaurant should be" report frontliners of this "outstanding" New French in Coral Gables where "each dish is an essay in perfection" overseen by chef Pascal and his wife Ann-Louise Oudin as well as an "impeccable" staff "committed to a fantastic experience"; complaints of "small portions" and "tight" quarters notwithstanding, most maintain it offers a "*magnifique*" meal at moderate prices; P.S. "don't miss out on the soufflé."

Paulo Luigi's | 19 | 16 | 18 | $23 |
3324 Virginia St. (Oak Ave.), Coconut Grove, 305-445-9000
☑ "Every town needs a dependable little" trattoria like this "cozy" "Grove oldie" where "families" and folks can get "massive" portions of "cheap", "good" "red-sauce" Italian including "superb garlic rolls" served in the "least pretentious setting in Miami"; alas, "inattentive" staff and food that's simply "standard" "disappoints" previous pals.

PEARL | 21 | 27 | 19 | $61 |
Penrod's, 1 Ocean Dr. (1st St.), Miami Beach, 305-673-1575; www.pearlsouthbeach.com
☑ "Celebrities", "models" and "wanna-bes" all "feel more beautiful" in the "creamsicle" lighting of this "over-the-top" SoBe club in the Penrod's complex; the "creative" seafood-focused Eclectic fare's "divine" and the staff in "crazy cleavage dresses" is "stunning", but it's the "futuristic decor" including "shag carpet chairs" as well as a "super-cool champagne bar" that grabs the spotlight; though you'll spend "money like it's water" for an experience some deem "overrated", most think it's "worth a peek."

Pelican Café ☽ | 23 | 22 | 18 | $33 |
Pelican Hotel, 826 Ocean Dr. (bet. 8th & 9th Sts.), Miami Beach, 305-673-1000; www.pelicanhotel.com
■ An outdoor perch on Ocean Drive affords "perfect people-watching" at this "cool" bistro in the eponymous Diesel-owned South Beach hotel, and the three squares served daily are equally "excellent" from "delicious omelets" to "great" New American dishes; the "high-tech" interior, "good service" and "decent" prices are also pleasers, plus it's a "wine lover's paradise."

Peppy's in the Gables | 22 | 18 | 23 | $30 |
216 Palermo Ave. (Ponce de Leon Blvd.), Coral Gables, 305-448-1240
■ "Service with a smile" both from the "friendly" staff and the "ever-present owner" are the start of an "enjoyable"

vote at zagat.com

Miami/Dade County F | D | S | C

experience at this "lovely" Northern Italian in the Gables; "terrific" dishes such as "wonderful ravioli" and "fantastic veal" are served in an "intimate", "converted-house" setting that makes for a "gem" of a "neighborhood" spot.

Perricone's Marketplace & Cafe 20 | 21 | 20 | $29
15 SE 10th St. (SE 1st Ave.), Miami, 305-374-9449
Despite its setting "in an old barn" (imported from Maine), this "unique" Brickell Village Italian ristorante-cum-*mercato* is just the prescription for a "sophisticated" "first date" with "sexy" outdoor seating; "great wines", "delicious" food, "incredible" desserts and "excellent" service are always "romantic", and it offers "wonderful" deli fare for "business types" on the run at lunchtime.

Pescado 18 | 25 | 16 | $47
Village of Merrick Park, 320 San Lorenzo Ave. (bet. Le Jeune Rd. & Ponce de Leon Blvd.), Coral Gables, 305-443-3474
With its "beautiful" decor that evokes the interior of a "boat" and "lush garden area", this Gables newcomer in Merrick Park is "worth the trip"; the seafood-focused Eclectic fare, however, reaps mixed reactions, with some saying it's "sublime" and others insisting it's "unimpressive", as is the "poor service"; here's hoping it's just "working out the kinks."

P.F. CHANG'S CHINA BISTRO 21 | 20 | 19 | $28
The Falls Shopping Ctr., 8888 SW 136th St. (US 1), Kendall, 305-234-2338
17455 Biscayne Blvd. (NE 171st St.), North Miami Beach, 305-957-1966
www.pfchangs.com
"It's not authentic and it's not neighborhood-y", but this chain has suburbanites lining up for a chance to eat "heaping servings" of "excellent", "gourmet" Chinese food in an "upscale" setting for a "decent price"; complaints are eclipsed by the raves, though some say they find the food merely "ok", the atmosphere "noisy" and the service "hit-or-miss"; N.B. it now takes reservations.

Piccadilly Cafeteria 13 | 8 | 11 | $12
Palm Springs Mall, 403 W. 49th St. (W. 4th Ave.), Hialeah, 305-822-4434
Westland Mall, 1645 W. 49th St. (W. 16th Ave.), Hialeah, 305-823-6601
Arch Creek Shopping Ctr., 13250 Biscayne Blvd. (NE 130th St.), North Miami, 305-892-9913
Trail Plaza, 1190 SW 67th Ave. (SW 8th St.), West Miami, 305-266-7603
8301 W. Flagler St. (NW 82nd Ave.), West Miami, 305-262-1319
www.piccadilly.com
For "basic comfort food that's cheaper than what you make at home", this Louisiana-based chain has its

Miami/Dade County   F D S C

champions who find the American and Southern eats "good" and the service "quick"; picky patrons, however, say the fare's "mediocre" and go only as a "last resort."

Piccadilly Garden ⊠   22 | 20 | 19 | $28
35 NE 40th St. (N. Miami Ave.), Miami, 305-573-8221
■ A Design District "secret" since the days "before the neighborhood was fashionable", this "great local place" offers "outstanding", "imaginative" Continental cuisine at a "great value" that's served "*sans* attitude" by a "good" staff; the interior's "dark" and "romantic", and there's also an "Andalusian-style garden with trickling fountains" and tropical foliage; N.B. it's unrelated to the cafeteria chain.

Picnics at Allen's Drugs   15 | 13 | 17 | $11
4000 Red Rd. (Bird Rd.), South Miami, 305-665-6964
◪ "You feel like you're back in the '50s" at this "old-fashioned soda fountain" in a South Miami "neighborhood drugstore"; the "all-American" fare is "best at breakfast" but it also serves "delicious milkshakes" and "vein-clogging banana pudding", though protesters who find it no picnic proclaim the food "tired" and "not worth the time."

Pilar   – | – | – | M
20475 Biscayne Blvd. (NE 203rd St.), Aventura, 305-937-2777; www.pilarrestaurant.com
Named for Hemingway's fishing boat, this New American seafooder sailed in under the helm of Scott Fredel (ex Rumi) on the site of a former bagel shop in Aventura; now instead of nova and lox you'll find salmon tartare, garlic and almond–encrusted black grouper and other creative dishes, at prices that won't sink the ship, served in a sleek, teak-accented room.

Pino's   21 | 17 | 20 | $30
3145 Commodore Plaza (bet. Grand Ave. & Main Hwy.), Coconut Grove, 305-567-9111
■ "Adorable" chef-owner Pino Saverino tries to "make your night perfect" (including favoring you with a song) when you dine at this "hidden gem" in Coconut Grove; "excellent pastas" and other dishes from a "fantastic menu" and "pleasant" surroundings also make it a "good place to go pre- or post-theater."

Piola ➊   23 | 18 | 18 | $20
1625 Alton Rd. (bet. Lincoln Rd. & 16th St.), Miami Beach, 305-674-1660; www.piola.it
■ "Killer thin-crust pizzas using the freshest ingredients" are the stock-in-trade of this chain imported from Italy with a "convenient" South Beach location "next to the movie theater"; the "cheap" *cucina* also includes "great" carpaccio and pasta served by a "congenial" staff, and the "cool", "loft"-like setting makes it an ideal "date spot" for movie buffs.

vote at zagat.com

Miami/Dade County | F | D | S | C |

PIT BAR-B-Q, THE | 26 | 8 | 14 | $13 |
16400 SW Eighth St. (Krome Ave.), Miami, 305-226-2272
■ Sure, it's a "little hole-in-the-wall near the Everglades", with "no air conditioning" and "limited" "bench seating", but BBQ junkies believe this veteran turns out the "best in South Florida"; the "feast" includes "wonderful shredded pork shoulder", ribs, frogs' legs and "light, fluffy fry biscuits with honey", and even though it's a "long drive" for a pit stop, acolytes aver "it's worth it."

Pizza Rustica ●≠ | 23 | 6 | 15 | $10 |
1447 Washington Ave. (Española Way), Miami Beach, 305-538-6009
863 Washington Ave. (9th St.), Miami Beach, 305-674-8244
■ "Square is cool", at least when it comes to the shape of the "huge slices" slung by this "zesty" trio of "popular" pizzerias in SoBe and Lauderdale purveying "incredibly delicious" "Roman-style" pies with "fresh, innovative toppings" like "addictive blue cheese and spinach"; there's "no atmosphere", but a near-dawn (till 6 AM) closing time makes them "perfect post-clubbing."

Porcão ● | 24 | 18 | 22 | $45 |
801 Brickell Bay Dr. (SE 8th St.), Miami, 305-373-2777; www.rodizioplace.com
■ Vets vow it "should be called 'pork-out'" because that's just what "gluttons" do at this "eat-meat-till-you're-beat" Brazilian rodizio with a "beautiful waterfront location" Downtown; there's also an "amazing salad bar" and "lethal" cocktails, but it's the "wonderful" churrascaria delivered (and delivered and delivered) by an "excellent" staff that makes for a "great experience."

Prezzo | 17 | 17 | 17 | $28 |
Loehmann's Fashion Island Mall, 18831 Biscayne Blvd. (NE 188th St.), Aventura, 305-933-9004
The Falls Shopping Ctr., 8888 SW 136th St. (US 1), Kendall, 305-234-1010
www.prezzo-international.com
■ "Surprisingly good food in a shopping mall" can be found at this "reliable" chain known for its "diverse menu" of "terrific", "solid" Italian dishes including "great salads" and "gourmet pizza" served in a "relaxing" setting; those "who loved it in the old days" lament "it's lost its glamour" and are irritated by "erratic service"; still, there's a "super" bar scene and you "can't beat" the prices.

Prime Grill | ∇ 21 | 25 | 20 | $44 |
3599 NE 207th St. (35th St.), Aventura, 305-692-9392; www.theprimegrill.com
■ Mavens are glatt for this Aventura newcomer, boasting it's the "best kosher steakhouse around", with "talented"

Miami/Dade County | F | D | S | C |

toques producing "excellent" beef and fish dishes as well as "great sushi" and non-dairy desserts served by an "attentive" staff in a "lovely" setting; only *machers* need apply, though, as this NYC import is "expensive."

Provence Grill | 19 | 16 | 19 | $32 |
1001 S. Miami Ave. (bet. SW 10th & 11th Aves.), Miami, 305-373-1940; www.provencegrill.com

◪ "Bon appetit!" cheer *amis* of this "lovely" "family-owned" Downtown Brickell Village French bistro with a "friendly" Gallic staff serving "consistent", "tasty" fare and "great wines" in a "comfortable", "country" atmosphere; non-sayers insist the food's "unremarkable" and lacks "variety", but admit to enjoying the occasional "bargain" lunch.

Puccini & Pasta ◐ | – | – | – | M |
Dadeland Mall, 7491 SW 88th St. (S. Dadeland Blvd.), Kendall, 305-669-4599

Another newcomer from the tireless Piero Filpi (Carpaccio, Carnevale, Splendido, et al.), this Italian in the Dadeland Mall in Kendall hits all the right notes with great pastas and pizzas at prices suited for those living *La Vie Boheme*; the rustic-looking interior provides tired shoppers with a getaway setting for a nice glass of vino.

Puerto Sagua ◐ | 20 | 7 | 18 | $17 |
700 Collins Ave. (7th St.), Miami Beach, 305-673-1115

◪ "When you get tired of the snobby South Beach food scene", this "great Cuban diner" will give you "hope", offering a refreshingly "non-trendy" setting for "excellent", "authentic" fare "without the fancy prices"; sure, it's "nothing special to look at", but the service is "outstanding", it's open till 2 AM and it'll "probably still be here after the last wanna-be model packs up and goes back to Iowa."

Punjab Palace | 17 | 9 | 15 | $21 |
11780 SW 88th St. (SW 117th Ave.), Kendall, 305-274-1300

◪ Proponents pontificate "if you do nothing else in your busy life, eat the tandoori chicken" at this "good-value" Indian serving "great" fare in a "mundane" Kendall strip mall; the service is "personalized" and "helpful", but a few disgruntled sorts take jabs at the "skimpy portions" and an interior that "needs redecorating."

Quinn's Restaurant | – | – | – | M |
Park Central Hotel, 640 Ocean Dr. (bet. 6th & 7th Sts.), Miami Beach, 305-673-6400

Chef-owner Gerry Quinn (ex A Fish Called Avalon) has opened a mighty "great addition to the SoBe dining scene" with this "creative", "excellent" seafooder in the Park Central Hotel; landlubbers will find "diverse offerings" including steak and pasta complemented by "terrific wines at fair prices", and it also boasts "great service" and "scenic" sidewalk seating overlooking Ocean Drive.

vote at zagat.com

Miami/Dade County

| | F | D | S | C |

Raja
33 NE Second Ave. (Flagler St.), Miami, 305-539-9551 — | — | — | I

"Ignore the surroundings" of this South Indian "dive" tucked away in a Downtown food court and "dig into" some "excellent", "fresh", "cheap" fare including "divine dosas" made by Raja and his wife who are "always smiling"; it's "good for a quick lunch" (closes at 6 PM), but alas, there's "no delivery."

Randazzo's Little Italy
150 Giralda Ave. (Ponce de Leon Blvd.), Coral Gables, 305-448-7002 — | — | — | M

An "ex boxing champ" turned chef-owner has opened this "NYC-style" "neighborhood" Italian in Coral Gables and he "really cares about your meal", offering "excellent" fare that's "not inventive but solid"; moderate prices and a "friendly" vibe make for an "overall good experience"; N.B. it's not related to Frank Randazzo's Talula.

Red Fish Grill
9610 Old Cutler Rd. (N. Kendall Dr.), Coral Gables, 305-668-8788 — 18 | 25 | 19 | $38

"Nestled at the end of Matheson Hammock Park" in a "secluded" beachside locale that "makes you feel like you're on vacation" in a "tropical" "paradise", this "special" Gables fish house definitely has "exceptional views"; the fin fare's "good" to "mediocre", but the "beautiful setting makes up for it" and the prices are "reasonable."

Red Lantern
3176 Commodore Plaza (Grand Ave.), Coconut Grove, 305-529-9998 — 18 | 15 | 19 | $24

For "upscale Chinese", this Coconut Grove "favorite" offers "consistent" albeit "unimaginative" choices at "reasonable prices", especially the "lunch bargains"; a "pleasant evening" can be had, although gripes about "grungy" digs indicate that takeout is a better option.

Red Thai Room
Promenade Shops, 20301 Biscayne Blvd. (NE 203rd St.), Aventura, 305-792-0232; www.redthai.com — 20 | 23 | 14 | $24

This "funky" Thai "treat" in Aventura offers a "beautiful", "fun", knickknack-bedecked setting and Siamese fare that's just as "creative" as well as "wonderful", "interesting" desserts; the "reasonable prices" still give you more Bangkok for your buck, but there's room for improvement in the service, as it's "slooow."

Renaisa
620 NE 78th St. (Biscayne Blvd.), Miami, 305-754-3985 — ∇ 26 | 10 | 22 | $22

Though few have discovered this "inexpensive" canalside Upper East Side Indian, the "word is spreading quickly" about its "fabulous" fare including "scrumptious" curries and Bangladeshi specialties – in fact, "you can't go wrong

subscribe to zagat.com

Miami/Dade County   F | D | S | C

with anything on the menu" at this renaissance place; its "crazy location" "across from a strip club" may turn off some, but the "food makes up for it"; P.S. "the lunch buffet is an outstanding bargain."

Restaurant St. Michel   23 | 23 | 22 | $41
Hotel Place St. Michel, 162 Alcazar Ave. (Ponce de Leon Blvd.), Coral Gables, 305-446-6572

■ A Coral Gables "grande dame" in a "lovely" landmark boutique hotel, this "consistently excellent" New American offers French-accented dishes, both "classic and creative", in an "exquisite", "antique"-filled space that works for a "quiet business breakfast" or a "romantic dinner"; the prices may be "steep", but the "special atmosphere" keeps cognoscenti "coming back year after year"; a new chef's arrival may outdate the Food score.

Ristorante La Bussola   24 | 24 | 25 | $44
264 Giralda Ave. (bet. Le Jeune Rd. & Ponce de Leon Blvd.), Coral Gables, 305-445-8783

■ "As good as gold every time", this "impressive", "old-world" Northern Italian offers "wonderful", "top-quality" fare in a "quiet", "classy", "beautifully designed space" in the Gables; the "professional" staff "makes you feel welcome", and though it's "not for the weak of wallet", the lunch may be the "best value in Florida."

River Oyster Bar, The ⌧   – | – | – | E
650 S. Miami Ave. (SW 7th St.), Miami, 305-530-1915; www.therivermiami.com

The former Fishbone Grill Downtown has morphed into this new seafooder just steps from the Miami River, and early reports rave about the "interesting" menu spotlighting "excellent" fin fare ("three words: fried whole snapper") and "terrific oysters"; the "cool" space features a large mahogany bar and low lighting.

Roadhouse Grill   16 | 12 | 16 | $21
12599 Biscayne Blvd. (NE 126th St.), North Miami, 305-893-7433; www.roadhousegrill.com

See review in Ft. Lauderdale/Broward County Directory.

ROMANO'S MACARONI GRILL   17 | 17 | 18 | $22
12100 SW 88th St. (SW 123rd Ave.), Kendall, 305-270-0621
8700 NW 18th Terrace (Galloway Rd.), Miami, 305-477-6676
16395 Biscayne Blvd. (163rd St.), North Miami Beach, 305-945-7990
www.macaronigrill.com

▲ "So what if it's not authentic", this Italian chain is "great for a family meal out" what with "cheap", "hearty portions" of "surprisingly satisfying" fare delivered to tables the "kids can color on" by a "bubbly" staff in a "fun ambiance"; purists pout the food's "bland" and "uneven at best", and the digs are "too damn loud."

Miami/Dade County | F | D | S | C |

ROMEO'S CAFE ⊠   26 | 20 | 26 | $62 |
2257 SW 22nd St./Coral Way (bet. 22nd & 23rd Aves.), Miami, 305-859-2228

■ "Charming" chef-owner Romeo Majano "customizes your dining experience" at this "tiny" Coral Way Northern Italian, where six "fabulous" "nightly changing" prix fixe courses ("no written menu") are "tailored to your taste" and "prepared to perfection"; "romantic atmosphere" and "personal" but "unobtrusive" service transform an "expensive" proposition into a "worthwhile splurge"; P.S. "book in advance" for the weekend seatings.

Rosinella   20 | 12 | 16 | $25 |
1040 S. Miami Ave. (bet. 10th & 11th Sts.), Miami, 305-372-5756
525 Lincoln Rd. (bet. Drexel & Pennsylvania Aves.), Miami Beach, 305-672-8777 ◐

■ There's a "real mama Rosinella" in at least one of the kitchens at these "charming" Downtown and South Beach twins (siblings of Sport Cafe), and the "honest", "delicious" Italian fare including the "best thin-crust pizza" tastes like "home cooking"; the "quaint" digs, "gentle" service and "excellent value" make them "great neighborhood" trattorias "even if they're not in your neighborhood."

Ruen Thai ◐   19 | 15 | 18 | $25 |
947 Washington Ave. (bet. 9th & 10th Sts.), Miami Beach, 305-534-1504

☑ For a "perfect sushi-Thai combo in the heart of South Beach", this "jewel" continues to shine with "reasonable prices" as well as "excellent food and service"; the "lack of parking is a big deterrent", but it's still a "good" choice for night-owls on weekends as the kitchen closes at 1 AM.

Rumi ◐   22 | 23 | 19 | $55 |
330 Lincoln Rd. (Washington Ave.), Miami Beach, 305-672-4353; www.rumimiami.com

☑ A "hip" "restaurant-cum-club" hidden away in a SoBe storefront, this "sexy" spot seduces supporters with "futuristic" decor, "groovy tunes" and an irresistible "VIP lounge"; before the "party" begins, "surprisingly good" New American fare gets the spotlight, though a few find "rumi for improvement" in the "overpriced" food, and the service dances between "impeccable" and "mediocre."

Rusty Pelican   15 | 22 | 17 | $36 |
3201 Rickenbacker Cswy. (Arthur Lamb Jr. Rd.), Key Biscayne, 305-361-3818

☑ Sure, it's "touristy", but "if you're lucky enough to get a table by the window" you'll enjoy "one of the best views in the city" at this "still-special" Key Biscayne seafooder known for its "outrageous brunch"; "it's a shame", however, that the "disappointing" food and "less than stellar service" "aren't half as good" as those "spectacular" vistas.

Miami/Dade County   F | D | S | C |

RUTH'S CHRIS STEAK HOUSE   25 | 22 | 23 | $52 |
2320 Salzedo St. (Aragon Ave.), Coral Gables, 305-461-8360; www.ruthschris.com

■ Staunch members of this "elegant" chain's gang argue it serves "the best steak north of Argentina" with its "signature" beef on "sizzling hot, butter-coated platters" and "great seafood" in "ample portions"; the "sophisticated, country club"–style setting and "experienced" staff who "treat customers like royalty" also please partisans, though a few ruthless sorts slam the "stiff prices."

Sakura   21 | 10 | 19 | $24 |
440 S. Dixie Hwy. (S. Le Jeune Rd.), Coral Gables, 305-665-7020
9753 NW 41st St. (NW 97th Ave.), Miami, 305-477-4477

◪ The Coral Gables branch "opened when no one ate" raw fish, and these Japanese siblings are still "favorites" for "fresh", "delicious" sushi and "great" bento box specials; the service is "quick" and "precise" and the settings are "comfortable", and though a few knock the fare as "nothing to write home about", they're certainly "always busy."

S&S Restaurant ∉   ▽ 18 | 9 | 18 | $12 |
1757 NE Second Ave. (NE 17th St.), Miami, 305-373-4291

■ With its counter-only seating that "can't have changed in its 75 years of existence", this Downtown dowager is a "little slice of history"; even if it's "seen better days", that doesn't deter "locals" in wingtips or flip-flops from gorging on the "best bargain breakfast in Miami" or the "gotta-try apple pie" and other all-American favorites.

San Loco ∉   20 | 9 | 15 | $10 |
235 14th St. (bet. Collins & Washington Aves.), Miami Beach, 305-538-3009

■ "If an evening of drinking has left you short of change", these "all-nighters" in Miami and Lauderdale "are the place to go" for "cheap", "excellent" Mexican including what some consider the "best tacos in Florida"; SoBe's "funky" setting next to a "world-famous" tattoo parlor only adds to the crazy scene.

Sara's ⓢ   18 | 7 | 14 | $17 |
2214 NE 123rd St. (Sans Souci Blvd.), North Miami, 305-891-3312

◪ "Heaven on earth for vegetarians", this North Miami eatery also gets "kudos for keeping it real" for kosher keepers, serving a "wide variety" of "outstanding" fare including pizza; "comfortable booths" and a "great family atmosphere" make it a "favorite" of 25 years' running.

Scotty's Landing   13 | 22 | 13 | $17 |
3381 Pan American Dr. (S. Bayshore Dr.), Coconut Grove, 305-854-2626

◪ "Drive your boat right up" to this "laid-back" "landmark" in Coconut Grove, a "great, old-time hangout" for sailors,

Miami/Dade County   F | D | S | C |

"dogs and kids"; the "so-so" burgers and seafood "won't win any prizes" and the service is "shaky" at best, but the "million-dollar view" and "Jimmy Buffet vibe" make it a "fab" destination.

Señor Frog's ◐   15 | 14 | 14 | $23 |
3480 Main Hwy. (Commodore Plaza), Coconut Grove, 305-448-0999
616 Collins Ave. (bet. 6th & 7th Sts.), Miami Beach, 305-673-5262
www.senorfrogsfla.com

■ A "rowdy", "young crowd" keeps these "lively" "Cancun imports" to Coconut Grove and South Beach hopping; the "predictable" Mexican eats are rather "ordinary" and the service is "hit-or-miss", but it's the "fantastic margaritas" and "party atmosphere" that attract the "spring breakers."

Sergio's ◐   17 | 9 | 14 | $14 |
8202 Mills Dr. (Kendall Dr.), Kendall, 305-279-3409
13600 SW 152nd St. (SW 137th Ave., near Metro Zoo), Kendall, 786-242-9790
3252 SW 22nd St./Coral Way (SW 32nd Ave.), Miami, 305-529-0047
9330 SW 40th St./Bird Rd. (SW 92nd Ave.), Westchester, 305-552-9626

■ For an "early-morning or late-night nosh, Cubano"-style, this mini-chain is "the place to be", serving "excellent" eats to the "masses"; "bargain breakfasts" and "good sandwiches" delivered "fast" mean they're "always busy."

Sheldon's   - | - | - | I |
9501 Harding Ave. (bet. 95th & 96th Sts.), Surfside, 305-866-6251
Take a "step back" in time to this "family-owned" "nifty retro soda fountain" in Surfside serving "cheap", "good" breakfasts and burgers as well as the "best egg creams in town"; you may have to put up with "grumpy servers" and a decor that "hasn't changed its look since it opened" in 1948, but it's "great for a nostalgia" trip.

SHIBUI ◐   28 | 21 | 24 | $31 |
10141 SW 72nd St. (102nd Ave.), Kendall, 305-274-5578;
www.shibuimiami.com

■ There may be a "zillion places" offering sushi in Miami, but this moderately priced family-owned "gem" in Kendall has been a "sentimental favorite" for over 20 years, and with reason – the "quality" fare's "fresh", "imaginative" and "consistent" and the service is "excellent"; vets advise "making reservations" to avoid a "long wait", and add the upstairs tatami rooms are "great for dates."

Shoji ◐   25 | 21 | 19 | $45 |
100 Collins Ave. (bet. 1st & 2nd Sts.), Miami Beach, 305-532-4245; www.shojisushi.com

■ Chef Shingo Inoue is a "true artist" creating "imaginative", "incredible", "high-end" sushi and other "exotic" fare

Miami/Dade County | F | D | S | C |

("try the seviche sampler and you'll want to eat here every day") at this South Beach Japanese; a "cool" interior and "beautiful" garden provide a "wonderful setting" for sipping "interesting martinis" and sampling what some call the "best" raw fin fare in "America."

Shorty's Barbecue | 20 | 12 | 17 | $15 |
9200 S. Dixie Hwy. (S. Dadeland Blvd.), South Miami, 305-670-7732
11575 SW 40th St./Bird Rd. (117th Ave.), Westchester, 305-227-3196
2255 NW 87th Ave. (bet. 21st & 25th Sts.), West Miami, 305-471-5554
www.shortys.com

■ "Yee-haw!" holler born-again hillbillies when they dig into the "heavenly ribs" with "thick, smoky-sweet sauce" and "butter-drenched corn on the cob" served at this "legendary" local BBQ duo with a Broward branch; all sport the same "fun Western decor" as the circa-1951 South Miami original in which you'll dine on "communal picnic tables" equipped with "rolls of paper towels", and though they ain't "fancy", the vittles sure are "affordable."

SHULA'S STEAK | 21 | 20 | 22 | $52 |
Alexander Hotel, 5225 Collins Ave. (north of Beach View Park), Miami Beach, 305-341-6565
6842 Main St. (Ludlam Rd.), Miami Lakes, 305-820-8047
7601 NW Miami Lakes Dr. (east of Palmetto Expwy.), Miami Lakes, 305-820-8102
www.donshula.com

☑ A chain "befitting the NFL's most successful coach ever" claim champions of Don Shula's "impressive" South Florida steakhouse team serving "huge portions" of "excellent" beef and "marvelous mashed potatoes" from a menu printed on pigskins; the "clubby" settings are festooned with "cool football paraphernalia" and the service is "helpful", but tightwads suggest you "drop back 10 and punt" the "overpriced" offerings.

Siam Lotus Room | 20 | 11 | 20 | $21 |
6388 S. Dixie Hwy. (Ludlam Rd.), South Miami, 305-666-8134

☑ Though its "building is a weird shade of green", the interior of this South Miami Siamese provides a "cute, homey" setting for what fans consider some of the "best Thai food in town" including "great curries" at a "good value"; those who feel the bloom is off the lotus, however, deem it "disappointing", with "mediocre" fare and a setting that "needs a major face-lift."

Siam Palace | 23 | 20 | 22 | $21 |
9999 Sunset Dr. (SW 102nd Ave.), South Miami, 305-279-6906

■ "Beautiful" "orchids galore" set the stage for this "must-visit" South Miami Thai, a "favorite" for "consistent", "delicious", "spicy" fare ("anything you order will be

Miami/Dade County

great"); the "authentic decor" evokes a "lush garden", and its "affordability" is another reason loyal subjects "love this place."

SMITH & WOLLENSKY ◐ — 23 | 22 | 22 | $56
1 Washington Ave. (S. Pointe Dr.), Miami Beach, 305-673-2800; www.smithandwollensky.com

■ "When money is no object" and "you just really need a great steak" coupled with "a rare Miami water view", this South Beach outpost of a New York–based chain is the "perfect spot"; the "super-prime" meats and "outstanding wines" are "impeccably" served by the "nicest staff in town", but it's the "unsurpassed" setting that solidifies its rep as a "wonderful dining experience."

Soyka — 19 | 21 | 19 | $30
5556 NE Fourth Ct. (Biscayne Blvd.), Miami, 305-759-3117

■ "One of the driving forces behind the Biscayne Boulevard renaissance", this "trendy" Upper East Side destination from Mark Soyka offers a "cool, industrial"-chic decor that attracts a "happening, mixed crowd"; the "well-priced" New American fare is "hearty" and "good" ("no matter what you're hungry for", it's on the "diverse menu"), and the service is "knowledgeable"; as might be expected in a "loftlike" space, it can get "noisy", so insiders prefer to go "during the week."

Spiga ◐ — 21 | 21 | 21 | $39
1228 Collins Ave. (bet. 12th & 13th Sts.), Miami Beach, 305-534-0079; www.spigarestaurant.com

■ "People always come back" to this "sweet", "charming" Northern Italian for the "excellent", "delicious" fare including "fantastic ravioli" and "amazing desserts" at a "good value" delivered by a "great staff"; the "handsome" but "tiny" space can get "crowded", but "happy" diners still feel far "away from the South Beach craziness."

Splendido — – | – | – | E
121 Alhambra Circle (Galiano St.), Coral Gables, 305-445-5252

Brand-new in the Gables and already renowned for its homemade pastas, this Italian has a distinguished pedigree; owner Piero Filpi, who made a name for himself with Carpaccio and Carnevale as well as his popular Mezzanotte duo, seems unable to fail with his recipe for a good time: fine food, decent prices, an attractive setting and good music.

Sport Cafe ◐ — 19 | 13 | 16 | $26
560 Washington Ave. (6th St.), Miami Beach, 305-674-9700

■ The "best place to watch international soccer matches" is this "small" sibling to Rosinella that doubles as a "great trattoria" serving "good", "tasty", "fresh", "inexpensive" fare including pizza, pastas and salads; another "rarity in South Beach" is its garden that provides an escape if you find the TVs "distracting."

Miami/Dade County | F | D | S | C |

Spris | 23 | 17 | 19 | $22 |
2305 Ponce de Leon Blvd. (Giralda Ave.), Coral Gables, 305-444-3388
731 Lincoln Rd. (bet. Euclid & Meridian Aves.), Miami Beach, 305-673-2020 ◐

■ "Take a break from Atkins" at this Lincoln Road "sidewalk cafe" in South Beach or its Gables *fratello* where the "people-watching is wonderful" and the "authentic thin-crust pizza" with a "range of unusual toppings" and "bountiful salads" are even "better"; "moderate prices", "warm", "unpretentious" service and "modern settings" are also "*molto buono.*"

Stefano's   ▽ | 20 | 17 | 19 | $43 |
24 Crandon Blvd. (Harbor Dr.), Key Biscayne, 305-361-7007

◩ Considering the "lack of better places with entertainment" on Key Biscayne, this classic Italian provides "great pasta" and other classic Italian dishes; however, one look at "the customers who gather around the bar" and you'll realize it's more of a "nightclub" as the "disco" scene keeps it "stayin' alive"; N.B. the dancing goes on till 4 AM on weekends.

Sundays on the Bay ◐ | 12 | 19 | 13 | $30 |
5420 Crandon Blvd. (W. Mashta Dr.), Key Biscayne, 305-361-6777; www.sundaysonthebay.com

◩ There are a few loyalists left who laud this "institution" on Key Biscayne for its "big waterfront deck" with "magnificent bay views", "great snacks" from a seafood menu and "good Sunday brunch"; bashers bayl out, however, citing "substandard" fare, "rickety" digs that "need a touch of paint" and "poor service."

Sunset Tavern ◐   ▽ | 14 | 15 | 15 | $17 |
7232 SW 59th Ave. (bet. Sunset Dr. & SW 73rd St.), South Miami, 305-665-9996; www.delilane-sunt.com

◩ Though few have stumbled into "Deli Lane's drunken brother" in South Miami, those who have tout the "nice portions" of "good", "tasty" Traditional American fare served by a "helpful" staff; a few knock it as "nothing special" ("I go to drink, not to eat"), but it's still "see and be seen on Sundays" for a "casual brunch outdoors."

Sunshine & AJ's
Food Without Fire | – | – | – | M |
747 Fourth St., Ste. 101 (Meridian Ave.), Miami Beach, 305-674-9960; www.foodwithoutfire.com

Picking up on the hottest, er, make that coolest new health food trend, this vegetarian market adjacent to a South Beach yoga shala makes dozens of delicious dips, salads, pizzas, lasagnas and desserts out of nuts and berries, fruits and veggies, none of which have been heated to above 118 degrees; N.B. no alcohol, but wheat grass is available.

vote at zagat.com

Miami/Dade County

F | D | S | C

Sushi Maki
19 | 13 | 18 | $25

23334 Ponce de Leon Blvd. (Aragon Ave.), Coral Gables, 305-443-1884

5812 Sunset Dr. (SW 58th Ave.), South Miami, 305-667-7677

◪ Despite the name, these "valued neighborhood spots" in the Gables and South Miami also serve "creative" Siamese dishes in portions large "enough for a small Thai village" along with "great sushi" that's an "excellent value"; a few detractors dis "gruff service" and "fast food"–joint decor, but fans counter they're "fast and reliable."

Su Shin
24 | 11 | 18 | $26

159 Aragon Ave. (1 block north of Coral Way), Coral Gables, 305-445-2584 ⓢ

10501 SW Kendall Dr. (107th Ave.), Kendall, 305-271-3235

■ If you are one of the "cognoscenti", perhaps one who has his or her "own chopsticks kept behind the bar", you already know about these "affordable" Japanese restaurants in Coral Gables and Kendall; if not, then you might be su-prised by the "unique", "delicious" rolls and "excellent" sushi you and the "locals" will vie for, including "intriguing daily blackboard specials."

Sushi Rock Cafe ◐
21 | 13 | 19 | $27

1351 Collins Ave. (14th St.), Miami Beach, 305-532-2133

■ This South Beach Japanese "really does rock" with "consistently good", "fresh", "interesting" sushi ordered from "album-cover menus" in a "funky" setting replete with "American pop culture" artifacts for decor and "loud music" for ambiance; the "small" space may "get a little cramped", but the "price is right" and it's a "fun hangout" for a "late-night" crowd.

Sushi Saigon ◐
∇ 19 | 15 | 15 | $35

(fka Peppercorn)

1131 Washington Ave. (bet. 11th & 12th Sts.), Miami Beach, 305-604-0599

■ Raw-fishionados and pho-natics alike are satisfied by this recently renamed Japanese-Vietnamese in South Beach serving a wide range of "wonderful" dishes in a renovated setting that's "much better"; its sidewalk tables in the middle of clubland make for great people-watching on weekends.

SUSHISAMBA DROMO ◐
24 | 24 | 18 | $47

600 Lincoln Rd. (Pennsylvania Ave.), Miami Beach, 305-673-5337; www.sushisamba.com

■ There's "never a dull moment" at this "colorful", almost "surreal" South Beach "hot spot" that sambaed down from New York City; its signature "eccentric mix of Japanese, Peruvian and Brazilian" cuisines "enchants" enthusiasts who single out the "high-quality", "inventive" sushi washed down by "large caipirinhas" and myriad sakes; some say

Miami/Dade County | F | D | S | C |

sayonara to "slow" service and bid adios to the "overpriced" fare, but more go for the "pulse-pounding atmosphere."

Sushi Siam | 21 | 15 | 17 | $31 |
632 Crandon Blvd. (bet. Enid & Sunrise Drs.), Key Biscayne, 305-361-7768
801 Brickell Bay Dr. (SE 8th St.), Miami, 305-579-9944 ⊠
647-649 Lincoln Rd. (bet. Jefferson & Washington Aves.), Miami Beach, 305-672-7112
5582 NE Fourth Ct. (NE 55th Terrace), South Miami, 305-751-7818
■ "When you're with a group that can't decide on cuisine", this local mini-chain provides a "haven" with an "excellent variety" of "wonderful", "delicious" Japanese and Thai dishes that are all "beautifully presented" in a "casual" setting; the "good value" is also vaunted, but the "service leaves a lot to be desired"; N.B. the NE Fourth Court location is sushi only.

Taco Rico Tex-Mex | 19 | 6 | 14 | $12 |
473 S. Dixie Hwy. (Le Jeune Rd.), Coral Gables, 305-663-3200
12055 SW 117th Ave. (bet. 120th & 122nd Sts.), Kendall, 305-232-8899
20537 Old Cutler Rd. (SW 92nd Ave.), Miami, 305-971-3435
■ "Blurring the line between restaurant and taco stand", these Tex-Mex "dives" delight "college kids" and others seeking a "quick and painless" fix of "dirt-cheap" and "delicious" fajitas, "ultra-size" burritos and other ricomended dishes; the decor's a bit "seedy", but the service is "fast" and they're definitely "worth the stop"; N.B. the Old Cutler Road locale is under separate ownership.

Talula | - | - | - | E |
210 23rd St. (bet. Collins Ave. & Dade Blvd.), Miami Beach, 305-672-0778; www.talulaonline.com
Acclaimed (and married) local talents Andrea Curto and Frank Randazzo have opened this charming New American in SoBe, and their collaboration has produced such dishes as halibut with purple rice, corn-pecan salsa and black bean puree and equally creative desserts; a warm interior with exposed brick and outdoor patio complete the picture.

Tambo Restaurant ⊠ | - | - | - | M |
275 Giralda Ave. (Salzedo St.), Coral Gables, 305-476-9025
Once a sexy South Beach hot spot, this popular Peruvian-Japanese eatery has just reopened in more modest Gables digs (the former site of Meza Art Gallery); along with its signature seviches, sushi and *tiraditos* (sashimi with South American seasonings), you'll also find beef and seafood dishes at gentle prices including a $12 early-bird.

Tango Grill | ∇ 16 | 8 | 18 | $29 |
328 Crandon Blvd. (East Dr.), Key Biscayne, 305-361-1133
■ Dancing under the radar of most surveyors, this "hangout" on Key Biscayne is "like a neighborhood place in Buenos

Miami/Dade County

| F | D | S | C |

TANTRA ●   21 | 26 | 18 | $62
1445 Pennsylvania Ave. (Española Way), Miami Beach, 305-672-4765; www.tantrarestaurant.com

■ It may not be "for the faint of heart" or "the kids", but the "exotic, erotic", "hypnotic" atmosphere of this "very SoBe" club/restaurant attracts lots of "pretty people" with "grass floors inside", "hookahs in the lounge" and "Indian soft-core porn" on the tube; the Eclectic eats are "exquisite" and "orgasmic", but those who feel stung say "tantric sex is the only way to forget the ridiculous prices" and sometimes "rude service."

TapTap Haitian   23 | 21 | 19 | $24
819 Fifth St. (bet. Jefferson & Meridian Aves.), Miami Beach, 305-672-2898

■ Loyalists "lovelove" this "unique" SoBe Haitian that "takes you into another world" with "delicious", "amazing" and "affordable" fish, lamb and goat served in a "festive" space that's "nicely decorated" with "beautiful" murals; occasional live music along with the "best mojitos in town" contribute to the "great tropical vibe."

Tasti D-Lite ⊠   - | - | - | I
4041 Royal Palm Ave. (41st St.), Miami Beach, 305-673-5483

"A ghetto for homesick New Yorkers", this pocket-sized newcomer on Miami Beach supplies "what every girl in a bikini needs": its namesake "great low-carb" frozen dessert delivers "ice cream flavor without ice cream results"; health food options like eggs and "good salads" and sandwiches are also on offer for breakfast, lunch and dinner (till 8 PM); N.B. closed Friday evenings and Saturdays.

TAVERNA OPA ●   21 | 15 | 16 | $29
36 Ocean Dr. (1st St.), Miami Beach, 305-673-6730
See review in Ft. Lauderdale/Broward County Directory.

Tequila Sunrise   14 | 17 | 14 | $27
3894 SW Eighth St. (Ponce de Leon Blvd.), Coral Gables, 305-446-8280

■ Amigos acclaim this "upscale" Coral Gables Mexican as a "fun place" serving "good", "interesting" food and "great margaritas"; those with less sunny dispositions deplore "uninspired" fare, a "noisy" atmosphere and a "shrill" mariachi band on weekends; your call.

Teté Restaurant ⊠   - | - | - | M
1444 SW Eighth St. (bet. 14th & 15th Aves.), Miami, 305-858-8801

"Innovative", "tasty" Eclectic fare that embraces Cuban, Med and Asian influences is served at this handsome Little Havana bistro; "interesting murals", "nice music" and

Miami/Dade County | F | D | S | C |

international wines add to the multicultural flair, though a few smite their heads over "ouch"-inducing prices.

Texas Taco Factory | 18 | 9 | 15 | $11 |
475 S. Dixie Hwy. (Le Jeune Rd.), Coral Gables, 305-662-2212
1608 Alton Rd. (16th St.), Miami Beach, 305-535-5757
◨ Hombres hankering for "terrific" Tex-Mex make their way to these Coral Gables and South Beach "favorites" for "fresh", "good", "cheap" chow including a "great salsa bar"; no-frills decor makes them "best for takeout" (and drive-thru at the Dixie Highway location).

Thai House South Beach ◐ | ▽ 19 | 14 | 20 | $24 |
1137 Washington Ave. (11th St.), Miami Beach, 305-531-4841
◨ "Repeat customers" over the past 10 years attest to the "excellent" Siamese fare like "great red curry" offered at this South Beach bastion boasting "efficient service" and locations "within stumbling distance" of nearby bars; it may be "pricier" than some would wish and the decor's a tad "kitschy", but the housebound will "put up with hokey wall hangings for good pad Thai."

Thai House II | 20 | 18 | 19 | $28 |
2250 NE 163rd St. (Biscayne Blvd.), North Miami Beach, 305-940-6075; www.thaihouse2.com
■ "Every neighborhood needs a local Thai place", and this Siamese-Japanese vet in NMB fills the bill admirably with "authentic", "delicious" dishes served in a "quiet", "intimate" setting by an "attentive" staff; "though prices have gone up over the years", it's still a "great deal" for such a "pleasant" experience; N.B. it's no longer affiliated with the South Beach outpost.

Thai Orchid | 20 | 15 | 17 | $24 |
317 Miracle Mile (bet. Le Jeune Rd. & Salzedo St.), Coral Gables, 305-443-6364
◨ "A great place for a leisurely meal" near the Actor's Playhouse in the Gables, this "excellent", "moderately priced" Thai impresses locals with "fresh orchids, fresh food and a lovely staff"; however, some slam the fare as "so-so" and declare the digs could use some "updating", and, worst of all, the "home-brewed beers are gone."

Thai Toni ◐ | 23 | 22 | 19 | $34 |
890 Washington Ave. (9th St.), Miami Beach, 305-538-8424
■ For a "good time", a "chic" crowd calls this "night-on-the-town" South Beach Thai boasting a "beautiful", "cool" interior in which to partake of "perfectly balanced curries", "amazing fish" and other "tantalizing" fare washed down by "fabulous" litchi martinis; "friendly", "unobtrusive" service and decent prices also make it "worth a trip."

vote at zagat.com

Miami/Dade County | F | D | S | C |

Timo
▽ 19 | 17 | 19 | $43

17624 Collins Ave. (bet. 175th Terrace & 178th St.),
Sunny Isles Beach, 305-936-1008; www.timorestaurant.com

An "enjoyable" experience is provided by this "welcome newcomer" in Sunny Isles Beach where the "excellent" Med-Italian fare includes some "adventurous" choices along with "simple" dishes served in a "jewel" of an interior that belies its strip-mall setting; "crowded" conditions make for a "noisy" ambiance and a sometimes "overwhelmed kitchen", but most maintain it's "off to a good start."

Tiramesu ●
21 | 18 | 19 | $30

721 Lincoln Rd. (Meridian Ave.), Miami Beach, 305-532-4538;
www.tiramesu.com

The "next-door sibling to Spris", this "commendable Italian" "hits all the high notes" with "delectable pastas and succulent seafood" served by a "friendly" staff in a South Beach setting that affords "a great view of all the Lincoln Road loonies"; penny-pinchers praise the 5–7:30 PM "beat-the-clock special", but prices in general are "reasonable."

Titanic Brewery ●
14 | 13 | 15 | $18

5813 Ponce de Leon Blvd. (Red Rd.), Coral Gables, 305-667-2537;
www.titanicbrewery.com

Its namesake ship may have sunk but this Gables "college hangout" is kept afloat by "excellent" microbrews and "good" American fare that "holds its own"; service can be "slow" and the bands that play most nights "annoying", but the prices are "reasonable."

Tobacco Road ●
16 | 12 | 16 | $19

626 S. Miami Ave. (SW 7th St.), Miami, 305-374-1198;
www.tobacco-road.com

"You gotta try the oldest bar in Miami" that may be the "ultimate dive" but is still "madly popular" after more than 90 years thanks to its "good", "well-priced" American grub with a side of "down-home" live blues and rock; P.S. the kitchen's open till 5 AM at this Downtown "legend."

Tokyo Bowl ●
13 | 8 | 12 | $16

860 Washington Ave. (9th St.), Miami Beach, 305-695-1802
12290 Biscayne Blvd. (bet. 123rd & 125th Sts.), North Miami,
305-892-9400

"Good" à la carte or all-you-can-eat sushi is served at this Dade/Broward Japanese chainlet that's a boon for "people on a budget", and the "fast" service is a bonus; blasé sorts are not bowled over by the "nothing-special" offerings or the decor, but for an "inexpensive, filling meal, it can't be beat."

TONI'S SUSHI BAR ●
25 | 19 | 20 | $34

1208 Washington Ave. (12th St.), Miami Beach, 305-673-9368

Though the SoBe "scene has changed over the last decade", this "fabulous" sushi "oasis" has remained true

Miami/Dade County | F | D | S | C |

to the "criteria set by" the owners, serving "splendid", "100-percent fresh" fish and "other wonderful Japanese delicacies" at "moderate prices"; "the beautiful people" and other "locals go once a week", and suggest that the "sunken tables" curtained by "beads" create "romantic" spots for rendezvous.

TONY CHAN'S WATER CLUB | 25 | 17 | 22 | $39 |
Doubletree Grand Hotel, 1717 N. Bayshore Dr. (1 block east of Biscayne Blvd.), Miami, 305-374-8888; www.miamihotelcondo.com

■ "No doubt about it", this Downtown Cantonese in the Doubletree Grand Hotel serves "superb", "upscale" Chinese food like "great Peking duck (and "fresh" sushi, too) in a setting that provides "fantastic water views"; it's also undoubtedly "pricey", but the service is "friendly" and it works for a "special evening out."

Tony Roma's | 18 | 13 | 16 | $22 |
18851 S. Dixie Hwy. (186th St.), Cutler Ridge, 305-255-4475 ◐
9525 N. Kendall Dr. (SW 95th Ave.), Kendall, 305-595-7427
3300 NW 87th Ave. (bet. NW 25th & 36th Sts.), Miami, 305-994-7511
6728 Main St. (67th Ave.), Miami Lakes, 305-558-7427
6601 S. Dixie Hwy. (67th Ave.), South Miami, 305-667-4806
18050 Collins Ave. (180th St.), Sunny Isles, 305-932-7907
www.tonyromas.com

■ Although founder "Tony Roma has gone to that great grill in the sky", he "left his recipes" for "awesome" babyback beef ribs and "the best onion loaf" to ensure that his Florida-based legacy would keep fans "licking their fingers"; even if the servers "take their own sweet, sticky time" and the decor "needs revamping", the "big portions" of "delectable" fare at "unbeatable prices" make it "great for families" (especially on Tuesday 'Kids' Nites').

Torero | – | – | – | M |
Bayside Market Place Mall, 401 Biscayne Blvd. (NE 4th St.), Miami, 305-579-2355; www.toreromiami.com

Toreadors looking to carbo-load before battling the bull will want to hoof it over to this Downtown Spanish newcomer (formerly Diego's) with sweeping bay views in the Bayside Marketplace; expect sublime sangrias and more than a dozen varieties of paella, as well as a festive nightclub atmosphere till 5 AM on weekends.

TOUCH ◐ | 23 | 26 | 20 | $56 |
910 Lincoln Rd. (Jefferson Ave.), Miami Beach, 305-532-8003; www.touchrestaurant.com

■ "It's the subtle, classy touches like the flame-swallowing belly dancers" that make this "South Beach–meets–Morocco" destination such a "scene", but the New

vote at zagat.com 83

Miami/Dade County | F | D | S | C |

American fare is "surprisingly delicious" and suitably "creative"; the "wild ambiance" is made more so by the "suggestive" shimmying, "sensual" decor and live music, and even if cynics suggest the "only thing touched is your wallet", others say "touché" to a "great overall experience."

Trattoria Luna | 23 | 20 | 23 | $33 |
9477 S. Dixie Hwy. (Datran Blvd.), Kendall, 305-669-9448; www.trattorialuna.com

■ Moonstruck supporters of this "postage stamp–size Italian in a Kendall strip mall" claim it "has it all", from "fabulous" food served by a "gracious", "superb" staff to an "intimate", "elegant" setting with a "wonderful ambiance"; with its "great-value lunch specials", it may just be the "best neighborhood" ristorante around.

Trattoria Sole | 21 | 19 | 20 | $33 |
5894 Sunset Dr. (US 1), South Miami, 305-666-9392

◪ You'll "feel like you're on vacation when sitting outdoors" eating "excellent", "high-quality" "classic" dishes at this "bustling" South Miami Italian, where the "chic locale and beautiful people" contribute to a "romantic but relaxed" vibe; service is usually "gracious", but on "jam-packed", "noisy" weekend nights the staff can be "distracted."

TROPICAL CHINESE | 27 | 19 | 22 | $30 |
Tropical Park Plaza, 7991 SW 40th St./Bird Rd. (SW 79th Ave.), Westchester, 305-262-7576; www.tropical-chinese.com

■ Despite its "unassuming" Westchester strip-mall locale, this "landmark" transports devotees to Hong Kong via "succulent", "delicate" and "delightful" dumplings served during daily dim sum lunches and "unusual", "great upscale Chinese" dishes; it's "fun to watch the kitchen behind a glass wall", the staff's "friendly" and though it can get "crowded", it remains a "locals' favorite."

Tuna's Waterfront ◐ | 16 | 11 | 16 | $31 |
Maule Lake Marina, 17201 Biscayne Blvd. (172nd St.), North Miami Beach, 305-945-2567

◪ "Good water views", "pleasant outdoor dining" and "fresh fish prepared a number of ways" are the hook at this North Miami Beach seafooder on the Intercoastal; however, critics say 'sorry, Charlie' about "mediocre" offerings, a "musty" odor and "decor that leaves a lot to be desired"; still, it's a "great late-night scene."

TUSCAN STEAK ◐ | 25 | 20 | 22 | $52 |
433 Washington Ave. (5th St.), Miami Beach, 305-534-2233

■ "Now we're talking portions" proclaim partisans of this "distinctive", "family-style" Italian steakhouse from the China Grill Management group, where the "world-class" T-bones, "excellent" risottos and "divine garlic bread" are all "conducive to sharing" (and "pricey"); it's "one of the few places in South Beach with great service", and even if

Miami/Dade County

| F | D | S | C |

the "handsome" space can get "very noisy", the "people-watching" and "hot bar scene" help compensate.

Tutto Pasta ☒ 22 | 14 | 20 | $23
1751 SW Third Ave. (SW 18th Rd.), Miami, 305-857-0709; www.tuttopasta.org
■ "Excellent", "honest" Italian fare at a "great price" pleases partisans at this "busy" Downtown "favorite"; it's not tutto noodles, though, as it serves "good" salads, fish and meat dishes in an attractive, low-key setting that works for lunch or a casual dinner.

Tutto Pizza ▽ 26 | 16 | 21 | $16
1753 SW Third Ave. (bet. SW 17th & 18th Rds.), Miami, 305-858-0909; www.tuttopizza.org
■ So successful was its Miami pasta-slinging sister next door that the Brazilian owners opened this small pie parlor purveying what dough-ting admirers maintain is the "best pizza in town", with "yummy thin crusts" and "imaginative" toppings; there's also a "perfect Caesar salad" or tiramisu that's a "winner."

1200 at the Biltmore 23 | 25 | 22 | $49
Biltmore Hotel, 1200 Anastasia Ave. (Granada Blvd.), Coral Gables, 305-445-1926; www.biltmorehotel.com
■ Whether it's a "power lunch", "romantic date" or "gargantuan Sunday brunch" you're after, this "always-wonderful" Mediterranean in the "landmark" Biltmore Hotel in Coral Gables is a "great place to empty your pockets"; the "lovely", "luscious" courtyard with fountain or "pretty" interior provide a suitable setting for the "delicious", "distinctive" dishes delivered by "polished" (if sometimes "slow") servers; the chef's recent departure may outdate the Food score.

1220 at the Tides 24 | 24 | 21 | $51
Tides Hotel, 1220 Ocean Dr. (bet. 12th & 13th Sts.), Miami Beach, 305-604-5130
■ Perhaps the "perfect place for an affair" is this "beautiful" hotel hideaway in the "heart of South Beach" featuring "tall booths" and "white-on-white" "minimalist decor" that create a "pocket of serenity from which to view frenetic Ocean Drive"; the "wonderful" New American fare is "attractively presented", and "elegant" service make it "worth the high price tag."

Two Chefs 22 | 17 | 22 | $42
8287 S. Dixie Hwy. (Ludlam Rd.), South Miami, 305-663-2100
◪ Groupies of this "gourmet gem" in South Miami adore the "imaginative", "exquisite" New American cuisine including "delicious steaks" and "ravishing soufflés" along with an "elegant" interior and "friendly" service that make it easy to ignore the strip-mall setting; contrarians consider it "overrated" and "not worth the price" (though

vote at zagat.com

Miami/Dade County F | D | S | C

there's an "excellent $25 early-bird"); N.B. though one chef has left, the food hasn't suffered.

Two Dragons 20 | 22 | 20 | $36
Sonesta Beach Resort, 350 Ocean Dr. (E. Heather Dr.), Key Biscayne, 305-361-0550

■ Serving "gourmet Chinese" as well as a "mix of other Asian dishes" including "very good sushi", this "surprise" in the Sonesta Beach Resort on Key Biscayne "doesn't feel like a hotel" restaurant; "original decor" including a serene Japanese garden provides an "elegant" setting, and though it's "expensive", it's worth it for such "awesome" fare.

Two Sisters ▽ 19 | 19 | 17 | $38
Hyatt Regency, 50 Alhambra Plaza (S. Douglas Rd.), Coral Gables, 305-441-1234

■ Though few have sussed out this "out-of-the-way" Coral Gables Spanish-Med in the Hyatt Regency, those who have think it "needs more exposure" because the "excellent" fare and "friendly" staff that "waits on you hand and foot" are not typical of the hotel experience; it also offers what some call the "best buffet brunch" around, as well as the opportunity to host a dinner where the "guests cook their meals under the guidance of the restaurant's chefs."

Van Dyke Cafe, The ● 15 | 17 | 15 | $27
846 Lincoln Rd. (Jefferson Ave.), Miami Beach, 305-534-3600; www.thevandyke.com

◪ "Location, location, location" are the top three reasons to hit Mark Soyka's "kissing cousin of the News Cafe" in South Beach, where the New American fare is "good" but the Sunday brunch "people-watching" is better; sure, the "service could improve", and yeah, it's a bit "overpriced", but the "casual" ambiance, "funky jazz scene after dinner" and "honest prices" make it a "great respite" for locals and tourists alike.

Versailles ● 21 | 14 | 18 | $20
3555 SW Eighth St. (SW 35th Ave.), Miami, 305-444-0240

■ You certainly get the "feel of Little Havana" at the "gold standard of Calle Ocho" where "Miami's Latin power brokers" sip "killer" cafecitos and eat "arguably the best Cuban food anywhere"; there may be "a long wait for a table" in the "raucous", "kitschy" dining room and it "helps to speak Spanish" (though "gringos are welcome"), but prices are "reasonable" and it's still the "place to be seen."

Vizio Cafe – | – | – | E
Arcade Town Ctr., 2995 NE 163rd St. (bet. Biscayne Blvd. & Collins Ave.), North Miami Beach, 305-947-3773; www.viziocafe.com

The name translates as 'vice', but North Miami Beachers can't give up this "lovely" "neighborhood Italian"-European serving "excellent" fare including its signature lobster

Miami/Dade County | F | D | S | C |

risotto and sesame-crusted tuna, all "nicely presented"; the stylish setting and "professional service" are also addictive.

White Lion Cafe ⌧ | – | – | – | M |
146 NW Seventh St. (bet. 1st & 2nd Sts.), Homestead, 305-248-1076
Though it remains under the radar of most, a pride of proponents "keeps coming back again and again" to this "Key West–style" American in Homestead where "fresh local produce" is used in a "variety" of "great" grub including "super sandwiches" and "homemade desserts"; "good service" and its setting festooned with antiques for sale make it a local mainstay.

WISH | 24 | 25 | 21 | $56 |
Hotel of South Beach, 801 Collins Ave. (8th St.), Miami Beach, 305-674-9474; www.wishrestaurant.com
■ A "magical garden" as "special as the food" attracts "romantic" sorts to this "quiet oasis in swinging South Beach" where the "exquisite", "serious" Brazilian-French fare from E. Michael Reidt provides a "symphony of unusual flavors"; the "ethereal" Todd Oldham–designed interior is matched by "fun" electronic martinis (cooled by blinking cubes), and though service can be a "bit slow", the staff's "courteous"; sure, some wish it were less "pricey", but more find it "leaves nothing to be desired."

World Resources ◐ | 21 | 18 | 17 | $33 |
719 Lincoln Rd. (Euclid Ave.), Miami Beach, 305-535-8987
■ "You get the best of both worlds" at this South Beach Thai-Japanese, including "delicious curries" and "great, fresh rolls" ("I could marry the sushi chef"); the "minimalist" setting's "relaxing", and there's a patio and sidewalk seating for "watching the passersby on the wonderful Lincoln Road"; P.S. resourceful types tout the "good-value bento boxes" for lunch.

Yambo ◐⌷ | – | – | – | I |
1643 SW First St. (bet. SW 16th & 17th Aves.), Miami, 305-649-0203
Step into this "friendly, interesting scene" in Little Havana for a taste of Nicaragua via imported tchotchkes and a chance to practice your *Español*; the fare's cheap and filling, and the "best *pollo* tacos" make it a "must-visit."

Yasuko's | ∇ 23 | 9 | 18 | $23 |
4041 Ponce de Leon Blvd. (Bird Rd.), Coral Gables, 305-476-1064
◼ This "great neighborhood Japanese" in Coral Gables offers a "little (very little)", "unpretentious" setting for "awesome sushi" and other "good", "typical" fare "served with a smile" by a "friendly" staff; sure, the "seating is tight" and the digs a tad "dingy", but it's "always dependable" and the tabs are as small as the surroundings.

vote at zagat.com

Miami/Dade County | F | D | S | C |

Yeung's Chinese | 13 | 10 | 15 | $20 |
954 41st St. (Alton Rd.), Miami Beach, 305-672-1144
☑ A "Miami Beach institution" for over 20 years, this "old-fashioned" Chinese churns out "good", "basic" dishes that may not be "inventive" but work when "you're too tired to cook"; it's not much on decor and the service is "below average", but it's "inexpensive" and "great for takeout."

Yuca ◐ | 20 | 19 | 19 | $46 |
501 Lincoln Rd. (Drexel Ave.), Miami Beach, 305-532-9822; www.yuca.com
☑ "It ain't like what mamasita used to make – it's better" boast boosters of the Nuevo Latino–Cubano fare at this "historically important culinary" cradle in South Beach; "imaginative", "sophisticated" dishes served in a "lovely" interior with outside seating for "Lincoln Road people-watching" make it a "must" for "out-of-towners", but the jaded call it "dated" and "overpriced."

Zuperpollo ◐ | ▽ 21 | 11 | 19 | $20 |
1247 SW 22nd St./Coral Way (bet. 12th & 13th Aves.), Miami, 305-856-9494
■ You'll find "fabulous rotisserie chicken" and "zuper *carne*" as well at this "great" Uruguayan-Argentine "dive" that draws the "Brickell crowd" for what may be "the best lunch special" in town; come zupper time, the "homey" digs can get "crowded" and "loud" (thanks in no small part to the "owner's accordion" styling), but the "friendly" service and "delicious" food help compensate.

The Keys/ Monroe County Restaurant Directory

The Keys/Monroe County F D S C

Most Popular
1. Outback Steakhse.
2. Louie's Backyard
3. Blue Heaven
4. Shula's on the Beach
5. Antonia's

Food
27 Café Solé
   Dining Rm./Little Palm Island
   Antonia's
26 Pierre's
   Cafe Marquesa

Decor
28 Pierre's
   Dining Rm./Little Palm Island
27 Louie's Backyard
25 Flagler's
   Morada Bay Bch. Cafe

Service
26 Dining Rm./Little Palm Island
   Pierre's
25 Antonia's
   Michaels
   Cafe Marquesa

A&B Lobster House 23 | 21 | 19 | $44
700 Front St. (Simonton St.), Key West, 305-294-5880
■ "Watch boats pull in and fish swim by" from two decks "overlooking the harbor" at this "touristy" bi-level Key West seafooder, as you consume "delectable" crustaceans and steaks served by a "knowledgeable" staff for "yacht-club prices" (upstairs) or the happy-hour half-price special some call "the best deal in town" (downstairs); meanwhile, a few grumble that "slow" service is "proof they operate on island time"; N.B. reservations required.

Abbondanza 20 | 19 | 17 | $24
1208 Simonton St. (Louisa St.), Key West, 305-292-1199
■ "Hungry with no money left? this is the place" to go say ciao-hounds of this "great family" Italian, where "reasonably priced", "very large" portions of "delicious" pasta render this "one of the best values on Key West"; an "extremely comfortable", "cute-as-a-bee's-knees" setting "with lots of cushy pillows" keeps 'em coming back.

Alice's at La-te-da 24 | 24 | 22 | $42
1125 Duval St. (Catherine St.), Key West, 305-296-6706;
www.lateda.com
■ "You can get anything you want at Alice's restaurant, including Alice" – Weingarten, that is, a "charming, witty" "local celeb" chef who "strolls from table to table" chatting with patrons as they dine on her "exquisite", "creative" Eclectic cuisine in a "tree-shaded poolside" hotel garden; a few complain of "hefty checks", but most agree this is "one of Key West's quirkiest and coolest hangouts."

Ambrosia 25 | 17 | 18 | $29
1100 Packer St. (Virginia St.), Key West, 305-293-0304
■ "Come with high expectations – they will be met" say finatics about this "inexpensive", "hard-to-find" 30-seat sushi specialist in a "residential" section of Key West where "delicious", "super-fresh" fish filleted by "fast and skilled" chefs will "melt in your mouth"; unfortunately, the service "isn't up to the same level"; N.B. reservations required.

The Keys/Monroe County F | D | S | C |

ANTONIA'S 27 | 23 | 25 | $45 |
615 Duval St. (bet. Angela & Southard Sts.), Key West, 305-294-6565; www.antoniaskeywest.com
■ "Dinner conversation consists of 'mmm' and 'wow'" as a "discerning clientele" enjoys "zuppa to savor", "wonderful homemade pasta" and "the Holy Grail of cappuccino" at this "expensive" Key West Italian, "an oasis of calm and civility" on "frenetic Duval Street"; the vibe is "sophisticated" and "romantic", so "dress up a little" and let the "welcoming", "knowledgeable" staff "make the experience remarkable."

Atlantic's Edge 24 | 24 | 24 | $51 |
Cheeca Lodge & Spa, US 1 (mile marker 82), Islamorada, 305-664-4651; www.cheeca.com
☑ "Get a seat by the window" or out on the deck to take in the "panoramic ocean view" at this "posh" New American at Islamorada's Cheeca Lodge, where an "attentive" staff serves up chef Andy Niedenthal's "imaginative dishes" made with "fresh, indigenous" ingredients; though some surveyors opine it's "overpriced", "even locals dine here on a regular basis."

Bagatelle 22 | 21 | 18 | $36 |
115 Duval St. (Front St.), Key West, 305-296-6609
■ "Sit on the balcony" to "watch the Duval Street crowd" from a safe distance at this "charming" Caribbean seafooder "reminiscent of an antebellum home" in Key West's Old Town; surveyors say the "delicious", "creative" fare is "reasonably priced", especially considering the "excellent location"; the only drawback, according to "grown-ups", is that it's been discovered by "rowdy" "spring-breakers."

Banana Cafe 22 | 18 | 18 | $24 |
1211 Duval St. (Louisa St.), Key West, 305-294-7227; www.banana-cafe.com
■ The a-peel of this "cute" bistro lies not just in "brilliant crêpes", "nice omelets", "terrific salads" and many other "reasonably priced" breakfasts and lunches served by an "attractive", "friendly" staff, but also in the opportunity it affords visitors to "enjoy a seat on the porch and people-watch" to get "the flavor of the Key West culture"; music lovers beg "bring back the live jazz!"

Barracuda Grill ☒ 26 | 16 | 23 | $35 |
US 1 (mile marker 49.5), Marathon, 305-743-3314; www.barracudagrill.com
■ "Ok, so it looks like an abandoned Dairy Queen from the outside" but inside this "quaint", "intimate" Marathon "find" is "amazing" New American seafood from a "husband-and-wife team" who "aren't afraid to push the envelope"; fans say it's "pricey but worth it", since service is "excellent" as well – but the no-reservations policy can make it a "battle" to get in.

vote at zagat.com

The Keys/Monroe County | F | D | S | C |

Bayside Grill | ▽ 20 | 16 | 16 | $24 |
US 1 (mile marker 100), Key Largo, 305-451-3380

◪ This small Key Largo reef 'n' beefer's "best feature" is its "panoramic view" of Sunset Cove, which makes it "a terrific place to watch the sun set"; respondents also report that for "great prices" you can get "decent if not distinguished" fare; if only there were "enough servers" to bring it promptly.

Benihana | 18 | 19 | 20 | $34 |
3591 S. Roosevelt Blvd. (next to Key West Airport), Key West, 305-294-6400; www.benihana.com

See review in Miami/Dade County Directory.

Bentley's ☒ | 21 | 11 | 19 | $31 |
US 1 (mile marker 82.7), Islamorada, 305-664-9094

■ The locals who pack this Traditional American in Islamorada don't care about its "blah exterior", "dated decor", "hustle-bustle environment" or setting "with no view" – they come for "pleasant service" from "superb owners" who dish out angus beef, "absolutely wonderful fish" and "shrimp as big as your hand"; as a result the place is "always busy, regardless of season", so "be prepared to wait."

Blue Heaven | 25 | 20 | 20 | $30 |
305 Petronia St. (Thomas St.), Key West, 305-296-8666; www.blueheavenkw.com

■ Paradise à la St. Francis, this "quirky", "rustic" Key West Floribbean is home to cats, dogs, "roosters and chickens and lizards, oh my", making for "fine barnyard dining" "under the stars and the banyan tree"; even more celestial, say fans, is the "worth-any-wait" food ("perfect pancakes", "must-have" pork tenderloin, "best-ever Key lime pie") served with "exuberant" "informality"; a few "cry fowl", though, clucking disapprovingly at all the poultry in motion.

B.O.'s Fish Wagon ⇗ | 23 | 14 | 16 | $14 |
801 Caroline St. (William St.), Key West, 305-294-9272

■ This "funky", "campy" Key West "shack" seems "straight out of *Gilligan's Island*" ("you order at a counter, there's no AC" and "cats and loose chickens" mill about), yet fans flock here for fried-fish sandwiches and conch fritters full of "artery-blocking deliciousness"; some warn, though, that this "quintessential seafood dive" is for "tourists."

B's Restaurant ☒ | – | – | – | M |
1500 Bertha St. (Flagler St.), Key West, 305-296-3140

For almost a quarter of a century, locals have popped into this "no-frills" Key West Cuban diner for "authentic", "terrific" island cuisine (plus Traditional American faves such as a "great Southern breakfast with café con leche and grits"); thanks to rough charm and "extremely reasonable" prices, the joint remains B-loved.

subscribe to zagat.com

The Keys/Monroe County F | D | S | C |

CAFE MARQUESA   26 | 24 | 25 | $52 |
Marquesa Hotel, 600 Fleming St. (Simonton St.), Key West, 305-292-1244; www.marquesa.com
■ "For the price of your meal here you could fly to the Marquesas Islands" josh judges, but "you don't mind paying" because this "classy" New American in the eponymous Key West hotel delivers "exceptional quality" – "outstanding" "gourmet" seafood, "a wonderful wine list" and "awesome desserts", served by a "top-notch" staff; though the 50-seat room with tables "thisclosetogether" is "formal" by Keys standards, "you can still wear shorts."

Café Med   23 | 21 | 21 | $33 |
Eden House, 425 Grinnell St. (Fleming St.), Key West, 305-294-1117; www.edenhouse.com
■ A "delightful" "newcomer" to Key West, this Italian-Mediterranean bower at the Eden House is "a bit off the beaten track" but "worth the hike from crazy Duval Street"; "sit outside" near the fountain in the "romantic" garden and "try the signature mushroom soufflé" or other "consistently" "solid" offerings from the "ambitious menu"; N.B. three-course prix fixe dinner available.

CAFÉ SOLÉ   27 | 22 | 24 | $42 |
1029 Southard St. (Frances St.), Key West, 305-294-0230; www.cafesole.com
■ A "locals' secret" no more, this "out-of-the-way" Key West Caribbean-French is this year's No. 1 for Food; besotted bon vivants revel in "exceptional" seafood such as "unreal hog snapper", "outstanding bouillabaisse" and conch carpaccio and commend a "wonderfully caring, attentive" staff, especially the "charming" chef-owner who likes to "mingle with his adoring fans" amid a "romantic, sexy" indoor-outdoor setting "that combines the tropics with Provence"; N.B. don't overlook the $20 two-course pre-theater special.

Calypso's Seafood Grille   ∇ 23 | 16 | 17 | $24 |
Ocean Bay Marina, 1 Seagate Blvd. (Ocean Bay Dr.), Key Largo, 305-451-0600
■ This cash-only "fun fishery" is "the kind of restaurant you want more of", with "top-of-the-line, fresh-off-the-line" seafood "incorporating tropical fruits and spices" and homemade sangria served "chilled in a child's beach bucket" by a "festive" staff in a "wide-open" "Jimmy Buffett"–esque Key Largo setting – though a few complain it can get "too noisy."

Camille's   21 | 17 | 17 | $25 |
1202 Simonton St. (Catherine St.), Key West, 305-296-4811; www.camilleskeywest.com
◾ Formerly housed in a "funkier downtown Duval Street location", this relocated yet still "reliable high-grade Key

vote at zagat.com   93

The Keys/Monroe County | F | D | S | C |

West coffee shop" (home to "imaginative" Traditional American food, including "the best breakfast in town", "lots of veg options" and "yummy specials" "well worth the price") now "seats many more"; however, you may have to wait anyway – some surveyors scold that "inattentive" staffers can be "too involved with themselves."

Castaways | – | – | – | M |
1406 Oceanview Ave. (mile marker 47.8 Oceanview), Marathon, 305-743-6247

Have a dock holiday by sailing right up to this "charming" half-century-old seafood hut (Marathon's most enduring); it's "nothing fancy when it comes to decor" but the food – including snapper Mazatlan and "great honey buns" – remains "reliable"; sit at the small outdoor bar when the tide is high to feast your eyes on the "nice view."

Chico's Cantina | 23 | 16 | 21 | $22 |
5230 US 1 (mile marker 4.5), Key West, 305-296-4714; www.chicoscantina.com

■ "Consistent, consistent, consistent" connoisseurs crow about this "casual" "family-owned" Key West Mexican, "popular with locals" for "cheap", "creative" *comida* full of the "explosive flavors of mole, poblano and chipotle" (plus "good sangria") at "reasonable prices"; opt for "the outside dining area", advise aficionados, and you "can't go wrong."

Commodore Waterfront Restaurant | ∇ 15 | 21 | 17 | $44 |
(fka Commodore Steak House)
700 Front St. (Simonton St.), Key West, 305-294-9191

■ This costly Key West surf 'n' turfer, formerly known as the Commodore Steak House, may be an "upscale joint" on the bight with a "wonderful view" of "the boats in the harbor" but "disappointing steaks" make it plain this is definitely "not New York City."

Conch Republic Seafood Co. ◐ | 16 | 17 | 16 | $27 |
631 Greene St. (Elizabeth St.), Key West, 305-294-4403; www.conchrepublicseafood.com

■ Inspiring conch-troversy among correspondents is this "loud" "warehouse-style" "monstrosity" – some consider it a "friendly", "inexpensive place" for "acceptable" seafood, while others complain that it turns out "overpriced", "mediocre", "tasteless fish"; either way, kids enjoy the "huge aquariums", their parents the 80-ft., 92-rum bar, and everyone the view of Key West's historic harbor.

Crack'd Conch Key Largo | 20 | 12 | 18 | $21 |
US 1 (mile marker 105), Key Largo, 305-451-0732; www.keysconch.com

■ An "offbeat" "food oasis" "on a dock" in Key Largo, "this charming little dive" is "a must" say the mollusk maniacs who love the "selection of" "great conch fritters", salads,

subscribe to zagat.com

The Keys/Monroe County   F | D | S | C

sandwiches, "honey biscuits to die for" and "even alligator"; "leave plenty of time" for waitresses who "have probably worked here since the '50s" to serve up your chow.

Cracked Conch Cafe ◐   21 | 11 | 17 | $19
US 1 (mile marker 49.5), Marathon, 305-743-2233; www.conchcafe.com

■ "You certainly get the flavor of the islands" at this "funky", "homey" – and perhaps "a little tacky" – "dive" in Marathon, "a better place than most" thanks to "inexpensive" fin fare like "great conch chowder" and "the best fritters this side of heaven"; N.B. the attached store offers the namesake delicacy by the pound.

Croissants de France   24 | 17 | 17 | $17
816 Duval St. (bet. Olivia & Petronia Sts.), Key West, 305-294-2624; www.croissantsdefrance.com

■ "You don't have to go all the way to Paris" for "sumptuous breakfasts" (e.g. "fantastic French toast"), "marvelous" lunchtime quiche or soup and "afternoon desserts" of "exquisite" "fresh-baked pastries" claim Key West carbo-cravers, who keep cool at this "balmy" Gallic via a "shady garden", "bistro umbrellas and electric fans."

Deli, The   ∇ 18 | 9 | 18 | $13
531 Truman Ave. (bet. Duval & Simonton Sts.), Key West, 305-294-1464

■ Opened in 1950, this "informal", "old-time Key West family restaurant" – more diner than deli – is "perfect" for "good, solid homestyle" fare "at a fair price"; finicky feeders report that "however you want your food, you will get it" (the amenable octogenarian chef will even "cook your catch"), and "locals love the place", fretting "if they close, we are doomed!"

Dennis Pharmacy   ∇ 18 | 12 | 18 | $11
1229 Simonton St. (United St.), Key West, 305-294-1577

■ The home of Jimmy Buffett's "original cheeseburger in paradise" is actually this "unique" "Cuban-inspired diner" in an "old-fashioned pharmacy" in Key West where you can chow down on "fabulous bean soups" and cheap "comfort food"; you can also "mingle with the bubbas" "and bikers" at a "lunch counter that's conducive to friendly chatter"; N.B. closed for dinner.

DINING ROOM AT   27 | 28 | 26 | $68
LITTLE PALM ISLAND RESORT
Little Palm Island Resort, US 1 (mile marker 28.5), Little Torch Key, 305-872-2551; www.littlepalmisland.com

■ "If you don't fall in love here, you're with the wrong person" rhapsodize romantics about this resort retreat, ranked the area's No. 1 for Service; in the "Polynesian-style" interior or at a torchlit table "ten feet from the water's edge" you can drink in "awesome sunsets" while feasting on

The Keys/Monroe County   F | D | S | C

"first-rate" Caribbean-French cuisine and 300-plus "quality wines"; "attentive, discreet" servers and the ferry ride from Little Torch Key help make this "very expensive" idyll "worth every cent."

Duffy's Steak & Lobster House   19 | 18 | 22 | $29
1007 Simonton St. (Truman Ave.), Key West, 305-296-4900
☑ All agree you'll feel "like you are family" at this casual, "comfortable" Key West seafooder with "lovely managers" and servers who "couldn't be friendlier" — but opinions diverge on the rest: pennywise patrons praise one of the "best lobster deals in town", but snootier sorts deem the fare "nothing spectacular" and the "sports-bar" setting "a little touristy."

Duval Beach Club   – | – | – | M
1405 Duval St. (South St.), Key West, 305-295-6550
"Dig your toes in the sand", dig the "impressive" Gulf view and dig into "standard beach fare" (moderately priced "breakfasts, burgers, fish sandwiches", nachos and salads, plus seafood and pasta) at Kelly McGillis' Traditional American near Key West's Southernmost Point; sunsters can even rent plastic chairs and consume a full-service meal with waves foaming over their feet — the easily burnt may prefer to "eat on the covered patio."

El Siboney ⓢ⌀   23 | 10 | 18 | $18
900 Catherine St. (Margaret St.), Key West, 305-296-4184
■ Compadres of Key West's "best-at-any-price", "authentic Cuban food" (e.g. "to-die-for roast pork" and "flan so good we came back and got one to go") brave "long lines" at this "no-frills", "way-off-the-beaten-path" spot, where "harried" "waitresses who greet you with affection" deliver portions so "tremendous" they provide "lunch for the next two days"; "get there before sunset" to ensure the kitchen hasn't "run out of entrees."

Finnegan's Wake Irish Pub ☾   18 | 18 | 18 | $24
320 Grinnell St. (bet. Eaton & James Sts.), Key West, 305-293-0222; www.keywestirish.com
■ It's easy being green at this "wee bit of Ireland", an "outstanding" pub "away from the hubbub" where locals go for "fabulous mutton stew" and "excellent pizza" ("go figure!") nightly till 2 AM, plus 25 obscure beers on draft; the staff, straight from the Emerald Isle, might be "amateurs" but they sure are "friendly"; N.B. reservations required.

Fish House   25 | 14 | 21 | $27
US 1 (mile marker 102.4), Key Largo, 305-451-4665; www.fishhouse.com
■ "I don't visit Key Largo without stopping in — and apparently neither does anyone else" report Conch Republicans of this generically named "ramshackle" "dive" where locals and tourists pack in "like sardines"; the

The Keys/Monroe County   F D S C

draw is an "extensive menu" of seafood "as fresh as if you had caught it yourself", which a "friendly and attentive" staff "serves up any way you can imagine"; N.B. there's more upscale dining next door at the Fish House Encore.

FLAGLER'S   23 | 25 | 22 | $42
Wyndham Casa Marina, 1500 Reynolds St. (Flagler Ave.), Key West, 305-296-3535; www.wyndham.com

■ The, er, flagship restaurant of Key West's "historical" Wyndham Casa Marina hotel (built in 1921 by railroad magnate Henry Flagler) tempts luxury-hungry diners to its swank whitewashed dining room with "great service", "excellent" steaks and seafood, a 1,000-label assemblage of wines and what some surveyors call "the best Sunday brunch"; though a minority deems the ambiance "a little stuffy", at least "the prices are not outrageous."

Frank Keys Cafe   ▽ 25 | 20 | 21 | $43
US 1 (mile marker 100.3), Key Largo, 305-453-0310; www.frankkeyscafe.com

■ This "quaint", "intimate" Victorian-style fish house in Key Largo is "a great little find" for "special nights out" gush gourmands who find the "level of service and food" "unexpectedly sophisticated", especially the "out-of-this-world Camembert fritters" and "phenomenal lobster."

Gallagher's Little Gourmet   – | – | – | E
Seashell Beach Resort, US 1 (mile marker 57.5), Grassy Key, 305-289-0454

Ok, so "there are no windows", but the "eclectic decor" – incorporating everything from "beer steins to a sunset mural" – provides its own brand of visual stimulation inside this "homey" 30-year-old at Grassy Key's Seashell Beach Resort; a "friendly" staff dishes out "large portions" of "excellent" Continental cuisine including "wonderful homemade rolls", steaks so big they "hang off the plate" and "must-have" desserts.

Ganim's   ▽ 19 | 11 | 23 | $16
99696 Overseas Hwy. (mile marker 99.6), Key Largo, 305-451-2895
102250 Overseas Hwy. (mile marker 102), Key Largo, 305-451-3337
102750 Overseas Hwy. (mile marker 102.5), Key Largo, 305-451-0900

■ Sadder-but-wiser surveyors who've woken up with "that queasy drank-too-much Keys stomach" recommend this family-owned Traditional American Largo chainlet for "great", "old-style artery-clogging breakfasts" that will tame the tum; at day's end, the Pennekamp outpost offers a $9.95 all-you-can-eat supper, while the Steak and Ribs location (mile maker 102.5) churns out "wood-smoked treats" solicitously served with Southern sides such as "the world's best sweet potato casserole."

vote at zagat.com

The Keys/Monroe County | F | D | S | C |

Grand Café Key West, The — — — M
314 Duval St. (Rose Ln.), Key West, 305-292-4816
Though few surveyors have discovered this Eclectic yearling on Duval Street, those who have say "don't miss the homemade soups and thin-crust pizza!"; an expansive wraparound porch adds to the charm as do the modern paintings by local artists for sale at moderate prices, like the menu items, which include plenty of pastas and French-influenced seafood as well.

Green Turtle Inn 16 | 15 | 17 | $30
US 1 (mile marker 81.5), Islamorada, 305-664-9595; www.greenturtleinn.com
☒ "Once a hot spot for the Southern traveler", this half-century-old Islamorada seafooder/cannery still attracts a few loyalists who "keep coming back" for "gotta-try turtle soup" and live entertainment (including magic shows and piano tunes) in "charming" digs; however, foes find this "worn-out haunt" "weird" and "kitschy" with "tired food."

Gus' Grille ∇ 16 | 21 | 20 | $36
Marriott Key Largo, US 1 (mile marker 103.8), Key Largo, 305-453-0029
☒ "Lovely views" of "beautiful sunsets" from a "beautifully decorated" room will make you "feel happy" at this higher-end seafood specialist lodged in the Marriott Key Largo, but critics caution the "overpriced" fare of "variable" quality and "inexperienced" service can be a downer.

Half Shell Raw Bar 20 | 17 | 18 | $23
231 Margaret St. (Caroline St.), Key West, 305-294-7496; www.halfshell-rawbar.com
■ "Eating it raw" with "pitchers of beer" in an "un-air-conditioned shack" cooled only by "sea breezes" "near the marina" is "what Key West is all about" gush groupies of this "cheap", "casual" fish house serving "fresh" seafood at "picnic tables"; locals lament it does get "noisy" when the "bus tours are dropped off."

Hard Rock Cafe ☻ 12 | 21 | 14 | $24
313 Duval St. (bet. Caroline & Eaton Sts.), Key West, 305-293-0230; www.hardrockcafe.com
See review in Miami/Dade County Directory.

Herbie's ⌧☞ 23 | 10 | 19 | $15
US 1 (mile marker 50.5), Marathon, 305-743-6373; www.herbies-restaurant.com
■ Though it might be considered a "dive" in "some parts of the country", this "funky, eclectic" "locals' place" in Marathon offers "consistently tasty", "fresh" seafood, including "melt-in-your-mouth fried oysters"; "fast service" from a staff that keeps it "real" and "great value" are other reasons it's a "Keys tradition."

The Keys/Monroe County | F | D | S | C |

Hog's Breath Saloon ◑ | 13 | 16 | 14 | $21 |
400 Front St. (Duval St.), Key West, 305-296-4222;
www.hogsbreath.com

◪ A "loud, sloppy kinda place" in Key West, this "biker bar/tourist trap" wins props for "excellent live music", "cold beer", "friendly" service and American grub that's a "bit better than fast food"; cynics are less than breathless over the "TGI-Friday's-as-an-old-roadhouse" ambiance.

Hot Tin Roof | – | – | – | VE |
Ocean Key Resort, 0 Duval St. (Front St.), Key West,
305-295-7057; www.oceankey.com

Key West's pricey "new hot spot" is a "great hideout" in a "beautiful" space "carved out of former hotel rooms" graced with "locally inspired" decor and a deck overlooking the harbor; early insiders declare the 'conch fusion cuisine' (a mix of Caribbean, Florida and Latin influences) "excellent."

Hurricane Grill, The ◑ | – | – | – | I |
(fka Hurricane Raw Bar)
US 1 (mile marker 49.5), Marathon, 305-743-2220;
www.hurricaneinmarathon.com

This inexpensive Marathon seafood stalwart has new owners who have revamped the menu to include landlubber "bar food" such as prime rib and wings, and spiffed up the space with new pool and foosball tables; cheap specials, "live music" on weekends and "great bartenders" are why cronies call it the "best nightlife this town has to offer."

Islamorada Fish Company | 19 | 19 | 17 | $25 |
US 1 (mile marker 81.5), Islamorada, 305-664-9271;
www.ifcstonecrab.com

■ For a "delightful dinner on the docks" to the beat of "live island music", finatics flock to this "moderately priced", "kid-friendly" Islamorada "seafood joint" where you can watch staffers "feed the sharks just a few feet from your table" though you tuck into some of the "freshest fish on land"; though some say the newer Dania Beach spot "pales in comparison" to the original, Broward locals can at least save themselves a "90-mile drive."

Jimmy Buffett's | 15 | 18 | 16 | $24 |
Margaritaville Cafe ◑
500 Duval St. (Fleming St.), Key West, 305-292-1435;
www.margaritaville.com

◪ A "must visit" for "tourists" and "parrot heads", this Key West "institution" is a "nice place to waste away" over margaritas, "great music" and "ok" American eats (including "cheeseburgers in paradise" "worthy of the song") in a room full of "novel decorations"; skeptics find the fare "overrated" and "disappointing", and "inconsistent" service leads smart-alecks to advise "bringing your own shaker of salt."

vote at zagat.com

The Keys/Monroe County   F | D | S | C

Kaiyó ☒   26 | 21 | 22 | $37
81701 Old Hwy. (mile marker 82), Islamorada, 305-664-5556; www.kaiyokeys.com
■ "Phenomenal" chef-owner Dawn Sieber (ex Atlantic's Edge) has "mastered the art of fusion cuisine" at her "awesome", "reasonably priced" Pan-Asian, Islamorada's "only sushi restaurant", where the "spectacular" tuna tataki wows "even the landlubbers"; the "cutting-edge decor" adds allure.

Kelly's Caribbean   19 | 23 | 18 | $33
Bar, Grill & Brewery
301 Whitehead St. (Caroline St.), Key West, 305-293-8484; www.kellyskeywest.com
☑ Even though it's "off the beaten path", Kelly McGillis' Caribbean-American microbrewery housed in the old Pan-Am offices is a "very busy" spot, thanks mainly to a "marvelous" setting and one of the "best outdoor patios in Key West"; while some witnesses find the "typical island fare" and house beers "surprisingly" "excellent", accusers describe the "expensive" eats as "bland" and "overcooked" and the service as "inattentive."

Keys Fisheries   ▽ 23 | 11 | 14 | $18
3502 Gulfview Dr. (mile marker 49), Marathon, 305-743-4353; www.keysfisheries.com
■ "Order and pick up" your "oh-so-good", "super-fresh" fin fare at the take-out window, then grab a seat at one of the "picnic tables" (where you can "bring your dogs") to "watch the sun set into the bay" at this self-serve "funky, old Florida-style" fish house; the all-you-can-eat golden crab special just might be the "best deal in Marathon."

La Trattoria   25 | 19 | 21 | $37
524 Duval St. (Applerouth Ln.), Key West, 305-296-1075; www.latrattoria.us
■ A taste of "Italy in Key West" is how paesani praise this family-run trattoria offering "generous portions" of "consistent", "comforting, rich yet delicate" Southern Italian cuisine and "excellent" service in a "romantic" setting with a "back entrance to a fabulous martini bar", Virgilio's, where "you won't mind the long wait for a table"; some feel the "price sheet needs a bit of a reality check", but defenders tout it as a "good value."

Leigh Ann's Coffee House ☒   ▽ 13 | 16 | 13 | $13
US 1 (mile marker 51.5), Marathon, 305-743-2001
■ This "funky" Marathon Italian "coffeehouse in a garden" wins praise for its "great home-baked muffins", frittatas, quiches and pastas as well as open-mike competitions and poetry nights; some sigh it's strictly for "locals" as "tourists" don't always "feel welcome"; N.B. it closes at 4 PM, except during the winter, when it stays open for dinner.

subscribe to zagat.com

The Keys/Monroe County F | D | S | C

Little Italy ▽ 18 | 11 | 18 | $21
US 1 (mile marker 68.5), Long Key, 305-664-4472

◪ "Very cheap", "big portions" of "good family fare" and "nice" "outdoor seating" have made this Long Key Italian a local fixture for some four decades, but Mott Street mavens dismiss it as a "food factory" in need of a "face-lift" and just say "fuhgeddaboudit."

Lorelei 15 | 17 | 16 | $25
US 1 (mile marker 82), Islamorada, 305-664-4656;
www.loreleifloridakeys.com

◪ "Drinks, music and a fabulous sunset" add up to a real "Keys experience" at this American seafooder in Islamorada, a popular "local hangout for charter boat captains", "fishermen" and "sketchy barefoot" types; the "weak" food is "not a good value" curmudgeons cavil, but insiders insist that once you take in the "great view", "you won't care how much you pay for your fish."

LOUIE'S BACKYARD 26 | 27 | 22 | $47
700 Waddell Ave. (Vernon St.), Key West, 305-294-1061;
www.louiesbackyard.com

■ It's the kind of place "you dream about" when you think of a "romantic Key West getaway" gush groupies about this "grande dame" of upscale dining with a "picture postcard setting" in a breathtaking Victorian house "overlooking the ocean", "exquisite", "polished" Caribbean-American cuisine and "super service"; it's such a "wonderful, laid-back experience" you "won't worry about the bill", but for those who always do, regulars recommend a less expensive lunch or "late-night drinks at the Afterdeck" bar.

Mangia Mangia 20 | 17 | 19 | $27
900 Southard St. (Margaret St.), Key West, 305-294-2469

■ "Too bad the word got out" lament Key West locals who must "wait in line" at this "out-of-the-way" yet "popular" Italian serving "cheap", "homemade pastas" and other "good, hearty" dishes in a "relaxed" "old conch house" with a "magical" outdoor garden; the "well-priced" wine list of more than 400 labels, "one of the largest on the island", "wows" even "casual" oenophiles.

Mangoes 21 | 21 | 20 | $33
700 Duval St. (Angela St.), Key West, 305-292-4606;
www.mangoeskeywest.com

■ "Sitting outside" in a "lovely" garden "beneath the twinkling lights" "on a corner of Duval Street" (the "perfect spot to people-watch") alone "would be enough to make this spot an enchanting venue", but "creative", "reliable" seafood-focused Caribbean cuisine, "killer frozen" cocktails and "attentive, friendly" service conspire to make it a "uniquely Key West" kind of place as well as a "favorite" "locals' hangout."

vote at zagat.com

The Keys/Monroe County | F | D | S | C |

Mangrove Mama's ▽ 24 | 21 | 21 | $24
US 1 (mile marker 20), Sugarloaf Key, 305-745-3030
■ Grouper and stone crabs in season (October–May) are so "awesome" at this "funky roadhouse" and seafood specialist in Sugarloaf Key that diehards "would walk from Key West" to get here; the "scrumptious" fin fare is served in a "casual" atmosphere by a "pleasant and friendly" staff.

Manny & Isa's Kitchen 22 | 8 | 19 | $18
Old US 1 (mile marker 81.6), Islamorada, 305-664-5019
■ The Key lime pie is "other-worldly" and the paella is a "must-try" (you should "order a day ahead") at this "venerable" Islamorada Cuban serving "authentic", "straightforward" fare in a "friendly, family atmosphere"; the "unpretentious" digs really do make you feel "like you're sitting in a kitchen", but the no-frills look undoubtedly helps to keep the "good prices" down.

Marker 88 – | – | – | E
US 1 (mile marker 88), Islamorada, 305-852-9315
Now under new ownership, this upscale Continental seafooder, a "longtime Islamorada favorite", still serves "classic" fin fare in "one of the prettiest outdoor settings in the Keys", though surveyors are split over the changing of the guard ("remains great" vs. "how the mighty have fallen"); recent renovations to the interior and gardens will be welcome news to those who felt it was "showing its age."

Martha's 18 | 18 | 19 | $35
3591 S. Roosevelt Blvd. (next to Key West Airport), Key West, 305-294-3466
☒ "Comfy", if somewhat "predictable", this Key West surf 'n' turfer near the airport offers "standard fare" in a "pleasant" space with "beautiful aquariums" and a "nice view" of the Atlantic; while foes feel that "time has passed this venue by", "gracious" service from a "patient" staff, "good early-bird prices" and a "great Sunday brunch" continue to make it a "favorite with the locals."

Martin's Cafe – | – | – | E
416 Applerouth Ln. (Duval St.), Key West, 305-296-1183
"Exquisitely light" German and Continental specialties are served in a "peaceful" setting "under a huge banyan tree" at this little-known hideaway at the end of a "quiet lane" that only seems far from the hustle and bustle of Duval Street; Europhiles will find it a welcome change from fried fish sandwiches and Key lime pie.

Meteor Smokehouse ◐ 22 | 15 | 18 | $21
404 Southard St. (bet. Duval & Whitehead Sts.), Key West, 305-294-5602; www.meteorsmokehouse.com
■ It's "not fancy", but it is "Key West's best" ("maybe only?") BBQ according to 'cuennoiseurs who queue up for "huge"

The Keys/Monroe County | F | D | S | C |

portions of "great dry-rubbed ribs" and "a selection of fixin's", including "spicy beans" "so good they'll make you jump up and slap your granny"; "friendly" service from some of the "nicest people" around is another plus.

MICHAELS | 25 | 23 | 25 | $46 |
532 Margaret St. (Southard St.), Key West, 305-295-1300; www.michaelskeywest.com
■ Carnivores call this "upscale" yet "casual" Key West Traditional American the "best place for meat on the island" thanks to "perfectly done steaks" (including a "fantastic filet al forno"), but it also wows with "excellent" seafood ("try the grouper Oscar"), "terrific fondue" and a "to-die-for" chocolate volcano dessert; "knowledgeable, efficient and courteous" service and a "quaint", "beautiful" garden setting are all part of the "fabulous dining experience."

Monte's Fish Market | 18 | 13 | 17 | $26 |
1970 N. Roosevelt Blvd. (1st St.), Key West, 305-294-1970
◪ Key West surveyors are split over this "much-anticipated" recent transplant from Summerland Keys, a "casual" seafood spot and market; while fans fawn over "super fresh" fin fare that's "not too expensive" and the "eat-on-the-deck" setting, critics find it "disappointing" so far and "hope for improvement" soon; the decor is still a work in progress.

MORADA BAY BEACH CAFE | 23 | 25 | 21 | $36 |
US 1 (Palm Ave.), Islamorada, 305-664-0604
■ With its "gorgeous" ocean views and "huge" beachfront setting, this Islamorada "beauty" "could serve dog food", but fortunately the Floribbean seafood is "excellent" and the key lime pie's the "best on the planet"; the more casual sister to Pierre's next door, it also offers live music and dancing (its full moon parties attract "everyone from babies to 99-year-olds") and "wonderful sunset" vistas.

Mo's ⊠⊄ | ∇ 26 | 11 | 24 | $23 |
1116 White St. (Eliza St.), Key West, 305-296-8955
■ "Worth going off the main strip" in Key West for "killer" French cuisine, this "hole-in-the-wall" is a "true local's favorite" that seems to open only "when [owner] Mo feels like it" (and is closed in summer), so cognoscenti counsel "call before you go"; the "brother-and-sister team" who run it provide "great service" and are "fun to hang out with" in a "diner-style" setting with "a lot of personality."

Mrs. Mac's Kitchen ⊠⊄ | - | - | - | - |
US 1 (mile marker 99.4), Key Largo, 305-451-3722
"Follow the locals" to this "roadside" "dive" in Key Largo serving "good, basic" and "cheap" American fare for breakfast, lunch and dinner including "delicious", "fresh" fish; the "eclectic" decor with "license plates everywhere" creates a "great" atmosphere conducive to catching up on the "latest town gossip."

vote at zagat.com

The Keys/Monroe County F D S C

Nicola Seafood ▽ 19 | 23 | 21 | $57
Hyatt Key West Resort & Marina, 601 Front St. (Simonton St.), Key West, 305-296-9900, ext. 54

■ "A pleasant surprise for hotel dining", this "friendly" "oceanfront" haven in the Key West Hyatt serves up "great" Caribbean-influenced seafood along with "beautiful sunset views" from the deck; of course, it's "convenient", especially if you are staying downtown or "after watching the show" on Mallory Square.

No Name Pub ▽ 18 | 16 | 12 | $19
N. Watson Blvd. (1½ mi. north of US 1), Big Pine Key, 305-872-9115; www.nonamepub.com

◪ "Good luck finding" this "most unusual pub", a true "dive" in the middle of Big Pine Key that was once a bait shop and is now "decorated with dollar bills on the walls"; the American fare's "great", but while some name-check the signature pizza as "fabulous", others who shall remain nameless nix it as "tasteless" and lament "lousy" service.

Old Tavernier ▽ 24 | 20 | 23 | $37
US 1 (mile marker 90.1), Tavernier, 305-852-8106

■ "What's not to like" at this "old-line" Tavernier taverna "favored by locals" for its "treasure trove" of "excellent" Italian and Continental dishes and a "beautiful", "relaxed" waterside setting with outdoor dining; a "great" staff helps "guarantee" an exceptional experience.

Old Town Mexican Cafe ▽ 18 | 14 | 15 | $23
609 Duval St. (bet. Angela & Southard Sts.), Key West, 305-296-7500

■ For a little "back-alley, south-of-the-border fun", this Mexican with a "California twist" offers "affordable", "interesting", "fresh", "delicious" fare in a "laid-back" and "conveniently located" spot on Key West's main drag; a "spritzer system keeps guests cool" and there's a deck overlooking Duval for primo "people-watching."

One Duval – | – | – | E
Pier House Resort & Spa, 1 Duval St. (Front St.), Key West, 305-296-4600; www.pierhouse.com

Key West's Pier House Resort's signature restaurant offers "delightful dining on the deck over the water" with views of that "famous sunset" at the very tip of Duval Street; the few respondents who've sampled the New American–Caribbean fare "love" it and appreciate the "good service", but others opine the "prices are out of line."

Opera Italian Restaurant ▽ 26 | 23 | 25 | $38
613½ Duval St. (bet. Angela & Southard Sts.), Key West, 305-295-2705; www.operarestaurant.com

■ Admirers sing arias to this "secret treasure" "hidden off Duval Street" for its "outstanding", "refined" Italian cuisine

subscribe to zagat.com

The Keys/Monroe County

including "gnocchi to rival your grandmother's" and "delicious rack of lamb", all "reasonably priced"; the setting is "charming" and "stylish" yet "comfortable", and it's always a "special treat" when chef-owner Andrea Benatti "comes out of the kitchen to greet you."

Origami   26 | 14 | 19 | $30

1075 Duval Sq. (bet. Truman Ave. & Virginia St.), Key West, 305-294-0092

■ "You can't go wrong" at this "awesome" Key West Japanese where "sparkling fresh fish" is artistically transformed into a "range" of "succulent", "excellent" sushi, each a "piece of heaven"; when you fold in "outdoor" seating, service "with a smile" and "moderate prices", it's a wonder there's nary a "tourist in sight."

OUTBACK STEAKHOUSE   19 | 14 | 18 | $26

US 1 (mile marker 80), Islamorada, 305-664-3344; www.outbacksteakhouse.com

☒ "The Aussie theme is worked a little hard" but devotees of this "dependable", "child-friendly" steakhouse chain (the Most Popular in the Keys) don't mind undergoing "ridiculous" waits for its "always-delicious" beef at "fair prices" and "fall-off-the-bone ribs" cooked on the barbie; bored blokes, however, blast the "noisy", "crowded" settings and sniff "stop at the bloomin' onion, 'cuz the bloom is off the rest of the menu."

Papa Joe's Landmark   18 | 19 | 17 | $24

US 1 (mile marker 79.7), Islamorada, 305-664-8109; www.papajoesmarina.com

■ "Arguably the best place for a Keys sunset", this marina mainstay (since 1937) in Islamorada offers "gorgeous views" from the outdoor tiki bar and some "reasonably priced", "great seafood", with the option of providing "your own fresh catch" for the kitchen to "fry up"; protesters pout it's a "tourist trap" serving simply "average" eats, but more maintain "the name says it all."

Papa's Restaurant ●   – | – | – | E

217 Duval St. (bet. Caroline & Greene Sts.), Key West, 305-293-7880; www.papasrestaurant.com

"Everyone needs a bit of Hemingway" while in Key West, and this seafooder located in a circa-1860 house provides the atmosphere with memorabilia and live jazz nightly; the Caribbean-accented "chow is good", particularly at breakfast, but a few who have and would rather have not insist "you can do better on Duval Street."

Pepe's Cafe & Steakhouse   23 | 16 | 19 | $25

806 Caroline St. (bet. Margaret & William Sts.), Key West, 305-294-7192

■ It "may look shady from the outside", but the "oldest restaurant in Key West" serves the "best breakfasts"

The Keys/Monroe County   F | D | S | C

("blueberry pancakes as big as tires") and "wonderful", "moderately priced", "down-to-earth" fare like oysters, burgers and steaks" washed down with "quality" cocktails; "wooden booths" in a "tiny" interior, a "worth-the-trip outdoor" space and "informal but good" service contribute to the "funky" ambiance; P.S. "plan ahead for Thursday Thanksgiving nights and Sunday BBQ."

PIERRE'S   26 | 28 | 26 | $60
US 1 (mile marker 81.6), Islamorada, 305-664-3225
■ Again topping the *Survey* for Decor in the Keys is this "gorgeous" oceanfront Islamorada Eclectic where "elegant" furniture and antiques from around the world evoke the "days of the British raj" and the terrace affords "memorable" sunset views; the "innovative" cuisine features "fresh, fantastic seafood" and the service is "impeccable", and though some take exception to the "expensive wines", more consider it "hands-down the best" place in the area.

Pisces   ∇ 24 | 25 | 24 | $58
(fka Cafe des Artistes)
1007 Simonton St. (Truman Ave.), Key West, 305-294-7100
■ The new incarnation of Cafe des Artistes "provides an expanded culinary experience as this Key West legend" that's still serving "terrific" fare but focusing more on New American–seafood dishes that are "beautifully prepared" and "elegant"; renovations have "upgraded the interior" and the decor features "wonderful Warhols on the walls" while the service remains "professional"; even if the offering's are "pricey" for the area, most maintain it's "worth it."

Porky's Bayside   ∇ 15 | 14 | 14 | $18
US 1 (mile marker 47.5), Marathon, 305-289-2065
◪ "It's what the Keys is all about" say buffs of this barbecue "dive" in Marathon where you "can sit out by the water" surrounded by "nautical decorations" while munching on smoky ribs and "great pork sandwiches"; foes liken it to a "B movie – you can laugh at it but it leaves you feeling unsatisfied" and still others opine it's "just plain poor."

PT's Late Night Bar & Grill ☻   20 | 12 | 16 | $19
920 Caroline St. (Grinnell St.), Key West, 305-296-4245
■ A "locals' favorite", this Key West institution serves "surprisingly great food for a sports bar" including "excellent" Traditional American "down-home" classics such as meatloaf at "reasonable prices"; the "dark" digs, "friendly atmosphere" and "late-night opening" (till 4 AM) make it an ideal post–"bar hopping" destination.

Quay, The   18 | 17 | 14 | $28
US 1 (mile marker 54), Marathon, 305-289-1810
◪ "The sunset is the best part" of this surf 'n' turf standby in Marathon where the "romantic" outdoor seating offers

The Keys/Monroe County   F | D | S | C

"extraordinary views"; assessments of the food range from "good" to "average" to "spotty", and the service is "distracted", but old hands insist the "patio more than makes up for" all that and you can always "grab a burger in the tiki bar."

Rusty Anchor   – | – | – | M
5510 Third Ave. (mile marker 5), Stock Island, 305-294-5369; www.rustyanchor.com
"It take years" to figure out how to find this American seafooder in Stock Island, but once you do, you're in on a "locals' favorite" for "reasonably priced", "consistently good" fin fare including stone crabs and "great fish sandwiches"; "nice, nautical decor" and "friendly service" are other reasons to drop anchor here.

Salute   ∇ 19 | 17 | 21 | $32
1000 Atlantic Blvd. (bet. Reynolds & White Sts.), Key West, 305-292-1117; www.salutekw.com
◪ Supporters salute this "gem" that's "right on the beach" at the southernmost tip of the Keys for its "terrific" Italian-Med specialties and "outstanding wines" served in a "wonderful", "casual" atmosphere; bashers object to paying "big bucks" and recommend you "try lunch when the food's still good but more reasonable."

Señor Frijoles   ∇ 18 | 18 | 21 | $16
US 1 (mile marker 103.9), Key Largo, 305-451-1592
◪ This "cute, casual" Mexican mainstay in Key Largo with an outdoor patio is "lots of fun", with a patio that's perfect for tippling "top-notch" sangria; after "diving all day", devotees dig into "great" grub, especially on Wednesdays for the "all-you-can-eat taco" special.

Seven Fish   26 | 16 | 22 | $35
632 Olivia St. (Elizabeth St.), Key West, 305-296-2777; www.7fish.com
■ Though it's "better hidden than a chameleon", this "off-the-beaten-trail" "treat" serves "spectacular" seafood in a "tiny" "storefront setting", including its "awesome" signature yellow snapper in Thai curry sauce as well as "delicious desserts" and "excellent beers and wines" at relatively "reasonable prices"; the service is "knowledgeable" and "friendly" and the decor, though "minimalist", is "pleasant", but you'll need to "make reservations" at this 40-seater.

Seven Mile Grill   20 | 16 | 19 | $16
US 1 (mile marker 47), Marathon, 305-743-4481
■ "A must-stop every time" for "one of the best fish sandwiches" around and other "quick", "cheap" Traditional American chow, this "cool old joint" has been a "middle Keys institution" since 1954; situated "right before the Seven Mile Bridge" in Marathon, it offers a "great location, great view and great happy hour."

The Keys/Monroe County F | D | S | C

SHULA'S ON THE BEACH 21 | 20 | 22 | $52
Wyndham Reach Resort, 1435 Simonton St. (South St.), Key West, 305-296-6144; www.donshula.com
See review in Miami/Dade County Directory.

Sloppy Joe's Bar 14 | 16 | 15 | $21
201 Duval St. (Greene St.), Key West, 305-294-5717; www.sloppyjoes.com
◪ "Throw on your cut-offs and head over" to the "greatest bar on earth" where the "frat-style party" has been running since 1933 in Key West with Ernest Hemingway as its most notable guest; "you don't come here for a romantic dinner", but there are "decent burgers" and other "standard pub fare" in a "loud" atmosphere made more so by live music; besides, "why eat and mess up a good buzz?"

Snapper's 20 | 18 | 18 | $25
139 Seaside Ave. (mile marker 94.5), Key Largo, 305-852-5956
◼ More than just another "typical seafood place", this "casual" Key Largo maritimer "on the water" is a "locals' favorite" for "fresh" fin fare, where "you'll feel as though you've escaped to a secluded island" – that is, one with a "great" Sunday brunch that you can tuck into while "enjoying the football game at the bar"; there's live music Thursdays–Saturdays for adults, while kids can entertain themselves by "feeding the fish."

Snook's Bayside ▽ 18 | 23 | 18 | $29
US 1 (mile marker 99.9), Key Largo, 305-453-3799; www.snooks.com
◪ Fans of this "hard-to-find" Key Largo New American say it's "worth the search" for "fine outside dining" "overlooking the water" with a view of "awesome sunsets" and a moderately priced, award-wining wine list; while the "specials show some flair", cynics feel snookered by the "delicious-sounding menu" that ultimately "disappoints."

Square One 24 | 22 | 24 | $44
Duval Sq., 1075 Duval St. (bet. Truman Ave. & Virginia St.), Key West, 305-296-4300; www.squareonerestaurant.com
◼ "Be square and be there" and "wear your nice clothes" to this "elegant", "upscale" New American "institution" that's "not a beer-slammin' margarita-tossin' kinda place", but "one of the best" spots in Key West nonetheless, thanks to "excellent" cuisine, "lethal, lewd" cocktails, "fabulous" service and an "entertaining" piano bar; N.B. the adjacent Café @ Square One is open for breakfast, lunch and Sunday brunch, and serves as a private room in the evenings.

Squid Row ▽ 24 | 12 | 24 | $29
US 1 (mile marker 81.9), Islamorada, 305-664-9865
◼ Go figure: an Islamorada seafooder that offers "wonderful food" but "no view", where you can "bring the fish you

The Keys/Monroe County — F | D | S | C

caught today" or order from the Traditional American menu that includes "great burgers" and some of the "best bouillabaisse in the Upper Keys", and "don't forget the Key lime pie"; the service is "friendly" and the "air-conditioned", wood-accented dining room provides a refuge from the "hot summer days and nights."

Sundowners on the Bay — 21 | 21 | 20 | $30
US 1 (mile marker 103.9), Key Largo, 305-451-4502
■ A "beautiful setting", "outrageous views" of Florida Bay and "delicious" "local seafood" make this aptly named veteran surf 'n' turf venue "worth a drive from Miami" to Key Largo; "a bit pricey" for some, it's nonetheless a "great place to go" for "spectacular sunsets."

Thai Cuisine — – | – | – | M
513 Greene St. (Ann St.), Key West, 305-294-9424; www.thaicuisinekeywest.com
Supporters are "glad to have" this "streetside" Siamese cafe in Key West where you can "sit outside and watch the parade of people" as you tuck into "good curries and soups"; despite mutters that it's a bit "overpriced", cronies consider it "just the thing for a Thai food fix."

Time Out Barbecue — ▽ 23 | 8 | 17 | $22
US 1 (mile marker 81.5), Islamorada, 305-664-8911
■ The digs are "not pretty", but this "cheap" Islamorada spot dishes out "real pit BBQ", slow-cooked outdoors, that'll make you think "you're in North Carolina" in a "casual", "friendly" setting; the menu also includes surf 'n' turf selections, but most come for the signature 'cue-sine that's "lick-your-fingers good."

Turtle Kraals — 20 | 18 | 17 | $25
Land's End Marina, 231 Margaret St. (Caroline St.), Key West, 305-294-2640; www.turtlekraals.com
■ "Outdoor dining doesn't get more casual or relaxing than this" "midpriced" Caribbean seafooder "on the docks" at Key West's Land's End Marina offering "fresh" "local specialties" and "great" raw bar items; while some dismiss it as a "loud" "tourist attraction", fans call it a "great scene for families" or anyone who "just came off a boat or the beach and doesn't feel like changing for dinner."

Two Friends Patio ◐ — 19 | 16 | 22 | $18
512 Front St. (bet. Duval & Simonton Sts.), Key West, 305-296-3124
■ A "perfect place to stop in Old Town" for "lunch after a day's shopping", brunch or a "good, quick breakfast", this Key West "tropical diner" also serves a dinner menu of seafood-centric Traditional American cuisine; it's a favorite among "tourists" for its "relaxing" outdoor patio that's "shaded from the sun", good-value happy hour and popular nightly karaoke.

The Keys/Monroe County

Whale Harbor Inn | 17 | 13 | 14 | $27 |

US 1 (mile marker 83.5), Islamorada, 305-664-4959; www.whaleharborinn.com

The queue goes "out the door" for this Islamadora American's all-you-can-eat seafood spread, "one of the best buffets you'll ever find" attest afishionados willing to "drive from Miami" for an "oyster overload"; the menu also includes landlubber favorites such as prime rib and NY strip, but many "take a pass on the food" and just "come for the music on the deck" or cocktails at the "laid-back bar" "overlooking the charter fishing fleet."

Ziggie's | 17 | 10 | 16 | $27 |

US 1 (mile marker 83), Islamorada, 305-664-3391

Amis advise "wear blinders for the tacky decor" of this Islamorada Cajun-Creole crab shack festooned with license plates and other kitschy knickknacks, 'cause it "eats way better than it looks", with a menu featuring Dungeness crabs, gumbo and jambalaya; moderate prices and "friendly, casual" service make it a "decent stop for lunch" or dinner with "the kids in tow."

Ft. Lauderdale/
Broward County

Broward County's Most Popular

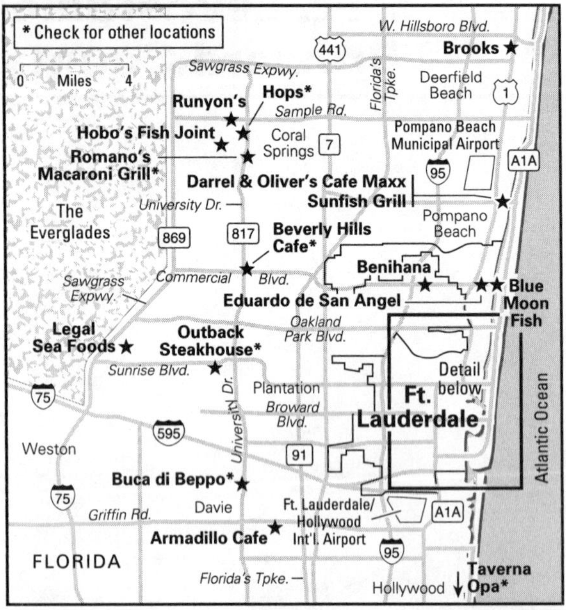

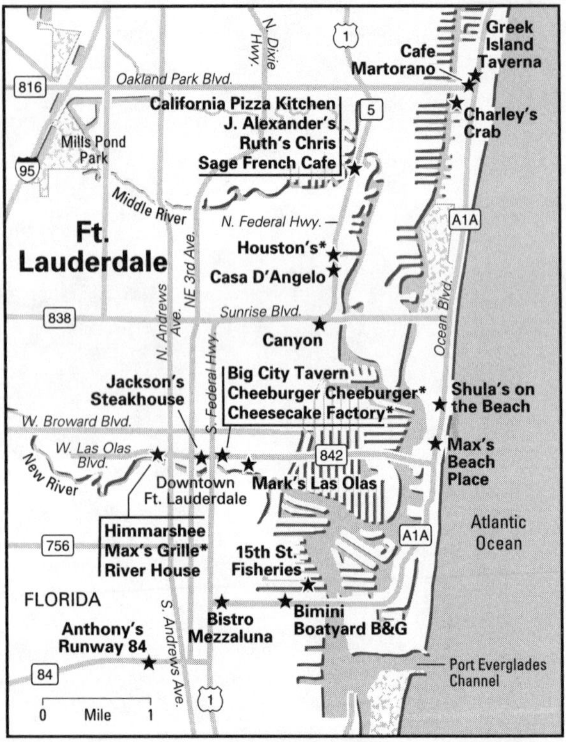

Broward County's Most Popular

1. Cheesecake Factory
2. Mark's Las Olas
3. Ruth's Chris
4. Houston's
5. Outback Steakhse.*
6. Casa D'Angelo
7. Blue Moon Fish
8. Charley's Crab
9. Darrel & Oliver's Cafe
10. Beverly Hills Cafe*
11. Big City Tavern
12. Cheeburger Cheeburger*
13. Eduardo de San Angel
14. Cafe Martorano
15. Shula's on the Beach*
16. Canyon
17. Taverna Opa
18. Hobo's Fish Joint
19. Romano's Macaroni Grill*
20. California Pizza Kit.
21. Bimini Boatyard
22. 15th St. Fisheries
23. Armadillo Cafe
24. Bistro Mezzaluna*
25. Benihana
26. Buca di Beppo
27. Hops*
28. Runyon's
29. Anthony's Runway 84
30. Himmarshee
31. J. Alexander's*
32. Sunfish Grill
33. River House
34. Jackson's Steakhse.
35. Brooks
36. Legal Sea Foods*
37. Max's Grille
38. Greek Island Taverna
39. Max's Beach Place
40. Sage French Cafe*

Many of the restaurants on the above list are among the area's most expensive. For a list of 60 Best Buys, see page 118. These are restaurants that give real quality at extremely reasonable prices.

---

* Indicates a tie with restaurant above

vote at zagat.com

Top Ratings

Top lists exclude restaurants with low voting.

Top 40 Food

- **27** Eduardo de San Angel
  - Sunfish Grill
  - La Brochette
  - Casa D'Angelo
  - La Spada's Hoagies
  - Mark's Las Olas
- **26** Cafe Martorano
  - Darrel & Oliver's Cafe
  - By Word of Mouth
  - Hobo's Fish Joint
  - Silver Pond
  - Canyon
- **25** Bistro Mezzaluna
  - Galanga
  - Black Orchid Cafe
  - Thai Spice
  - Rainbow Palace
  - Ruth's Chris
- **24** Grill Room
  - Armadillo Cafe
  - Darrel & Oliver's Bistro
  - Victoria Park
  - Runyon's
  - Blue Moon Fish
  - Jasmine Thai
  - Tom Jenkins BBQ
  - Primavera
  - Brooks
  - Himmarshee
  - Cafe Seville
  - East City Grill
- **23** Greek Island Taverna
  - Calypso/Raw Bar
  - La Tavernetta
  - Cafe Claude
  - Gianni's*
  - Hi-Life Cafe
  - Cafe Vico/Downtown
  - Fulvio's 1900
  - Il Toscano

By Cuisine

American (New)
- **27** Sunfish Grill
  - Mark's Las Olas
- **26** Darrel & Oliver's Cafe
  - By Word of Mouth
- **25** Bistro Mezzaluna

American (Traditional)
- **23** River House
- **21** Houston's
- **20** Cheesecake Factory
  - Gibby's Steaks/Seafood
  - Ambry, The

Caribbean
- **23** Calypso/Raw Bar
  - Max's Beach Place
- **22** Las Vegas
  - Padrino's
- **20** Sugar Reef

Chinese
- **26** Silver Pond
- **25** Rainbow Palace
- **21** Christina Wan's
- **19** Bamboo Garden

Continental
- **25** Black Orchid Cafe
- **24** Runyon's
  - Brooks
- **22** Food Lover's Cafe
- **20** Yesterday's

French
- **23** Cafe Claude
  - Sage
- **22** La Vie en Rose
- **21** Grandma's French Cafe
- **20** French Quarter

Italian
- **27** Casa D'Angelo
- **26** Cafe Martorano
- **24** Primavera
- **23** La Tavernetta
  - Gianni's

Mediterranean
- **27** La Brochette
- **23** Greek Island Taverna
- **21** Taverna Opa
- **20** Giorgio's Grill
- **19** Casablanca Cafe

114   subscribe to zagat.com

Top Food

Seafood
- *27* Sunfish Grill
- *26* Hobo's Fish Joint
- *24* Blue Moon Fish
- *23* Calypso/Raw Bar
  River House

Steakhouses
- *25* Ruth's Chris
- *23* Jackson's
  Hollywood Prime
- *22* Andre's
- *21* Shula's on the Beach

By Special Feature

Brunch
- *24* Armadillo Cafe
  Blue Moon Fish
- *23* River House
  Sage
- *22* La Vie en Rose

Early-Bird
- *24* Himmarshee
- *22* La Vie en Rose
- *21* Max's Grille
- *20* Ambry, The
  Yesterday's

Business Dining
- *27* Sunfish Grill
  Casa D'Angelo
  Mark's Las Olas
- *26* Darrel & Oliver's Cafe
- *25* Black Orchid Cafe

Newcomers/Unrated
- Bonefish Grill
- Cohiba Brasserie
- JB's on the Beach
- Josef's
- Sublime

Dock & Dine
- *24* Blue Moon Fish
- *23* La Tavernetta
- *22* Rustic Inn Crabhse.
- *21* Taverna Opa
- *20* Mezzanotte

People-Watching
- *27* Mark's Las Olas
- *26* Cafe Martorano
  Canyon
- *25* Bistro Mezzaluna
- *24* Himmarshee

By Location

Ft. Lauderdale/Greater Ft. Lauderdale
- *27* Eduardo de San Angel
  Casa D'Angelo
  La Spada's Hoagies
  Mark's Las Olas
- *26* Cafe Martorano

West/West Central Broward
- *26* Silver Pond
- *24* Armadillo Cafe
  East City Grill
- *23* Il Toscano
- *22* Ichiban

Northeast Broward
- *27* Sunfish Grill
- *26* Darrel & Oliver's Cafe
- *24* Brooks
- *23* Calypso/Raw Bar
  Cafe Claude

Southeast Broward
- *23* Hollywood Prime
  Fulvio's 1900
- *21* Christina Wan's
  Taverna Opa
- *20* Sugar Reef

Northwest Broward
- *27* La Spada's Hoagies
- *26* Hobo's Fish Joint
- *24* Runyon's
  Jasmine Thai
- *22* La Vie en Rose

Southwest Broward
- *27* La Brochette
- *21* Capriccio
  Nami
- *20* Roasted Pepper
- *19* Bahama Breeze

Top 40 Decor

26 Hollywood Prime
    Mai-Kai
25 Galanga
    River House
24 Jackson's Steakhse.
    Grill Room
    Mark's Las Olas
23 Blue Moon Fish
    Samba Room
    Seawatch
    Rainbow Palace
    Yesterday's
22 East City Grill
    La Vie en Rose
    Canyon
    Eduardo de San Angel
    Max's Beach Place
    Bahama Breeze
    Ruth's Chris
    French Quarter
    Runyon's
    Tarantella Rist.
21 Il Toscano
    Black Orchid Cafe
    Casa D'Angelo
    Buca di Beppo
    Casablanca Cafe
    Brasserie Las Olas
    Martha's Supper Club
    Brooks
    Primavera
    Giorgio's Grill
20 Max's Grille
    3030 Ocean
    Hi-Life Cafe
    Bimini Boatyard
    Timpano Chophse.
    Houston's
    Shula's on the Beach
    Bistro Mezzaluna

Outdoors

Bimini Boatyard
Blue Moon Fish
Brasserie Las Olas
15th St. Fisheries
Himmarshee
Houston's
JB's on the Beach
Joe's Riverside Grille
Shirttail Charlie's
Shooters Waterfront

Romance

Cafe Seville
Casablanca Cafe
Eduardo de San Angel
Hi-Life Cafe
Josef's
La Vie en Rose
Max's Beach Place
River House
Sugar Reef
Victoria Park

Rooms

Bungalow 9
French Quarter
Galanga
Hollywood Prime
Jackson's Steakhse.
La Barraca
La Vie en Rose
Mai-Kai
Mark's Las Olas
Samba Room

Views

Aruba
Giorgio's Grill
JB's on the Beach
La Tavernetta
Martha's Supper Club
Max's Beach Place
Max's Grille
Seawatch
3030 Ocean
Yesterday's

Top 40 Service

- **26** Eduardo de San Angel
- **25** La Brochette
  - Runyon's
  - Victoria Park
  - Casa D'Angelo
- **24** Darrel & Oliver's Cafe
  - Rainbow Palace
  - Hi-Life Cafe
  - Sunfish Grill
  - Black Orchid Cafe
- **23** Ruth's Chris
  - Primavera
  - By Word of Mouth
  - Canyon
  - Jackson's Steakhse.
  - Mark's Las Olas
  - Cafe Seville
  - East City Grill
  - Cafe Vico
  - Grill Room
- **22** Brooks
  - Bistro Mezzaluna
  - Galanga
  - Hobo's Fish Joint
  - Hollywood Prime
  - Jasmine Thai
  - Shula's on the Beach
  - Capriccio
  - Darrel & Oliver's Bistro
  - Fulvio's 1900*
  - Thai Spice
- **21** Blue Moon Fish
  - River House
  - Cafe Claude
  - Himmarshee
  - Food Lover's Cafe
  - Ambry, The
  - Max's Beach Place
  - La Tavernetta
  - Old Florida Seafood

Best Buys

Top 40 Bangs for the Buck

1. La Spada's Hoagies
2. Bellante's Pizza
3. San Loco
4. Pizza Rustica
5. Las Vegas
6. Shorty's BBQ
7. Cheeburger Cheeburger
8. Mario the Baker
9. Tom Jenkins BBQ
10. Christina Wan's
11. Lester's Diner
12. Bamboo Garden
13. Jasmine Thai
14. California Pizza Kit.
15. Padrino's
16. Piccadilly Cafeteria
17. Calypso/Raw Bar
18. Beverly Hills Cafe
19. Swiss Chalet
20. Whale's Rib
21. Grandma's French
22. Thai Spice
23. Conca D'Oro
24. Bahama Breeze
25. Bonefish Willy's
26. Romano's Macaroni
27. Cheesecake Factory
28. Carlos & Pepe's
29. Tarantella Rist.
30. Buca di Beppo
31. Galanga
32. Hops
33. Nami
34. Islamorada Fish
35. Greek Island Taverna
36. Roasted Pepper
37. Il Mulino
38. Roadhouse Grill
39. Tokyo Bowl
40. Houston's

Other Good Values

Café La Bonne Crepe
Caspian Persian Grill
Catfish Dewey's
Chez Andrée
Cohiba Brasserie
Ferdo's Grill
Food Lover's Cafe
Geronimos
Hong Kong City
India House
Jalapeños
La Vie en Rose
Madras Café
Old Florida Seafood
Sage
Siam Cuisine
Su Shin
Tumi
Wan's Sushi
Wine Cellar

Ft. Lauderdale/ Broward County Restaurant Directory

Ft. Lauderdale/Broward County | F | D | S | C |

Ambry, The 20 | 16 | 21 | $38
3016 E. Commercial Blvd. (Bayview Dr.), Ft. Lauderdale, 954-771-7342; www.ambryrestaurant.com

■ "Close your eyes and you're in beautiful Bavaria" sigh surveyors over the "superb" German-American fare ("excellent salad bar", sauerbraten and "tried-and-true steaks") served at this "old standby" in Northeast Lauderdale; the "cozy, authentic" setting and "welcoming", "excellent" service (not to mention apple strudel) also help to transform a meal here into a "relaxing" Deutsch "treat."

Andre's Steakhouse 22 | 20 | 21 | $46
3031 E. Commercial Blvd. (Bayview Dr.), Ft. Lauderdale, 954-489-7411; www.andressteakhouse.com

◪ "Incredible steaks" are the attraction at this "wonderful addition to Ft. Lauderdale", a new outpost of a South Florida mini-chain that offers beef "cooked to perfection" as well as seafood and a host of side dishes; the service is "attentive" but "not overbearing", and the exposed brick walls and mahogany paneling create a comfortable setting; even though naysayers snipe "it needs some aging to reach its prime" and protest "New York prices", more believe it rivals the "big names."

Angelo of Mulberry Street 22 | 19 | 20 | $43
2861 E. Commercial Blvd. (Bayview Dr.), Ft. Lauderdale, 954-689-3542; www.angelmulberry.com

◪ "It's a slice of Little Italy transported to Ft. Lauderdale" say surveyors about this "first-class" *fratello* to a Manhattan classic, offering the same "excellent" "old-fashioned cooking" with "flair" that even New York expats proclaim "the real thing"; the atmosphere's "elegant" yet "homey", and even though foes find fault with "slow" service, ardent admirers argue "I love this place!"

Anita's Gourmet Mexicano ▽ 25 | 23 | 26 | $35
10288 W. Sample Rd. (Coral Springs Dr.), Coral Springs, 954-255-1778

◪ "The fantastic little sister" to Eduardo de San Angel from Señor Pria's brothers Jose and Luis, this Coral Springs newcomer serves up a "varied menu" of "simple" but "imaginative" Mexican dishes imbued with "subtle spices" in a haciendalike setting; the "pleasant" staff is "attentive", and though a few pout you'll part with too many pesos, more insist it's a "hidden treasure" that "never disappoints."

Anthony's Runway 84 21 | 16 | 19 | $39
330 State Rd. 84 (SW 4th Ave.), Ft. Lauderdale, 954-467-8484

■ "Sinatra would be at home" at this "classic New York"–style Italian in Southwest Lauderdale that's known as an "amazing" "people-watching hot spot" and boasts a "unique" setting evoking airplane decor; Old Blue Eyes certainly would have sung out for the "honest drinks" and

Ft. Lauderdale/Broward County | F | D | S | C |

"copious portions" of "excellent" food, and might've advised adversaries who complain of "long waits", "even with reservations", to "get to know the maitre d'."

Argentango Grill | – | – | – | M |

1822 Young Circle (Harrison St.), Hollywood, 954-920-9233

This Argentine newcomer in Hollywood is a definite step up from a *parillada* though meat-loving gauchos will be happy to find a beef bonanza; it also offers creative seafood and other dishes in a sleek, stylish storefront, and prices are easy on the wallet; N.B. a new branch is scheduled to open in Miami in 2004.

ARMADILLO CAFE | 24 | 19 | 21 | $41 |

3400 S. University Dr. (1 mile south of 595), Davie, 954-423-9954; www.armadillocafe.com

☑ "Great care" and "attention to detail" are evident in the "superb", "inventive", even "exciting" Southwestern cuisine served at this "upscale" Davie destination that's also known for its "good wine list"; a few fume that it's "lost its character" since the move to larger digs several years ago, and the service swerves from "superb" to "inattentive", but more find it "unbelievable that a place of this quality isn't in a big city."

Aruba Beach Cafe | 16 | 18 | 15 | $25 |

1 E. Commercial Blvd. (east of Ocean Blvd.), Lauderdale-by-the-Sea, 954-776-0001

☑ An "enjoyable tropical" environment is the lure at this "informal", "lively" Lauderdale-by-the-Sea "people-watching" perch "right on the beach"; though it's known more as a "great place for drinks" than a dining destination, the Caribbean fare's "well prepared" (especially the "over-the-top" conch fritters) and the service is "upbeat."

Athena by the Sea | 18 | 16 | 19 | $26 |

4400 Ocean Dr. (Commercial Blvd.), Lauderdale-by-the-Sea, 954-771-2900; www.athenabythesea.com

☑ "It's like *My Big Fat Greek Wedding*" exclaim enthusiasts who "love" this Lauderdale-by-the-Sea eatery, a "fun place on weekends" with belly dancing and plate smashing all overseen by an "excellent" staff; the "great", "incredibly priced" Hellenic fare includes the "best" hummus, and though a few phyllo-stines fume it's a "glorified diner", they're overruled by folks who cheer "*opa!*"

Bahama Breeze ◐ | 19 | 22 | 19 | $25 |

11000 Pines Blvd. (N. Hiatus Rd.), Pembroke Pines, 954-450-6450
Sawgrass Mills, 2750 Sawgrass Mills Circle (W. Sunrise Blvd.), Sunrise, 954-845-9311
www.bahamabreeze.com

See review in Miami/Dade County Directory.

vote at zagat.com

Ft. Lauderdale/Broward County F | D | S | C

Bamboo Garden 19 | 12 | 17 | $17
10041 Pines Blvd. (Palm Ave.), Pembroke Pines, 954-433-3939
See review in Miami/Dade County Directory.

Bavarian Village 18 | 18 | 19 | $29
1401 N. Federal Hwy. (bet. Hollywood Blvd. & Sheridan St.), Hollywood, 954-922-7321

◪ Fans of this "old German standby" in Hollywood hail its "good", "hearty" fare including "succulent Wiener schnitzel" at "moderate prices" as well as a "cute", *gemütlich* setting with "accordion music as the crowning touch"; skeptics snarl the food's "the same old, same old" and decry the "dreary" digs but most agree it's a "fun" "place to take mama."

Bellante's Pizza & Pasta ∉ 13 | 10 | 15 | $7
8357 W. Atlantic Blvd. (Ramblewood Dr.), Coral Springs, 954-510-1591
10281 Pines Blvd. (Palm Ave.), Pembroke Pines, 954-435-7090
3128 N. Federal Hwy. (NE 31st St.), Pompano Beach, 954-788-6860
See review in Miami/Dade County Directory.

Benihana 18 | 19 | 20 | $34
276 E. Commercial Blvd. (NE 3rd Ave.), Lauderdale-by-the-Sea, 954-776-0111; www.benihana.com
See review in Miami/Dade County Directory.

BEVERLY HILLS CAFE 17 | 12 | 16 | $18
Countryside Shops, 5544 S. Flamingo Rd. (Stirling Rd.), Cooper City, 954-434-2220
4000 N. 46th Ave. (Stirling Rd.), Hollywood, 954-963-5220
Plantation Promenade Plaza, 10001 W. Cleary Blvd. (Nob Hill Rd.), Plantation, 954-452-2990
The Gardens, 7041 W. Commercial Blvd. (University Dr.), Tamarac, 954-722-8211
See review in Miami/Dade County Directory.

BIG CITY TAVERN ☻ 20 | 19 | 18 | $33
609 E. Las Olas Blvd. (Federal Hwy.), Ft. Lauderdale, 954-727-0307; www.bigtimerestaurants.com
See review in Palm Beach County Directory.

Bimini Boatyard Bar & Grill 17 | 20 | 17 | $29
1555 SE 17th St. (17th St. Bridge), Ft. Lauderdale, 954-525-7400

◪ The "million-dollar view" from the patio of this "people-watching" perch in a Lauderdale marina will make you "thank your lucky stars you're in Florida", but though partisans praise the "big salads" and "tasty specialty bread", the rest of the American menu is "nothing special"; still, it's "reasonably priced" and all will be forgiven after "drinks at sundown."

Ft. Lauderdale/Broward County F | D | S | C |

Bin 595   ▽ 22 | 25 | 21 | $41 |
Renaissance Hotel, 1230 S. Pine Island Rd. (State Rd. 84), Plantation, 954-308-4595; www.bin595.com

◼ Though few have discovered this "surprisingly good" grill in Plantation's Renaissance Hotel, those who have admire its "imaginative" New American fare tweaked with Pan-Asian and Caribbean influences; other pluses are a well-stocked wine bar and "friendly staff", though less bin-eficent sorts believe it's "overpriced" and "nothing special."

BISTRO MEZZALUNA   25 | 20 | 22 | $43 |
741 SE 17th St. (S. Federal Hwy.), Ft. Lauderdale, 954-522-6620

◼ A "chic clientele" goes to "see and be seen in Ft. Lauderdale" at this "trendy" 10-year-old in a strip mall that's "still going strong" offering "consistently outstanding" New American fare featuring "excellent meats and pastas" matched by a "great wine list"; though the service can be "knowledgeable", the staff can be "snarly" when it's "busy" (no reservations are taken), so some suggest you "get there early" to "enjoy" a more "gracious" atmosphere.

BLACK ORCHID CAFE   25 | 21 | 24 | $50 |
2985 N. Ocean Blvd. (Oakland Park Blvd.), Ft. Lauderdale, 954-561-9398; www.blackorchidcafe.com

■ This "exotic" Ft. Lauderdale cafe has definitely got game, serving such "daring", "exquisitely prepared" specialties as buffalo, elk, pheasant and ostrich along with "outstanding" Continental fare; the service is "pampering", the "romantic", "intimate" atmosphere's made more so by a "great" jazz guitarist, and even though it's "expensive", "you won't find another experience like it in South Florida."

BLUE MOON FISH CO.   24 | 23 | 21 | $42 |
4405 W. Tradewinds Ave. (E. Commercial Blvd.), Ft. Lauderdale, 954-267-9888; www.bluemoonfishco.com

■ Its "gorgeous" waterfront patio by the Intracoastal in Lauderdale-by-the-Sea lures locals and visitors seeking "a view with food to match" so they can "watch the yachts go by" while feasting on "fabulous", "interesting" fish dishes; the interior's "elegant" and the service is "attentive" and "friendly"; even if a few feel a bit blue when they get the bill, regulars recommend the "great two-for-one lunches" and "marvelous" prix fixe Sunday brunch.

Bonefish Grill   – | – | – | I |
1455 N. University Dr. (Shadow Wood Blvd.), Coral Springs, 954-509-0405; www.bonefishgrill.com

The Coral Springs link in this chain of sleek, contemporary seafood houses from the Outback Steakhouse folks is snaring suburbanites with fresh fish that's cooked over an oak-burning grill and topped with a variety of sauces such as warm mango salsa or lemon basil; it's affordably priced for a classy yet casual night out.

---

vote at zagat.com

Ft. Lauderdale/Broward County | F | D | S | C |

Bonefish Willy's
20 | 11 | 16 | $20

Ramblewood Plaza, 1269 University Dr. (Ramblewood Dr.), Coral Springs, 954-345-8448

■ During football season, fans mob this "neighborhood keeper" in Coral Springs, watching games on 13 satellite TVs and chowing down on "great stuffed quahogs", "all-you-can-eat crab legs" or a blackened dolphin sandwich that "alone is worth a visit"; just be warned it can get "too loud", but overall it's a "comfortable place to meet old friends."

Bongusto! Ristorante
▽ 21 | 14 | 23 | $37

5640 N. Federal Hwy. (NE 56th St.), Ft. Lauderdale, 954-771-9635

■ If you "always wished for an Italian grandmother, you'll be very happy" at this small, "friendly" family-run business in Ft. Lauderdale where the "excellent" homestyle dishes like "melt-in-your-mouth stuffed veal" and "great service" make for a "relaxing dinner"; though aesthetes aver it's "looking a little tired", *amici* assert it "gets better all the time."

Brasserie Las Olas
20 | 21 | 18 | $31

333 E. Las Olas Blvd. (SE 3rd Ave.), Ft. Lauderdale, 954-779-7374; www.brasserielasolas.com

☑ A "hip atmosphere" and "pleasant" patio and courtyard lure shoppers and "theatergoers" to this "casual" "oasis" in Ft. Lauderdale; most maintain the "moderately priced" New American food's "still good under new owners" with an especially "great Sunday brunch", but a few are brassed off over "routine" fare and the "dining room din."

Brooks
24 | 21 | 22 | $44

500 S. Federal Hwy. (¼ mi. south of Hillsboro Blvd.), Deerfield Beach, 954-427-9302; www.brooks-restaurant.com

☑ Mavens hail this "haven of civilization in Deerfield Beach" for its "wonderful", "consistent" Continental cuisine including rack of lamb "seasoned to perfection" and "fantastic" dessert soufflés as well as its "classy", "formal" but "comfortable" setting and "excellent" service; while a few rebels yell it's "stuffy" and the food's "uninspired", more maintain it's a "special place for special occasions"; P.S. the "prix fixe dinner is a good value."

Buca di Beppo
18 | 21 | 20 | $26

3355 S. University Dr. (SW 30th St.), Davie, 954-577-3287
5975 N. Federal Hwy. (Imperial Point Dr.), Ft. Lauderdale, 954-229-0922
www.bucadibeppo.com

☑ "Where else can you dine with a pope's head at your table" proclaim patrons who know "the best way to experience" these "crazy" links is with a "large group" and a "big appetite" for "huge portions" of "family-style" Southern Italian cooking served by an "upbeat" staff; party-poopers protest "mediocre" food and "long waits", but fans counter "it's the most fun you'll have eating out."

Ft. Lauderdale/Broward County   F | D | S | C

Bungalow 9   ▽ 22 | 24 | 21 | $40
3101 N. Federal Hwy. (E. Oakland Park Blvd.), Ft. Lauderdale, 954-565-5678; www.bungalownine.com

"Super-modern yet romantic decor" and "alluring dancers behind screens" draw "hipsters" to this "beautiful" newcomer in Ft. Lauderdale, a restaurant/club hybrid with a "throbbing bar scene"; the New American fare's "excellent" and "savory", the "service is up to par" and even those who ruminate "there's room for improvement" add "we'll try it again."

BY WORD OF MOUTH   26 | 13 | 23 | $41
3200 NE 12th Ave. (E. Oakland Park Blvd.), Ft. Lauderdale, 954-564-3663; www.bywordofmouthfoods.com

"Connoisseurs" just can't help mouthing off about this "hideaway nestled in the depths" of Northeast Lauderdale, where the "daily changing" New American offerings are "fabulous" and the "to-die-for" desserts and baked goods are "the best"; there's no printed menu, but the staff "takes you to a display case to show you the selections", creating a "bonding experience", and despite (or because of) the "small", "snug" setting, it's a "good date place."

Cafe Claude   23 | 17 | 21 | $37
Cove Shopping Ctr., 1544 SE Third Ct. (E. Hillsboro Blvd.), Deerfield Beach, 954-421-7337

"The owner greets guests like old friends" at this "excellent" "little French bistro" in the Cove Shopping Center; the food is "wonderful", with some "exceptional" dishes such as the "best duck in town", "good" wines are "fairly priced" and the early-bird special may be the "best-kept secret in Deerfield Beach"; though a few sniff the "decor's dated", its champions consider it "charming."

Café La Bonne Crepe   19 | 15 | 17 | $24
815 E. Las Olas Blvd. (bet. SE 8th & 9th Aves.), Ft. Lauderdale, 954-761-1515

A "quaint place" that's "quite popular with shoppers" on Ft. Lauderdale's Las Olas Boulevard, this "small" French bistro offers "light but filling", "delicious" crêpes, both savory and sweet, along with "excellent" omelets and other "well-prepared" dishes; the "cozy" interior's "romantic", and even if critics complain about "*l'attitude des garçons*", it's a "good alternative to the pricier" options nearby.

CAFE MARTORANO   26 | 16 | 20 | $57
3343 E. Oakland Park Blvd. (N. Ocean Blvd.), Ft. Lauderdale, 954-561-2554

"It's a real trip, but what a way to go" say legions of loyalists who endure "long waits" to dine at this "tiny" no-reservations, no-menu Lauderdale Italian; "spectacular" standards like "the best meatballs" and "wonderful scampi" have supporters "singing along" with the "blaring Sinatra

Ft. Lauderdale/Broward County   F | D | S | C

tunes", and later in the evening the "disco ball" descends and there's "dancing in the aisles"; even if the staff can err on the side of "arrogance" and prices are "outrageous", it's still the "coolest place" in town.

Cafe Seville ⊠   24 | 18 | 23 | $34
2768 E. Oakland Park Blvd. (Bayview Dr.), Ft. Lauderdale, 954-565-1148; www.cafeseville.com

■ A "true feeling of Spain" pervades this "small", "family-run" "charmer" in Northeast Ft. Lauderdale where "authentic" fare such as "excellent tapas" and "outstanding paella" are paired with "wonderful sangria" and "fine" Iberian vinos; the "romantic" setting, "personable" owners and "pleasant" service also help make it a "favorite"; N.B. an on-site wine bar has opened post-*Survey*.

Cafe Vico/Vico's Downtown   23 | 20 | 23 | $34
1 E. Broward Blvd., Ste. 108 (NE 1st St.), Ft. Lauderdale, 954-463-4414 ⊠
IHOP Plaza, 1125 N. Federal Hwy. (NE 11th Ave.), Ft. Lauderdale, 954-565-9681
www.cafevico.com

■ "White linens at checkerboard prices" create a "satisfying experience" at this "fine Italian" "treasure" "tucked away" in a Northeast Ft. Lauderdale shopping center; the "recently expanded" interior provides a "lovely" setting for "outstanding" fare including "superb" seafood, and the "excellent" service rounds out an "enjoyable" evening; N.B. its new downtown sibling is unrated.

CALIFORNIA PIZZA KITCHEN   19 | 14 | 18 | $19
2301 N. Federal Hwy. (bet. Oakland Park & Sunrise Blvds.), Ft. Lauderdale, 954-565-1196; www.cpk.com

■ "Even though it's a chain", this "pizza lover's paradise" has the "right formula": the "diverse", "delicious", "designer" pies "keep kids happy" and the "wine list keeps parents happy"; the servers are "sweethearts", the atmosphere's "bright" and "cheerful" and the prices are "excellent."

Calypso Restaurant & Raw Bar   23 | 14 | 19 | $22
460 S. Cypress Rd. (5th St.), Pompano Beach, 954-942-1633;
www.calypsorestaurant.com

■ When Pompano Beach babies are jonesing for a "taste of the islands", they head to this "hole-in-the-wall" in a "little strip mall" for "unique", "excellent" and "well-prepared" Caribbean seafood featuring the "best jerk seasoning"; the raw bar, "good beers", "fantastic staff" and "casual" atmosphere are all "winners" too.

CANYON   26 | 22 | 23 | $42
1818 E. Sunrise Blvd. (N. Federal Hwy.), Ft. Lauderdale, 954-765-1950; www.canyonfl.com

■ The "incredible" prickly pear margaritas sparkle at this "small" "gem" in Ft. Lauderdale, but it's the "unique",

Ft. Lauderdale/Broward County F | D | S | C

"elegant" Southwestern cuisine that has burnished its reputation for nearly 10 years; it's still "trendy" and "popular" (and doesn't take reservations), however, so seasoned surveyors suggest "go early to avoid the crowds and noise" and sample the "heavenly" fare served by a "terrific", "knowledgeable" staff – and "ask for a private booth."

Capriccio 21 | 19 | 22 | $38
2424 N. University Dr. (bet. Davie Rd. & Sheridan St.), Pembroke Pines, 954-432-7001; www.capriccios.net
◪ "Ah! the violinist" is a "total delight" at this Pembroke Pines Italian where the owner may "belt out" an aria as a captive audience tucks into "excellent" signature dishes like osso buco in a "romantic" setting with a "great ambiance"; dissonant diners declare it's "overrated" and "needs a major update", but the "reasonable prices" and "attentive" service still rate bravos.

Cap's Place Island 15 | 18 | 17 | $35
2765 NE 28th Ct. (take ferry from dock), Lighthouse Point, 954-941-0418; www.capsplace.com
◪ A "must for out-of-town visitors", this "fish shack" in Lighthouse Point has a "wonderful history" as a gambling house frequented by Al Capone and a destination for the likes of FDR and Churchill; however, critics carp the seafood dishes "leave a lot to be desired" and the "boat ride over is the best part", but it still provides a "taste of old Florida."

Carlos & Pepe's 19 | 17 | 17 | $23
1302 SE 17th St. (Cordova Rd.), Ft. Lauderdale, 954-467-7192
◪ Sombreros off to this veteran Ft. Lauderdale cantina for its "large portions" of "reliable" and "economical" Mexican food including "fresh salsa" and "delicious tuna dip" as well as "killer margaritas" consumed in a "nice, dark atmosphere" that gets "livelier" and "louder" on the weekends; a few dyspepe-tic sorts, however, sneer the food's "run of the mill" and "Americanized."

Casablanca Cafe 19 | 21 | 18 | $30
3049 Alhambra St. (Atlantic 1st Ave.), Ft. Lauderdale, 954-764-3500
■ Bogie and Bergman would blush over the "truly romantic" atmosphere at this Med seafooder in a "cozy" restored 1920s home on Ft. Lauderdale beach with "gorgeous ocean views"; "good", "reliable" fare, "attentive service" and a "great two-for-one lunch deal" are others reasons everybody comes here, and the nightly live entertainment "will leave you saying 'play it again, Sam.'"

CASA D'ANGELO 27 | 21 | 25 | $46
Sunrise Sq. Plaza, 1201 N. Federal Hwy. (bet. E. Sunrise Blvd. & NE 13th St.), Ft. Lauderdale, 954-564-1234; www.casa-d-angelo.com
■ "Master" chef-owner Angelo Elia brings a "touch of Tuscany" to Lauderdale with his "fantastic" Italian fare,

vote at zagat.com

Ft. Lauderdale/Broward County   F | D | S | C |

from "divine" "homemade pastas" and "exceptional risottos" to "sublime fish" along with "terrific (if pricey) wines"; the "wonderful" staff along with a "classy yet unpretentious" interior contribute to the "fantastic dining experience", but it's the "dependably" "top-flight" food that accounts for the fact that "it's always busy."

Caspian Persian Grill   – | – | – | M |

7821 W. Sunrise Blvd. (N. University Dr.), Plantation, 954-236-9955
This "homey" haven in a Plantation shopping center is "the only Iranian restaurant in town", and folks hankering for "something different" delight in its "wonderful", "nicely prepared" specialties that "make great use of herbs" as well as its "interesting" decor and Persian music.

Catfish Dewey's   19 | 10 | 17 | $22 |

4003 N. Andrews Ave. (bet. Commercial & Oakland Park Blvds.), Oakland Park, 954-566-5333

▣ Down-home devotees get dewey-eyed over the "best damn fried catfish" served at this "country-style" Southern "charmer" in Oakland Park, and other "pig-outs" include the "great hushpuppies" and "good all-you-can-eat stone crabs"; the digs are "shack"-like but "comfortable", and the "affordable" vittles make it a "family" destination; P.S. there's "foot-stompin' music" the first Sunday of each month.

CHARLEY'S CRAB   19 | 19 | 19 | $40 |

1755 SE Third Ct. (Riverview Rd.), Deerfield Beach, 954-427-4000
3000 NE 32nd Ave. (Oakland Park Blvd.), Ft. Lauderdale, 954-561-4800
www.muer.com

▣ "Don't let the name fool you", it's "white tablecloths all the way" at these "old stalwarts", all offering "great water views", "accommodating service" and "wonderful" "classic" seafood dishes; foes fuss it's "boring mooring", with "overpriced", "so-so" fare and "lackluster" settings, but admit the "early-bird's a bargain"; N.B. the Palm Beach outpost, while still open, is undergoing a renovation.

CHEEBURGER CHEEBURGER   18 | 11 | 15 | $14 |

Trafalgar Sq., 1853 Univeristy Dr. (Atlantic Blvd.), Coral Springs, 954-346-6666
708 E. Las Olas Blvd. (bet. SE 6th & 8th Aves.), Ft. Lauderdale, 954-524-8824
5409 N. University Dr. (W. Commercial Blvd.), Lauderhill, 954-749-4666
2010 N. Flamingo Rd. (bet. Sheridan & Taft Sts.), Pembroke Pines, 954-441-9799
1793 Belltower Ln. (Bonaventure Blvd.), Weston, 954-659-1115
www.cheeburger-cheeburger.com

■ "What can I say, what can I say" – this "retro-style" diner chain serves some "delicious gargantuan-sized burgers" "cooked the way you like 'em" as well as the "best onion

Ft. Lauderdale/Broward County F | D | S | C

rings in town" and "habit-forming milkshakes"; though a few gripe "grease is the word", even vegetarians "fall off the chuckwagon" for those "big, fat" patty melts.

CHEESECAKE FACTORY ● 20 | 19 | 18 | $25
600 E. Las Olas Blvd. (S. Federal Hwy.), Ft. Lauderdale, 954-463-1999
Sawgrass Mills Oasis, 2612 Sawgrass Mills Circle (Flamingo Rd.), Sunrise, 954-835-0966
www.thecheesecakefactory.com
With its fabled "menu longer than the latest Harry Potter" and portions large enough "to serve an entire canasta" group, these "dependable" chain links attract "masses" who "line up" for "good" American fare and "dynamite desserts"; sure, they're "noisy" and the lines can be "prohibitively long", but the staff's "quick and efficient" and the "well-done corporate formula" is "great for the kids"; N.B. it's voted Most Popular in Lauderdale and Palm Beach.

Chez Andrée - | - | - | M
1000 N. Broadwalk (Michigan St.), Hollywood, 954-922-1002
A welcome addition to Hollywood, this beachfront bistro on the Broadwalk serves classic French fare as well as regional dishes from the country's southwest region; locals are just getting acquainted with the repertoire of owner Franck Chaumes, who grew up near Bordeaux, and chef Xavier Michaud, who brings years of expertise from the Riviera and Monte Carlo.

Christina Wan's Mandarin House 21 | 14 | 20 | $20
2031 Hollywood Blvd. (Dixie Hwy.), Hollywood, 954-923-1688
■ "Christina is always there to greet you with a smile" at this "trusted" Hollywood "favorite" for the "best Chinese in the area" including "varied vegetarian selections"; despite "unexciting decor", "lots of regulars are here all the time", wan over by the "excellent" service, a "warm atmosphere" and "fair prices."

Chuck's Steakhouse 18 | 13 | 17 | $27
2428 E. Commercial Blvd. (N. Federal Hwy.), Ft. Lauderdale, 954-772-2850
1207 SE 17th St. (S. Federal Hwy.), Ft. Lauderdale, 954-764-3333 ●
www.chucksflorida.com
Pioneers of the steak and salad bar concept, the Ft. Lauderdale and Boca Raton links of this chain are "casual" "old standbys" that corral carnivores with "large portions" of "good" beef, "pleasant" digs and "reasonable prices"; protesters say they're "predictable" and "past their prime."

Cohiba Brasserie ⌧ - | - | - | M
17864 NW Second St. (NW 178th Ave.), Pembroke Pines, 954-442-8777
Foodies are buzzing over this handsome, moderately priced newcomer located in an out-of-the-way medical complex

vote at zagat.com

Ft. Lauderdale/Broward County   F | D | S | C

in Pembroke Pines, the showcase for chef Roberto Ferrer's Eclectic cuisine, a fusion of Latin and Asian cooking with French influences that includes such dishes as saffron risotto paella and Peking duck with ginger sweet-potato mash; there's live music and flamenco on weekend nights.

Conca D'Oro   19 | 13 | 17 | $20
1833 Tyler St. (bet. Hollywood Blvd. & US 1), Hollywood, 954-927-6704
☒ Open since 1976, this "longtime local favorite" in downtown Hollywood has expanded to three rooms over the years, but it's still run by a "wonderful family" and serves "good Italian food" like homemade gnocchi and lasagna and "great pizza"; dissenters deem it "overrated", but fans are fond of the "friendly" staff and nightly entertainment.

Costello's ☒   - | - | - | M
2345 Wilton Dr. (NE 8th Ave.), Wilton Manors, 954-563-7752
This gay-friendly Wilton Manors New American draws a steady clientele with its "calm, comfortable and upscale" setting, "romantic" atmosphere and "top-drawer appetizers and entrees" like calamari and fresh fish; its Gin Mill martini bar adds to the men's club feel.

Creolina's   23 | 13 | 18 | $26
209 SW Second St. (3rd Ave.), Ft. Lauderdale, 954-524-2003
☒ A "little piece of the Big Easy" in South Florida, this "low-key" Ft. Lauderdale cafe slings "awesome", "sometimes brilliant" Cajun-Creole creations "spiced just right" with "Emeril"-worthy sauces (not to mention "saucy" waitress Rosie O'Neal); design doyennes who declare the "dark" interior "needs work" will be happy to hear it's been painted and spruced up with new art post-*Survey*.

Crepe Christina   ▽ 23 | 14 | 22 | $26
2736 N. Federal Hwy. (bet. E. Oakland Park Blvd. & 26th St.), Ft. Lauderdale, 954-566-2880
■ Christine and Pierre Morin turn out "unbeatable", "delicious crêpes" along with other "great French comfort food" in this "sweet, little" "staple" in Ft. Lauderdale; a "personable staff", a "comfortable", "quiet" space and an "unrushed", "old-time Gallic atmosphere" explain its enduring popularity; N.B. open October–late spring.

Dan Marino's Fine Food & Spirits   18 | 17 | 16 | $25
Coral Square Mall, 901 University Dr. (Atlantic Blvd.), Coral Springs, 954-341-4658
Riverfront Mall, 300 SW First Ave. (Broward Blvd.), Ft. Lauderdale, 954-522-1313
www.danmarinosrestaurant.com
☒ "Dan, Dan, you da man!" cheer fans of this Broward and Miami trio of "upscale sports bars"–cum–"casual" steakhouses owned by the former Dolphins quarterback, who sometimes "drops" back into the pocket of its "dark,

Ft. Lauderdale/Broward County | F | D | S | C |

clubby'' digs; while it gains plenty of yardage with "good" burgers, fish and salads ("there's something for everyone") and "friendly" service, it gets blitzed by bashers who knock it as "no touchdown."

Darrel & Oliver's Bistro 17 ● | 24 | 18 | 22 | $49 |
Renaissance Hotel, 1617 SE 17th St. (Eisenhower Blvd.), Ft. Lauderdale, 954-626-1701

A "great surprise" "tucked into the lobby" of the Renaissance Hotel in Ft. Lauderdale, this "attractive" "sibling to Cafe Maxx" is acclaimed as "another triumph" for Darrel Broek and Oliver Saucy with "sensational, innovative" New American cuisine brought to table by an "educated", "impeccable" staff; alas, doubters deem the room too "dark" and "claustrophobic", adding it's "overpriced", but the faithful still find it a "favorite."

DARREL & OLIVER'S CAFE MAXX | 26 | 19 | 24 | $54 |
2601 E. Atlantic Blvd. (east of N. Federal Hwy.), Pompano Beach, 954-782-0606; www.cafemaxx.com

A longtime Pompano Beach "favorite", this "superb" New American–Eclectic in an "unpretentious" storefront offers "consistent", "exceptional" cuisine that "blends" flavors from "Florida and the rest of the world"; the interior's "comfortable" (if "plain"), the service is "outstanding" and though it's "pricey", "every bite's worth the premium cost"; P.S. "no cocktails", but the wines are "top-notch."

East City Grill | 24 | 22 | 23 | $41 |
Weston Town Ctr., 1800 Belltower Ln. (Arvida Pkwy.), Weston, 954-659-3339; www.eastcitygrill.com

Yet another "happening" "hot spot" from Darrel Broek and Oliver Saucy, this "welcome oasis near the Everglades" wows Westonians with "superb" New American dishes like the signature snapper and "killer skirt steak" as well as "right-on-target" service; though a few fume it's "pricey" for the suburbs and others miss its prior "fun beach" location, it does have a "pleasant" terrace overlooking a lake and the interior boasts "great lighting that makes you feel sexy."

EDUARDO DE SAN ANGEL ☒ | 27 | 22 | 26 | $46 |
2822 E. Commercial Blvd. (bet. Bayview Dr. & 28th Ave.), Ft. Lauderdale, 954-772-4731; www.eduardodesanangel.com

Chef-owner Eduardo Pria will "change your views of south-of-the-border cuisine", and the "sublime" fare proffered at this Mexican that garners Ft. Lauderdale's No. 1 Food score; from "fresh fish to mango crème brûlée", the "unique", "delicate" dishes are "artfully" presented (accompanied by "great wines" but "no margaritas"), and the "solicitous service" is equally "refined"; the "romantic", "old-world" setting in a "small" storefront adds to the "wonderful experience"; P.S. "reservations are a must during the season."

vote at zagat.com

Ft. Lauderdale/Broward County F | D | S | C

811 Bourbon Street — | 18 | 18 | $22
811 S. University Dr. (SW 10th St.), Plantation, 954-424-8110

This sprawling West Broward eatery is no longer as jazzed about serving Cajun-Creole and has revamped its menu that now includes such Continental dishes as Châteaubriand and rack of lamb along with a few New Orleans hits like jambalaya; critics complain it's "noisy", but others prefer a lively atmosphere and the personal attention from the owner, a "master schmoozer."

Ferdo's Grill ☒ ▽ 19 | 16 | 21 | $20
4300 N. Federal Hwy. (NE 43rd St.), Ft. Lauderdale, 954-492-5552

"Bring dollars for the wonderful belly dancer" on Saturday nights at this small Middle Eastern storefront in a Ft. Lauderdale strip mall, and bring a few more for the "tasty", "fresh" fare including "damn fine gyros"; it's "not fancy but it's not bare-bones either", and the "spirited" staff helps make for a "pleasant experience."

15th St. Fisheries 18 | 17 | 17 | $36
Lauderdale Marina, 1900 SE 15th St. (1 mi. south of Broward Blvd.), Ft. Lauderdale, 954-763-2777; www.15streetfisheries.com

"From the pelican feedings" to the "beautiful view of the Intracoastal" overlooking "mega yachts", this "rustic", "old-style" Southeast Ft. Lauderdale seafood house "feels like Florida", making it "a great place to take visitors"; the "fresh" fin fare's "good" if "unimaginative", the bread's "delicious" and the staff "well informed", but a few harpoon "dated" decor and "overpriced" offerings; N.B. reservations required for the more formal upstairs section.

Food Lover's Cafe 22 | 15 | 21 | $34
1576 E. Oakland Park Blvd. (16th Ave.), Ft. Lauderdale, 954-566-9606

Lovers of this "secret hideaway" tucked in a "barn-shaped" building in Ft. Lauderdale are in ecstasy over its "excellent", "gourmet" Continental cuisine with "fine" French flair that provides "good value"; the atmosphere is "comfortable", the service is "pleasant" and even though some consider it merely "average", more call it a "great little find"; N.B. the exterior had a fresh paint job and landscaping post-*Survey*.

Frankie's Pier 5 ▽ 18 | 18 | 15 | $33
124 S. Federal Hwy. (Hallandale Beach Blvd.), Hallandale, 954-454-2410

This Hallandale institution is run by a father-and-son team "who know good food", serving "enjoyable" Southern Italian dishes like chicken scarparillo; longtimers "love the piano player" performing Tuesday–Sunday, and a recent redo may counter complaints of "old-fashioned" decor.

Ft. Lauderdale/Broward County F | D | S | C |

French Place ◐ ▽ 18 | 13 | 18 | $31
360 SE McNab Rd. (bet. 18th Ave. & US 1), Pompano Beach, 954-785-1920

Though few can place this "cute", "little" "family-run" French cafe/bakery in Pompano Beach, a committed coterie acclaims its "lovely" signature dishes of duck, rack of lamb, escargot and "the best bread around" from an "authentic" menu unchanged in 29 years; however, a few fashionistas fulminate the "tired" digs "need grooming."

French Quarter ⌀ 20 | 22 | 18 | $41
215 SE Eighth Ave. (Las Olas Blvd.), Ft. Lauderdale, 954-463-8000

Despite its name, indoor brick courtyard and wrought-iron filigree touches, this "romantic" Lauderdale longtimer more typifies "a corner of Paris than New Orleans", serving "delicious", "comforting" French classics; those who give it no quarter quibble the food's "fussy" and service "snobby", but more maintain it's still a "special-occasion" destination.

Fulvio's 1900 23 | 20 | 22 | $41
1900 Harrison St. (19th Ave.), Hollywood, 954-927-1900

"New York–quality dining with a neighborhood feel" helps explain the "loyal following" of this Hollywood Northern Italian that dishes up "excellent" fare and offers a "great wine list" in a "quaint", "homey" setting; wallet-watchers wail it's "way too expensive", but defenders demur they're "never disappointed."

GALANGA 25 | 25 | 22 | $32
2389 Wilton Dr. (NE 8th Ave.), Wilton Manors, 954-202-0000

It's named for a "robust" spice relative of ginger, and this "outstanding" newcomer has taken root in Wilton Manors with its "exciting", "sophisticated" Thai-Japanese cuisine that's a "culinary adventure" as well as "wonderful" sushi; the "knockout", "Zen-like" decor and "pretty outdoor dining area" (not to mention "excellent" service) add to the "exotic" experience at this "winner."

Geronimos Bar & Grill ◐ ▽ 19 | 9 | 13 | $19
3528 S. University Dr. (south of Rte. 595), Davie, 954-474-9992; www.geronimosbar.com

Brothers Geronimos and Louie Dimitrelos "put their hearts, souls" and "charisma" into this casual Davie American "hangout" that "looks like a dive" but is actually "the best-kept secret" in town, serving "great" fare with "Greek flair" plus a late-night menu till 3 AM; the "friendly" staff actually "seems happy to be serving the customers."

Gianni's 23 | 14 | 19 | $29
1601 E. Atlantic Blvd. (NE 16th Ave.), Pompano Beach, 954-942-1733

"A wonderful family" "favorite" in Pompano Beach, this "popular" Southern Italian offers "large portions" of

Ft. Lauderdale/Broward County F | D | S | C

"exceptional" salads and "delicious" garlic-laden pastas at "reasonable prices"; even though it's often "crowded and noisy", paesani proclaim it "pleasingly" so and insist it's "worth the trouble" for such "terrific" fare.

Gibby's Steaks & Seafood 20 | 17 | 20 | $34
2900 NE 12th Terrace (E. Oakland Park Blvd.), Oakland Park, 954-565-2929; www.gibbysrestaurant.com
■ Supporters of this seasoned Ft. Lauderdale "favorite" cite the "sensational" American fare including "excellent" beef and "tasty" seafood, "great early-bird specials", "pleasant" service and "clubby", "relaxed" atmosphere; naysayers nix the "inconsistent", "formulaic" food and "'70s-flashback" decor, but they're overruled by vets who say "there's a reason it's been around so long."

Giorgio's Grill 20 | 21 | 16 | $32
606 N. Ocean Dr. (Indiana St.), Hollywood, 954-929-7030; www.giorgiosgrill.com
■ "Sit outside" and "drool" over the mega-yachts that glide by this "classic" Hollywood villa, a "stunner on the Intracoastal" with "contemporary" decor and "fantastic views"; the kitchen "delivers consistent Mediterranean favorites" including "exceptional" seafood, and the service is "efficient"; the "noise" can be "overwhelming", however, as it moonlights as a nightclub.

Grandma's French Cafe 21 | 15 | 20 | $23
3354 N. Ocean Blvd. (NE 34th St.), Ft. Lauderdale, 954-564-3671
■ For over 30 years, Francophiles have thronged this "tiny" cafe–cum–ice cream shop on Galt Ocean Mile in Lauderdale for "lovely salads", the "best crêpes", "impressive" Gallic classics and "divine homemade" *crème glacée*; the "charming" setting, "excellent" service and "great value" help make for a "pleasant experience"; N.B. new owners don't plan to change a thing.

Greek Island Taverna 23 | 15 | 20 | $27
3300 N. Ocean Blvd. (Oakland Park Blvd.), Ft. Lauderdale, 954-565-5505
■ Proponents gladly participate in an "orgy of oregano and olive oil" at this "festive" Hellenic on Galt Ocean Mile and don't mind "standing in line" for saganaki "that would leave Plato speechless" and "lamb you'll gnaw to the bone"; the "simple, tasteful decor" evokes an "authentic" Greek taverna, the service is "personable", the "prices are moderate" and the "lively" atmosphere becomes more so as the evening progresses.

GRILL ROOM 24 | 24 | 23 | $50
Riverside Hotel, 620 E. Las Olas Blvd. (SE 8th Ave.), Ft. Lauderdale, 954-467-2555; www.riversidehotel.com
■ The "hip crowd may fall asleep" but "genteel diners" gush about the "pampering" provided at this "sophisticated"

Ft. Lauderdale/Broward County F | D | S | C

New American in the Riverside Hotel; "superb" steaks and other "wonderfully prepared" dishes are complemented by "outstanding" wines served by a "gracious" staff in a "lovely", "upscale" setting; sure, it's a bit "old-fashioned" and may be best for the "expense-account crowd", but it's "great for a romantic occasion" capped off by a drink in the "fun" piano bar.

Hi-Life Cafe 23 | 20 | 24 | $38
Plaza 3000, 3000 N. Federal Hwy. (south of Oakland Park Blvd.), Ft. Lauderdale, 954-563-1395; www.hilifecafe.com

■ It's "hard to find" but this "sensational" "treasure" in a Ft. Lauderdale strip shopping center is "worth tracking down" for its "delicious, creative" New American dishes, "great flourless chocolate cake" and "wonderful wine" selection; the decor is "warm" and "romantic", and owner Chuck Smith and his "wonderful" staff "make everyone feel important", which is why its extended "family" including a "large gay clientele" considers it an "all-time favorite."

Himmarshee Bar & Grille 24 | 18 | 21 | $38
210 SW Second St. (Moffat Ave.), Ft. Lauderdale, 954-524-1818; www.himmarshee.com

■ "Theatergoers" and Lauderdale "hipsters" head to this "unassuming little gem" "near the Broward Center" for "daily changing" "outrageously delicious" Eclectic–New American dishes including "excellent seafood and steak", "adventurous" wines, "stellar" service and a "minimalist", "candlelit" setting; its "popularity" can translate into "lots of noise", but those in-the-know advise sitting outside to savor the "bustling street scene" with a "touch of SoHo."

HOBO'S FISH JOINT 26 | 18 | 22 | $43
Palm Spring Plaza, 10317 Royal Palm Blvd. (Coral Springs Dr.), Coral Springs, 954-346-5484

☑ This "cool, little out-of-the-way place" in a "nondescript" Coral Springs storefront may "have a silly name, but boy can they cook seafood" affirm afishionados who also acclaim the "huge" portions, "incredible" "mix-and-match" options, "nice wine list" and "courteous" service; ho-bohemians bash it as "overpriced" and bemoan the "waits" due to the reservations policy (only for parties of six or more).

HOLLYWOOD PRIME ☒ 23 | 26 | 22 | $65
Westin Diplomat Resort & Spa, 3555 S. Ocean Dr., Hollywood, 954-602-6000

☑ The "dark", "dramatic" interior of this steakhouse in the "classy" Westin Diplomat Resort has earned it the No. 1 spot for Decor in this *Survey* and plaudits from fans who also praise "fantastic food" and "wines for every taste"; dissers call it "all dressed up with no place to go" and oppose the "overpriced" offerings, but more are happy to shell out for "gourmet" fare in a "gentlemen's club atmosphere."

vote at zagat.com

Ft. Lauderdale/Broward County   F | D | S | C

Hong Kong City BBQ   ▽ 24 | 8 | 17 | $21
5301 N. State Rd. 7 (Commercial Blvd.), Tamarac, 954-777-3832
■ This "Chinatown-style storefront with ducks hanging up front" helps transform this Tamarac mainstay into an "authentic" destination known for its "delicious dim sum", casseroles and "real Asian barbecue", all at "unbelievably low" prices; the "plain" digs may be "far from elegant", but the "excellent" food keeps it "popular" with insiders.

Hops   16 | 15 | 16 | $21
2600 University Dr. (bet. Royal Palm Blvd. & Sample Rd.), Coral Springs, 954-340-3868
S. Harbor Plaza, 1430 SE 17th St. (Federal Hwy.), Ft. Lauderdale, 954-527-1594
11555 Pines Blvd. (bet. Hiatus & N. Flamingo Rds.), Pembroke Pines, 954-441-4599
Jacaranda Plaza, 8285 W. Sunrise Blvd. (University Dr.), Plantation, 954-236-3710
3571 N. Federal Hwy. (Sample Rd.), Pompano Beach, 954-941-7787
www.hopsonline.com
See review in Palm Beach County Directory.

HOUSTON'S   21 | 20 | 20 | $29
1451 N. Federal Hwy. (13th St.), Ft. Lauderdale, 954-563-2226
2821 E. Atlantic Blvd. (Federal Hwy.), Pompano Beach, 954-783-9499
www.houstons.com
■ These "trendy" chain links in Broward, Miami and Palm Beach (the Pompano branch boasting a "beautiful" waterfront setting) are "real standouts", thanks to "consistently good" American fare like the "wonderful spinach-artichoke dip" and "great salads and steaks"; the "warm", "wood"-lined interiors and "excellent" service contribute to their "popularity", and an "unbeatable bar scene" ameliorates the "long waits" for a table.

Ichiban   22 | 17 | 19 | $31
Shoppes of Arrowhead, 2411 S. University Dr. (Nova Dr.), Davie, 954-370-0767
✍ "Good, reliable sushi" and bento boxes please buffs of these Japanese "oases" in Davie and Boca, while groupies of grill power "love the hibachi" (at the PB county locale only) with "entertaining chefs"; critics complain they're merely "ok", but others opine they're "worth a visit."

Il Mulino   20 | 14 | 19 | $24
1800 E. Sunrise Blvd. (US 1), Ft. Lauderdale, 954-524-1800
■ A "date-night" destination by the Gateway Cinema in Ft. Lauderdale, this "wonderful" Italian offers the "comfort of carbs", serving "out-of-this-world" pastas, "garlic rolls that absolutely reek" and "great wines", all providing "excellent value"; a "winning combination" of "friendly

Ft. Lauderdale/Broward County   F | D | S | C

service" and "relaxed" atmosphere "keeps loyal customers waiting at the door."

Il Toscano   23 | 21 | 20 | $34
Waterway Shoppes, 2282 Weston Rd. (Arvida Pkwy.), Weston, 954-385-5883; www.iltoscanoweston.com

■ "Incredible" Northern Italian fare with "flair" draws faithful followers to this "spacious", "pretty" Weston "charmer" with a patio overlooking a lake (albeit artificial); "excellent" service and a "friendly bar scene" add to the attraction, and the "consistent" food is "worth the money."

India House   ▽ 22 | 10 | 22 | $23
563 W. Oakland Park Blvd. (bet. Andrews Ave. & Powerline Rd.), Ft. Lauderdale, 954-565-5701; www.indiahouserestaurant.com

◪ "Don't be put off by the strip-mall location" – this Ft. Lauderdale Indian offers "outstanding" food, including "delicious naan", "fiery vindaloo" and other "authentic", "flavorful" dishes as well as a "great lunch buffet"; though a few dis the "dark" digs, the "reasonable prices" and "personal" service keep its cronies cumin in.

Indigo   19 | 18 | 19 | $34
Riverside Hotel, 620 E. Las Olas Blvd. (SE 8th Ave.), Ft. Lauderdale, 954-467-0671; www.riversidehotel.com

◪ The flavors of Singapore, Malaysia and Indonesia attract the adventurous to this "quiet oasis" in the Riverside Hotel in Ft. Lauderdale; the Southeast Asian dishes are "excellent" and "prepared with finesse", and the setting's "elegant" within and "enjoyable" on the sidewalk that affords "people-watching" on Las Olas; however, a few are blue that the "concept's better than the execution" and assert the staff should be better "trained" about the "interesting" menu.

Islamorada Fish Company   19 | 19 | 17 | $25
Outdoor World, 220 Gulf Stream Way (Griffin Rd.), Dania, 954-927-7737; www.ifcstonecrab.com

See review in Keys/Monroe County Directory.

JACKSON'S STEAKHOUSE   23 | 24 | 23 | $53
Las Olas Ctr., 450 E. Las Olas Blvd. (5th Ave.), Ft. Lauderdale, 954-522-4450; www.jacksonssteakhouse.com

◪ An "elegant", "English-club" decor and "some of the best beef anywhere, period" pulls in a crowd of "good ol' boys" and "romance"-seekers to this Las Olas steakhouse in Ft. Lauderdale; the service is "impeccable" and the atmosphere's "wonderful", but naysayers assert it's "not worth the big bucks"; N.B. members-only at lunch.

Jalapeños Mexican Kitchen   – | – | – | I
207 N. University Dr. (Pines Blvd.), Pembroke Pines, 954-965-8088
8229 W. Sunrise Blvd. (N. University Dr.), Plantation, 954-473-5351

Chef-owner Alberto Partida brings a taste of Michoan in Central Mexico to his colorful cantinas in Pembroke Pines

Ft. Lauderdale/Broward County F | D | S | C |

and Plantation, importing authentic ingredients to cook up regional specialties like sopa Azteca, chicken smothered in red Oaxacan mole and pork loin marinated in the juice of bitter oranges.

J. Alexander's   19 | 19 | 19 | $27 |
2415 N. Federal Hwy. (21st St.), Ft. Lauderdale, 954-563-9077
8550 W. Broward Blvd. (Pine Island Rd.), Plantation, 954-916-8837
www.jalexanders.com

◪ This "casual" American chain with links in Lauderdale, Plantation and Boca Raton "does the basics a bit better", particularly the "hearty salads", "fabulous prime rib" and "rattlesnake pasta" (actually chicken) that shake up "ladies who lunch"; the "service is great", the "dark" setting's "pleasant" and if a few find it "overpriced" for "average" fare, supporters insist it's "a step above" the competition.

Japanese Village Steakhouse   – | – | – | E |
350 E. Las Olas Blvd. (bet. S. Federal Hwy. & 3rd Ave.),
Ft. Lauderdale, 954-525-8386

Village people praise this "flavorful" addition on Las Olas, a casual cousin of Tokyo Sushi offering flashy, "Americanized Japanese" grilled fare and high jinks from entertaining hibachi chefs; diners also have the option of ordering from a limited selection of sushi; N.B. its sibling is closed for renovations and is expected to open late fall 2003.

Jasmine Thai   24 | 17 | 22 | $23 |
Cocogate Plaza, 5103 Coconut Creek Pkwy. (State Rd. 7),
Margate, 954-979-5530

■ A Margate "landmark", Ann and Peter Hongnopkhun's "outstanding", "reliable" Siamese is "known for its quality" and "reasonable prices"; "authentic", "well-prepared" Thai and Asian dishes such as roast duckling, panang curry and sticky rice with mangoes are a "cut above the strip mall where it's located."

JB's on the Beach   – | – | – | M |
300 N. Ocean Blvd. (Hillsboro Blvd.), Deerfield Beach,
954-571-5220; www.jbsonthebeach.com

Ocean views, tropical breezes and contemporary decor set the stage for this new oceanfront seafooder/steakhouse in Deerfield Beach, where a casual but upscale menu that covers familiar surf and turf with dishes such as Key West stuffed shrimp, lobster salad, babybacks and porterhouse steaks; with two bars and live bands on weekends, it's quickly becoming a scene.

Joe's Crab Shack   ∇ 15 | 15 | 14 | $30 |
4402 N. University Dr. (44th St.), Lauderhill, 954-749-2722;
www.joescrabshack.com

◪ "Be prepared to wait" at this Lauderdale link of the national seafood chain where "tourists" and families with "kids" gather for "good, cheap" stone crabs and assorted

Ft. Lauderdale/Broward County   F | D | S | C |

fin fare, as well as landlubber choices, served in a "cheesy" space that's a "cross between a hippie pad and Toys 'R' Us"; the "visual stimulation" notwithstanding, however, cold fish carp over "not-special" eats and a "way-too-noisy" scene.

Joe's Riverside Grille   17 | 16 | 15 | $34 |
Sands Harbor Resort, 125 N. Riverside Dr. (Atlantic Blvd.), Pompano Beach, 954-941-2499
◪ "Tasty seafood" and "fantastic views" of the Intracoastal from a "top-notch" outdoor deck are the draw at Joe and Erica Cascio's "friendly" maritimer housed in Pompano Beach's Sands Harbor Resort; critics caution it's "just not the same experience" unless you "take a table outside", as the fare's "not as wonderful" as the "romantic" alfresco setting.

Josef's ⊠   – | – | – | M |
9763 W. Broward Blvd. (Nob Hill Rd.), Plantation, 954-473-0000
Chef-owner Josef Schibanetz (ex Miami's Doral Golf Resort and Spa) and his wife Beth operate this cozy Northern Italian tucked away in a Plantation shopping center, the showcase for his creative Austrian-influenced menu highlighting the flavors of the northeasternmost of Italy's 20 regions; the cozy, candlelit room, dressed in tans and other muted colors, exudes warmth.

La Barraca   – | – | – | E |
1831 N. Pine Island Rd. (W. Sunrise Blvd.), Plantation, 954-693-9757
"Close your eyes and you're in Spain" attest amigos who've discovered this charming, if pricey, new Iberian tapas-try in a Plantation shopping plaza where chef-owner Jorge Luis Fernandez cooks up hot and cold tapas, as well as traditional dishes such as paella, paired with a thoughtful selection of Spanish wines; there's live flamenco on Wednesday and Friday nights and accordion players Saturdays and Sundays.

LA BROCHETTE BISTRO   27 | 18 | 25 | $37 |
Embassy Lakes Plaza, 2635 N. Hiatus Rd. (Sheridan St.), Cooper City, 954-435-9090
■ "New innovations and classic favorites" plus "a solid wine list" set apart this "quaint" Cooper City charmer championed for its "memorable" Mediterranean cuisine, particularly the juicy meats served on a skewer and "the freshest seafood" "at reasonable prices"; despite its strip-mall setting, the interior's "elegant" but "homey", and the "professional", "informed" staff helps make this "the perfect place to celebrate a special occasion."

La Carreta ❶   17 | 11 | 14 | $19 |
301 N. University Dr. (Pines Blvd.), Pembroke Pines, 954-966-8161
See review in Miami/Dade County Directory.

vote at zagat.com

Ft. Lauderdale/Broward County F | D | S | C |

La Creperie – | – | – | M |
Sun Village Plaza, 4589 N. University Dr. (NW 44th St.), Lauderhill, 954-741-9035

A quaint charmer that's easy to miss, this midpriced "little bistro" in Lauderhill's Sun Village Plaza has attracted a loyal local following for more than a decade with a "limited" menu of "consistently" "delicious", "authentic" French fare, including a long list of crêpes.

LA SPADA'S ORIGINAL HOAGIES ⊘ 27 | 7 | 19 | $10 |
7893 W. Sample Rd. (bet. Riverside & Woodside Drs.), Coral Springs, 954-345-8833
Shops of Arrowhead, 2645 S. University Dr. (Nova Dr.), Davie, 954-476-1099
4346 Seagrape Dr. (Commercial Blvd.), Lauderdale-by-the-Sea, 954-776-7893

■ The "authentic Philly-style" hoagies at this sandwich trio are simply "sub-lime", "stuffed so large" with "tasty toppings" that "taking a bite is a challenge" and well "worth the slightly higher prices"; there's "no decor" and "not much room", and you can expect a "line out the door", but it "moves quickly if you know what you want", and it's "fun to watch" the "expert staff."

Las Vegas 22 | 11 | 20 | $15 |
2807 E. Oakland Park Blvd. (Bayview Dr.), Ft. Lauderdale, 954-564-1370
9905 Pines Blvd. (bet. NW 98th & Palm Aves.), Pembroke Pines, 954-431-6883
7015 W. Broward Blvd. (NW 70th Ave.), Plantation, 954-584-4400

■ For "authentic" Cuban cooking "and plenty of it" "at prices you can afford", amigos aver you "can't beat" this quintet operated by Antonio Vilarino and his family; "friendly" service leaves loyalists with "nothing to complain about"; N.B. post-*Survey* renovations at the Plantation and Lauderdale locations may outdate the above Decor score.

La Tavernetta 23 | 17 | 21 | $40 |
926 NE 20th Ave. (south of Sunrise Blvd.), Ft. Lauderdale, 954-463-2566; www.latavernetta.net

◪ The "romantic" "waterfront ambiance" is "well worth the trouble of finding" this "out-of-the-way" "gem" in Ft. Lauderdale, where you can "look at the boats" while diving into "impeccable" Northern Italian fare served by a "warm, friendly" staff; critics contend "it isn't the same" since a change in ownership, citing "bland" cooking and "average" service, but for many it's still a "keeper."

La Vie en Rose Cafe 22 | 22 | 20 | $30 |
2950 N. State Rd. 7 (Coral Lake Dr.), Margate, 954-977-0110

◪ Rueful regulars report their "best-kept secret" in Margate is now a "popular" destination for "fabulous" French-

140 subscribe to zagat.com

Ft. Lauderdale/Broward County F | D | S | C

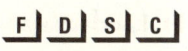

American fare that's "always a good value", especially the $49 lovers' dinner for two and early-bird 'twilight menu' that starts from $9.95; the "beautiful", "charming" decor and "romantic", "European" ambiance help mollify Miss Manners types miffed at service that can be "curt at times."

Le Cafe de Paris   18 | 17 | 18 | $33

715 E. Las Olas Blvd. (SE 8th Ave.), Ft. Lauderdale, 954-467-2900

☑ A "consistent French favorite of Ft. Lauderdale's upper crust", this "standby" on "fashionable" Las Olas also appeals to wallet-watchers with "well-priced" "comfort food" including "awesome" crêpes, while voyeurs can enjoy "great people-watching" from the tables outside; some feel it's in need of a "face-lift", but most "never hesitate to bring a guest" here for "classic, old-school" dining.

Legal Sea Foods   19 | 18 | 17 | $34

Oasis at Sawgrass, 2602 Sawgrass Mills Circle (N. Flamingo Rd.), Sunrise, 954-846-9011; www.legalseafoods.com

☑ Finatics are hooked on the "fantastic New England clam chowder", "great lobster rolls" and other maritime fare at this "busy" trio of outposts of a "welcome Northeast import", including the newest "trendy" addition in CityPlace in West Palm; although the "striking" "modern" decor wins praise, wags wonder whether the "overpriced" eats, "long waits" and "deplorable" "attitude" "work better in Boston."

Lester's Diner ◐   15 | 10 | 17 | $16

250 State Rd. 84 (bet. SW 2nd & 3rd Aves.), Ft. Lauderdale, 954-525-5641
4701 Coconut Creek Pkwy. (NW 46th Ave.), Margate, 954-979-4722
1393 NW 136th Ave. (Sunrise Blvd.), Sunrise, 954-838-7473

☑ An "institution" for the "blue-collar crowd", "boaters" and "late-night club-goers" alike, this "classic" 24/7 coffee shop trio is a popular stop for a "late-night piece of pie" or "early morning breakfast", dished out by "servers who've been there for ages"; cynics find the fare "adequate", but concede the prices are "reasonable."

Louie Louie   17 | 17 | 18 | $30

1313 E. Las Olas Blvd. (S. Federal Hwy.), Ft. Lauderdale, 954-524-5200

☑ "Immense servings" of "NY-style" Italian "favorites" and "friendly", "attentive" service keep this "sophisticated", "upbeat" spot on Las Olas Boulevard and in Delray Beach "busy" with the "beautiful people"; naysayers knock the "limited" selection of "somewhat generic" dishes, but more insist they "haven't lost any sparkle."

Madras Café   – | – | – | M

1434 S. Powerline Rd. (Hammondville Rd.), Pompano Beach, 954-977-5434

Aficionados applaud this "authentic" Indian newcomer to Pompano Beach that offers a 'Wednesday Regional', when

Ft. Lauderdale/Broward County　F | D | S | C

the menu features the cuisine from a specific part of the subcontinent; the service may be a "little slow", but reasonable tabs and "excellent" food are "worth" the wait.

Maguire's Hill 16　▽ 18 | 16 | 19 | $18
535 N. Andrews Ave. (bet. Broward & Sunrise Blvds.),
Ft. Lauderdale, 954-764-4453

■ "Now this is what they mean by an Irish pub" toast touters of this "classic" bit of "the old sod" in Northeast Lauderdale; "simple", "traditional" food like corned beef and cabbage, a mostly Gaelic staff, a "friendly atmosphere" and "good" live music on weekends are other reasons to riverdance on over.

MAI-KAI　15 | 26 | 19 | $38
3599 N. Federal Hwy. (NE 31st St.), Ft. Lauderdale, 954-563-3272;
www.maikai.com

☑ A "'50s holdover" that's "so out it's in", this Polynesian Lauderdale "landmark" hidden behind "palm trees, tikis and torches" is mai-tee "kitschy" but it sure is "fun"; the "lush" decor and "must-see" dance show trump the "overpriced" Pacific Rim–Cantonese fare, but the appetizers are "good" and the cocktails "exotic."

Mangos ◐　16 | 16 | 17 | $25
904 E. Las Olas Blvd. (SE 9th Ave.), Ft. Lauderdale, 954-523-5001

☑ "Its laid-back atmosphere makes you think you're on vacation" so Lauderdale professionals join tourists at this "casual" American on Las Olas with "good food" and "live music"; though bashers boo "boring" eats, the "people-watching" from "great sidewalk" seating is "entertaining."

Mario the Baker　20 | 7 | 16 | $15
2220 N. University Dr. (bet. Sunset Strip & W. Sunrise Blvd.),
Sunrise, 954-742-3333
See review in Miami/Dade County Directory.

MARK'S LAS OLAS　27 | 24 | 23 | $54
1032 E. Las Olas Blvd. (SE 11th Ave.), Ft. Lauderdale,
954-463-1000; www.chefmark.com

☑ The "crown jewel of Las Olas" in downtown Ft. Lauderdale shines with "beautiful food for beautiful people" from chef Militello, one of the "oft-copied but rarely matched originators of Floribbean" cuisine; the food's "always fabulous" and "innovative", the wines are "unbelievable" and the "chic", "modern" decor's "magical"; foes feel it misses the mark, with "snooty service", a "noisy" atmosphere and "stiff tabs", but they're overruled by those who feel it "exceeds expectations."

Martha's Supper Club　19 | 21 | 20 | $36
6024 N. Ocean Dr. (E. Dania Beach Blvd.), Hollywood,
954-923-5444

☑ The "beautiful view of the Intracoastal" makes this Hollywood dinner/dancing destination a natural for a

Ft. Lauderdale/Broward County   F | D | S | C

"special occasion" as well as a "great" place "to take grandma" for "reliable", "good" American cuisine with an emphasis on seafood; a few hipsters, however, find the fare a "let-down" and say the digs "need sprucing up."

Max's Beach Place   23 | 22 | 21 | $39
Beach Pl., 17 S. Atlantic Blvd. (north of Las Olas Blvd.), Ft. Lauderdale, 954-525-5022
■ "On a moonlit night" the "stunning views" are "as romantic as it gets" sigh sweethearts who snag a table "overlooking the beach" at this New American–Caribbean in Lauderdale known for its "delicious" fare including "to-die-for" salmon; "stylish decor", "excellent service" and a "real-deal" happy hour that won't max out your credit card help explain why a "trendy crowd" keeps it "busy."

Max's Grille   21 | 20 | 19 | $33
Las Olas Riverfront Complex, 300 SW First Ave. (Las Olas Blvd.), Ft. Lauderdale, 954-779-1800
2210 Weston Rd. (Arvida Pkwy.), Weston, 954-217-0212
☐ "Good" New American fare, a "friendly staff", "upscale decor" and an "unbeatable" 3-for-1 happy hour conspire to keep this "hip" duo in Lauderdale and Weston at the top of the local food chain; even if it gets "loud", the outdoor seating and "people-watching" "seduces" supporters, especially at the Riverfront location.

Melting Pot, The   20 | 18 | 19 | $37
10374 W. Sample Rd. (Coral Springs & University Drs.), Coral Springs, 954-755-6368
See review in Palm Beach County Directory.

Mezzanotte   20 | 19 | 19 | $37
Las Olas Riverfront Complex, 300 SW First Ave. (Las Olas Blvd.), Ft. Lauderdale, 954-761-8787
See review in Miami/Dade County Directory.

Michael's Kitchen   – | – | – | M
Dania Square, 433 E. Sheridan St. (US 1), Dania, 954-926-5556; www.michaels-kitchen.com
A local favorite in Dania Beach, chef-owner Michael Blum's midpriced cafe pairs inventive New American dishes such as 'fire cracker tuna martini' (tartare over seaweed and cucumber) and candied pecan-crusted black grouper with selections from an impressive wine list; yellow walls and high ceilings create a bright and airy atmosphere.

Nami   21 | 16 | 18 | $25
8381 Pines Blvd. (NW 83rd Ave.), Pembroke Pines, 954-432-2888
☐ Both "authentic", "tasty" tepanyaki dishes prepared tableside and "excellent" sushi are on tap at this Pembroke Pines Japanese; the service is "always good" at this "solid" strip-mall denizen, but detractors find it of nami-nal interest, saying "there are better alternatives out there."

vote at zagat.com   **143**

Ft. Lauderdale/Broward County F | D | S | C

O'Hara's Hollywood ◐   13 | 18 | 15 | $28
1903 Hollywood Blvd. (bet. 19th & 20th Aves.), Hollywood, 954-925-2555; www.oharasjazzcafe.com

☒ Hepcats are jazzed by the "great" live bands swinging at Kitty Ryan's "lovely" Hollywood cabaret where diners can order jambalaya and Traditional American eats but the kitchen "doesn't sing a sweet tune"; the food's "secondary" anyway, so mavens elect to enjoy the music over "drinks."

Old Florida Seafood House   22 | 14 | 21 | $27
1414 NE 26th St. (east of Dixie Hwy.), Wilton Manors, 954-566-1044

■ This "reliable" Wilton Manors seafood house "may not be fancy" but it's always "busy" thanks to the "huge portions" of "decently priced", "good", "fresh fish" and its ever-popular fried jumbo shrimp plus "super early-bird deals"; sure, after 25 years, it could use "updating", but it's "comfortable" and the staff "truly aims to please."

OUTBACK STEAKHOUSE   19 | 14 | 18 | $26
650 Riverside Dr. (Ramblewood Dr.), Coral Springs, 954-345-5965
6201 N. Federal Hwy. (Bayview Dr.), Ft. Lauderdale, 954-771-4390
1801 SE 10th Ave. (SW 18th St.), Ft. Lauderdale, 954-523-5600
7841 Pines Blvd. (N. University Dr.), Pembroke Pines, 954-981-5300
1823 Pine Island Rd. (Sunrise Blvd.), Plantation, 954-370-9956
www.outbacksteakhouse.com

See review in Keys/Monroe County Directory.

Padrino's   22 | 14 | 18 | $21
2500 E. Hallandale Beach Blvd. (S. Ocean Dr.), Hallandale, 954-456-4550
The Fountains Plaza, 801 S. University Dr. (bet. Broward Blvd. & Peters Rd.), Plantation, 954-476-5777

■ "Cuban food the way you want it to be – bountiful, inexpensive and tasty" is the name of the game at this "all-star" mini-chain in Broward and Boca; "to-die-for pork sandwiches" are favorites at these "pleasant" "staples."

Pellegrino's Ristorante   ∇ 19 | 16 | 16 | $46
847 SE Eighth Ave. (9th St.), Deerfield Beach, 954-418-0611

☒ "It's like Sunday dinner with a big Italian family" at this Deerfield Beach destination for "good", "authentic" home cooking in an "atmospheric" room with a "jukebox pumping out doo-wop and Sinatra"; it may be "pricey" and the service could be better, but *amici* adore the "New York" style of this relation to Gotham's famed Rao's.

Piccadilly Cafeteria   13 | 8 | 11 | $12
4697 N. State Rd. 7 (south of Commercial Blvd.), Lauderdale Lakes, 954-735-5729
7200 N. University Dr. (1 block north of W. McNab Rd.), Tamarac, 954-726-3674
www.piccadilly.com

See review in Miami/Dade County Directory.

Ft. Lauderdale/Broward County   F | D | S | C

Pizza Rustica ◐   23 | 6 | 15 | $10
3327 E. Oakland Park Blvd. (Ocean Blvd.), Ft. Lauderdale, 954-567-2992
See review in Miami/Dade County Directory.

Primavera   24 | 21 | 23 | $42
Primavera Plaza, 830 E. Oakland Park Blvd. (west of N. Dixie Hwy.), Oakland Park, 954-564-6363; www.trueitalian.com

◪ Chef-owner Giacomo Dresseno "really wants to please his customers and he usually hits the mark" with his "creative", "authentic" Northern Italian cuisine affirm admirers of this upscale, "white-tablecloth" classic in an Oakland Park shopping center; critics carping about "crowded" quarters and "not-too-trendy decor" will be happy to hear that the place was remodeled over the summer (which puts the above score in question).

RAINBOW PALACE   25 | 23 | 24 | $46
2787 E. Oakland Park Blvd. (Bayview Dr.), Ft. Lauderdale, 954-565-5652

■ "For the most exceptional Chinese cuisine in Lauderdale", happy little bluebirds fly to this "elegant" "haven" for "excellent", "refined", "beautifully" presented fare and "terrific wines" served by "pampering", "tux-clad" waiters in a "lovely setting"; "of course, you pay a hefty price for such a treat", but it's "worth the splurge."

Red Coral   – | – | – | M
401 E. Las Olas Blvd. (SE 5th Ave.), Ft. Lauderdale, 954-523-4330; www.redcorallasolas.com

A red-hot newcomer on Las Olas, this sleek Pan-Asian sports a minimalist interior with a lounge and mezzanine as well as outdoor seating; offerings include sushi, pad Thai, lo mein, teriyaki as well as salads and wraps, and plans for a DJ will make it a one-stop destination for Lauderdale partiers.

Redfish Bluefish   – | – | – | M
906 E. Hallandale Beach Blvd. (US1), Hallandale, 954-454-8878

No, it's not a paean to Dr. Seuss (no green eggs or ham here); instead, this Hallandale piscatorium doubles as a seafood grille and sushi spot, serving cooked fresh catches and raw fin fare, paired with an impressive wine list, in a sleek, multilevel dining room with cozy banquettes.

Regalo ☒   22 | 18 | 20 | $29
4215 N. Federal Hwy. (bet. Commercial & Oakland Park Blvds.), Ft. Lauderdale, 954-566-6661; www.regalorestaurant.com

◪ This "warm" Ft. Lauderdale Italian "is the type of spot you'd like to have in your neighborhood" just so "you could be a regular" say fans impressed with the "excellent" food, "wonderful atmosphere" and "charming" setting; though a few complain it's "inconsistent" and could do without the valet parking, more maintain it's a "perfect date place."

vote at zagat.com

Ft. Lauderdale/Broward County | F | D | S | C |

RIVER HOUSE | 23 | 25 | 21 | $42 |
301 SW Third Ave. (bet. Broward Blvd. & 2nd St.), Ft. Lauderdale, 954-525-7661; www.ftlauderdaleriverhouse.com

■ "One of the most beautiful settings in town", this "romantic" American seafooder in a "historic home" overlooking the New River in Lauderdale "is a wonderful place to entertain visitors"; "fabulous", "fresh" fish and other "delicious" dishes and "great wines by the glass" are complemented by the "elegant" decor and "excellent" service, and the "lovely view" of yachts gliding by helps make for a "memorable meal"; P.S. try the "terrific brunch."

Roadhouse Grill | 16 | 12 | 16 | $21 |
1580 N. University Dr. (bet. Atlantic & Royal Palm Blvds.), Coral Springs, 954-346-6344
1900 S. University Dr. (Hwy. 595), Davie, 954-370-3044
401 N. Federal Hwy. (2 blocks north of Hillsboro Blvd.), Deerfield Beach, 954-428-9080
3300 E. Commercial Blvd. (N. Federal Hwy.), Ft. Lauderdale, 954-772-3700
8525 Pines Blvd. (N. University Dr.), Pembroke Pines, 954-438-0599
www.roadhousegrill.com

☑ "There's nothing glamorous" about this "family-friendly" Traditional American chain in South Florida where cowpokes chow down on "big portions" of "good" steaks and burgers along with "free peanuts"; kids love the "fun", "loud" atmosphere, not to mention "throwing shells on the floor", but neatniks yell "yuck!"

Roasted Pepper, The | 20 | 14 | 18 | $24 |
9893 Pines Blvd. (N. Palm Ave.), Pembroke Pines, 954-450-8800; www.theroastedpepper.com

☑ A "high-energy" atmosphere replete with "live music" and a "friendly", "singing staff" make this Pembroke Pines Southern Italian a "fun family place" with "enormous portions" of "good", "consistent" classics for the kids and "huge martinis" for the grown-ups; though some feel "remodeling" might help and others are over the conga lines, it's an "inexpensive" way to have a "celebratory" dinner.

ROMANO'S MACARONI GRILL | 17 | 17 | 18 | $22 |
1695 University Dr. (NW 16th St.), Coral Springs, 954-345-0808
13620 Pines Blvd. (136th Ave.), Pembroke Pines, 954-704-2331
100 N. University Dr. (W. Broward Blvd.), Plantation, 954-473-5770
See review in Miami/Dade County Directory.

Ruggero's | – | – | – | M |
1025 N. Federal Hwy. (E. Sunrise Blvd.), Ft. Lauderdale, 954-523-2225

Easy to miss in a small strip mall, this upscale Lauderdale Italian attracts a loyal following with hearty dishes such as encrusted lamb and osso buco and lighter fare such as grilled calamari; the inviting space is decorated with

146 subscribe to zagat.com

Ft. Lauderdale/Broward County   F | D | S | C

antiques, and filled with the strains of a jazz guitarist on Mondays and Tuesdays.

Runyon's ◐ 24 | 22 | 25 | $44
9810 W. Sample Rd. (west of University Dr.), Coral Springs, 954-752-2333; www.runyonsrestaurant.com

☑ Listen to the "piano man" while digging into "awesome" steaks, "delicious" prime rib and other "outstanding" Continental fare at this "Coral Springs classic"; "excellent" service and a "great atmosphere" add to a "consistently good" experience, and though a few protest the "high prices" and "dated decor", more laud it as a "favorite."

Rustic Inn Crabhouse 22 | 13 | 16 | $30
4331 Anglers Ave. (Griffin Rd.), Ft. Lauderdale, 954-584-1637; www.crabhouse.com

■ "It's better than a trip to Maryland" claim the crowds lining up for "excellent" crustaceans including the "best-in-the-universe garlic crabs" "by the bucketful" at this "rustic" Ft. Lauderdale seafood "institution" on the Intracoastal; a "casual" setting with "newspaper-covered tables" and the sound of mallets "banging away" isn't for the "headache"-prone, but hey, "it's part of the fun" and the "rewards come at the end."

RUTH'S CHRIS STEAK HOUSE 25 | 22 | 23 | $52
2525 N. Federal Hwy. (bet. Oakland Park & Sunrise Blvds.), Ft. Lauderdale, 954-565-2338; www.ruthschris.com
See review in Miami/Dade County Directory.

Sage French Cafe 23 | 19 | 20 | $32
Union Planter Shopping Plaza, 2378 N. Federal Hwy. (NE 26th St.), Ft. Lauderdale, 954-565-2299; www.sagecafe.net

■ "Oh, to live in the neighborhood" of this "intimate" French bistro, a "hidden gem" in a Lauderdale shopping center touted as one of "the best values in town" for "superb" fare like "awesome" duck; the "charming" decor evokes a "country cafe", and if it sometimes gets "noisy", it's always a "treat"; N.B. sage surveyors will seek out the wine tastings on the first Tuesday of the month.

Sakana Japanese Restaurant – | – | – | M
Emerald Woods Plaza, 3940 N. 46th Ave. (bet. N. Hills & Stirling Rds.), Hollywood, 954-894-3611

Appropriately, its name means "fish", and this unassuming Hollywood storefront attracts schools of supporters with its vast menu of sushi as well as cooked Japanese fare; it also rewards regulars by allowing them to create their own rolls that remain in permanent rotation.

Samba Room 20 | 23 | 19 | $36
350 E. Las Olas Blvd. (SE 3rd Ave.), Ft. Lauderdale, 954-468-2000

☑ A "beautiful people's place" on Las Olas in Lauderdale, this "*très* cool" Nuevo Latino lures a "lively" crowd with a

Ft. Lauderdale/Broward County F | D | S | C

"dark, hip space", the "best mojitos" and "delicious", "interesting" dishes "with a twist"; service can be "inconsistent" and the ambiance "ear-splitting" as the evening wears on, but you can opt for the "outdoor couches" that "create a living room on the sidewalk."

San Loco ● — 20 | 9 | 15 | $10
204 SW Second St. (SW 2nd Ave.), Ft. Lauderdale, 954-463-2003
See review in Miami/Dade County Directory.

Satine — ▽ 23 | 25 | 23 | $48
Westin Diplomat Resort & Spa, 3555 S. Ocean Dr. (Hallandale Beach Blvd.), Hollywood, 954-602-8330; www.satine.net

■ "South Beach pizzazz hits Hollywood" at the Westin Diplomat Resort & Spa's "memorable" young waterfront star (named after the siren in *Moulin Rouge*) where "eclectic" and "expensive" Asian-accented Floribbean cuisine is served in a sultry setting; the "ambiance heats up" later in the evenings, when the "Satine girls" "shake their stuff."

Scopa — – | – | – | M
International Bldg., 2447 E. Sunrise Blvd. (Bayview Dr.), Ft. Lauderdale, 954-630-8058

The latest occupant of a revolving door of a location in the International Building across from The Galleria in Ft. Lauderdale, this Southern Italian newcomer serves up dishes such as rigatoni with smoked mozzarella and prosciutto di Parma, as well as an ultra-rich chocolate soufflé, in a cozy, intimate space with dark-wood accents; there's also a small outdoor patio.

Seafood World — ▽ 23 | 13 | 18 | $28
Main Street Plaza, 4602 N. Federal Hwy. (¾ mi. north of Sample Rd.), Lighthouse Point, 954-942-0740

■ For nearly 30 years, this midpriced seafood veteran in Lighthouse Point has been luring afishionados with some of the "best stone crabs", "sweetest shrimp in town" and fish so fresh it "tastes like it jumped from the sea to your plate", all of which goes far in quieting any quibbles over the humble digs.

Seawatch — 19 | 23 | 19 | $32
6002 N. Ocean Blvd. (1 mi. north of Commercial Blvd.), Lauderdale-by-the-Sea, 954-781-2200

◪ A "stunning" "beach location" with a "million-dollar" "oceanfront" vista is the main draw of this Lauderdale-by-the-Sea stalwart, overshadowing the "serviceable" seafood and "kitschy" decor, though fans find the "reasonably" priced fin fare "perfectly adequate" in such a "scenic" setting; "early-bird diners" flock here for "good deals" and because the "ocean view ends at sunset", which is why savvy insiders "go for lunch and avoid the crowds."

Ft. Lauderdale/Broward County F | D | S | C

Shirttail Charlie's 16 | 16 | 18 | $27
400 SW Third Ave. (SW 6th St.), Ft. Lauderdale, 954-463-3474; www.shirttailcharlies.com
◪ Whether you come for "casual" dining downstairs (complete with a swimming pool "for the kids") or a "romantic" rendezvous in the upscale upstairs space, this "hard-to-find" Downtown seafooder boasting a "beautiful view of New River" is "an experience"; the fare may be "nothing special", but the "free boat ride" across the water to the Broward Center is a "great gimmick" and "perfect" for "pre-theater" repasts.

Shooters Waterfront Cafe U.S.A. 14 | 17 | 16 | $25
3033 NE 32nd Ave. (NE 30th St.), Ft. Lauderdale, 954-566-2855
◪ While the "crowd is a mix of ages and status" at this "lively" Ft. Lauderdale waterfront surf 'n' turf, all agree you're "paying for the view" – from "yachts going by" on the Intracoastal to "hard-body watching" and "bikini contests"; the fare is "only fair" by comparison, but the "hefty drinks" and "location" make it "worth going."

Shorty's Barbecue 20 | 12 | 17 | $15
5989 S. University Dr. (Stirling Rd.), Davie, 954-680-9900; www.shortys.com
See review in Miami/Dade County Directory.

SHULA'S ON THE BEACH 21 | 20 | 22 | $52
Yankee Trader Hotel, 321 N. Atlantic Blvd. (bet. Bayshore Dr. & Granada St.), Ft. Lauderdale, 954-355-4000; www.donshula.com
See review in Miami/Dade County Directory.

Siam Cuisine ▽ 23 | 13 | 20 | $26
2010 Wilton Dr. (NE 20th St.), Wilton Manors, 954-564-3411
◪ Pad-antic types pronounce this longtime local "favorite" in Wilton Manors the "best Thai in Ft. Lauderdale" offering "fabulous" fare; although the digs may not "compete with other trendy" spots in the area, the "friendly" service makes up for it, and "the sake certainly doesn't hurt, either."

SILVER POND 26 | 10 | 15 | $25
4285 N. State Rd. 7 (south of Commercial Blvd.), Lauderdale Lakes, 954-486-8885
■ "It's the real thing" cheer champions of this bit of "Chinatown in the tropics" serving "affordable", "authentic", "superb" Hong Kong–style cuisine in a Lauderdale Lakes strip mall; sure, the decor's "average", but the "outstanding" and "unusual" dishes and "big portions" ensure this "popular" "find" is "packed during winter."

Solo Trattoria ⑤ ▽ 19 | 12 | 20 | $33
208 SW Second St. (Andrews Ave.), Ft. Lauderdale, 954-525-7656
■ "Now that's Italian" croon cronies of this tiny Riverfront "find" near the Broward Center; "always consistent", "good-value" Northern cuisine and "fast" service from the

vote at zagat.com 149

Ft. Lauderdale/Broward County | F | D | S | C |

"personable" staff make it a "wonderful" option for a "quick pre-theater dinner", but the "close quarters" mean it's tough to "find a seat inside", so if sidewalk dining isn't for you, it's best to "reserve early."

Sublime | – | – | – | M |

1431 N. Federal Hwy. (13th St.), Ft. Lauderdale, 954-615-1431; www.sublimeveg.com

A far cry from nuts and berries, this Lauderdale newcomer offers a fully vegan menu of artfully presented Eclectic dishes, paired with a large selection of organic wines, beers and spirits; the elegant space (made with environmentally friendly building materials) boasts cascading waterfalls, skylights and Italian glass tile.

Sugar Reef | 20 | 16 | 16 | $32 |

600 N. Surf Rd. (bet. Fillmore & New York Sts.), Hollywood, 954-922-1119; www.sugarreef.us

■ "Whatever you wear, you're overdressed" for this "quirky", "festive" spot wedged between the gyro shops and "pizza joints" on Hollywood's boardwalk, where Patrick Fernault's "creative" French-Caribbean cooking always "surprises with its interesting mix of flavors"; "friendly service" and a "great ocean view" help take some of the sting out of the somewhat tall tabs.

SUNFISH GRILL ⊠ | 27 | 15 | 24 | $45 |

2771 E. Atlantic Blvd. (Intracoastal Waterway), Pompano Beach, 954-788-2434; www.sunfishgrill.com

■ "A tiny place with big ambitions", this "fantastic" New American seafooder is tucked into a "nondescript" Pompano Beach strip mall but offers "the best fish in town" thanks to "terrific" chef Anthony Sindaco, whose "scrumptious" appetizers, "inventive" entrees and "sinful desserts" are enhanced by "super wines"; the staff's "extraordinarily knowledgeable" and the setting, though "modest", is "relaxed"; even if it's "expensive", sun worshipers insist "it's worth every penny."

Su Shin | ▽ 28 | 15 | 18 | $27 |

4595 N. University Dr. (bet. Commercial & Oakland Park Blvds.), Lauderhill, 954-741-2569

■ "Fresh, tasty" sushi and other "delicious entrees" (the hot "sauce from hell" "will clear your sinuses") are served in a "friendly environment" at this Lauderhill Japanese, where the sporting staff will regale you with an "entertaining" tableside rendition of 'Happy Birthday' on your big day; N.B. it's independent of the duo in Coral Gables and Kendall.

Swiss Chalet | 14 | 8 | 13 | $14 |

751 E. Commercial Blvd. (bet. N. Dixie Hwy. & 6th Ave.), Ft. Lauderdale, 954-776-1630

◪ "Very good value for the money" is the chief appeal of this Lauderdale outpost of a Canadian rotisserie chicken-

Ft. Lauderdale/Broward County F | D | S | C

and-ribs chain (with a Delray Beach branch) where fans come for "good" eats in a "clean", though "uninspiring" setting; however, critics cluck over the "unmemorable" fare.

Tarantella Ristorante 20 | 22 | 20 | $27
Weston Town Ctr., 1755 Bell Tower Ln., Weston, 954-349-3004; www.tarantellas.net

■ Named after the lively folk dance of Southern Italy, this moderately priced spin-off of Capriccio located in the Weston Town Center "is definitely a keeper", serving "well-prepared" Italian fare "you can count on" in a room "beautifully decorated" with Sicilian ceramic tiles; on weekends it gets "packed with child-toting families."

Tarpon Bend 15 | 16 | 15 | $22
200 SW Second St. (SE 2nd St.), Ft. Lauderdale, 954-523-3233
Weston Town Ctr., 1630 Bell Tower Ln. (bet. Arvida Pkwy. & Bonaventure Blvd.), Weston, 954-888-9118
www.tarponbend.com

◪ While fans say "you can't beat" the "extremely fresh" seafood "for the price" at this casual Himmarshee maritimer, most think of it "more as a watering hole than eatery", thanks to the "very hot bar with nightly specials" and a "huge singles scene on Fridays"; N.B. the lakefront location at Weston Town Center is a popular destination for families.

TAVERNA OPA ● 21 | 15 | 16 | $29
3051 NE 32nd Ave. (NE 30th Ct.), Ft. Lauderdale, 954-567-1630
410 N. Ocean Dr. (1 block north of Hollywood Blvd.), Hollywood, 954-929-4010
www.tavernaoparestaurant.com

◪ "The party is as much a part of eating as the food" (which includes "divine" lamb and "wonderful" mezes) at this "crazy", "loud" Greek trio in Broward and Miami where "belly dancers" and "handsome waiters" "will get you" shimmying "on the tables"; arrive early or you'll be waiting "half a lifetime", especially on weekends.

THAI SPICE 25 | 18 | 22 | $27
1514 E. Commercial Blvd. (east of Dixie Hwy.), Ft. Lauderdale, 954-771-4535

■ "Don't be fooled by its purple neon sign" or "strip-mall location" say fans of this Lauderdale Thai offering "superb", "top-notch" fare in the "relaxing" ambiance of a recently expanded space; "you can tell the owners care" from the "wonderful portions" and "exquisite" service, which is why many anoint it one of the "best in Broward."

3030 Ocean 22 | 20 | 21 | $43
Marriott Harbor Beach Resort & Spa, 3030 Holiday Dr. (Seabreeze Blvd.), Ft. Lauderdale, 954-765-3030; www.3030ocean.com

■ "A surprise at the Marriott" in Ft. Lauderdale, this "upscale" New American–seafooder goes "beyond the

Ft. Lauderdale/Broward County   F | D | S | C

usual hotel dining experience"; chef Dean Max is making a splash with "terrific" fish as well as other "outstanding" dishes at "reasonable prices", the "lovely" interior affords "beautiful ocean views" and the service is "excellent"; the "bar is also a hit", offering "wonderful" cocktails, and a "stroll on the beach" caps off an "enjoyable" night.

Timpano Italian Chophouse ◐   21 | 20 | 20 | $42
450 E. Las Olas Blvd. (SE 3rd Ave.), Ft. Lauderdale, 954-462-9119; www.e-brands.net

■ "Sinatra could walk in any minute" at this "upscale", "retro" Las Olas steakhouse that's a "mainstay of the Downtown work crowd" for its "delicious" surf 'n' turf "with an Italian flair" (including mussels "to die for"), "nicely appointed" space with leather seating and lots of wood, and "decent bar scene"; while a few find it "overpriced", many recommend it as a "great place to take a client or a date."

Tokyo Bowl   13 | 8 | 12 | $16
1361 E. Commercial Blvd. (NE 13th Ave.), Ft. Lauderdale, 954-776-2847
1720 S. Federal Hwy. (SE 17th St.), Ft. Lauderdale, 954-524-8200
See review in Miami/Dade County Directory.

Tokyo Sushi   ∇ 25 | 12 | 23 | $27
17 Causeway Plaza, 1499 SE 17th St. (SE 15th Ave.), Ft. Lauderdale, 954-767-9922

◪ This Ft. Lauderdale Japanese on the 17th Street Causeway isn't "much on atmosphere" or decor, but the "consistently good" cuisine (that includes "fresh" sushi and "always-excellent" hot appetizers) is downright "beautiful" to the few fans who've discovered it.

Tom Jenkins BBQ ⌧⇆   24 | 8 | 15 | $16
1236 S. Federal Hwy. (Davie Blvd.), Ft. Lauderdale, 954-522-5046

■ The owners of this Ft. Lauderdale BBQ "treasure", Harry Harrell and Gary Torrence, started cooking from a trailer in a parking lot, but now offer "amazingly good" "down-home" fare in a casual sit-down place with "picnic tables"; a "cross-section" of fans are drawn by the "smoke billowing out of the chimney" to find this "local institution" (the "hordes of cars" in the "small parking lot" are another clue to the 'cue); N.B. cash only.

Tony Roma's   18 | 13 | 16 | $22
2445 University Dr. (Royal Palm Blvd.), Coral Springs, 954-340-8665
606 E. Hallandale Beach Blvd. (US 1), Hallandale, 954-454-7427
7920 Pines Blvd. (University Dr.), Pembroke Pines, 954-962-7427
www.tonyromas.com
See review in Miami/Dade County Directory.

Ft. Lauderdale/Broward County   F | D | S | C |

Tropical Acres   16 | 12 | 18 | $28 |
2500 Griffin Rd. (½ mi. west of I-95), Ft. Lauderdale, 954-761-1744; www.eatattropicalacres.com
◪ A Lauderdale "landmark", this "trusty, old" steakhouse seems like it's "been around forever" (since 1949, to be precise), and it remains a "must stop" for a mostly "senior" following that comes for "good, affordable" beef in a "traditional", "clubby" atmosphere; there's "nothing fancy" about it – and "nothing memorable" either, sneer cynics, other than "tired" digs that "need a face-lift."

Tumi   ▽ 19 | 11 | 19 | $20 |
5917 Johnson St. (bet. N. 59th Ave. & State Rd. 7), Hollywood, 954-985-8358
■ A "nice find" in Hollywood, this midpriced Peruvian offers a "refreshing change of pace" with its "down-home" fare, including seviche that's "loved by all" and "fresh" fish dishes; the "extremely friendly" staff will "help you order", and live music adds to the experience; N.B. a recent redo may outdate the Decor score.

Victoria Park   24 | 18 | 25 | $37 |
900 NE 20th Ave. (Sunrise Blvd.), Ft. Lauderdale, 954-764-6868
■ Cognoscenti commend this "hidden treasure" in Ft. Lauderdale as a "lovely little place that makes you feel as if you're on the islands", offering a "small but excellent menu" of "delectable" Eclectic fare in a "cozy", "quiet" space sporting a "funky Key West–type decor"; "fabulous service" is another reason it's such a "good value."

Wan's Sushi House   – | – | – | M |
3327 Sheridan St. (Park Rd.), Hollywood, 954-987-1388
Although perhaps not as well known as its sibling, Christina Wan's, this small, midpriced Japanese in Hollywood's Park Sheridan Plaza is "number Wan for sushi" according to those in-the-know; cooked fare such as tempura and noodle dishes are also a "good value for the money."

Whale's Rib, The   20 | 13 | 20 | $22 |
2031 NE Second St. (A1A), Deerfield Beach, 954-421-8880
◪ "Locals love" this "funky, little" seafood "joint" near the Deerfield Beach pier for its "fresh, honest", "inexpensive" fin fare, "wonderful location" and "beachy atmosphere" where you'll feel equally at home in "cut-offs or a business suit"; even "limited" parking, "cramped" tables and "dated" digs do not deter diehards willing to brave "long lines."

Wine Cellar   18 | 17 | 20 | $26 |
Panama Plaza, 199 E. Oakland Park Blvd. (N. Andrews Ave.), Ft. Lauderdale, 954-565-9021
■ "Forget the cholesterol for one night" urge cellar-brants of this "old-style" Ft. Lauderdale Continental, a "favorite of

vote at zagat.com

Ft. Lauderdale/Broward County F | D | S | C

seniors" for its "reliable" German and Hungarian fare served in an Alpine-style setting; the "tasty food" is an "excellent value", especially for "early-birders", while birders of a different feather should find the mini-aviary "fascinating."

Wings 'N Things ⌽   ∇ 21 | 9 | 14 | $13
3556 W. Broward Blvd. (35th Ave.), Ft. Lauderdale, 954-587-2475
◪ Fans flock to this Ft. Lauderdale "landmark" for "cheap", "big portions" of "awesome garlic wings and blue cheese dressing" and "curly fries with vinegar", but the rest of the menu is "nothing special"; so far a recent major renovation has yet to put any wind in the wings of the Decor score.

Wolfgang Puck Grand Cafe   20 | 20 | 18 | $28
Sawgrass Mills Mall Oasis, 2610 Sawgrass Mills Circle (Sunrise Blvd.), Sunrise, 954-846-8668; www.wolfgangpuck.com
◪ Cronies crow it's "what you'd expect from the Puck name" at this Cal-Asian located in the Oasis at Sawgrass Mills – namely, an "interesting range" of "creative", "well-prepared" dishes served by a "fast, friendly" staff in a "beautifully decorated" space, but "no LA scene to deal with"; you might add to that "long lines" and "high prices" carp critics, but still, most deem it a "good choice when shopping" or before a concert at the arena.

Yesterday's   20 | 23 | 20 | $36
3001 E. Oakland Park Blvd. (bet. Intracoastal Waterway & Oakland Park Blvd.), Ft. Lauderdale, 954-563-4168
◪ "Be sure to request a table by the water" at this Ft. Lauderdale Continental located on the Intracoastal, an "old favorite" that's been wooing tourists and locals alike since 1974 with its "elegant" space, "fabulous" view and "excellent early-bird menu"; the food may not "match the scenery", but the "romantic", "candlelit" setting "makes for a delightful evening."

Palm Beach/
Palm Beach County

Palm Beach County's Most Popular

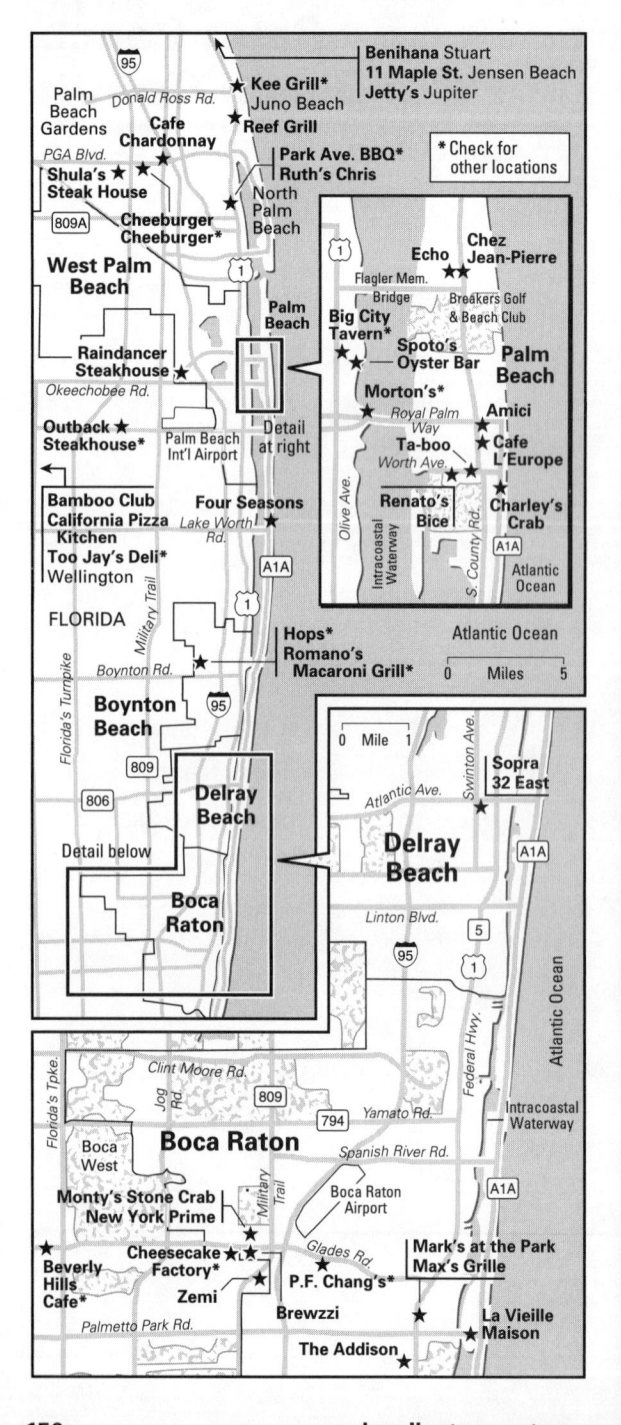

*Check for other locations

- **Benihana** Stuart
- **11 Maple St.** Jensen Beach
- **Jetty's** Jupiter

Palm Beach Gardens
- Cafe Chardonnay
- Shula's Steak House
- Cheeburger Cheeburger*

Juno Beach
- Kee Grill*
- Reef Grill

North Palm Beach
- Park Ave. BBQ*
- Ruth's Chris

West Palm Beach
- Raindancer Steakhouse
- Outback Steakhouse*

Palm Beach
- Echo
- Chez Jean-Pierre
- Big City Tavern*
- Spoto's Oyster Bar
- Morton's*
- Ta-boo
- Amici
- Renato's Bice
- Cafe L'Europe
- Charley's Crab
- Breakers Golf & Beach Club

Wellington
- Bamboo Club
- California Pizza Kitchen
- Too Jay's Deli*

- Four Seasons

Boynton Beach
- Hops*
- Romano's Macaroni Grill*

Delray Beach
- Sopra
- 32 East

Boca Raton
- Monty's Stone Crab
- New York Prime
- Cheesecake Factory*
- Zemi
- Beverly Hills Cafe*
- P.F. Chang's*
- Brewzzi
- The Addison
- Mark's at the Park
- Max's Grille
- La Vieille Maison

156   subscribe to zagat.com

Palm Beach County's Most Popular

1. Cheesecake Factory
2. Kee Grill
3. Cafe L'Europe
4. Ruth's Chris
5. Chez Jean-Pierre
6. Morton's
7. Outback Steakhse.
8. La Vieille Maison
9. P.F. Chang's
10. Four Seasons
11. Ta-boo
12. New York Prime
13. Too Jay's Deli
14. Zemi
15. Max's Grille
16. Bice Rist.
17. Charley's Crab
18. Reef Grill
19. 32 East
20. Cafe Chardonnay
21. Beverly Hills Cafe
22. Amici Rist.
23. Big City Tavern*
24. Cheeburger Cheeburger
25. Shula's Steak Hse.
26. Renato's
27. Raindancer Steakhse.
28. Sopra*
29. Romano's Macaroni Grill
30. California Pizza Kit.
31. Spoto's Oyster Bar
32. Bamboo Club
33. Echo*
34. Monty's Stone Crab
35. Addison, The
36. Benihana
37. Park Ave. BBQ
38. 11 Maple Street
39. Hops*
40. Brewzzi
41. Mark's at the Park*
42. Jetty's

Many of the restaurants on the above list are among the area's most expensive. For a list of over 50 Best Buys, see page 162. These are restaurants that give real quality at extremely reasonable prices.

---

* Indicates a tie with restaurant above

vote at zagat.com

Top Ratings

Top lists exclude restaurants with low voting.

Top 40 Food

28 11 Maple Street
Chez Jean-Pierre
Four Seasons
27 L'Escalier
26 Cafe L'Europe
New York Prime
La Vieille Maison
Marcello's La Sirena
25 Zemi
Le Mistral
Cafe Chardonnay
Kathy's Gazebo
Kee Grill
Reef Grill
Ruth's Chris
24 Echo
Spoto's Oyster Bar
Morton's
Sapori
Splendid Blendeds
Raindancer Steakhse.
Kyoto Sushi
32 East
Flagler Steakhse.
Rhythm Cafe
Renato's
23 John G's
Renzo's of Boca
Arturo's
Out of Denmark
Uncle Tai's
La Petite Maison
Cuban Cafe
Trevini*
Cabana
Little Moirs Food*
Lazy Loggerhead
Sopra
River House
Tsunami

By Cuisine

American (New)
28 11 Maple Street
Four Seasons
25 Zemi
Cafe Chardonnay
24 32 East

Asian
24 Echo
Kyoto Sushi
23 Uncle Tai's
Tsunami
21 P.F. Chang's

Caribbean
25 Reef Grill
23 Cuban Cafe
Cabana
22 Padrino's
20 Pineapple Grille

Continental
26 Cafe L'Europe
25 Kathy's Gazebo
22 Ta-boo
Addison, The
21 Boulevard Grille

French
28 Chez Jean-Pierre
27 L'Escalier
26 La Vieille Maison
25 Le Mistral
23 La Petite Maison

Italian
26 Marcello's La Sirena
24 Sapori
Renato's
23 Renzo's of Boca
Arturo's

Seafood
25 Kee Grill
Reef Grill
24 Spoto's Oyster Bar
23 Little Moirs Food
River House

Steakhouses
26 New York Prime
25 Ruth's Chris
24 Morton's
Raindancer
Flagler

subscribe to zagat.com

Top Food

By Special Feature

Breakfast
- *23* John G's
  Lazy Loggerhead
- *21* Hurricane Café
- *20* Hamburger Heaven
  Off the Vine

Brunch
- *22* Ta-boo
- *21* De La Tierra
- *20* Cheesecake Factory
  Off the Vine
  Pineapple Grille

Dock & Dine
- *23* River House
- *20* Jetty's
- *18* Sailfish Marina
- *17* Conchy Joe's

Early-Bird
- *25* Kee Grill
  Reef Grill
- *23* Tom's Place
- *22* Café Protégé
- *21* Okeechobee Steakhse.

Hotel Dining
- *28* Four Seasons
  Four Seasons
- *27* L'Escalier
  Breakers, The
- *24* Flagler Steakhse.
  Breakers, The
- *21* De La Tierra
  Sundy Inn
  Shula's Steak Hse.
  PGA Nat'l Resort

Newcomers/Unrated
- Café Boulud
- Max & Eddie's
- Nirvana
- Palm Beach Fish
- Sunset Grill

People-Watching
- *27* L'Escalier
- *26* Cafe L'Europe
  New York Prime
- *25* Kathy's Gazebo
- *24* Echo

By Location

Central County
- *28* Chez Jean-Pierre
  Four Seasons
- *27* L'Escalier
- *26* Cafe L'Europe
  Marcello's La Sirena

North Central County
- *25* Le Mistral
  Cafe Chardonnay
  Ruth's Chris
- *23* River House
- *22* Carmine's Ocean Grill

North County
- *25* Kee Grill
  Reef Grill
- *23* Little Moirs Food
  Lazy Loggerhead
- *22* Buonasera

South County
- *26* New York Prime
  La Vieille Maison
- *25* Zemi
  Kathy's Gazebo
  Kee Grill

vote at zagat.com

Top 40 Decor

- **28** La Vieille Maison
  Four Seasons
  L'Escalier
- **27** De La Tierra
  Cafe L'Europe
  Tsunami
  Addison, The
- **26** Renato's
- **25** Sopra
- **24** Echo
  Le Mont
- **23** 11 Maple Street
  Leopard Lounge
  Zemi
  Sailfish Marina
  Bizaare Ave. Cafe
  Flagler Steakhse.
  DaDa
  River House
  Kathy's Gazebo
- **22** La Petite Maison
  Trevini
  Bamboo Club
  Kee Grill
  Chez Jean-Pierre
  Bimini Twist
  Ta-boo
  Ruth's Chris
  City Cellar Wine
  Bice Rist.
  Mark's CityPlace
- **21** Cafe Chardonnay
  Morton's
  New York Prime
  Uncle Tai's
  Spoto's PGA
  Cabana
  Brasserie Mon Ami
  Pete's Boca Raton
  Mario's Tuscan Grill

Outdoors

Bellagio
Bice Rist.
De La Tierra
11 Maple Street
Mark's at the Park

Pineapple Grille
Renato's
River House
Sailfish Marina
Spoto's Oyster Bar

Romance

Addison, The
Café Boulud
Cafe L'Europe
Kathy's Gazebo
La Vieille Maison

Le Mistral
Le Mont
L'Escalier
Renato's
Trevini

Rooms

Cafe L'Europe
Chez Jean-Pierre
City Cellar Wine
Echo
Johannes

La Vieille Maison
Le Mont
Lucca
Ta-boo
Tsunami

Views

Bellagio
De La Tierra
Four Seasons
Jetty's
John G's

Lazy Loggerhead
Le Mont
Lucca
Rottie's
Sailfish Marina

Top 40 Service

- **28** L'Escalier
- Four Seasons
- **26** Chez Jean-Pierre
- **25** La Vieille Maison
- Flagler Steakhse.
- Cafe L'Europe
- **24** Renato's
- 11 Maple Street
- Linda B. of Boca Raton
- Rhythm Cafe
- **23** Ruth's Chris
- Morton's
- Kathy's Gazebo
- Raindancer Steakhse.
- Arturo's
- La Petite Maison
- River House
- Le Mistral
- New York Prime
- **22** Cafe Chardonnay
- Trevini
- La Belle Epoque
- Kee Grill
- Zemi
- Capri Blu
- Shula's Steak Hse.
- Mario's Tuscan Grill
- Café Protégé
- Addison, The
- Marcello's La Sirena
- **21** Ta-boo
- Sapori
- Flagler Grill
- Spoto's Oyster Bar
- Le Mont
- Cafe Bellino
- Uncle Tai's
- Sopra
- Spoto's PGA
- Echo

Best Buys

Top 40 Bangs for the Buck

1. Pizza Girls Pizza
2. Lazy Loggerhead
3. Tin Muffin Café
4. John G's
5. Cheeburger Cheeburger
6. Hamburger Heaven
7. Harry & the Natives
8. Park Ave. BBQ
9. Cuban Cafe
10. Green's Pharmacy
11. California Pizza Kit.
12. Padrino's
13. Hurricane Café
14. Beverly Hills Cafe
15. Mississippi Sweets
16. Don Ramon's
17. Too Jay's Deli
18. Swiss Chalet
19. Blue Anchor Pub
20. Bizaare Ave. Cafe
21. Romano's Macaroni Grill
22. Little Moirs Food
23. Dune Deck Cafe
24. John Bull Pub
25. Cheesecake Factory
26. Brewzzi
27. Havana
28. Dave's Last Resort
29. Hops
30. Tom's Place
31. Bamboo Club
32. P.F. Chang's
33. Bimini Twist
34. Cabana
35. E.R. Bradley's Saloon
36. Conchy Joe's Seafood
37. DaDa
38. Mondo's
39. Sorrento
40. Tony Roma's

Other Good Values

Boston's
Brogue's
Cardello's Pizza
Crazy Buffet
Eilat Cafe
El Colonial
Gallery Grille
Grille, The
Hurricane Café
La Tre
Mario's of Boca
Off the Vine
Old Key Lime Hse.
Schooner's Seafood

Palm Beach/
Palm Beach County
Restaurant Directory

Palm Beach/Palm Beach County   F | D | S | C

Addison, The 22 | 27 | 22 | $51
2 E. Camino Real (S. Dixie Hwy.), Boca Raton, 561-395-9335; www.theaddison.com

The "perfect pop-the-question" place may just be this "divine" "treat" located in Addison Mizner's restored 1925 office building near his famous Boca Raton resort; the "old-world" multiroomed interior evokes the "back lot of MGM", with Spanish details and a "spectacular garden courtyard" complete with "lovely fountain", and the "classic" Continental fare is "delicious"; service can be "professional" or "spotty", and penny-pinchers protest it's "overpriced", but that "beautiful" setting makes for a "memorable experience."

America Restaurant Bar ☾ 18 | 18 | 16 | $29
1 N. Clematis St. (Flagler Dr.), West Palm Beach, 561-835-1633

Patriots approve of the "big portions" of "affordable", "good" American "comfort food the way you wish your mother cooked" (especially the "great desserts" like fried Twinkies and "unbeatable chocolate soufflé") served at this bistro on Clematis in West Palm Beach; it's also a "stylish", "late-night place" for locals, though a few seditious sorts note it's "noisy" and "service could be faster."

Amici Ristorante 21 | 18 | 20 | $47
288 S. County Rd. (Royal Palm Way), Palm Beach, 561-832-0201

"Watch the rich and the famous misbehave" at this "tony" Palm Beach Italian considered the "island gathering place" where you can rub elbows (literally) with "celebs" and "beautiful people" in the "crowded", bright digs; the "overpriced" "food is incidental" – though "great" pasta and wood-oven pizza get a nod – as it's all about the "table-hopping" "scene" presided over by "personable" host-owner Maurizio Ciminella.

Anchor Inn 16 | 9 | 15 | $29
2810 Hypoluxo Rd. (bet. I-95 & S. Congress Ave.), Lantana, 561-965-4794

For nearly 30 years, Lantanans have dropped anchor at this "laid-back" fish house on Lake Osborne, attracted to the "fresh", "tasty" fin fare (particularly the "terrific" planked salmon) and "good value"; a few mutineers mutter about "lackluster decor" and "uneven service", but admit the waterside location is "pleasant."

Angelo & Maxie's Steakhouse 20 | 20 | 19 | $47
CityPlace, 651 Okeechobee Blvd. (Rosemary Ave.), West Palm Beach, 561-833-6550; www.mootwo.com

It may be an "upscale urban steakhouse", but this CityPlace chain outpost offers the "best early-bird bargain" in downtown West Palm Beach, and Kravis Center–bound

Palm Beach/Palm Beach County F | D | S | C

carnivores hit it pre-show for "huge portions" of "succulent" beef and "great" chicken in a "comfortable" (if a bit "dark") setting; however, the jaded jeer it's "disappointing" when compared to the New York City original and say the service could use "improvement."

Arturo's Ristorante 23 | 20 | 23 | $49
6750 N. Federal Hwy. (1 mi. north of Yamato Rd.), Boca Raton, 561-997-7373; www.arturosrestaurant.com
◪ "Authentic", "excellent" Northern Italian cuisine including some "pasta dishes cooked tableside" has drawn the "moneyed" set to this Boca classic for over 20 years; the "rolling antipasti chariot" is a "thing of beauty", the "old-world" surroundings are "soothing" and "attractive" and the service can be "impeccable"; doubters declare it "dated" and "costly", but more maintain it's the obvious choice for a "special occasion"; N.B. jackets suggested.

Bamboo Club, The 19 | 22 | 18 | $27
The Mall at Wellington Green, 10300 W. Forest Hill Blvd. (US 441), Wellington, 561-753-6606; www.thebambooclub.com
◪ "It's hard to believe it's a chain" say supporters of this Wellington Green Pan-Asian (with an Aventura offshoot) that's known for "sophisticated", "delicious" dishes that "encourage sharing", "interesting" cocktails and "sexy", "relaxing", "pretty" decor; a few nonmembers feel "bamboozled" by the "overpriced" fare and "disappointing" service, but admit it "beats eating at the food court."

Banana Boat ◐ 14 | 18 | 15 | $24
739 E. Ocean Ave. (SE 6th St.), Boynton Beach, 561-732-9400
◪ Both boaters and landlubbers "in the mood to party" meet on the waterfront decks at this "feel-good place" in Boynton Beach where a "casual seafood" menu offers "lots of options", "drinks are great" and the atmosphere's "jumping"; a "little live reggae" adds to the "vacation" vibe, and though a few mutineers say the "food's not appealing", you "go here for the scene."

Bellagio 19 | 20 | 18 | $33
CityPlace, 600 S. Rosemary Ave. (Okeechobee Blvd.), West Palm Beach, 561-659-6160
◪ "The ideal spot to feel the energy of West Palm Beach" may be this CityPlace Northern Italian offering a "great alfresco setting" with "wonderful views" of "dancing water fountains" as well as the "best people-watching" in town; the food's "good" and "simple", and even if there's less gushing and more grumbling about the "indifferent", "slow" service, the "fantastic location" still lures loyalists.

Benihana 18 | 19 | 20 | $34
3602 SE Ocean Blvd. (S. Dixie Hwy.), Stuart, 772-286-0740; www.benihana.com
See review in Miami/Dade County Directory.

vote at zagat.com

Palm Beach/Palm Beach County F | D | S | C

Ben's Steakhouse 19 | 14 | 18 | $29
3400 S. Congress Ave. (bet. Lake Worth Rd. & 10th Ave. N.), Palm Springs, 561-967-3400; www.bensteakhouse.com
◪ An "excellent salad bar", "great", "reasonably priced" steaks and a "perfect early-bird" have been the hallmarks of this "reliable" Palm Springs "classic" since 1975; there's also "good service" and a "nice lounge" with live entertainment, although those who've Ben there, done that deride the "dark", "dated decor."

BEVERLY HILLS CAFE 17 | 12 | 16 | $18
8228 Glades Rd. (Eastlake Blvd.), Boca Raton, 561-482-3227
13860 Wellington Trace (bet. Greenview Shores Blvd. & Paddock Dr.), Wellington, 561-791-2604
See review in Miami/Dade County Directory.

BICE RISTORANTE 22 | 22 | 21 | $53
313½ Worth Ave. (bet. Cocoanut Row & Hibiscus Ave.), Palm Beach, 561-835-1600; www.biceristorante.com
◪ Providing a "paradigm" for a "posh" "see-and-be-seen" scene are these "*très chic*" Palm Beach and Coconut Grove outposts of an "alluring worldwide" chain of "upscale" Italians; the food can be "top drawer" and "delicious" and the "classy" setting's certainly "pretty", but the service swings from "professional" to "condescending"; still, despite high tabs, "pandemonium" prevails in season.

BIG CITY TAVERN ◐ 20 | 19 | 18 | $33
5250 Town Center Circle (bet. Glades & Palmetto Park Rds.), Boca Raton, 561-361-4551
224 Clematis St. (N. Olive Ave.), West Palm Beach, 561-659-1853
www.bigtimerestaurants.com
◪ There are "good times to be had" at these "bustling" neighborhood joints in Palm Beach and Broward, as "large cocktails" and a "well-conceived wine list" draw "high-energy" after-work crowds while "lovely" interiors with "romantic booths", "delicious" New American fare and "reasonable" tabs bring "young" hopefuls with "date place" on their minds; a few hayseeds, however, call the food "unremarkable" and atmosphere "too noisy."

Bimini Twist 21 | 22 | 19 | $29
8480 Okeechobee Blvd. (Andros Isle), West Palm Beach, 561-784-2660
◪ "You'd think they're giving the food away" at this "mobbed" new West Palm seafooder from the owners of Kee Grill; as it is, though, the "terrific", "delicious" dishes are "reasonably priced" topped by "to-die-for Key lime pie", the decor's "simple" but "gorgeous" and service is "friendly"; a few foes, however, have their knickers in a twist over the "noisy" ambiance and "long waits" ("life's too short for beepers") due to the no-reservations policy.

Palm Beach/Palm Beach County F | D | S | C

Bistro, The   20 | 18 | 19 | $43
Driftwood Plaza, 2133 S. US 1 (Olympus Circle), Jupiter, 561-744-5054

■ It's "the besto" boast regulars of this Jupiter newcomer where "wonderful hospitality" from "affable" Irish owner Declan Hoctor (ex Roly's) serves as prelude to "delicious", "imaginative" Continental cuisine served in a "hideaway" by an "attentive" staff; "high noise levels make conversation difficult", but most report a "lovely" experience.

Bistro Zenith   19 | 17 | 18 | $34
Regency Court Shopping Ctr., 3011 Yamato Rd. (Jog Rd.), Boca Raton, 561-997-2570

◪ Opinions run the gamut from A to Z on this Boca bistro in Regency Court; admirers applaud the "interesting" and "consistently good" New American fare, a "comfortable", "sophisticated" setting and "attentive staff", while others zap the "unmemorable" fare and "loud" ambiance; most would agree that it "holds up for an informal meal."

Bizaare Avenue Cafe ⊠   21 | 23 | 20 | $25
921 Lake Ave. (S. H St.), Lake Worth, 561-588-4488

◪ For a "Greenwich Village experience in Lake Worth", faux-hemians flock to this "fun, funky" "fleamarket" of an eatery, where the decor's "marvelous" and the stuff's "for sale" ("even what you're sitting on"); the Eclectic fare's "great" (and "not too bizarre"), the wines are "lovely" and the prices are "reasonable" at this "quirky", "romantic" spot.

Blue Anchor British Pub   16 | 17 | 17 | $21
804 E. Atlantic Ave. (Palm Sq.), Delray Beach, 561-272-7272; www.theblueanchor.com

■ This "cheap and cheerful" Delray pub catapults expats back to "merry old England" with its "authentic" atmosphere (many features were imported "from across the pond"), "good pints" and "great" Traditional British fare; it's a "sociable" hangout" during the week, though live bands have the place "packed to the gills" Fridays and Saturdays.

Bohemian Gardens   14 | 11 | 14 | $24
5450 Lake Worth Rd. (Haverhill Rd.), Greenacres, 561-968-4111

◪ "A touch of Mitteleuropa" in west Lake Worth since 1947", this "homey" Continental packs in lots of early-birders "drinking Manhattans and decaf" to wash down a "wide variety" of "good", "traditional", "reasonably priced" dishes; trendier sorts sigh it's "dark, uninviting" and "over the hill", and aver the food's merely "average."

Boston's ◐   14 | 13 | 14 | $24
40 S. Ocean Blvd. (Atlantic Ave.), Delray Beach, 561-278-3364; www.bostonsonthebeach.com

◪ Brahmins and other "displaced" New Englanders boast this "great" restaurant/bar in Delray is "not for Yankee

vote at zagat.com

Palm Beach/Palm Beach County F | D | S | C |

fans" as it's filled with "Boston [Red Sox] memorabilia"; there's also an upper deck with "beautiful views", the better for dining on "good", "simply prepared" Traditional American and fin fare at "decent" prices; alas, rivals revile the "so-so" sustenance and "offhand" service.

Boulevard Grille 21 | 19 | 19 | $46

Royal Palm Plaza, 514 Via de Palmas (Mizner Blvd.), Boca Raton, 561-391-4194

☒ Most agree the "change of chefs" "hasn't hurt" this "elegant" New American–Continental in east Boca's Royal Palm Plaza where the "appetizers alone" are "worth the trip" and the other dishes are "excellent", complemented by "terrific wines" and served in a "calm atmosphere"; though antagonists taunt it's "time for a makeover" and grill it as "overpriced", locals know to "go off-season" when the menu is discounted.

Brasserie Mon Ami 18 | 21 | 18 | $31

University Commons Plaza, 1400 Glades Rd. (I-95), Boca Raton, 561-394-2428; www.brasseriemonami.com

☒ Friends of this "always jumping" east Boca bistro across from FAU favor its "Parisian feel" and "charming" decor, a "casual", "pleasant" setting for "reasonably priced", "delicious" New American and French fare ferried by a "smiling", "efficient" staff; foes feel the "faux" setting "belongs at Epcot", adding the food should be "as good as the owner's other restaurants" (Burt Rapoport's Max's Grill and Prezzo).

Brewzzi 18 | 18 | 18 | $23

2222 Glades Rd. (bet. I-95 & St. Andrews Blvd.), Boca Raton, 561-392-2739
700 S. Rosemary Ave. (Okeechobee Blvd.), West Palm Beach, 561-366-9753
www.brewzzi.com

■ Ale and hearty types tout these "awesome brewpubs" serving "fresh distilled beers" in Boca and West Palm Beach shopping areas; the "surprisingly good" Italian-American fare arrives in "mountainous" portions and includes "gourmet pizzas" and "terrific sandwiches", and the "sporty" digs evoke a "bigger, nicer *Cheers*"; sure, they're "loud" and service "needs improvement", but penny-pinchers proclaim "the price is right."

Brogue's – | – | – | M |

621 Lake Ave. (bet. K & L Sts.), Lake Worth, 561-585-1885

This new downtown Lake Worth Irish pub serves up "tasty", "typical" Gaelic grub like "great shepherd's pie and corned beef sandwiches" and "good times" in the form of live music nightly; a few neatniks note it "needs to iron out a few wrinkles", but ex-Pats enjoy the opportunity to "hang out with local soccer hooligans" at the big bar or patio.

Palm Beach/Palm Beach County F | D | S | C

Buonasera   22 | 15 | 19 | $45
2145 S. US 1 (½ mi. south of Indiantown Rd.), Jupiter, 561-744-0543
■ Evoking an "upscale" trattoria "on the Amalfi coast", this Jupiter Italian offers "excellent", "authentic" pastas and "worthy fish and veal" in an "attractive", "intimate" interior or on the "delightful patio"; though the service ranges from "professional" to "pretentious" and the fare's certainly "pricey", it's "not as expensive as a trip" to the old country, "yet the result is the same."

Busch's Seafood   14 | 20 | 15 | $34
840 E. Atlantic Ave. (Intracoastal Waterway), Delray Beach, 561-278-7600
■ "Location, location, location" is the charm of this east Delray Beach seafooder, as a "lovely patio" where you can "watch the boats" on the Intracoastal Waterway makes it a "great place to while away the hours"; unfortunately, the staff's performance "leaves a lot to be desired" and, most agree, so does the "pedestrian" food, which seems caught in a "'50s time warp."

Cabana   23 | 21 | 21 | $30
118 S. Clematis St. (bet. Flagler Dr. & Narcissus Ave.), West Palm Beach, 561-833-4773
■ "*Caliente!*" cheer surveyors who have visited this "upbeat" Nuevo Latino–Cuban in downtown West Palm Beach; like its two NYC siblings, it embodies "urban Hispanic chic" via an "imaginative" "fusion" of cuisines, "the best mojitos in town" and "lively", "stylish" decor ("eat outside" to take in "the people and the fountain" in the nearby park); thanks to a "helpful, attentive" staff and "reasonable" prices, it's a definite "crowd-pleaser."

Cafe Bellino   21 | 15 | 21 | $34
180 S. Federal Hwy. (SE 2nd St.), Boca Raton, 561-393-2844
■ "If you're from out of town, it's hard to find" this strip-plaza Tuscan trattoria in Boca Raton, but locals retrace their steps to this "cozy" "favorite" for "moderately priced", "well-prepared" "homemade pasta" and a staff that "makes you feel like an old friend"; some lament "cramped" digs, but others insist the "great little garden" compensates.

Café Boulud   – | – | – | VE
Brazilian Court Hotel, 301 Australian Ave. (Hibiscus Ave.), Palm Beach, 561-655-6060; www.danielnyc.com
Super-chef Daniel Boulud's long-awaited Palm Beach outpost in the renovated Brazilian Court Hotel offers a menu reflecting that of the NYC original, offering his signature mix of traditional and interpretive French dishes; Provence-inspired decor fills the sunny dining rooms, and other options include a courtyard with fountain and two private areas; acolytes are advised to book early, as it's destined to be one of the hottest tickets in town during the season.

vote at zagat.com

Palm Beach/Palm Beach County F | D | S | C

Cafe Cellini ▽ 21 | 17 | 23 | $43
Palm Beach President, 2505 S. Ocean Blvd. (north of Lake Worth Bridge), Palm Beach, 561-588-1871
■ The "owner knows his frequent guests" at this "flower-decorated" Continental in the Palm Beach President condo: a "mature crowd" that appreciates "peace, quiet and calm dining", "consistently good food", a "high-end wine list" and an "eager-to-please" staff; the "old-fashioned" restaurant isn't for everyone, but it's perfect "for taking grandma out", especially before 6 PM ("after that, prices skyrocket"); N.B. closed on winter Mondays.

CAFE CHARDONNAY 25 | 21 | 22 | $48
Garden Square Shoppes, 4533 PGA Blvd. (Military Trail), Palm Beach Gardens, 561-627-2662; www.cafechardonnay.com
■ A "time-tested favorite" in Palm Beach Gardens, this New American may prove to be the "classiest dining experience you'll ever have in a strip mall"; "outstanding", "artfully prepared" dishes including "incredible seafood" are paired with "fabulous wines", and the staff is "happy to educate the customer"; though a few find the decor "drab" and digs "cramped", others acclaim it as "lovely."

Cafe du Parc ☒ ▽ 22 | 17 | 20 | $52
612 Federal Hwy. (bet. Blue Heron & Northlake Blvds.), Lake Park, 561-845-0529
■ This petite Lake Park French is Gallic "to its bones", "without much variation from what you'd expect", and while some gourmands glorify "excellent" entrees like lamb, fish and cassoulet, others term them "too classical" (not to mention "overpriced"); though the "service retains its patina", the "traditional" "small house" setting gives off a "dated" vibe and "could use some sprucing up."

CAFE L'EUROPE 26 | 27 | 25 | $67
331 S. County Rd. (Brazilian Ave.), Palm Beach, 561-655-4020; www.cafeleurope.com
■ The "killer decor" at this "still-going-strong Palm Beach staple" "says 'you have arrived, dahling'", with "gorgeous" flowers and the "beautiful people" ("see the wonders Botox has wrought") adorning the recently refreshed room; the Continental cuisine is "marvelous" and "flawlessly prepared", and the wine list is "extraordinary"; even though the service ranges from "pampering" to "pompous" and the offerings are "extremely expensive", vets advise "dress up", "break the bank and live the good life."

Café Protégé ☒ 22 | 21 | 22 | $35
Florida Culinary Institute, 2400 Metrocenter Blvd. (I-95 at 45th St. exit), West Palm Beach, 561-687-2433; www.cafeprotege.com
■ There's "always something" different at this New American, the "upscale" "training kitchen" at the Florida

Palm Beach/Palm Beach County F | D | S | C

Culinary Institute in West Palm Beach where "beautifully prepared", "creative" dishes are presented by "students" who "try hard"; though some say it's "a little too pricey" and "service can be spotty", the pre–6 PM sunset specials ("an excellent value") and $14 buffet lunch make it "worth a visit."

Caffe Luna Rosa   20 | 18 | 17 | $35

34 S. Ocean Blvd. (E. Atlantic Ave.), Delray Beach, 561-274-9404; www.caffelunarosa.com

☑ "The big sell here is the ocean" sprawling out across the street from this "breezy", "islandy" alfresco Italian in Delray Beach, which serves "new twists on the classics" all day (plus, for hungover brunchers, "the best Bloody Mary in the area"); the staff is "cheery if not always efficient" and "parking's awkward", but "even jaded Floridians" say "it's perfect on a moonlit night."

CALIFORNIA PIZZA KITCHEN   19 | 14 | 18 | $19

The Gardens mall, 3101 PGA Blvd. (Kew Gardens Ave.), Palm Beach, 561-625-4682
The Mall at Wellington Green, 10300 W. Forest Hill Blvd. (Range Line Rd.), Wellington, 561-793-1601
Palm Beach Int'l Airport, West Palm Beach, 561-683-0834
www.cpk.com

See review in Ft. Lauderdale/Broward County Directory.

Capri Blu   21 | 16 | 22 | $44

116 N. Dixie Hwy. (bet. Banyan Blvd. & Clematis St.), West Palm Beach, 561-832-4300

■ "*Magnifico!*" rave the tru-blu "loyal clientele" of this "old-fashioned Italian" family operation in West Palm Beach, where the fare has a "wonderful flair" ferried by servers who "care"; however, some report that its "awkward location keeps it from being busier", while others blame the prices: "it's a little too expensive for what you get"; P.S. check out the "fun opera nights" every Monday in season.

Cardello's Pizza   ∇ 15 | 13 | 15 | $20

Abacoa, 1447 10th St. (Northlake Blvd.), Lake Park, 561-848-0123; www.cardellos.com

■ Known for its all-you-can-eat early-bird special, this "casual", cavernous family-oriented Lake Park pizzeria also lays out a "fantastic lunch buffet"; the "great salad bar" is "large and fully stocked with too much of everything" including "hot, garlicky rolls" and "ok pasta."

Carmine's Ocean Grill   22 | 19 | 18 | $39

Prosperity Ctr., 2460 PGA Blvd. (Prosperity Farms Rd.), Palm Beach Gardens, 561-624-1141; www.carminesoceangrill.com

☑ "Attractive" trendies nibble on "consistently good" fish at this Italian seafoodery and raw bar in Palm Beach Gardens; though the "dark" room can be "crowded and loud" owing to the "chaotic" "meat market" "bar action"

Palm Beach/Palm Beach County   F | D | S | C

and the service is "spotty", most voters say it's "worth it" for a "diverse" menu "big enough to make everyone happy."

Cay Da   ▽ 22 | 11 | 20 | $23
7400 N. Federal Hwy. (NE 74th St.), Boca Raton, 561-998-0278

■ Despite its "bare-bones storefront setting", this modest Boca Raton Vietnamese is a "delightful little place" where a "pleasant" staff proffers "fresh", "crisp and tasty" eats; add in "reasonable" prices and "personal service" and the result is far better than o-Cay.

CHARLEY'S CRAB   19 | 19 | 19 | $40
456 S. Ocean Blvd. (Worth Ave.), Palm Beach, 561-659-1500; www.muer.com

See review in Ft. Lauderdale/Broward County Directory.

CHEEBURGER CHEEBURGER   18 | 11 | 15 | $14
200 S. Federal Hwy. (E. Palmetto Park Rd.), Boca Raton, 561-392-1969
450 E. Atlantic Ave. (5th Ave.), Delray Beach, 561-265-1959
819 Lake Ave. (bet. S. Dixie Hwy. & S. J St.), Lake Worth, 561-383-1949
5520 PGA Blvd. (Central Blvd.), Palm Beach Gardens, 561-627-1793
CityPlace, 760 S. Rosemary Ave. (Fern St.), West Palm Beach, 561-833-1997 ⑤
www.cheeburger-cheeburger.com

See review in Ft. Lauderdale/Broward County Directory.

CHEESECAKE FACTORY ●   20 | 19 | 18 | $25
5530 Glades Rd. (Butts Rd.), Boca Raton, 561-393-0344
CityPlace, 701 S. Rosemary Ave. (Okeechobee Blvd.), West Palm Beach, 561-802-3838
www.thecheesecakefactory.com

See review in Ft. Lauderdale/Broward County Directory.

CHEZ JEAN-PIERRE BISTRO ⑤   28 | 22 | 26 | $62
132 N. County Rd. (bet. Sunrise & Sunset Aves.), Palm Beach, 561-833-1171

■ Fans "fly to Palm Beach just to eat" at this "premier" French "favorite of the old guard and NP (new people)" alike; the "exquisite yet unpretentious" preparations are "masterpieces" (the "best sea bass" and "to-die-for sorbets"), and the "wonderful", "longtime" staff along with "charming" owners Jean-Pierre and Nicole Leverrier "make you feel at home"; the "lovely" setting with "zany" trompe l'oeil art completes the picture, and if it's all "a little overpriced", it's worth a "splurge."

Chuck & Harold's   16 | 17 | 17 | $34
207 Royal Poinciana Way (N. County Rd.), Palm Beach, 561-659-1440; www.muer.com

☒ "Chuck and Harold have gone" but you can still watch the "glamorous world go by" if you "sit outside" on the

Palm Beach/Palm Beach County F | D | S | C

patio at this Traditional American, a "quintessential Palm Beach" "standby" where enthusiasts enjoy a "reliable Sunday brunch" and signature crab cakes (though not "erratic service"); critics charge it's now "tourist, tourist, tourist" and "surviving on reputation only."

Chuck's Steakhouse ● — 18 | 13 | 17 | $27
21618 St. Andrews Blvd. (Palmetto Park Rd.), Boca Raton, 561-338-5570; www.chucksflorida.com
See review in Ft. Lauderdale/Broward County Directory.

City Cellar Wine Bar — 21 | 22 | 20 | $34
CityPlace, 700 S. Rosemary Ave. (Okeechobee Blvd.), West Palm Beach, 561-366-0071; www.bigtimerestaurants.com
■ Oenophiles ooh and aah over West Palm Beach's "most beautiful cellar", a glassed-in floor-to-ceiling rack at this "vibrant" Mediterranean on the second floor of CityPlace; the "extensive list" of 300-plus labels (including 40 by-the-glass offerings) is matched by "generous portions" of "inventive" fare presented by a "friendly" if sometimes "amateurish" staff, so that overall the "impressive yet reasonable" restaurant rates a big "bravo!"

City Oyster — 21 | 19 | 20 | $37
213 E. Atlantic Ave. (N. Railroad Ave.), Delray Beach, 561-272-0220; www.bigtimerestaurants.com
■ "Get a table out on the sidewalk" to "hang and people-watch" at this "happening" fish place on Delray Beach's East Atlantic; inside the "chic", "warm" (and "noisy") dining room, it's "wall to wall" with "hip" "singles" downing "creative", "fresh" fare that goes way beyond bivalves; an "attractive" staff, including "great bartenders", helps make this a "favorite everyday spot."

Cobblestone Cafe ☒ — 17 | 16 | 18 | $35
Gallery Sq. N., 383C Tequesta Dr. (Seabrook Rd.), Tequesta, 561-747-4419
☒ "Wonderful hospitality" is the strength of this "intimate" New American bistro, a "charming" "find" in Tequesta's Gallery Square where the eats are "interesting" and the decor "cute" and "clever"; though the room is "small and a little noisy" and critics cluck it's "lost its former character and quality", it's considered "generally ok."

Conchy Joe's Seafood — 17 | 18 | 16 | $24
3945 N. Indian River Dr. (Jensen Beach Blvd.), Jensen Beach, 772-334-1130
■ For evocative "local flavor", "wear your shorts" and "flip-flops" to this "giant", "reasonably priced" Jensen Beach reef-and-beefer with its "thatched chickee roof", a "lively" "Caribbean atmosphere" (including live reggae on weekends) and a "spectacular view of the Indian River"; hooked devotees "wish they'd give the recipe" for the "incredibly delicious conch chowder."

vote at zagat.com 173

Palm Beach/Palm Beach County F D S C

Couco Pazzo — | — | — | E
915 Lake Ave. (S. Dixie Hwy.), Lake Worth, 561-585-0320
This Lake Worth Italian favorite was sold this summer, but the new owners say they'll stick to the popular menu, just adding their own tweaks; the small but bustling room has an adjoining cafe/pizzeria that will be more casual, but you can expect many of the same pies and panini – the cooks who trained under Marty Servido stayed on.

Courtyard Grill, The ▽ 23 | 20 | 24 | $50
11970 SE Dixie Hwy. (south of Bridge Rd.), Hobe Sound, 772-546-2900
☒ Some surveyors enthuse you'll be "greeted like family" by the "well-dressed" servers at this out-of-the-way Hobe Sound Continental, where a "charming" atmosphere enhances "delicious" (if "expensive") fare; others sniff that the place "can be noisy" due to "railroad tracks and passing trains" out front and protest the "pompous staff."

Crab Pot ▽ 13 | 11 | 14 | $21
386 E. Blue Heron Blvd. (bet. Intracoastal Waterway & Lakeshore Dr.), Riviera Beach, 561-844-2722; www.waterfrontdining.net
■ Expect a "laid-back Key West" experience at this Riviera Beach fishery; it's "not expensive", so "don't look for fine china or even fine food" – just "lots of fried offerings" and "good drinks" – but with "seagulls sitting at your elbow" it will remind you "of what Florida used to be."

Crazy Buffet 17 | 13 | 14 | $24
2030 Palm Beach Lakes Blvd. (Robbins Dr.), West Palm Beach, 561-616-9288; www.gocrazybuffet.com
■ The crowds "constantly coming and going" prove this "wacky" West Palm Beach self-serve is a "local favorite" for families ("kids love this place!") and workday lunchers; it offers 50 kinds of all-you-can-eat sushi and a "wide variety of ethnic food", including Japanese and Chinese fares, grilled meats and pizza – plus "the price is right."

Cuban Cafe 23 | 14 | 20 | $22
Plumtree Ctr., 3350 NW Boca Raton Blvd. (Spanish River Blvd.), Boca Raton, 561-750-8860
■ Whether you're on a "romantic date" or eating a "casual meal" at this "cute", "red-checkered-tablecloth" Cuban in mid-Boca, you'll be Havana good time, thanks to "large portions" of "affordable", "outstanding", "authentic food" served by an "attentive" and "friendly" staff.

Cucina Dell' Arte ◐ 17 | 16 | 17 | $35
257 Royal Poinciana Way (bet. Bradley Pl. & N. County Rd.), Palm Beach, 561-655-0770
■ Denizens of this "solid", "reasonable" Palm Beach Italian report that new proprietors "have put life back in

Palm Beach/Palm Beach County F | D | S | C

it": the updated menu offers "healthier" options including "imaginative" pizzas and salads; the staff is "eager to please" and the renovated interior is more spacious – which means this "unpretentious retreat" can also be a "noisy, noisy, noisy" "nightspot" (food's served until 3 AM).

DaDa ●   18 | 23 | 17 | $27
52 N. Swinton Ave. (1st St.), Delray Beach, 561-330-3232
◪ "An eclectic crowd" fills four "adorable" "bohemian" rooms at this downtown Delrayer where "lovers talk and cuddle" on "huge furniture that makes you want to stay all night" and others "find themselves doodling" with chalk on the "slate-topped tables"; the "great" New American food and "killer drinks" help compensate for "lax" service.

Dakotah 624 ●   20 | 18 | 19 | $41
270 E. Atlantic Ave. (2nd Ave.), Delray Beach, 561-274-6244; www.dakotah624.com
◪ Even fans of this "chic" Delray American say it "needs mimes for waiters" to combat "extreme noise" – but cope by swilling "the best $10 martinis" in town and savoring "inventive food"; an "upscale, young crowd" likes to "eat outdoors" to "see and be seen", while thrifties advise "just order tapas or apps" to fill up "without breaking the bank."

Dave's Last Resort & Raw Bar ●   16 | 12 | 14 | $19
632 Lake Ave. (bet. K & L Sts.), Lake Worth, 561-588-5208; www.daveslastresort.com
◪ There's "typical bar and finger food" along with "excellent salads and fish" at this Lake Worth sports pub; it's an "always-busy" "hangout" for locals who "watch the football game" on 25 TVs and a "fun little place", and it's also a reliable resort where shoppers or beachgoers can "bring the kids"; owing to high-decibel high jinks, though, all agree it's "not for the conversation-minded."

De La Tierra   21 | 27 | 19 | $46
Sundy Inn, 106 S. Swinton Ave. (Atlantic Ave.), Delray Beach, 561-272-5678; www.sundyhouse.com
■ A "turn-of-the-century home" on a "spectacular" setting with "delightful gardens" creates an "unsurpassed dining environment" at this "special-occasion" place that's part of the "romantic" Sundy Inn in Delray Beach; chef Johnny Vinczencz's "innovative", "outstanding" Floribbean fare and "show-stopping desserts" are also "memorable", but it's the "exquisite" landscape that makes it a "must for out-of-town guests."

Don Ramon's   18 | 11 | 17 | $18
6230-10 Indiantown Rd. (Central Blvd.), Jupiter, 561-741-3378
Promenade Plaza, 9920 Alt-A1A (Holly Dr.), Palm Beach Gardens, 561-625-1061

(continued)

Palm Beach/Palm Beach County F | D | S | C |

(continued)
Don Ramon's
7101 S. Dixie Hwy. (Forest Hill Blvd.), West Palm Beach, 561-547-8704
502 S. Military Trail (bet. Gun Club Rd. & Summit Blvd.), West Palm Beach, 561-687-0161
☑ "Especially when on a budget", surveyors hail this "consistent" "real Cuban" quartet, where "generous portions" of "juicy ropa vieja" & "delicious" pulled pork can be "a terrific bargain" (early-bird specials cost less than $8); add in a "cheerful" staff, and people willingly shrug off the "cheesy dinerlike decor" – "the food is so good I never care."

Dune Deck Cafe ⌀   17 | 12 | 17 | $20 |
100 N. Ocean Blvd. (Ocean Ave.), Lantana, 561-582-0472; www.dunedeckcafe.com
■ "Have lunch without changing out of your wet suit" at this "welcoming" "beachside" "back-porch" cafe next to the Ritz in Lantana, where the Traditional American breakfasts and brunches are so "surprisingly good" that it's often jammed ("have an alternate location in mind") and there's no decor to speak of except a "superb view of the Atlantic Ocean"; N.B. credit cards accepted only at dinner January–May.

ECHO   24 | 24 | 21 | $50 |
230A Sunrise Ave. (N. County Rd.), Palm Beach, 561-802-4222; www.echopalmbeach.com
■ This "happening" Palm Beach Asian-fusion showplace is "so chic" you'll "wonder whether you're hip enough to dine there"; the menu is a "brilliant broad brush" stroke of eastern offerings including "fresher-than-fresh sushi" and "the best Beijing duck for miles" as well as "wonderful" drinks, all "beautifully presented" by a staff with "impressive knowledge" – just expect the experience to be "pricey"; N.B. delivery available.

Eilat Cafe   22 | 12 | 15 | $26 |
Wharfside, 6853 SW 18th St. (Powerline Rd.), Boca Raton, 561-368-6880; www.eilatcafe.com
☑ "They do wonders with fish" at this family-run Boca glatt spot, where "vegetarians and kosher seekers" can find "delicious" dairy and seafood offerings that look so "elegant" "you'd think the chef went to art school"; several grumble, though, that "service is erratic", plus the dining room has "no atmosphere", making "outdoor dining" on the wharfside deck "the only choice."

El Colonial ⌀   ▽ 21 | 13 | 20 | $19 |
1017 N. Federal Hwy. (Jasmine Dr.), Lake Park, 561-882-1762
■ "The price is right" at this neighborhood Cuban in Lake Park, where regulars "relish the flavors" of "bueno"

Palm Beach/Palm Beach County F | D | S | C

"authentic" eats in a "friendly" "luncheonette" atmosphere; what with the "generous portions" and "so much help, it's hard to figure out how it makes money" – especially when you consider the renowned $7 early-bird special.

11 MAPLE STREET 28 | 23 | 24 | $46
3224 NE Maple Ave. (11th Ave.), Jensen Beach, 772-334-7714
■ Its "low-key atmosphere" belies the "haute" New American cuisine served at this downtown Jensen Beach "charmer" that surveyors have voted No. 1 for Food; chef-owner Mike Perrin uses the "freshest ingredients" to create "novel", "astonishing", "beautifully presented" dishes, and his "gracious" wife Margie "greets you like an old friend"; the "delightful" "converted old house" setting alone is "worth the drive" for a "special date"; N.B. beer and wine only; closed Mondays and Tuesdays.

E.R. Bradley's Saloon ● 15 | 16 | 17 | $23
104 Clematis St. (Flagler Dr.), West Palm Beach, 561-833-3520; www.erbradleys.com
☑ "Most patrons aren't here for the food" and that's probably just as well say surveyors of this well-known West Palm Beach "true happy-hour spot", where decor and service may be "average" but a "lively young crowd" is happy to down drinks, munch on "ordinary" pub grub and take in a "magnificent" Intracoastal view; DJs inspire "20-year-olds" to dance into the wee hours.

Falcon House ⌧ ∇ 22 | 19 | 21 | $34
116 NE Sixth Ave. (1st St.), Delray Beach, 561-243-9499; www.thefalconhouse.com
■ Located in a historic house in east Delray Beach, this "sophisticated dive" draws a "trendy" crowd, especially after 10 PM; voters say they're attracted by "great drinks" ("the bar is worth seeing") but come away "very impressed" with "amazing" Contemporary American fare served tapas-style; in all, this "cozy", "fun place" is "good for out-of-town visitors."

Flagler Grill 23 | 19 | 21 | $40
47 SW Flagler Ave. (Joan Jefferson Way), Stuart, 772-221-9517
☑ Surveyors are split on this Stuart Floribbean: fans toast "creative" "gourmet food" and a "stellar wine list" served up by "nice" staffers in a "quaint, old" setting that "hasn't changed in years"; foes flame "plain-vanilla decor" and "nothing-special" fare, adding it costs "too much money for too little food"; your call.

Flagler Steakhouse, The 24 | 23 | 25 | $59
The Breakers, 2 S. County Rd. (bet. Royal Palm & Royal Poinciana Ways), Palm Beach, 561-659-8471; www.thebreakers.com
■ It's where Palm Beach's elite meet to eat meat: this beefery overlooking The Breakers' links feels so much

Palm Beach/Palm Beach County F | D | S | C |

"like a private club" that many "don't realize it's open to the public"; those who do agree it's "superb", with "fantastic service" that makes "you feel as if the staff knows you", "elegant" earth-toned decor and "unbelievable steak" – at "unbelievable prices", admittedly, but "worth it."

FOUR SEASONS - THE RESTAURANT 28 | 28 | 28 | $68 |

Four Seasons, 2800 S. Ocean Blvd. (Lake Ave.), Palm Beach, 561-582-2800; www.fourseasons.com 633-3750

■ "A tribute to the talents" of "master" chef Hubert Des Marais, this "faultless" Four Seasons hotel New American "continues to amaze" with "phenomenal" fish and other "extraordinary" dishes using regional ingredients that are all a "joy to behold"; the "superior" staff is "there before you know you need something", and the setting, while "formal", is "luxurious" and "beautiful"; naturally, it's "expensive", but "perfect for special occasions."

Gallery Grille ▽ 20 | 19 | 20 | $26 |

383 Tequesta Dr. (Seabrook Rd.), Tequesta, 561-575-3775

■ Guys and gals greet this "great newcomer" to the Tequesta art-and-antique plaza, a "cute" bistro-esque Contemporary American that serves only breakfast and lunch; it's "always a fun meal" since you can "sit at the counter and meet the locals" over a cup of joe, a gourmet sandwich or the popular Sunday brunch; prices are "reasonable" too, so feel free to splurge on that painting.

GiGi's Tavern ◐ 19 | 20 | 19 | $34 |

Mizner Park, 346 Plaza Real (N. Federal Hwy.), Boca Raton, 561-368-4488; www.gigis.com

■ A "Benzes-and-Ferraris" "Boca crowd" boogeying to live music and boozing with "beautiful bartenders" makes this deco-inflected Mizner Park French bistro a "happening" "singles scene"; "food seems secondary", but many praise "delectable" fin fare "at a reasonable price"; those who shun the after-dark "meat market" advise "have lunch outside" since there's "no better place to people-watch."

Ginger Wok ▽ 16 | 6 | 16 | $19 |

208 N. Dixie Hwy. (W. Lantana Rd.), Lantana, 561-588-9997

❚ It's got "no atmosphere" and "no liquor" either, but this humble east Lantana "not-just-a-regular Chinese" serves up "imaginative fresh fish", "good vegetarian selections" and a "crispy chicken that's actually crisp under the sauce"; surveyors caution that you'll "have to be patient" with servers, who "are fast, but don't speak much English."

Gotham City Restaurant and Bar – | – | – | E |

16950 Jog Rd. (Morikami Park Rd.), Delray Beach, 561-381-0200; www.gothamcityrestaurant.com

The hip Delray Beach dining scene moves west with this urban-chic bower; it features courtyard seating and a

Palm Beach/Palm Beach County F | D | S | C

show kitchen that turns out wood-grilled steaks, chops and chicken as well as pastas and other Continental fare.

Green's Pharmacy   15 | 5 | 16 | $14
151 N. County Rd. (Sunrise Ave.), Palm Beach, 561-832-0304
■ It's "great to find a five-and-dime experience" in Palm Beach, darlings, and this is it: a "landmark" 1938 pharmacy "fixture" offering "the most affordable", "unpretentious" Traditional American breakfasts and lunches on the island; you'll find "your broker, a bum and everyone in between" sipping "thick, tall milkshakes" and pigging out on "patty melts worth every fat gram"; critics wish housekeeping was more rigorous.

Grille, The ⍉   18 | 16 | 17 | $33
5101 Congress Ave. (Yamato Rd.), Boca Raton, 561-912-9800
■ A "corporate crowd" frequents this "good ol' American" in Boca for its "tasty" lunches of traditional grill fare plus "hot" "homemade biscuits"; dinner denizens appreciate the "large portions" served in a "classy", "clubby" yet casual wood-and-brass setting by a "friendly, sweet staff", and everyone's glad it's "less expensive than others of its ilk."

Hamburger Heaven ⍉   20 | 10 | 18 | $16
314 S. County Rd. (bet. Brazilian Ave. & Royal Palm Way), Palm Beach, 561-655-5277
■ Carnivores are on cloud nine at this diner, a "Palm Beach fixture for generations" where a "real mix of customers" will "wait for hamburgers – what does that tell you?"; "go hungry", grab a "table or booth" ("kids love to sit at the counter") and let "crusty" staffers bring you "fabulous" beef patties and "amazing shakes and desserts"; P.S. it "finally accepts credit cards."

Harry and the Natives   17 | 20 | 17 | $18
11910 S. Federal Hwy. (SE Bridge Rd.), Hobe Sound, 772-546-3061; www.harryandthenatives.com
■ An "absolutely wild" Hobe Sound "institution", Harry and his mom's Traditional American is a "funky", "kitschy", "old Florida" "experience"; come "in shorts and flip-flops", park beside "a Harley or a Bentley" and take in the "infectious informality" along with "decent food" at "great prices"; "be sure to read everything on the walls"; N.B. closed in August.

Havana   18 | 10 | 16 | $19
6801 S. Dixie Hwy. (Forest Hill Blvd.), West Palm Beach, 561-547-9799; www.havanacubanfood.com
■ Java junkies, never fear: "wonderful café con leche" that "will keep you up for days" can be had 24/7 from the walk-up window at this moderately priced West Palm Beach Cuban, along with "warm empanadas", "excellent sandwiches" and other "simple", "tasty" fare served by a

vote at zagat.com

Palm Beach/Palm Beach County F | D | S | C

"professional" staff; it's "good for takeout" say surveyors, since the decor is "early cafeteria-style."

Henry's
20 | 19 | 18 | $36

Addison Pl. N., 16850 Jog Rd. (bet. Carter & Morikami Park Rds.), Delray Beach, 561-638-1949

☑ Habitués hail this "homey" American bistro in Delray Beach as a "good value", with a "wide range" of "creative comfort food" "stylishly presented" by a "friendly" staff, but disparagers disagree, dissing "stodgy", "erratic" fare, "inattentive" servers and "mobbed" conditions – and everyone dislikes the "sometimes overwhelming" "noise level"; still, the proprietors "must be doing something right" if you "can't get a last-minute reservation."

Hops
16 | 15 | 16 | $21

545 N. Congress Ave. (Old Boynton Ave.), Boynton Beach, 561-731-3313
1725 S. Federal Hwy. (SE Central Pkwy.), Stuart, 772-288-6900
Pine Trail Shopping Ctr., 4576 Okeechobee Blvd. (Military Trail), West Palm Beach, 561-616-5074
www.hopsonline.com

☑ Surveyors are at lagerheads about this "informal" "easy-on-the-pocketbook" chain of microbreweries; advocates stoutly support the "extra-large portions" of "decent", "dependable" steaks, salads and sandwiches (and especially the "out-of-this-world" "hot honey-butter croissants"), while bashers are bitter about "incidental" food, "iffy service" and "uninspiring" "cookie-cutter" interiors; in short, a critical free-for-ale.

HOUSTON'S
21 | 20 | 20 | $29

1900 NW Executive Center Circle (Glades Rd.), Boca Raton, 561-998-0550; www.houstons.com
See review in Ft. Lauderdale/Broward County Directory.

Hurricane Café
21 | 13 | 18 | $20

14050 US 1 (Donald Ross Rd.), Juno Beach, 561-630-2012
■ Still something of a secret, this chef-owned American a block from the beach in Juno Beach is a "little gem" to those in the know; it's "cozy", "clean and bright", with a "friendly" staff and "reliable", "excellent" edibles that attract fans "again and again" for "reasonably priced" "light dinners, lunches" and especially breakfasts; P.S. "it's packed in season."

I & J's Station House
21 | 10 | 18 | $38

233 W. Lantana Rd. (Dixie Hwy.), Lantana, 561-547-9487; www.stationrestaurants.com

☑ "Put on that bib" and "get your lobster fix" at this "informal", "New England"–esque seafood "shack" next to the railroad tracks in Lantana, known for its "value-priced", "unadorned", "fresh-from-the-tank" crustaceans that claw connoisseurs consider "as good as up in Maine";

Palm Beach/Palm Beach County F | D | S | C

if a few crab that the "not-much-to-look-at" digs are overly "crowded", even they concede "you know it's fresh" since the place is "always busy."

Ichiban 22 | 17 | 19 | $31
8841 Glades Rd. (Lyons Rd.), Boca Raton, 561-451-0420
See review in Ft. Lauderdale/Broward County Directory.

Il Trullo 22 | 19 | 20 | $44
Fisherman's Wharf Plaza, 287 E. Indiantown Rd. (Intracoastal Pointe Dr.), Jupiter, 561-745-8040
210 E. Ocean Ave. (east of US 1), Lantana, 561-586-2912
■ "Classy Northern Italian" favorites "done right" are the hallmark of this Lantana-Jupiter trattoria twosome, which is also appreciated for its "warm, intimate" atmosphere made "even more inviting" by the "attentive" owners and staff (they clearly "care about their customers"); boosters don't blink at prices as "rich" as the "terrific" dishes ("you'd think you were in NY").

J. Alexander's 19 | 19 | 19 | $27
University Commons, 1400 Glades Rd. (east of I-95), Boca Raton, 561-347-9875; www.jalexanders.com
See review in Ft. Lauderdale/Broward County Directory.

Jetty's 20 | 20 | 19 | $34
1075 A1A N. (US 1), Jupiter, 561-743-8166
■ Given its "picture-postcard-perfect" view of Jupiter's red lighthouse, "delicious", "value"-priced "traditional Florida seafood" and "sweet, thoughtful" service, it's no surprise that "the wait can be an hour and a half" in season at this "large", "unpretentious" and "popular" Jupiter fish house ("if only they took reservations!"); insiders suggest "come early" – you can eat for $12.95 between 5–6 PM – and "try to get a table by the water."

Johannes ∇ 22 | 19 | 22 | $78
47 E. Palmetto Park Rd. (N. Federal Hwy.), Boca Raton, 561-394-0007
■ "You may need a GPS" to find this "tiny" (30 seats), "funky" New American in east Boca Raton, but once you get there you'll feel a bit like a guest at a "dinner party in a fabulous home", thanks to its sofa seating and "intimate" setting; if an "intimidated" few eschew the "too-nouveau" vibe and "way-expensive" tabs, most sing the praises of "talented" chef-owner Johannes Fruhwirt and his "creative" cuisine.

John Bull English Pub ● 21 | 18 | 19 | $25
Village Commons Shopping Plaza, 801 Village Blvd. (Palm Beach Lakes Blvd.), West Palm Beach, 561-697-2855; www.bigtimerestaurants.com
■ "Everything's British but the accents" (think "English pub, squared") at this "dark, cozy" West Palm Beach standby, a "locals'" favorite for shepherd's pie and the like washed

vote at zagat.com

Palm Beach/Palm Beach County F | D | S | C |

down with "a pint or two"; supporters seated in the "pleasant" outdoor courtyard or beside the "nice blazing fire" inside ignore the "shopping mall" milieu.

John G's ⊉   23 | 12 | 20 | $16 |
10 S. Ocean Blvd. (Lake Ave.), Lake Worth, 561-585-9860; www.johngs.com
■ Even in a "hurricane" there'd likely "still be a line" out the door at this "unpretentious" American "landmark on Lake Worth Beach", but those in-the-know actually "hope for" a wait since "John G. himself offers" up chocolate-covered fruits to make the time pass sweetly; there's "not much decor" to speak of, unless you count the "beautiful ocean view", but no one's complaining considering the "fabulous breakfasts and lunches" in "plentiful" portions ("go hungry"); N.B. it's cash-only and closes at 3 PM.

Juno Beach Fish House   16 | 13 | 15 | $26 |
13980 US 1 (Donald Ross Rd.), Juno Beach, 561-626-2636; www.junobeachfishhouse.com
☑ The "platters are huge" and early-bird specials the "best around" according to admirers of this "informal" Floribbean seafooder a block off Juno Beach; however, the "unimpressed" cite "cafeteria-quality" eats, "plain, diner-type" digs and "uninspired service", but even critics concede it's somewhat better "when the owner is there."

KATHY'S GAZEBO CAFE ☒   25 | 23 | 23 | $54 |
4199 N. Federal Hwy. (Spanish River Rd.), Boca Raton, 561-395-6033; www.kathysgazebo.com
☑ For more than 20 years, the Boca brigade has "dressed up" to dine at this "upscale", "traditional" Continental where the "Dover sole imported from heaven" is the signature and other "top-notch" dishes are "prepared with care"; though the "comfortable", "beautiful" setting is "stuffy" to some, and the "skilled" staff can be "frosty" "if you're not a regular", cafe society decrees it "the greatest."

KEE GRILL   25 | 22 | 22 | $41 |
17940 N. Military Trail (bet. Champion Ave. & Clint Moore Rd.), Boca Raton, 561-995-5044
14020 US 1 (Donald Ross Rd.), Juno Beach, 561-776-1167
☑ These Palm Beach county seafooders offer "consistently superb" fin fare as well as steaks and "fantastic side dishes", all at a "great value"; the "attractive", "casual" settings with "tropical" decor and "smooth-as-silk" service help ameliorate the "long waits" (no reservations in Juno but Boca books three weeks out) at these "favorites."

Kyoto Sushi ☻   24 | 20 | 20 | $34 |
25 NE Second Ave. (Atlantic Ave.), Delray Beach, 561-330-2275; www.kyotosushisake.com
■ "Very cool" conclude visitors to this downtown Delray Beach sushi specialist whose "SoBe vibe" and "club-

Palm Beach/Palm Beach County F | D | S | C

music sounds" draw "lively", "see-and-be-seen" sorts who "watch the video monitors" as chefs prepare "amazing, creative" rolls as well as "to-die-for" cooked Japanese dishes; take your chopsticks out in the courtyard or dine in the "spartan", "modern" main room, but know that ordering from the "big" à la carte menu and sake list can "run up the bill."

La Belle Epoque   22 | 19 | 22 | $49
253 SE Fifth Ave. (Atlantic Ave.), Delray Beach, 561-272-5800
■ The "lovely owners greet you" at this "elegant" New French in east Delray, a prelude to the "wonderful", "artistic" food and "great wines" ferried by the "friendly" staff; the setting's "modern" yet "charming", but it leaves critics "cold" along with the "overrated", "pricey" offerings; P.S. a new cafe has opened within the restaurant, serving "lighter fare" at lighter tariffs.

La Fonda Del Sol   – | – | – | E
730 US 1 (bet. N. Lake & PGA Blvds.), North Palm Beach, 561-844-0710
While surveyors mostly abstained from commenting on this Latin-Continental in North Palm Beach, those who did are fonda the "interesting" menu featuring paella and "delicious shrimp"; there's also a "romantic ambiance" in the dark interior with Spanish Colonial decor; N.B. dinner only.

Lake Avenue Grill   – | – | – | M
(fka Daniel's Lake Avenue Grill)
Gulf Stream Hotel, 1 Lake Ave. (Golfview Rd.), Lake Worth, 561-227-7230
Lake Worth's circa-1925 Gulfstream Hotel on the Intracoastal is undergoing an extensive renovation, as is its restaurant – a "hip, boutique" concept is in the works for both; the popular Sunday brunches and pool parties remain intact, though augmented by contemporary Continental fare; at press time, the eatery's scheduled to reopen late November.

Lana's Cafe   ∇ 18 | 10 | 21 | $35
78 S. Federal Hwy. (Palmetto Park Rd.), Boca Raton, 561-750-2494
■ A "diamond in the rough" in a "small storefront" setting, this Boca Raton neophyte shines with its "superb" New American fare such as "good crab cakes" and chocolate parfait for dessert; though there's "not much atmosphere", it's "not overpriced" either, and the "food is far superior to the surroundings."

L'Anjou   20 | 19 | 19 | $36
717 Lake Ave. (bet. J & K Sts.), Lake Worth, 561-582-7666
■ Providing a "taste of France" for over 25 years to the inhabitants of "quaint, Key West"-esque Lake Worth, this bistro offers some excellent old-school dishes like "delicious" escargot and "good boeuf bourguignon" at

Palm Beach/Palm Beach County | F | D | S | C |

"bargain" prices; the staff's "friendly" and there's "great late-night jazz" on weekends, but a few protesters walk away from "pedestrian" food and decor that "needs work."

La Petite Maison 🚫 | 23 | 22 | 23 | $46 |
366 E. Palmetto Park Rd. (US 1), Boca Raton, 561-750-7483
☑ "Say '*oui*'" to "a taste of France without the seven-hour flight" as devotees do when dining at this "cozy" "Paris-in-Boca" bistro serving "excellent", "elegant" Med-influenced fare; a "charming", "attractive" setting and "friendly" service help make it a "favorite", but a few find the offerings "pricey" and the food "old-fashioned."

La Trattoria | 21 | 16 | 20 | $33 |
Village Corner Stores, 6060 SW 18th St. (Palm D'oro Rd.), Boca Raton, 561-750-1296; www.bocatrattoria.com
■ A "hidden beauty" tucked into a Boca Raton shopping plaza, this "classy, little" Italian "gets raves" for its "outstanding" traditional dishes "sparked" by "surprising", "super specials"; the setting's "charming", the service is "excellent" and it's a "good value", but now that "the word's gotten out", you can expect "waits on Saturday nights."

La Tre | ∇ 23 | 9 | 19 | $27 |
249 E. Palmetto Park Rd. (Mizner Blvd.), Boca Raton, 561-392-4568
☑ Smug Boca Ratoners believe they're "lucky to have such a wonderful" Vietnamese in the area with a "creative menu" of "excellent" dishes "you'd have a hard time finding" elsewhere; despite "spartan decor" and "bad acoustics", it's "still a favorite" after nearly 15 years.

L'Avenue 🚫 | ∇ 24 | 19 | 13 | $15 |
4 S. O St. (Lake Ave.), Lake Worth, 561-540-4166
☑ Though still undiscovered by many, there's nonetheless a "wait" during the season for the "good, French-accented sandwiches" and "faves like salade niçoise" served at this "heavenly", "little" lunch-only bistro on Lake Worth's east side; regulars overlook occasional "rude" service and limited seating at this "jewel" for some of the "best" light fare around.

LA VIEILLE MAISON | 26 | 28 | 25 | $63 |
770 E. Palmetto Park Rd. (NE Olive Way), Boca Raton, 561-391-6701
☑ After more than 25 years, this Boca Raton "icon" remains "unwavering in its commitment to wonderful classic French cuisine" and devotees declare it "deserves its great reputation" for "fabulous" food, "exceptional wines" and "outstanding" service in its "gorgeous", multiroomed setting that garners the top Decor score in this *Survey*; even if *non*-sayers opine this old house is "past its prime" and deplore "snooty service", more maintain it's still "the gold standard."

Palm Beach/Palm Beach County F | D | S | C

La Villetta 21 | 18 | 20 | $44
4351 N. Federal Hwy. (43rd & 44th Sts.), Boca Raton, 561-362-8403
◪ The whole snapper baked in a salt crust is the star of a menu that "offers a wealth of choices" at this "upbeat" northeast Boca Raton Italian, and other dishes are "delicious" as well; the "caring service" and "elegant", "charming" atmosphere make it easy to "ignore the strip-mall setting" and "zero in on the food" instead.

Lazy Loggerhead Café 23 | 14 | 20 | $15
401 N. A1A (Carlin Park), Jupiter, 561-747-1134
■ Come direct from the dunes in your bathing suit for a "magically delicious" breakfast or lunch at this "casual", "excellent beachside cafe" in Jupiter's Carlin Park; "kids love" the "great", affordable American eats like hot dogs, and the "best dolphin sandwich"; there's only one hitch at this "raffishly charming" "hut" – "no reservations."

Le Brittany – | – | – | M
899A Prima Vista Blvd. (US 1), Port St. Lucie, 772-871-2231
Though few have traveled to this "oasis in the dining desert that is Port St. Lucie", those who have hail the "wonderful" French-Continental fare that focuses on seafood; perhaps the small storefront eatery in the corner of a shopping plaza is "not much on decor", but the bargain prix fixe dinners "delight" devotees.

Legal Sea Foods 19 | 18 | 17 | $34
CityPlace, 550 S. Rosemary Ave. (Okeechobee Blvd.), West Palm Beach, 561-838-9000; www.legalseafoods.com
See review in Ft. Lauderdale/Broward County Directory.

LE MISTRAL 25 | 19 | 23 | $47
Northbeach Plaza, 12189 US 1 (PGA Blvd.), North Palm Beach, 561-622-3009
■ This North Palm Beach "favorite" has Francophiles exclaiming "ooh-la-la!" over the "consistently" "delicious" Gallic fare presented in a "charming", "beautiful" interior featuring "comfortable banquettes"; though "perfect for special occasions", it's also acclaimed for its "good summer prix fixe menu", so boosters advise "bring your hunger and ignore your cholesterol."

Le Mont ⓢ 19 | 24 | 21 | $56
Northbridge Ctr., 515 N. Flagler Dr. (bet. 4th & 5th Sts.), West Palm Beach, 561-820-2442
◪ You "can't beat" the "million-dollar view" "overlooking the Gold Coast" from this Pittsburgh import high up in the Northbridge Center (aka the Darth Vader building) in downtown West Palm; while some insist the Continental cuisine is "excellent", more earthbound sorts say it "needs improvement"; still, it's "great for a business lunch" and the "early-bird is an excellent value."

vote at zagat.com

Palm Beach/Palm Beach County | F | D | S | C |

Leopard Lounge | 19 | 23 | 20 | $48 |
Chesterfield Hotel, 363 Cocoanut Row (Australian Ave.), Palm Beach, 561-659-5800; www.redcarnationhotels.com

◪ "Where nouveau billionaires mix with old-money aristocrats", this "Palm Beach original" in the Chesterfield Hotel is "quite the scene", serving "wickedly strong drinks" in a room dominated by "naked ladies painted on the ceiling" and "black, red and leopard-print decor"; the New American fare's "good, not great" and some wags tag it "spotty", but in season (when jackets are required), it's undeniably "people-watching heaven."

L'ESCALIER ☒ | 27 | 28 | 28 | $81 |
The Breakers, 1 S. County Rd. (Royal Palm Way), Palm Beach, 561-659-8480; www.thebreakers.com

■ For "world-class dining", it "doesn't get better" than this "opulent" New French stairway to heaven in Palm Beach's fabled Breakers Hotel; the "incredible" cuisine provides "total ecstasy on a plate" (a Versace plate, that is), the "exquisite", "romantic" setting is "the pinnacle of elegance" and the service is "top-notch" but "unpretentious" (earning it the No. 1 score in this *Survey*); though it's assuredly "expensive", even jaded connoisseurs confess they "never felt so good about spending so much."

Le Vieux Paris ☒ | ▽ 23 | 21 | 22 | $34 |
170 W. Camino Real (SW 2nd Ave.), Boca Raton, 561-368-7910

■ "Ladies who lunch" drop into this "homey French" bistro "off the beaten track" near downtown Boca after shopping while the "senior set" "enjoys the inexpensive dinners"; the "wonderful", "authentic" fare and "lovely surroundings" create a "relaxed", pleasant experience."

Linda B. of Boca Raton | 22 | 19 | 24 | $47 |
41 E. Palmetto Park Rd. (Federal Hwy.), Boca Raton, 561-367-0200

■ The "charming" "Linda B. makes everyone feel welcome" at this surf 'n' turfer near Boca's downtown, where the "excellent" food is "well prepared" and "delicious" ("don't miss the strawberry Napoleon") and the "small" storefront space in a shopping strip is "one of the loveliest in town"; an "older crowd" appreciates the "professional service" and the "personal attention" from the owner.

Little Moirs Food Shack ☒ | 23 | 13 | 19 | $24 |
103 US 1 (E. Indiantown Rd.), Jupiter, 561-741-3626

■ "From the looks and the name you'd expect a burger joint", but the specialty of this Jupiter "hole-in-the-wall" is "unbelievably fresh", "imaginative" seafood with "tropical flair", via a "chef sideshow in full view"; an enthusiastic crowd of "surfing and fishing" types apparently doesn't mind the "cramped" interior, "faux-island" decor and

Palm Beach/Palm Beach County F | D | S | C

"lackadaisical" servers some grouse about; N.B. closed for dinner Sunday–Tuesday.

Louie Louie ◐   17 | 17 | 18 | $30
201 E. Atlantic Ave. (SE 2nd Ave.), Delray Beach, 561-276-3600
See review in Ft. Lauderdale/Broward County Directory.

Lucca   ▽ 23 | 27 | 23 | $60
Boca Raton Resort & Spa, 501 E. Camino Real (Palmetto Dr.), Boca Raton, 561-447-5822; www.myriadrestaurantgroup.com
■ It's "tough to get a reservation" (members and guests only) at Drew Nieporent's "stunning" Northern Italian in the private Boca Raton Resort, but it's worth the effort to experience the "magnificent" views of the Intracoastal along with "rich", "divine" Tuscan-inspired fare; the setting's "magnificent" and the service is "top of the line", though a few mutter it's "overpriced"; P.S. there's a "fabulous private room" with a chef's table for special occasions.

Luna Pazza   – | – | – | E
171 E. Palmetto Park Rd. (Mizner Blvd.), Boca Raton, 561-391-1515
This new Boca Italian is known by few surveyors, but avid admirers are over the moon about the "interesting" cuisine using "fresh ingredients" and "wonderful sauces" for pasta; many feel that with its "fun atmosphere", it has the potential to "shine."

Maggiano's Little Italy   18 | 20 | 19 | $29
21090 St. Andrews Blvd. (bet. Glades & Palmetto Park Rds.), Boca Raton, 561-361-8244; www.maggianos.com
■ "Eat yourself into a stupor" at this chain link behind Boca Raton's Town Center mall where the "family-style" Italian offerings guarantee "doggy bags"; the food's "good", the staff's "super friendly" and the "big" space is "beautiful" and "upscale", but it's also "crowded" and "noisy", leading detractors to dis it as "much ado about average" ciao.

Maison Carlos ⌧   ▽ 22 | 20 | 21 | $40
207 Clematis St. (Narcissus Ave.), West Palm Beach, 561-659-6524
■ Providing a "breath of fresh air" in downtown West Palm Beach, this new bistro (a sibling to Renato's) attracts a "fun crowd" with a "wonderful combination of French and Italian dishes" including "good seafood" in a "casual" yet "sophisticated" atmosphere; "terrific" husband-and-wife team Lanie and Carlos Farias "make a concerted effort to please", and though grumps gripe it's "pricey", it's still a "great addition to Clematis Street."

MARCELLO'S LA SIRENA   26 | 19 | 22 | $50
6316 S. Dixie Hwy. (Forest Hill Blvd.), West Palm Beach, 561-585-3128; www.lasirenaonline.com
■ "A little bit of Mulberry Street" "hidden" in West Palm Beach, this "excellent" "New York–style" Italian

Palm Beach/Palm Beach County F | D | S | C

offers "delicious", "creative" cuisine using the "freshest ingredients" accompanied by "superb wines"; the "pleasant surroundings" create a "peaceful oasis" in an "out-of-the-way" location, and though the service can be "desultory" and the fare's "pricey", it remains a "longtime favorite"; N.B. closed July and August.

Marc's Chophouse   19 | 17 | 19 | $41
Fisherman's Wharf, 337 E. Indiantown Rd. (US 1), Jupiter, 561-747-2522

☑ "Excellent", "well-prepared" steaks hit the marc for mavens of this "elegant" "monument to chophouses" in Jupiter's Fisherman's Wharf, as do the "good early-dining specials" and "great piano bar entertainment"; even if naysayers nix the fare as "nothing special" and the interior as "tired", more report a "first-rate experience" (that includes dance bands Wednesday–Saturday).

Mario's of Boca   19 | 15 | 17 | $28
Holiday Inn, 1901 N. Military Trail (Glades Rd.), Boca Raton, 561-392-5595; www.mariosofboca.com

■ "All of Boca has managed to find" this Italian "mainstay" since its recent move to the Holiday Inn near the Interstate, and though the "new digs are nicer" and even "more impressive", it still serves the same "heavenly garlic rolls" and "sizable portions" of "good", "typical specialties like chicken parm" at "terrific" prices; the fact that you'll "wait for a table" doesn't deter devotees from descending on this "busy" spot.

Mario's Tuscan Grill   22 | 21 | 22 | $42
1450 N. Federal Hwy. (Glades Rd.), Boca Raton, 561-362-7407; www.mariostuscangrill.com

■ The "upscale" sibling to Mario's of Boca, this Northern Italian offers "sophisticated", "first-rate" fare that's "beautifully presented" in a "romantic", "comfortable" setting with a garden; "wonderful" service helps make it a "great place for impressing visitors", and even though it's "pricey", it's worth the "splurge" for such an "excellent experience"; P.S. it also has a "fun, little bar" that's a destination for "drinks and antipasti."

Mark's at the Park   22 | 21 | 20 | $45
Mizner Park, 344 Plaza Real (Mizner Blvd.), Boca Raton, 561-395-0770; www.chefmark.com

☑ "Everything's wonderful from bread to dessert" at Mark Militello's Mizner Park satellite, a Boca "hot spot" offering an "innovative" menu of "terrific", "high-quality" Med fare with regional accents served in a "classy", modern interior by an "excellent" staff; locals also laud the "great people-watching" provided by dining outside "under the umbrellas", though a few fume it's a "pricey" and "disappointing spin-off."

Palm Beach/Palm Beach County F | D | S | C

Mark's CityPlace   21 | 22 | 19 | $43
CityPlace, 700 S. Rosemary Ave. (Okeechobee Blvd.), West Palm Beach, 561-514-0770; www.chefmark.com
Chef Militello's West Palm CityPlace outpost is a "winner", with "beautiful", "chic" surroundings in which to dine on "marvelous" New American fare that includes "great pizzas" as well as "incredible" and "interesting" sushi like lobster maki; though the staff's "caring", "service can be harried" and the ambiance "loud", but most report an "extraordinary experience" that's "worth the price."

Max & Eddie's Cucina   – | – | – | M
2441 Beach Court (Blue Heron Blvd.), Singer Island, 561-842-5200
An experienced husband-wife team runs this small Italian just yards off Riviera Beach's shoreline with their down-pat formula for solid favorites – traditional Roma and American with an accent; the warm, red-brick and wood interior is a cozy backdrop for relaxing over a glass of vino from an award-winning list, and there's also delivery service to nearby hotels.

MAX'S GRILLE   22 | 20 | 20 | $36
Mizner Park, 404 Plaza Real (N. Federal Hwy.), Boca Raton, 561-368-0080; www.maxsgrille.com
"The beat goes on" at this "very Boca" Mizner Park "mainstay" where "power lunchers", shoppers and hipsters hail the "innovative" New American menu that features "consistently wonderful" dishes like its "outstanding" signature grouper along with an "extensive wine list"; the decor's "smart" and "casual" yet "romantic", the service is "considerate" and the prices are "reasonable"; P.S. "sit outside if you can and watch the beautiful people."

Maxwell's Chophouse   21 | 20 | 19 | $55
501 E. Palmetto Park Rd. (Intercoastal Waterway), Boca Raton, 561-347-7077
"A throwback" to the "great New York steakhouses", this "plush", "upscale" Boca meat market is a magnet for a "classy" crowd that stampedes for the "excellent" beef and "top" sides along with "great" cocktails mixed in a bar that affords "terrific eavesdropping opportunities"; a few are maxed out on the "condescending" service and "overpriced" offerings, but even if "it costs an arm and a leg", loyalists claim it's "worth every limb."

McCarty's ●   14 | 17 | 14 | $39
Royal Poinciana Plaza, 50 Cocoanut Row (south of Royal Poinciana Way), Palm Beach, 561-659-1899
Diners are divided about this Palm Beach newcomer near the Poinciana Playhouse, with proponents proclaiming it a "much-needed addition" serving "great" Traditional American fare from "delicious steaks, fish and mac 'n'

Palm Beach/Palm Beach County F | D | S | C

cheese to eggs and bacon at midnight"; cons call it "overpriced", with food that "misses", "slow service" and "uncomfortable chairs."

Melting Pot, The 20 | 18 | 19 | $37
5455 N. Federal Hwy. (north of NW 51st St.), Boca Raton, 561-997-7472
Palm Coast Plaza, 3044 S. Military Trail (10th Ave. N.), Lake Worth, 561-967-1009
www.meltingpot.com

■ Fondue's not only "back, it's in style", and this chain delights the DIY delegation with its "unique" "self-cooked" meals using "fresh", "fantastic ingredients" from "cheese to steak to chocolate" along with "exciting sauces for dipping"; neighsayers knock it as a "one-trick pony" and pout the place "reeks of oil", but more say it's "wonderful with a group" and for the "kids."

Mississippi Sweets BBQ 20 | 10 | 17 | $19
Charleston Sq., 6604 Hypoluxo Rd. (Jog Rd.), Lake Worth, 561-432-8555

■ Less-than-sweet surveyors "hope everyone rates this" Lake Worth BBQ joint "poorly" so they "won't have to wait in line" for their share of "the best", "messiest" babyback ribs and Brunswick stew (and the "sweet potato fries ain't chopped liver"); there's "no decor to speak of" and the dining area's "miniscule", but these are minor matters for "excellent" fare that's so well priced it's almost "free" served by a "happy staff"; the North Palm Beach branch has closed, dang it.

Mondo's 19 | 16 | 18 | $25
713 US 1 (Lighthouse Dr.), North Palm Beach, 561-844-3396

■ "You can't go wrong" with the "creative" New American–Mediterranean fare at this "clubby, warm" North Palm Beach "neighborhood" sports bar where "yuppies and newly retired" folks gather along the long dark-wood bar or in "comfortable booths"; the "menu has something for everyone" and provides "good value" as well.

Montezuma – | – | – | M
5607 S. Dixie Hwy. (Bunker Rd.), West Palm Beach, 561-586-7974

You might want to "practice Spanish" before going to this "no-atmosphere" storefront Mexican cantina in West Palm Beach as frequent fans have unexpectedly ordered some "odd but good" meals; overall, the food's "authentic", "outstanding" and "well priced", "especially at lunch."

Monty's Stone Crab 18 | 16 | 17 | $39
2300 Executive Center Dr. NW (Glades Rd.), Boca Raton, 561-994-5626; www.montysstonecrab.com
See review in Miami/Dade County Directory.

Palm Beach/Palm Beach County F | D | S | C

MORTON'S, THE STEAKHOUSE   24 | 21 | 23 | $56
Boca Ctr., 5050 Town Center Circle (Military Trail), Boca Raton, 561-392-7724
Phillips Point Office Bldg., 777 S. Flagler Dr. (Lakeview Ave.), West Palm Beach, 561-835-9664
www.mortons.com

You know what you're getting at this "dependable", "excellent" chain – "steer-sized steaks", preceded by "wonderful appetizers" followed by a "decadent" Godiva chocolate cake and other desserts served in an "old-school", "gentlemen's club ambiance"; the service, if slightly "pretentious", is "exceptional", but the offerings are "overpriced, even for good food" and many maintain this "franchise doesn't make the grade."

Mrs. Smokey's BBQ   – | – | – | I
3804 Northlake Blvd. (Sandtree Dr.), Palm Beach Gardens, 561-799-0885

What a New Yorker knows about barbecue might be questionable, but the owner of this casual newcomer off the interstate in Palm Beach Gardens has a good rep up north for ribs and chicken; bring the family and find out if the I.'Cue of the Gotham native cuts it in Southern Florida.

Mykonos   18 | 13 | 16 | $31
(fka Culinaros)
Wharfside Plaza, 6897 SW 18th St. (Powerline Rd.), Boca Raton, 561-338-3646

On weekends at this Boca Hellenic (formerly Culinaros), it's "like *My Big Fat Greek Wedding*": "customers and servers dance on tables" and "break dishes on purpose"; though the "decor's a little tacky" and the "music's awfully loud", the "outrageous" portions make it "a good value" "for a big group"; "eat before 7 PM" or outdoors by the lake to avoid the ruckus.

Nando's Beefeeder's Steakhouse   ▽ 21 | 15 | 20 | $32
3208 Forest Hill Blvd. (Congress Ave.), West Palm Beach, 561-649-4545

In addition to serving "amazing prime rib" and other steakhouse classics, this West Palm Beach "treat" offers "quality" Italian dishes including "to-die-for scampi" and the "best osso buco" supplemented by a "good salad bar"; "dark, old-school" decor, "pleasant service" and moderate prices are other reasons "you can't go wrong here."

NEW YORK PRIME   26 | 21 | 23 | $61
2350 Executive Center Dr. NW (Glades Rd.), Boca Raton, 561-998-3881; www.newyorkprime.com

"Yabba dabba Boca!" exclaim "devoted carnivores" before tucking into "gargantuan portions" of "excellent" steaks, "amazing" seafood and "great salads and sides" served at this "fabulous" "beef parlor"; the interior is

Palm Beach/Palm Beach County F | D | S | C

"beautiful" and service "doting", but its status as the "ultimate power scene" has parvenus pouting it's almost "impossible to get a reservation" at this "pricey" place as "only steady customers are taken care of"; still, loyalists believe it's "in a league of its own."

Nirvana – | – | – | E

Catalina Shops, 1701 N. Congress Ave. (Gateway Blvd.), Boynton Beach, 561-752-1932

This new slice of heaven in a Boynton shopping plaza is turning heads and palates with an unusual mix of Indo-Caribbean dishes from a talented toque; roti with tamarind chutney starts the meal and unusual dishes like the ginger-glazed sea bass with a Haden mango rum sauce are on offer.

No Anchovies! 16 | 12 | 16 | $24

PGA Plaza, 2650 PGA Blvd. (Prosperity Farms Rd.), Palm Beach Gardens, 561-622-7855; www.noanchovies.com

◪ For "good", "basic" Italian fare like pizza and pasta at "great prices", this Palm Beach Gardens storefront is a "solid", family-"friendly" choice; though naysayers aver the food's "average" and decry the "crowded", "noisy" atmosphere, more consider it an "enjoyable" alternative.

Off the Vine 20 | 19 | 17 | $29

5530 PGA Blvd. (Central Blvd.), Palm Beach Gardens, 561-799-6655

◪ Cafe Chardonnay's younger, more "casual" sibling in Palm Beach Gardens offers a "delightful", "broad" menu of American "comfort food" with "innovative twists" at "reasonable prices" for breakfast, lunch and dinner; the "charming" ambiance within and "wonderful outdoor dining" attract gaggles of golfers and locals, and those incensed by "inconsistent" service can visit the attached gourmet market for takeout.

Okeechobee Steakhouse 21 | 14 | 19 | $35

2854 Okeechobee Blvd. (Palm Beach Lakes Blvd.), West Palm Beach, 561-683-5151

◪ A circa-1947 "landmark", this West Palm steakhouse is considered a "classic" thanks to "consistently excellent" meats, a "superb salad bar" and "good desserts" at "reasonable prices"; the service is "prompt", and even though the decor has "seen better days", its fans hope this "old-fashioned" destination is around "forever."

Old Key Lime House 14 | 16 | 15 | $26

300 E. Ocean Ave. (bet. A1A & US 1), Lantana, 561-582-1889

◪ "Right on the Intracoastal" in a "historic" Lantana house, this circa-1889 seafooder is a "great" "old Florida–style" place to "bring the guests" or "pull up to in your boat"; even though the "usual fish and burger fare" is "not *très* gourmet", it is "satisfactory", and the "kid-friendly" setting and "beautiful views" make for a "relaxing" meal.

Palm Beach/Palm Beach County F | D | S | C

Orchids of Siam 17 | 13 | 17 | $23
Forest Hills Shopping Ctr., 3027 Forest Hill Blvd. (Congress St.), West Palm Beach, 561-969-2444

◪ For two decades, this "great neighborhood Thai" in a West Palm Beach shopping center has offered "terrific", "genuine" fare on "plates decorated with orchids" in a "relaxed atmosphere"; though a few feel it's "on the decline", cognoscenti are confident the "curry will keep you coming back"; P.S. try the "good early-bird."

OUTBACK STEAKHOUSE 19 | 14 | 18 | $26
6030 SW 18th St. (Palm D'Oro Rd.), Boca Raton, 561-338-6283
1300 Linton Blvd. (Wallace Dr.), Delray Beach, 561-272-7201
103 A-1 S. US 1 (Indiantown Rd.), Jupiter, 561-743-6283
6266 Lantana Rd. (Jog Rd.), Lake Worth, 561-963-7010
3101 SE Federal Hwy. (Indian St.), Stuart, 772-286-2622
871 Village Blvd. (Palm Beach Lakes Blvd.), West Palm Beach, 561-683-1011
www.outbacksteakhouse.com
See review in Keys/Monroe County Directory.

Out of Denmark ⌿ 23 | 18 | 20 | $41
1715 S. Federal Hwy. (Linton Blvd.), Delray Beach, 561-276-4950; www.outofdenmark.com

◪ "A delightful bit of Scandinavia" in Delray Beach, this "fabulous" "family-run" "find" delivers "delicious" Danish fare including complimentary gravlax and an "unbelievable appetizer smorgasbord" that's included with each entree; the "wonderful" owners and staff "care about their customers", and though a few waist-watchers dis-dane "too much food" and the "tiny" space can get "crowded", fervent followers claim "to know it is to love it."

Paddy Mac's ∇ 21 | 21 | 19 | $27
Garden Sq. Shoppes, 10971 N. Military Trail (PGA Blvd.), Palm Beach Gardens, 561-691-4366

■ You "can't go wrong" with this pub in a Palm Beach Gardens shopping center where the "traditional" Gaelic fare is "outstanding", the staff is "dynamite", the music is "excellent" and the prices are "good"; a "friendly" publican is "always there to help", and "lots of regulars" reason it's "just the way an Irish bar should be."

Padrino's 22 | 14 | 18 | $21
Mission Bay Plaza, 20455 State Rd. 7 (Glades Rd.), Boca Raton, 561-451-1070
See review in Ft. Lauderdale/Broward County Directory.

Painted Horse Café ⌧ ∇ 24 | 20 | 22 | $37
2417 S. Dixie Hwy. (north of Belvedere Rd.), West Palm Beach, 561-833-1490

■ Set in a "lovely" "renovated house" near downtown West Palm Beach, this New American colt could be the "find of

vote at zagat.com 193

Palm Beach/Palm Beach County F | D | S | C

the year"; the dishes are "hearty", "delectable" and "interesting" (but not "out there"), the wines are "excellent" (no liquor) and the "knowledgeable" staff's "on top of everything"; the "warm", "charming" interior with fireplaces makes it a "pleasant surprise that's worth a return visit."

Palm Beach Fish Market & Bistro — | — | — | M
3815 S Dixie Hwy. (Southern Blvd.), West Palm Beach, 561-835-0300; www.pbfishmarketandbistro.com
This new seafooder took over and polished up a previous market/restaurant on Antique Row in West Palm Beach and carries out the same theme – fresh fin fare at the market and on the plate; lighter lunches include chowder, salads and sandwiches, while you can hook stone crabs (in season) and fish cooked your way for dinner.

Palm Beach Grill 21 | 19 | 20 | $40
Royal Poinciana Plaza, 340 Royal Poinciana Way (Cocoanut Row), Palm Beach, 561-835-1077; www.palmbeachgrill.com
■ A "Houston's dressed up for the smart set", this "upscale" chain link delivers "outstanding" New American and steakhouse fare from high ("wonderful Dover sole") to low (the "best burgers") at "reasonable prices"; the setting's "great" for "informal" get-togethers "before the theater", and the "smiling" staff is "efficient"; its "popularity", however, can mean "long waits", even with reservations.

Park Ave. BBQ 21 | 11 | 18 | $17
4796 N. Congress Ave. (Hypoluxo Rd.), Boynton Beach, 561-357-7427
2401 N. Dixie Hwy. (Cornell Dr.), Lake Worth, 561-586-7427
525 US 1 (Anchorage Dr.), North Palm Beach, 561-842-7427
769 N. Federal Hwy. (US 1), Stuart, 772-692-0111
236 US 1 (Tequesta Dr.), Tequesta, 561-747-7427
13897 Wellington Trace Blvd. (Greenview Shores Blvd.), Wellington, 561-795-7427
2215 Palm Beach Lakes Blvd. (Village Blvd.), West Palm Beach, 561-689-7427
■ This "terrific" local 'cue chain may be more *Green Acres* than Park Avenue ("not pretty", decorwise), but it offers some of the "best", most "finger-lickin'" ribs and chicken around, along with "to-die-for potato salad and beans" and an "all-you-can-eat catfish special"; the grub's "inexpensive", service is "speedy", the joints are "clean" and "they play oldies – what more could you want?"; N.B. a Delray Beach branch is set to open at press time.

Peter's Stone Crabs 18 | 13 | 17 | $38
(nka Jimmy's Stone Crabs)
411 E. Atlantic Ave. (west of US 1), Delray Beach, 561-278-0036; www.petersstonecrabs.com
◪ "It's not Joe's", but then "neither are the prices" at this fin-and-claw specialist (now called Jimmy's) in downtown

194 subscribe to zagat.com

Palm Beach/Palm Beach County F | D | S | C

Delray Beach where the "stone crabs are great" and the service comes with a "smile"; landlubbers lament the rest of the offerings, however, maintaining they're "mediocre", and deplore the "depressing decor."

Pete's Boca Raton 19 | 21 | 20 | $41
7940 Glades Rd. (Florida Tpke.), Boca Raton, 561-487-1600; www.petesbocaraton.com
◪ "Enjoyable waterfront dining" in a "beautiful", "glitzy" setting draws "large parties" and "singles" to this longtime seafooder/steakhouse in west Boca; there may be "no surprises" on the menu, but the fare can be "terrific", the early-bird's "a steal" and the service is always "efficient"; if the "crowded, noisy" bar scene can seem "overwhelming", it also offers the benefit of "great people-watching."

P.F. CHANG'S CHINA BISTRO 21 | 20 | 19 | $28
University Commons, 1400 Glades Rd. (NW 10th Ave.), Boca Raton, 561-393-3722
The Gardens, 3101 PGA Blvd. (Campus Dr.), West Palm Beach, 561-691-1610
www.pfchangs.com
See review in Miami/Dade County Directory.

Piccadilly Cafeteria 13 | 8 | 11 | $12
2007 Palm Beach Lakes Blvd. (I-95), West Palm Beach, 561-686-4169; www.piccadilly.com
See review in Miami/Dade County Directory.

Pineapple Grille 20 | 20 | 19 | $33
Palm Trail Plaza, 800 Palm Trail (George Bush Blvd.), Delray Beach, 561-265-1368; www.pineapplegrille.com
■ There's "serious good cooking" going on at this "laid-back", "charming" Delray Beach "favorite", where the "excellent" Caribbean cuisine's "creative", spotlighting "delicious fish" and the wine list is "good and reasonably priced"; the interior's "cozy" and "bright", but "alfresco is easier on the ears" (unless you object to a "serenading guitarist"), and the "trusty staff makes it a perennial delight."

Pizza Girls Pizza 21 | 8 | 14 | $11
114 S. Clematis St. (bet. Flagler Dr. & Narcissus Ave.), West Palm Beach, 561-833-4004; www.pizzagirls.com
■ "As close to NYC pizza as you're gonna get" in SoFla, this "happening" parlor across from the fountain in downtown West Palm slings "generous slices" and "great-tasting" pies with "fantastic", "interesting" toppings; fans are also fired up over the "cute" decor and "super-friendly service" and insist "it's worth the drive from wherever you are."

Portofino's Italian Grill – | – | – | M
2447 N. Ocean Ave. (Beach Rd.), Singer Island, 561-844-2162
This oceansider on Riviera Beach has been around for a long time, but a new owner has revamped the menu with

vote at zagat.com

Palm Beach/Palm Beach County | F | D | S | C |

"excellent" "family-style Italian" dishes including pizza now served in an opened-up dining room with indoor-outdoor seating; regulars report it's "as good now as ever."

Pranzo | 18 | 18 | 17 | $37 |

Mizner Park, 402 Plaza Real (bet. Glades & Palmetto Park Rds.), Boca Raton, 561-750-7442

■ *Amici* of this Boca trattoria in Mizner Park call it a "great surprise" serving "delicious" Italian fare including "homestyle" pastas and the "freshest mozzarella" in a "nice" wood-lined setting; bashers insist it's "more of a bar scene", with "decent" food that's "close but no cigar."

Prezzo | 17 | 17 | 17 | $28 |

Stanford Corporate Plaza, 7820 Glades Rd. (Arvida Pkwy.), Boca Raton, 561-451-2800
Wellington Green Mall, 10300 W. Forest Hill Blvd. (US 441), Wellington, 561-333-1030
www.prezzo-international.com
See review in Miami/Dade County Directory.

RAINDANCER STEAKHOUSE | 24 | 18 | 23 | $42 |

2300 Palm Beach Lakes Blvd. (west of I-95), West Palm Beach, 561-684-2810; www.raindancer-steakhouse.com

■ "Well established" and locally owned, this West Palm steakhouse "favorite" is "top-notch" say surveyors who savor its "outstanding, fresh food", including a "fabulous salad bar" and some of the "best beef in the area", served by an "accommodating yet un-hovering" staff in a "romantic twilight" atmosphere; "the problem", impatient people purport, is that there's "always" a "long wait", "season or no season."

Redfire Grill | 22 | 20 | 21 | $35 |

2000 PGA Blvd. (west of US 1), Palm Beach Gardens, 561-776-0222

☑ "Creative, tasty grilled meats" and "fantastic seafood" add up to "good-value" "food without a lot of affectation" at this popular Palm Beach Gardens New American; oenophiles also toast the "great selection of wines" served by a "knowledgeable" staff in the "large room that manages to feel intimate", but fans of "dinner conversation" hope the new owners will work on the "deafening" noise.

REEF GRILL | 25 | 14 | 20 | $30 |

12846 US 1 (Juno Isles Blvd.), Juno Beach, 561-624-9924
251 S. US 1 (Indiantown Rd.), Jupiter, 561-746-8857

■ "Don't tell your friends" – these "local" "favorites" in Juno and Jupiter are "crowded enough", though regulars with reef madness don't mind the waits for "spectacular" seafood from an "awesome menu" of "exciting", Caribbean-accented dishes in "large" portions; even if the "casual" settings border on "divey", the "excellent" wines (no cocktails) are served in "quality" Reidel stemware.

196   subscribe to zagat.com

Palm Beach/Palm Beach County F | D | S | C

Renato's — 24 | 26 | 24 | $59
87 Via Mizner (Worth Ave.), Palm Beach, 561-655-9752; www.renatospalmbeach.com
■ It's "old money and old cuisine done right" at this "romantic" Italian "hideaway" in one of Palm Beach's vias off Worth Avenue, where the "beautiful" "European atmosphere" (including "lovely china" and "white-glove service") complements the "sumptuous" fare; it's "pricey" but "worth it", so "take a first date" and "eat outside" in the "perfect atmosphere" of its "beautiful" bougainvillea-draped courtyard — it could be "wine and roses forever."

Renzo's of Boca — 23 | 15 | 21 | $39
5999 N. Federal Hwy. (north of Yamato Rd.), Boca Raton, 561-994-3495; www.renzosofboca.com
◪ Owner Renzo Sciortino "makes you feel like you are dining in his home" at this "traditional" Italian in Boca Raton that "beats the competition" thanks to "flavorful" Sicilian fare; true, it's "a little pricey" and "not the prettiest" place around (and the "no-reservations" policy irks some), but an "expansion to two rooms" means "getting in is easier."

Rhythm Cafe ⊠ — 24 | 19 | 24 | $36
3800 S. Dixie Hwy. (½ block north of Southern Blvd.), West Palm Beach, 561-833-3406; www.rhythmcafe.cc
■ With its "hip", "kitschy", "rummage-sale" decor, this converted drugstore on West Palm Beach's Antique Row marches to the beat of a different drummer; a "cool" crowd is keen on the "creative", "fabulous" New American fare, "good wine selection" and "wonderful desserts" (it's "hard to resist the warm chocolate chip cookies"), and the "laid-back" staff and owners are "friendly" and "fun."

Riggin's Crabhouse — 20 | 13 | 19 | $28
607 Ridge Rd. (bet. I-95 & Lantana Rd.), Lantana, 561-586-3000; www.rigginscrabhouse.com
■ It's Maryland blue, stone and garlic "crab heaven" at this rustic, "good ol' boy" seafood shack tucked behind a shopping center off Lantana's I-95 exit; though it's "not fancy", the crustaceans are "delicious" (albeit "messy"), the portions are "huge" and "economically priced" and everyone "goes home happy as a clam."

River House — 23 | 23 | 23 | $43
2373 PGA Blvd. (Prosperity Farms Rd.), Palm Beach Gardens, 561-694-1188; www.riverhouse-restaurant.com
■ A "fab location" on the Intracoastal in PBG makes a "window seat" de rigueur at this "longstanding" "favorite" where the fare goes beyond the "standard surf 'n' turf" in the form of "exciting", "beautifully presented", "delicious" steak and seafood and a "wonderful, fresh" salad bar; the "no-reservations policy is a hassle" but is easily remedied by "having a drink on the deck and watching the yachts."

vote at zagat.com

Palm Beach/Palm Beach County F | D | S | C

ROMANO'S MACARONI GRILL   17 | 17 | 18 | $22
Executive Ctr., 2004 NW Executive Center Dr. (Military Trail), Boca Raton, 561-997-5492
Catalina Plaza, 1501 N. Congress Ave. (bet. Gateway Blvd. & Old Boynton Rd.), Boynton Beach, 561-734-0661
www.macaronigrill.com
See review in Miami/Dade County Directory.

Rottie's   ▽ 23 | 26 | 23 | $44
10900 S. Ocean Dr. (½ mi. north of Jensen Beach Cswy.), Jensen Beach, 772-229-7575; www.rottiescuisine.com
■ From the "wonderful ocean views" and "beautiful decor" to the "fabulous", "high-quality" American fare with "excellent wines" and the "friendly service", this "romantic" Jenson Beach seafooder "has everything"; it's a bit "pricey", but "worth it" for a "special occasion", and the "tiki bar offers live jazz and more casual dining."

RUTH'S CHRIS STEAK HOUSE   25 | 22 | 23 | $52
661 US 1 (Lighthouse Dr.), North Palm Beach, 561-863-0660; www.ruthschris.com
See review in Miami/Dade County Directory.

Saigon Sun ☒   – | – | – | I
545 Northlake Blvd. (US 1), North Palm Beach, 561-881-0882
For "authentic, delicious" Vietnamese, North Palm Beachers proclaim this tiny, family-run eatery a "great find" for house specialties like soups and chicken dishes and desserts like fried bananas; don't expect much in the decor department, but it's sun-sationally wallet-friendly.

Saigon Tokyo   – | – | – | M
2902 Jog Rd. (10th Ave. N.), Greenacres, 561-966-1288
The soups at this strip-mall storefront Asian in Greenacres are "so huge" and "delicious" they make an "inexpensive meal" when eaten alone, but don't pass up the "fresh", "beautifully presented" sushi and "nice combos"; if you want to be even thriftier, tap the "personable" servers for the Vietnamese menu, as the offerings are "half the price" of the Japanese dishes, and "just as tasty."

Sailfish Marina   18 | 23 | 16 | $29
98 Lake Dr. (¼ mile south of Blue Heron Blvd.), Palm Beach Shores, 561-842-8449; www.sailfishmarina.com
■ You don't have to own a yacht in order to appreciate the "consistently good" fish (and steaks for landlubbers) served at this old salt in Palm Beach Shores as it's on the water taxi route; the "very fresh" seafood may come from the charter boats that dock here, and it manages to be both "casual" and "romantic" indoors and out thanks to those "great marina views"; N.B. an oyster bar is planned.

Palm Beach/Palm Beach County F | D | S | C

Sandbar & Grill, The 18 | 16 | 17 | $26
Fisherman's Coast, 311 E. Indiantown Rd. (US 1), Jupiter, 561-743-7788

▣ "Tasty salads and seafood" satisfy supporters of this Jupiter shopping center New American that's a "great place for casual dining" with its "reasonable prices", "pleasant service" and "tropical decor"; critics carp that while it's "excellent for lunch", it's "only so-so for dinner" and find the ambiance "too loud" to be relaxing.

SAPORI ⓢ 24 | 18 | 21 | $40
Royal Palm Plaza, 301 Via de Palmas (bet. Federal Hwy. & SE 3rd St.), Boca Raton, 561-367-9779

■ Chef-owner Marco Pindo "is a maturing artist" whose "clever menu" features "fantastico" seafood and a "wonderful" selection of the "finest" pastas with "original" sauces at this upscale Boca Raton shopping center Italian; the setting is "charming", the staff "pays attention to detail" and if the offerings are a *poco* "expensive", it's worth it to be in on such an "impressive" "little secret."

Savanna's PB 12 | 14 | 14 | $43
375 S. County Rd. (Peruvian Ave.), Palm Beach, 561-832-2799

▣ Diners "either love or hate" this sister to Amici with a Southampton twin; pros proclaim it a "nice addition to the Palm Beach" scene, serving an "offbeat selection" of "good" New American fare in a "relaxing setting" that features "great outdoor seating"; cons consider the food "mediocre" and "overpriced" and the service "uneven"; N.B. closed in summer.

Schooner's Seafood 17 | 10 | 16 | $27
1001 N. A1A (US 1), Jupiter, 561-746-7558

■ Join the "locals" who make this "casual" fishery in Jupiter their "neighborhood" "hangout", and sit in the "open-air dining room" enjoying "great" fisherman's stew or burgers followed by "freshly baked desserts", all at "good prices"; even though the "young", "well-trained" staff is "efficient", you can expect the typical South Florida "wait in season."

Seaside Meeting Place ⓢ – | – | – | M
9120 SE Bridge Rd. (US 1), Hobe Sound, 772-545-3579

This seafooder near the bridge in Hobe Sound is "trying hard" and succeeding with "delicious" lobster rolls and its signature fried Ipswich clam roll, with other fare rating merely "standard"; it's a cheery place with diner-esque decor, serving breakfast, lunch, Sunday brunch and dinner Wednesday–Saturday till 8 PM.

SHULA'S STEAK HOUSE 21 | 20 | 22 | $52
PGA National Resort & Spa, 400 Ave. of the Champions (PGA Blvd.), Palm Beach Gardens, 561-627-4852

See review in Miami/Dade County Directory.

Palm Beach/Palm Beach County   F | D | S | C

Siam Gourmet   _|_|_| M
Sandalfoot Plaza, 23034 Sandalfoot Plaza Dr.
(bet. Hillsboro Blvd. & Palmetto Park Rd.), Boca Raton,
561-487-8414
The owner's daughter is the chef at this "lovely" Thai in a west Boca shopping center, and some insist the cuisine's the "best" in town, with "wonderfully flavorful" curries and spicy fish dishes; the service is "pleasant" and prices are reasonable, especially if you opt for the lunch and dinner prix fixe.

Sinclair's Ocean Grill   ∇ 23 | 21 | 19 | $43
Jupiter Beach Resort, 5 N. A1A (E. Indiantown Rd.),
Jupiter, 561-745-7120
A "hidden treasure" in a Jupiter resort, this New American is "overlooked" by many but may warrant hunting down for its "innovative" dishes including "excellent" seafood served in an "elegant", "lovely" setting; critics carp the "menu promises more than it delivers" and are "underwhelmed" by a "costly" experience.

Snappers   22 | 14 | 17 | $26
398 N. Congress Ave. (Old Boynton Rd.), Boynton Beach,
561-375-8600; www.snappers.com
Supporters snap up the "outstanding" signature planked halibut and other "terrific", "moderately priced" fish dishes served by a "friendly" staff at this "popular", "superior seafooder" in Boynton Beach; there's also an "extraordinary list of wines by the glass", which may help you endure the "long waits" due to the no-reservations policy.

Sopra   23 | 25 | 21 | $55
110 E. Atlantic Ave. (bet. 1st & 2nd Aves.), Delray Beach,
561-274-7077
It's advisable to "dress to kill" at this downtown Delray Beach "scene for the beautiful people", where the "chic" setting dotted with a "good-looking", "leather-clad" staff makes for a "Manhattan-like" experience; the Italian fare is equally "exquisite", arriving in "impressive portions" (try the "oversized" 18-layer chocolate cake), but "sky-high prices" and "attitude from the management" spur some to say it's "not worth the effort."

Sorrento   _|_|_| M
(fka No Anchovies!)
Village Commons, 771 Village Blvd. (Palm Beach Lakes Blvd.),
West Palm Beach, 561-684-0040
This Southern Italian in the cluster of restaurants on Village Boulevard in West Palm "recently changed hands and name", and new owners have dressed it up a bit with white tablecloths and more mature service; the menu's traditional though it offers nightly specials, and the all-you-can-eat buffet lunch is a rare bargain.

Palm Beach/Palm Beach County F | D | S | C

SPLENDID BLENDEDS CAFE ⓢ 24 | 13 | 20 | $37
432 E. Atlantic Ave. (S. Federal Hwy.), Delray Beach, 561-265-1035

■ "They really know what they're doing" at this "amazing but understated" Eclectic in downtown Delray that delivers "fabulous", "uniquely prepared dishes" including the "best snapper Française anywhere" (the "house specialty that's worthy of the designation"); the "charming" staff provides "outstanding" service, so the only drawback is the "small" "storefront facility" that's "cramped" and "noisy", and the "sidewalk tables afford fine views of the Atlantic Avenue action"; N.B. wine and beer only.

SPOTO'S OYSTER BAR 24 | 18 | 21 | $34
125 Datura St. (bet. N. Flagler Dr. & S. Narcissus Ave.), West Palm Beach, 561-835-1828

■ "The real deal for shellfish lovers" is this "terrific, little" seafooder, the "hip, hot and happening" "place to be" in downtown West Palm Beach; connoisseurs won't clam up about the "wonderful raw bar" and "extensive menu" of "flavorful fish" and "irresistible pastas", all at a "great value", served by "pros" in a "quaint", "casual" and "crowded" setting with sidewalk seating; N.B. Parrot Head alert: Jimmy Buffett's been known to stop by.

Spoto's PGA 22 | 21 | 21 | $37
4560 PGA Blvd. (Military Trail), Palm Beach Gardens, 561-776-9448

☑ An "offshoot of the West Palm Beach" original, this "trendy" PBG newcomer offers some of the "best and freshest seafood in the county", with its "outstanding raw bar", "fantastic crabmeat cocktail" and other classic fin fare; the staff's "excellent", which is critical to such a "popular" joint with "big crowds" and "small tables", even if a few contrarians complain of "disorganized" service and "long waits."

Stresa 22 | 12 | 20 | $33
2710 Okeechobee Blvd. (bet. Congress Ave. & Military Trail), West Palm Beach, 561-615-0200

☑ Its "strange location" in a West Palm Beach strip mall and "so-so decor belie the delicious food" proffered at this "small", "authentic" Italian; "large portions" of "excellent" pastas, "spectacular veal" and other dishes delivered by an "impeccable" staff that's "sooo fast it almost detracts" from the experience; even if it's "crowded" and "noisy", the "low prices" (especially at lunch) make it a "favorite" option.

Suite 225 ☽ – | – | – | E
225 E. Ocean Ave. (Dixie Hwy.), Lantana, 561-582-2255; www.suite225.net

This Asian fusion newcomer in east Lantana near the beach is a "nice change of pace" for the Palm Beach dining

Palm Beach/Palm Beach County F | D | S | C |

scene; a "chef who loves to please" oversees "excellent sushi" including rolls for those who don't do raw fish (lamb, beef), wok specialties and creative salads in the restaurant set under old oaks; an outdoor bar and a planned breakfast service sweeten the deal.

Sunset Grill — | — | — | M |
2500 Broadway (24th St.), West Palm Beach, 561-832-2722; www.sunsetbarandgrill.net
An imaginative take on American comfort food has Northwood denizens waiting anxiously for the sun to set, so they can sample the diverse offerings at this newcomer; contemporary art, mirrors and booths create an attractive setting, and the vibe's appropriate to its refurbished neighborhood in West Palm Beach.

Sushi Rok ∇ 22 | 14 | 19 | $31 |
106 N. Olive Ave. (Clematis St.), West Palm Beach, 561-802-9906
■ Chop-sticklers cheer this "trendy", "modern" downtown West Palm Beacher for serving "the best sushi around" along with other Japanese specialties as well as a range of sakes; lawyers and courthouse workers say it's "great for lunch" ("always good" and "fresh"), but don't look for rok-bottom prices, as it tends toward the "expensive" side.

Swiss Chalet 14 | 8 | 13 | $14 |
Delray Sq., 4961B W. Atlantic Ave. (Military Trail), Delray Beach, 561-496-5299
See review in Ft. Lauderdale/Broward County Directory.

Tabica Grill 20 | 18 | 20 | $31 |
The Woods Shopping Plaza, 901 W. Indiantown Rd. (Penock Ln.), Jupiter, 561-747-0108; www.tabica.com
■ "Forgive me, mother, but the best meatloaf" around is served at this "great neighborhood bistro" set in a Jupiter shopping center; the other New American offerings are "creative" and "all-around good", including "excellent pastas", and the "early-bird special is such a deal" (and includes several free drinks on select nights); though the "down-to-earth" digs can get "noisy" and "crowded", the staff's "friendly" and it remains a "locals' favorite."

TA-BOO 22 | 22 | 21 | $46 |
221 Worth Ave. (bet. Hibiscus Ave. & S. County Rd.), Palm Beach, 561-835-3500; www.tabooresturant.com
■ "After a hard day of shopping on Worth Avenue", the "rich and famous" nip into this "delightful" "old reliable" in Palm Beach for "outstanding" wine and "excellent" New American–Continental fare that ranges from "pizza to caviar"; the "gorgeous" interior is sprawled over several rooms (and has hosted the likes of the Windsors and Sinatra), and the servers "treat everyone well" under the owner's watchful eye; obviously, it's "elbow-to-elbow in

Palm Beach/Palm Beach County F | D | S | C

season", but since the elbows in question belong to local "household names", nobody seems to mind.

Testa's 15 | 14 | 16 | $33
221 Royal Poinciana Way (S. County Rd.), Palm Beach, 561-832-0992; www.testasrestaurants.com

A "Palm Beach fixture" since 1921, this Italian-American serves up "old-fashioned" breakfasts like the "best blueberry pancakes" and "fabulous desserts" like the signature strawberry pie; even though detractors "detesta" the "heavy, uninspired offerings" at dinner and bewail the "worn-out" decor, it still provides "good people-watching from the outdoor tables."

32 EAST 24 | 20 | 20 | $43
32 E. Atlantic Ave. (bet. SE 1st & Swinton Aves.), Delray Beach, 561-276-7868; www.32east.com

Chef Nick Morfogen "just keeps getting better" at this "high-velocity" Delray Beach Contemporary American on Atlantic Avenue where the "fresh, impeccably prepared" cuisine is "urbane without being pretentious", the 250-bottle wine list is "incredible" and the "excellent" staff "memorizes a new menu daily"; the "very W Hotel"–esque dining room features an open kitchen, and though it gets "noisy", there's a "relaxing" space upstairs; even if some pout it's "a little pricey for Florida", regulars retort "it never disappoints."

Tin Muffin Café, The 22 | 17 | 20 | $16
364 E. Palmetto Park Rd. (bet. Federal Hwy. & SE 4th Ave.), Boca Raton, 561-392-9446

"The perfect destination for a casual ladies' lunch", this east Boca Raton "favorite stop" offers what may be the "best mint lemonade", "incredible salads and sandwiches", "delightful desserts" and, of course, "great muffins"; the "adorable" space in a "tiny" house also features outdoor seating, and "even the bathrooms are charming"; N.B. closes at 5 PM.

Tom's Place 23 | 12 | 16 | $23
7251 N. Federal Hwy. (bet. Lindell Blvd. & Yamato Rd.), Boca Raton, 561-997-0920

"Get the bib ready" for some real "down-home soul food" at this "family-owned" east Boca barbecue vet vaunted for its "fantastic ribs" but also offering "amazing" Southern fried chicken, "must-try" catfish and "phenomenal cornbread"; perhaps the 300-seat interior's a bit "no-frills", but there's always takeout, and it's "worth the wait" anytime for the "best BBQ sauce" around.

Tony Roma's 18 | 13 | 16 | $22
365 N. Congress Ave. (Boynton Beach Blvd.), Boynton Beach, 561-736-6263; www.tonyromas.com
See review in Miami/Dade County Directory.

Palm Beach/Palm Beach County | F | D | S | C |

Too Bizaare ⊠   18 | 23 | 17 | $27 |
287 E. Indiantown Rd. (Intracoastal Pointe Dr.), Jupiter, 561-745-6262
■ No longer affiliated with its Lake Worth progenitor, this Jupiter "hot spot" offers a "comfortable", "interesting" setting with antiques for sale and a "nice variety" of Eclectic fare and "terrific" tapas as well as "excellent" wines; "great" "live music most nights" and a "friendly staff" keep it "boogeying."

TOO JAY'S GOURMET DELI   19 | 11 | 15 | $18 |
Polo Shops, 5030 Champion Blvd. (bet. Clint Moore Rd. & Military Trail), Boca Raton, 561-241-5903
Regency Court Plaza, 3013 Yamato Rd. (Jog Rd.), Boca Raton, 561-997-9911
The Bluffs, 4050 US 1 (Marcinski Rd.), Jupiter, 561-627-5555
419 Lake Ave. (S. Federal Hwy.), Lake Worth, 561-582-8684
Royal Poinciana Plaza, 313 Royal Poinciana Way (Cocoanut Row), Palm Beach, 561-659-7232
Loehman's Plaza, 4084 PGA Blvd. (I-95), Palm Beach Gardens, 561-622-8131
Regency Sq., 2504 SE Federal Hwy. (Monterey Rd.), Stuart, 772-287-6514
Treasure Coast Plaza, 555 21st St. (US 1), Vero Beach, 772-569-6070
Wellington Green Mall, 10300 Forest Hill Blvd. (Rte. 441), Wellington, 561-784-9055
www.toojays.com
◪ Some "New York transplants" think they've died and gone to the "Lower East Side" when they "satisfy their pastrami cravings" at this "great deli" chain offering "heaps of meat" on "delicious rye bread" as well as "chicken soup like mom's" and "awesome black-and-white cookies" served by an appropriately "sassy" (even "surly") staff; the jay-ded claim "Katz's it ain't" and lament the "long lines", but more maintain it's "worth it" for a "fix."

Trevini   23 | 22 | 22 | $50 |
Esplanade Bldg., 150 Worth Ave. (bet. Ocean Blvd. & S. County Rd.), Palm Beach, 561-833-3883;
www.treviniristorante.com
■ This "jewel" in Palm Beach's Esplanade sparkles with "beautifully prepared", "inspired" fare from a "diverse and interesting" Italian menu served in an "elegant", even "breathtaking" setting; the "polished" staff is "gracious" (and the "host will charm the pants off you"), and even though this Stresa sibling is "expensive", it's a "good addition to Worth Avenue."

Tropical Bistro ⊠   – | – | – | M |
940 Park Ave. (10th St.), Lake Park, 561-845-5436
A "real find – if you can find it", this "cute" "hole-in-the-wall" in Lake Park provides "excellent" Caribbean fare

Palm Beach/Palm Beach County F | D | S | C |

Tsunami 23 | 27 | 18 | $54 |
CityPlace, 651 Okeechobee Blvd. (Rosemary Ave.),
West Palm Beach, 561-835-9696; www.tsunamirestaurant.com
☒ "So stylish you won't believe it's in West Palm Beach", this new CityPlace "stunner" appeared "like a hurricane" and the "ultra-beautiful people" who've been swept up call it "a knockout"; though the "gorgeous" decor takes top billing, the Asian fusion fare is also "exquisite" including "excellent" sushi, and the "*très* groovy" bar shakes up some "great" cocktails; though the "inexperienced" service and "pricey" offerings have some storming off, most "hope it makes it."

264 the Grill 17 | 18 | 18 | $39 |
264 S. County Rd. (Royal Palm Way), Palm Beach, 561-833-6444
☒ The "Palm Beachiest crowd in town" ("you might even see men wearing jackets") descends upon this "solid performer" for the "excellent early-bird" special; the "good", "consistent" American-Continental fare spotlighting steaks and seafood, "comfortable" setting and a "friendly" staff suit supporters, but a few foes feel the cuisine's "unimaginative" and deem the decor "dated."

Uncle Tai's 23 | 21 | 21 | $36 |
Boca Ctr., 5250 Town Center Circle (bet. Glades & Palmetto Park Rds.), Boca Raton, 561-368-8806
☒ "As upscale as Boca Chinese gets", this longtimer in Town Center Circle is considered a "must-go" for "elegant presentations" of "outstanding" Hunan-style dishes "cooked to order"; the "chic" setting is "lovely" and service is "excellent", but many are fit to be tai'ed over the "small portions" and "overpriced" fare.

Vangelli's Greek Taverna ● ▽ 21 | 18 | 18 | $30 |
319 Clematis St. (Olive St.), West Palm Beach, 561-655-4681
■ Though few have discovered this "wonderful" taverna since its recent opa'ning in downtown West Palm Beach, those who have cheer its "excellent food" with "enough variety" on the meze menu to "share a bunch of appetizers" as the "oversized interior" makes it "great for groups"; on weekend nights you're advised to "bring your dancing shoes" and warned "don't fall off the table!"

Wilt Chamberlain's ● 13 | 15 | 15 | $21 |
Somerset Shoppes, 8903 W. Glades Rd. (Lyons Rd.), Boca Raton, 561-488-8881
☒ The late Dipper "would be proud" to see his "sports-themed" namesake "still thriving" boast boosters of this Boca "family" destination where "TVs, hoops and video

| Palm Beach/Palm Beach County | F | D | S | C |

games" and "Wilt paraphernalia" are a "treat for dads and kids" ("bring lots of quarters"); "inexpensive", "big portions" of "standard sports bar fare" and more "health-conscious selections" score points, while the "bar scene" is a zone for the "twenties set", but the "below-average" eats and "over-the-top" noise get a facial from foes.

ZEMI 25 | 23 | 22 | $50

Boca Ctr., 5050 Town Center Circle (S. Military Trail), Boca Raton, 561-391-7177; www.dinezemi.com

■ "Boca to the max", this "posh" New American provides primo "people-watching" while you feast on "superb", "innovative" and "well-executed" New American fare with an "Asian twist" and select from an "eclectic wine list"; the "cool" decor is "understated" and "sophisticated", and "dining outside is always a treat"; either way, the "service is excellent", and though wallet-watchers whisper it's "expensive", it's "fun" to "spoil yourself rotten."

Indexes

CUISINES
LOCATIONS
SPECIAL FEATURES

Indexes list the best of many within each category.

All restaurants are in Miami/Dade County unless otherwise noted (B=Broward County; K=Keys/Monroe County; P=Palm Beach County).

Cuisine Index

CUISINES

American (New)
Atlantic's Edge/K
Barracuda Grill/K
Barton G.
Big City Tavern/B
Big City Tavern/P
Bin 595/B
Bistro Mezzaluna/B
Bistro Zenith/P
Boulevard Grille/P
Brasserie Las Olas/B
Brasserie Mon Ami/P
Bungalow 9/B
By Word of Mouth/B
Cafe Chardonnay/P
Cafe Marquesa/K
Café Protégé/P
Cobblestone Cafe/P
Costello's/B
DaDa/P
Dakotah 624/P
Darrel/Oliver's Bistro/B
Darrel/Oliver's Cafe/B
East City Grill/B
11 Maple St./P
Falcon House/P
Four Seasons/P
Gallery Grille/P
Grill Room/B
Hi-Life Cafe/B
Himmarshee/B
Icebox Café
Jake's
Johannes/P
Lana's Cafe/P
Leopard Lounge/P
Mariposa
Mark's CityPlace/P
Mark's Las Olas/B
Max's Beach Pl./B
Max's Grille/B
Max's Grille/P
Metro Kitchen
Michael's Kitchen/B
Mondo's/P
Nemo

Norman's
One Duval/K
Painted Horse/P
Palm Beach Grill/P
Pelican Café
Pilar
Pisces/K
Redfire Grill/P
Restaurant St. Michel
Rhythm Cafe/P
Rumi
Sandbar & Grill/P
Savanna's PB/P
Sinclair's/P
Snook's/K
Soyka
Square One/K
Sunfish Grill/B
Tabica Grill/P
Ta-boo/P
Talula
3030 Ocean/B
32 East/P
Touch
1220 at the Tides
Two Chefs
Van Dyke Cafe
Zemi/P

American (Traditional)
Ambry/B
America/P
Aquatica Beach Bar
Bentley's/K
Beverly Hills Cafe
Beverly Hills Cafe/B
Beverly Hills Cafe/P
Big Pink
Bimini Boatyard/B
Boston's/P
Brewzzi/P
B's Rest./K
Camille's/K
Charley's Crab/B
Charley's Crab/P
Chart House

Cuisine Index

Cheeburger Cheeburger/P
Cheesecake Factory
Cheesecake Factory/B
Cheesecake Factory/P
Christine Lee's
Chuck & Harold's/P
Dan Marino's
Dan Marino's/B
Dave's Last Resort/P
Dune Deck Cafe/P
Duval Beach Club/K
11th St. Diner
E.R. Bradley's/P
Flanigans Loggerhead
Fox's Sherron Inn
Front Porch Cafe
Ganim's/K
Geronimos Bar & Grill/B
Gibby's Steaks/B
Gordon Biersch Brewery
Green's Pharmacy/P
Grille, The/P
Hard Rock Cafe
Hard Rock Cafe/K
Harry and the Natives/P
Henry's/P
Hog's Breath Saloon/K
Hops/B
Hops/P
Houston's
Houston's/B
Houston's/P
Hurricane Café/P
J. Alexander's/B
J. Alexander's/P
Jimmy Buffett's/K
Joe Allen
John G's/P
Kelly's Caribbean/K
Lazy Loggerhead/P
Lorelei/K
Louie's Backyard/K
Magnum
Mangos/B
Martha's Supper Club/B
Max & Eddie's/P
McCarty's/P
Michaels/K
Mrs. Mac's Kitchen/K
News Cafe
Off the Vine/P
O'Hara's Hollywood/B
Old Cutler Inn
Piccadilly Caf.
Piccadilly Caf./B
Piccadilly Caf./P
PT's Late Night/K
River House/B
Roadhouse Grill
Roadhouse Grill/B
Rottie's/P
Rusty Anchor/K
S&S Rest.
Seven Mile/K
Sheldon's
Sloppy Joe's/K
Squid Row/K
Sunset Grill/P
Sunset Tavern
Swiss Chalet/B
Swiss Chalet/P
Testa's/P
Tin Muffin/P
Titanic Brewery
Tobacco Rd.
Two Friends Patio/K
264 the Grill/P
Whale Harbor Inn/K
White Lion
Wilt Chamberlain's/P
Wings 'N Things/B

Argentinean
Argentango Grill/B
Graziano's
Las Vacas Gordas
Novecento
Tango Grill
Zuperpollo

Barbecue
Bar-B-Q Barn
Hong Kong City BBQ/B
Meteor Smokehse./K
Mississippi Sweets/P

Cuisine Index

Mrs. Smokey's BBQ/P
Park Ave. BBQ/P
Pit Bar-B-Q
Porky's Bayside/K
Shorty's BBQ
Shorty's BBQ/B
Time Out BBQ/K
Tom Jenkins BBQ/B
Tom's Place/P
Tony Roma's
Tony Roma's/B
Tony Roma's/P

Brazilian
Porcão
SushiSamba dromo
Wish

Cajun
Creolina's/B
811 Bourbon St./B
Ziggie's/K

Californian
Wolfgang Puck Cafe/B

Caribbean
Azul
Bagatelle/K
Bahama Breeze
Bahama Breeze/B
Bin 595/B
Café Solé/K
Caffe Vialetto
Calypso Rest./Raw Bar/B
Christine's Roti Shop
Citronelle
Dining Rm./Little Palm/K
Grass Lounge
Hot Tin Roof/K
Kelly's Caribbean/K
Louie's Backyard/K
Mangoes/K
Max's Beach Pl./B
Nicola Seafood/K
Nirvana/P
One Duval/K
Ortanique on Mile
Papa's/K
Pineapple Grille/P
Reef Grill/P
Sugar Reef/B
Tropical Bistro/P
Turtle Kraals/K

Chinese
(* dim sum specialist)
Bamboo Garden
Bamboo Garden/B*
Christina Wan's/B
Christine Lee's
Ginger Wok/P
Hong Kong City BBQ/B*
Mai-Kai/B
New Chinatown
Pao
P.F. Chang's
P.F. Chang's/P
Rainbow Palace/B
Red Lantern
Silver Pond/B
Tony Chan's
Tropical Chinese*
Two Dragons
Uncle Tai's/P
Yeung's Chinese

Coffeehouses
Cafe Demetrio
Leigh Ann's Coffee/K

Coffee Shops/Diners
Bagels & Co.
Camille's/K
Deli, The/K
Dennis Pharmacy/K
11th St. Diner
Flamingo
Gables Diner
Green's Pharmacy/P
Jumbo's
Lester's Diner/B
Manny & Isa's/K
News Cafe
Picnics at Allen's
S&S Rest.
Sheldon's

Colombian
Mama Vieja

Cuisine Index

Continental
Addison/P
Biscayne Wine
Bistro, The/P
Bizcaya Grill
Black Orchid Cafe/B
Bohemian Gardens/P
Boulevard Grille/P
Brooks/B
Cafe Cellini/P
Cafe L'Europe/P
Courtyard Grill/P
Crystal Cafe
811 Bourbon St./B
Finnegan's Wake Pub/K
Fleming
Food Lover's Cafe/B
Gallagher's Gourmet/K
Gotham City/P
Kathy's Gazebo /P
La Fonda Del Sol/P
Lake Avenue Grill/P
La Paloma
Le Brittany/P
Le Mont/P
Marker 88/K
Martin's Cafe/K
Old Tavernier/K
Piccadilly Garden
Runyon's/B
Ta-boo/P
Tropical Bistro/P
264 the Grill/P
Wine Cellar/B
Yesterday's/B

Creole
Creolina's/B
811 Bourbon St./B
Ziggie's/K

Cuban
Ayestaran
Bahamas Fish Mkt.
Bongos
B's Rest./K
Cabana/P
Café Cardozo
Casa Larios
Cuban Cafe/P
David's Cafe
Disco Fish
Don Ramon's/P
El Colonial/P
El Siboney/K
Havana/P
Havana Harry's
Islas Canarias
Joe's Seafood
La Carreta
La Carreta/B
La Casita
Lario's
Las Culebrinas
Las Vegas/B
Latin American
Lila's
Lincoln Road Café
Little Havana
Manny & Isa's/K
Molina's
Padrino's/B
Padrino's/P
Puerto Sagua
Sergio's
Versailles
Yuca

Danish
Fleming
Out of Denmark/P

Delis
Arnie & Richie's Deli
Bagel Emporium
Bagels & Co.
Deli Lane Cafe
Dennis Pharmacy/K
Too Jay's Deli/P

Dessert
By Word of Mouth/B
Escopazzo
Grandma's French Cafe/B
Outback Steakhouse

Eclectic
Alice's at La-te-da/K
Aura
Balans

vote at zagat.com

Cuisine Index

Berries
Bizaare Ave. Cafe/P
Café Cardozo
Café Tu Tu Tango
Cohiba Brasserie/B
Crazy Buffet/P
Darrel/Oliver's Cafe/B
Globe Cafe & Bar
Grand Café Key West/K
Himmarshee/B
Hot Tin Roof/K
Icebox Café
Mango's
Nexxt Cafe
Nikki Beach
One Ninety
Pearl
Pescado
Pierre's/K
Splendid Blendeds/P
Sublime/B
Tantra
Teté Rest.
Too Bizaare/P
Victoria Park/B

English
Blue Anchor Pub/P
John Bull English Pub/P

Floribbean/New World
Baleen
Blue Heaven/K
Chef Allen's
De La Tierra/P
Flagler Grill/P
Juno Beach Fish/P
Kaiyó/K
Mark's Las Olas/B
Mark's South Beach
Morada Bay Beach/K
Norman's
Satine/B

Fondue
Melting Pot
Melting Pot/B
Melting Pot/P

French
Brasserie Mon Ami/P
Café Boulud/P
Cafe du Parc/P
Café Solé/K
Chez Jean-Pierre/P
Crepe Christina/B
Croissants de France/K
Dining Rm./Little Palm/K
Forge, The
French Bakery Cafe
French Place/B
French Quarter/B
Green Street Cafe
La Sandwicherie
La Vieille Maison/P
Le Brittany/P
Le Cafe de Paris/B
Les Deux Fontaines
Maison Carlos/P
Melody Inn
Mo's/K
Palme d'Or
Sugar Reef/B

French (Bistro)
A La Folie
Banana Cafe/K
Cafe Claude/B
Café La Bonne Crepe/B
Café Pastis
Chez Andrée/B
Cobblestone Cafe/P
GiGi's Tavern/P
Grandma's French Cafe/B
La Creperie/B
L'Anjou/P
La Petite Maison/P
L'Avenue/P
Le Bouchon du Grove
Le Festival*Casa
Lemon Twist
L'Entrecôte de Paris
Le Provençal
Les Halles
Le Vieux Paris/P
Provence Grill
Sage French/B

Cuisine Index

French (New)
Azul
B.E.D.
Blue Door
Hanna's Diner
La Belle Epoque/P
La Vie en Rose/B
Le Mistral/P
L'Escalier/P
Pascal's on Ponce
Wish

German
Ambry/B
Bavarian Village/B
Dab Haus
Edelweiss
Fritz & Franz Bierhaus
Martin's Cafe/K

Greek
Athena by the Sea/B
Greek Island Taverna/B
Mykonos
Mykonos/P
Ouzo's Greek
Taverna Opa
Taverna Opa/B
Vangelli's/P

Haitian
TapTap

Hamburgers
Beverly Hills Cafe
Beverly Hills Cafe/B
Beverly Hills Cafe/P
Big Pink
Cheeburger Cheeburger/B
Cheeburger Cheeburger/P
Gables Diner
Hamburger Heaven/P
Hard Rock Cafe
Hard Rock Cafe/K
Hog's Breath Saloon/K
Jimmy Buffett's/K
Roadhouse Grill
Roadhouse Grill/B

Scotty's Landing
Tobacco Rd.

Health Food
Artichoke's
Berries
Granny Feelgood's
Here Comes the Sun
Miami Juice
Oasis Cafe
Sublime/B
Sunshine & AJ's
Tasti D-Lite

Hot Dogs
Dogma

Ice Cream Parlor
Grandma's French Cafe/B
Picnics at Allen's
Tasti D-Lite

Indian
Anokha
Christine's Roti Shop
House of India
Imlee
India House/B
Kebab Indian
Madras Café/B
Nirvana/P
Punjab Palace
Raja
Renaisa

Indonesian
Bali Café
Indigo/B

Irish
Brogue's/P
Finnegan's Wake Pub/K
John Martin's
Maguire's Hill 16/B
Paddy Mac's/P

Italian
(N=Northern; S=Southern)
Abbondanza/K
Ago (N)

vote at zagat.com 213

Cuisine Index

Amalfi
Amici Ristorante/P
Anacapri
Angelo of Mulberry/B
Anthony's Runway 84/B (S)
Antonia's/K
Arturo's/P (N)
Basilico (N)
Bellagio/P
Bella Luna (N)
Bellante's Pizza
Bellante's Pizza/B
Bice Ristorante (N)
Bice Ristorante/P (N)
Big Cheese
Big Fish
Bistro Zinc
Bongusto! Rist./B
Botticelli
Brewzzi/P
Buca di Beppo/B (S)
Bugatti, Art of Pasta (N)
Buonasera/P
Cafe Avanti (N)
Cafe Bellino/P (N)
Cafe Martorano/B
Cafe Med
Café Med/K
Cafe Prima Pasta (N)
Café Ragazzi
Cafe Vico/B (N)
Caffe Abbracci (N)
Caffe Da Vinci
Caffe Luna Rosa/P
Caffe Milano (N)
Caffe Vialetto
Capri Blu/P
Capriccio/B
Cardello's Pizza/P
Carmine's Ocean Grill/P
Carnevale (N)
Carpaccio
Casa D'Angelo/B
Casa Tua
Conca D'Oro/B
Couco Pazzo/P
Cucina Dell' Arte/P

da Ermanno (S)
da Leo Trattoria (N)
Escopazzo
Fancy's (S)
Fish 54
Frankie's Pier 5/B (S)
Fulvio's 1900/B (N)
Gianni's/B (S)
Gil Capa's Bistro
Grappa (N)
Grazie Cafe (N)
Hosteria Romana
Il Mulino/B (N)
Il Sole (N)
Il Toscano/B (N)
Il Trullo/P (N)
Josef's/B (N)
La Gastronomia
La Loggia (N)
La Lupa di Roma
La Palma (N)
La Tavernetta/B (N)
La Trattoria/K (S)
La Trattoria/P
Laurenzo's Cafe
La Villetta/P
Le Festival*Casa
Leigh Ann's Coffee/K
Little Italy/K
Locanda Sibilla (N)
Lombardi's
Louie Louie/B
Louie Louie/P
Lucca/P (N)
Luna Pazza/P (N)
Macaluso's
Maggiano's Little Italy/P (S)
Maison Carlos/P
Mama Jennie's
Mangia Mangia/K
Marcello's La Sirena/P
Mario's of Boca/P
Mario's Tuscan/P (N)
Mario the Baker (S)
Mario the Baker/B (S)
Max & Eddie's/P
Mezzanotte

subscribe to zagat.com

Cuisine Index

Mezzanotte/B
Nando's Beefeeder's/P
No Anchovies!/P
Oggi Caffe
Old Tavernier/K
Opera Italian/K
Osteria del Teatro (N)
Paulo Luigi's
Pellegrino's/B (S)
Peppy's in Gables (N)
Perricone's
Pino's (N)
Piola (N)
Portofino's/P
Pranzo/P (N)
Prezzo
Prezzo/P
Primavera/B (N)
Puccini & Pasta
Randazzo's (S)
Regalo/B
Renato's/P
Renzo's of Boca/P
Ristorante La Bussola (N)
Roasted Pepper/B (S)
Romano's Mac. Grill
Romano's Mac. Grill/B
Romano's Mac. Grill/P
Romeo's Cafe (N)
Rosinella (S)
Ruggero's/B
Salute/K
Sapori/P
Scopa/B (S)
Solo Trattoria/B (N)
Sopra/P (N)
Sorrento/P (S)
Spiga (N)
Splendido
Sport Cafe
Stefano's
Stresa/P (N)
Tarantella/B
Testa's/P
Timo
Timpano Italian/B
Tiramesu (N)

Trattoria Luna (N)
Trattoria Sole (N)
Trevini/P
Tuscan Steak (N)
Tutto Pasta
Vizio Cafe

Japanese
(* sushi specialist)
Ambrosia/K*
Benihana/B
Benihana/K
Benihana/P
Benihana/Samurai
Blue Sea*
Bond St. Lounge*
Doraku*
Fujihana*
Galanga/B*
Hiro Japanese*
Ichiban/B
Ichiban/P
Japanese Village Steakhse./B
Kaiyó/K
Kampai*
Kyoto Sushi/P*
Maiko*
Mark's CityPlace/P*
Matsuri*
Miyako*
Nami/B
Nobu Miami Beach*
Origami/K*
Redfish Bluefish/B*
Ruen Thai*
Saigon Tokyo/P*
Sakana/B*
Sakura*
Shibui*
Shoji*
Suite 225/P*
Sushi Maki*
Su Shin*
Su Shin/B
Sushi Rock*
Sushi Rok/P*
Sushi Saigon*

vote at zagat.com 215

Cuisine Index

SushiSamba dromo*
Sushi Siam*
Tambo Rest.
Thai House II*
Tokyo Bowl*
Tokyo Bowl/B*
Tokyo Sushi/B*
Toni's Sushi*
Tsunami/P*
Wan's Sushi/B*
World Resources*
Yasuko's*

Korean
Kyung Ju

Kosher
Eilat Cafe/P
Moroccan Nights
Prime Grill
Sara's

Lebanese
Khoury's

Malaysian
Indigo/B

Mediterranean
Abbey Dining Rm.
Aria
Athena by the Sea/B
Bizcaya Grill
Café Ibiza
Cafe Med
Café Med/K
Casablanca Cafe/B
City Cellar Wine/P
Elia
Giorgio's Grill/B
Green Street Cafe
Il Fico
Khoury's
La Brochette /B
La Dorada
La Petite Maison/P
Mark's at Park/P
Mondo's/P
Nina Rest.
Oasis Cafe
Salute/K
Timo
1200 at the Biltmore
Two Sisters

Mexican
Anita's Mexicano/B
Baja Fresh Mexican Grill
Carlos & Pepe's/B
Chico's Cantina/K
Eduardo de San Angel/B
El Rancho Grande
El Toro Taco
Jalapeños Mexican Kitchen/B
La Valentina
Montezuma/P
Mrs. Mendoza's
Old Town Mexican/K
San Loco
San Loco/B
Señor Frijoles/K
Señor Frog's
Tequila Sunrise

Middle Eastern
Daily Bread
Ferdo's Grill/B
Maroosh
Miami Juice
Original Daily Bread

Moroccan
Moroccan Nights

Nicaraguan
El Novillo
Guayacan
Los Ranchos
Yambo

Nuevo Latino
Cabana/P
Cacao 1737
Carmen
Chispa
La Fonda Del Sol/P
Samba Rm./B
Yuca

subscribe to zagat.com

Cuisine Index

Pan-Asian
Bamboo Club
Bamboo Club/P
Bin 595/B
Cafe Sambal
China Grill
Echo/P
Grass Lounge
Lan
Pacific Time
Red Coral/B
Suite 225/P
Tsunami/P
Two Dragons
Wolfgang Puck Cafe/B

Persian
Caspian Persian Grill/B

Peruvian
Chalán/El Chalán
Francesco
Nobu Miami Beach
SushiSamba dromo
Tambo Rest.
Tumi/B

Pizza
Andiamo! Pizza
Archie's Pizza
Bellante's Pizza
Bellante's Pizza/B
Blu la Pizzeria
Bugatti, Art of Pasta
California Pizza Kit.
California Pizza Kit./B
California Pizza Kit./P
Cardello's Pizza/P
Cucina Dell' Arte/P
La Gastronomia
Mario the Baker
Mario the Baker/B
Mark's CityPlace/P
No Anchovies!/P
No Name Pub/K
Piola
Pizza Girls Pizza/P
Pizza Rustica

Pizza Rustica/B
Prezzo
Prezzo/P
Solo Trattoria/B
Spris
Tutto Pizza

Portuguese
Old Lisbon

Pub Food
Bar, The
Blue Anchor Pub/P
Brogue's/P
John Bull English Pub/P
John Martin's
Maguire's Hill 16/B
No Name Pub/K
Paddy Mac's/P

Puerto Rican
Old San Juan

Sandwiches
Arnie & Richie's Deli
Bagel Emporium
Bagels & Co.
Cafe Demetrio
Deli, The/K
Deli Lane Cafe
Gallery Grille/P
La Sandwicherie
La Spada's Hoagies/B
L'Avenue/P
Paninoteca
Perricone's
Too Jay's Deli/P

Seafood
A&B Lobster/K
A Fish Called Avalon
AltaMar
Anchor Inn/P
Argentango Grill/B
Aruba Beach Cafe/B
Bagatelle/K
Bahamas Fish Mkt.
Baleen
Banana Boat/P

Cuisine Index

Bayside Grill/K
Bayside Seafood
Big Fish
Bimini Twist/P
Blue Moon Fish/B
Bonefish Grill/B
Bonefish Willy's/B
B.O.'s Fish Wagon/K
Busch's Seafood/P
Cafe Marquesa/K
Calypso Rest./Raw Bar/B
Calypso's Seafood/K
Cap's Place Island/B
Captain's Tavern
Carmine's Ocean Grill/P
Casablanca Cafe/B
Castaways/K
Catfish Dewey's/B
Charley's Crab/B
Charley's Crab/P
Chart House
City Oyster/P
Commodore Waterfront/K
Conch Republic/K
Conchy Joe's Seafood/P
Crab House
Crab Pot/P
Crack'd Conch/K
Cracked Conch Cafe/K
Dave's Last Resort/P
Disco Fish
Duffy's Steak/K
15th St. Fisheries/B
Fish 54
Fish House/K
Fish Joynt
Flagler's/K
Francesco
Frank Keys Cafe/K
Garcia's
Gibby's Steaks/B
Green Turtle Inn/K
Grillfish
Gus' Grille/K
Half Shell Raw Bar/K
Herbie's/K
Hobo's Fish Joint/B

Hurricane Grill/K
I & J's Station Hse./P
Islamorada Fish/B
Islamorada Fish/K
JB's on the Beach/B
Jetty's/P
Joe's Crab Shack/B
Joe's Riverside Grille/B
Joe's Seafood
Joe's Stone Crab
Juno Beach Fish/P
Kee Grill/P
Keys Fisheries/K
La Vie en Rose/B
Lazy Loggerhead/P
Legal Sea Foods/B
Legal Sea Foods/P
Les Deux Fontaines
Linda B./Boca Raton/P
Little Moirs Food /P
Lorelei/K
Mangoes/K
Mangrove Mama's/K
Marker 88/K
Martha's/K
Monte's Fish Mkt./K
Monty's Stone Crab
Monty's Stone Crab/P
Morada Bay Beach/K
Nicola Seafood/K
Old Cutler Oyster
Old Florida/B
Old Key Lime/P
Palm Beach Fish/P
Papa Joe's/K
Papa's/K
Pepe's Cafe/K
Pescado
Peter's Stone Crabs/P
Pete's Boca Raton/P
Pilar
Pisces/K
Quay, The/K
Quinn's Rest.
Redfish Bluefish/B
Red Fish Grill
Reef Grill/P

Cuisine Index

Riggin's Crabhse./P
River House/B
River House/P
River Oyster Bar
Rottie's/P
Rustic Inn Crabhse./B
Rusty Anchor/K
Rusty Pelican
Sailfish Marina/P
Schooner's Seafood/P
Scotty's Landing
Seafood World/B
Seaside Meeting Pl./P
Seawatch/B
Seven Fish/K
Shirttail Charlie's/B
Shooters/B
Shula's on the Beach/K
Snapper's/K
Snappers/P
Spoto's Oyster/P
Spoto's PGA/P
Squid Row/K
Sundays on Bay
Sundowners on the Bay/K
Sunfish Grill/B
Tarpon Bend/B
3030 Ocean/B
Timpano Italian/B
Tuna's Waterfront
Turtle Kraals/K
Whale Harbor Inn/K
Whale's Rib/B

Singaporean
Indigo/B

Soul Food
Tom's Place/P

Southern
Catfish Dewey's/B
Jumbo's
Piccadilly Caf.
Piccadilly Caf./B

Southwestern
Armadillo Cafe/B
Canyon/B

Spanish
(* tapas specialist)
Alcazar
Cafe Seville/B
Casa Juancho
Casa Paco
Casa Panza
Diego's
La Barraca/B*
La Dorada
Las Culebrinas
Torero
Two Sisters

Steakhouses
A&B Lobster/K
Andre's Steakhse./B
Angelo & Maxie's/P
Argentango Grill/B
Bayside Grill/K
Benihana/B
Benihana/K
Benihana/P
Benihana/Samurai
Ben's Steakhse./P
Capital Grille
Christy's
Chuck's Steakhse./B
Chuck's Steakhse./P
Commodore Waterfront/K
Conchy Joe's Seafood/P
Dan Marino's
Dan Marino's/B
Duffy's Steak/K
El Novillo
Flagler's/K
Flagler Steakhse./P
Forge, The
Ganim's/K
Gibby's Steaks/B
Graziano's
Hollywood Prime/B
Jackson's Steakhse./B
JB's on the Beach/B
Las Vacas Gordas
Linda B./Boca Raton/P
Linda B. Steakhse.
Los Ranchos
Marc's Chophse./P

vote at zagat.com

Cuisine Index

Martha's/K
Maxwell's Chophse./P
Morton's
Morton's/P
Nando's Beefeeder's/P
New York Prime/P
Okeechobee/P
Outback Steakhouse
Outback Steakhouse/B
Outback Steakhouse/K
Outback Steakhouse/P
Palm
Palm Beach Grill/P
Pepe's Cafe/K
Pete's Boca Raton/P
Prime Grill
Quay, The/K
Raindancer Steakhouse/P
River House/P
Ruth's Chris
Ruth's Chris/B
Ruth's Chris/P
Shooters/B
Shula's on the Beach/B
Shula's on the Beach/K
Shula's Steak
Shula's Steak House/P
Smith & Wollensky
Sundowners on the Bay/K
Tango Grill
Timpano Italian/B
Tropical Acres/B
Tuscan Steak

Swiss
Melody Inn

Tex-Mex
Paquito's
Taco Rico
Texas Taco

Thai
Bangkok Bangkok
Bangkok Bangkok
Fujihana
Galanga/B
Jasmine Thai/B
Kampai
Orchids of Siam/P
Panya Thai
Red Thai Rm.
Ruen Thai
Siam Cuisine/B
Siam Gourmet/P
Siam Lotus
Siam Palace
Sushi Maki
Sushi Siam
Thai Cuisine/K
Thai House So. Bch.
Thai House II
Thai Orchid
Thai Spice/B
Thai Toni
World Resources

Uruguayan
Zuperpollo

Vegan
Sublime/B
Sunshine & AJ's

Vegetarian
Christina Wan's/B
Granny Feelgood's
Here Comes the Sun
Sara's

Vietnamese
Cay Da/P
Hy-Vong
La Tre/P
Little Saigon
Miss Saigon
Saigon Sun/P
Saigon Tokyo/P
Sushi Saigon

Location Index

LOCATIONS

MIAMI/DADE COUNTY

Coconut Grove/Kendall/South Miami
Anokha
Bahama Breeze
Baleen
Bangkok Bangkok
Benihana/Samurai
Berries
Beverly Hills Cafe
Bice Ristorante
Big Cheese
Bizcaya Grill
Blu la Pizzeria
Botticelli
Cafe Med
Café Pastis
Café Tu Tu Tango
Casa Larios
Casa Paco
Chart House
Cheesecake Factory
Dan Marino's
Deli Lane Cafe
Flanigans Loggerhead
Fox's Sherron Inn
Fujihana
Gil Capa's Bistro
Grappa
Green Street Cafe
Kampai
Khoury's
La Carreta
La Casita
Lan
Las Culebrinas
Latin American
Le Bouchon du Grove
Los Ranchos
Mezzanotte
Monty's Stone Crab
New Chinatown
Old Cutler Inn
Original Daily Bread
Outback Steakhouse
Paulo Luigi's
P.F. Chang's
Picnics at Allen's
Pino's
Prezzo
Puccini & Pasta
Punjab Palace
Red Lantern
Romano's Mac. Grill
Scotty's Landing
Señor Frog's
Sergio's
Shibui
Shorty's BBQ
Siam Lotus
Siam Palace
Sunset Tavern
Sushi Maki
Su Shin
Sushi Siam
Taco Rico
Tony Roma's
Trattoria Luna
Trattoria Sole
Two Chefs

Coral Gables
Amalfi
Archie's Pizza
Bagel Emporium
Baja Fresh Mexican Grill
Bangkok Bangkok
Bar, The
Bugatti, Art of Pasta
Cacao 1737
Cafe Demetrio
Café Ibiza
Caffe Abbracci
Caffe Vialetto
Carmen
Chispa
Christy's

vote at zagat.com

Location Index

Diego's
Francesco
Fritz & Franz Bierhaus
Gables Diner
Globe Cafe & Bar
Havana Harry's
House of India
Houston's
Jake's
John Martin's
La Casita
La Dorada
La Gastronomia
La Palma
Latin American
Le Festival*Casa
Le Provençal
Les Halles
Los Ranchos
Mariposa
Maroosh
Melody Inn
Miss Saigon
Moroccan Nights
Norman's
Ortanique on Mile
Palm
Palme d'Or
Pascal's on Ponce
Peppy's in Gables
Pescado
Randazzo's
Red Fish Grill
Restaurant St. Michel
Ristorante La Bussola
Ruth's Chris
Sakura
Splendido
Spris
Sushi Maki
Su Shin
Taco Rico
Tambo Rest.
Tequila Sunrise
Texas Taco
Thai Orchid
Titanic Brewery

1200 at the Biltmore
Two Sisters
Yasuko's

Design Dist./Upper East Side
Andiamo! Pizza
Citronelle
da Ermanno
Dogma
Edelweiss
Grass Lounge
Il Fico
Magnum
One Ninety
Piccadilly Garden
Renaisa
Soyka
Sushi Siam

Downtown/Biscayne
(Including Brickell Area and Miami River)
Azul
Bali Café
Big Fish
Bongos
Cafe Sambal
Capital Grille
Deli Lane Cafe
Garcia's
Gordon Biersch Brewery
Granny Feelgood's
Hard Rock Cafe
Joe's Seafood
Jumbo's
La Loggia
Las Culebrinas
Lombardi's
Los Ranchos
Miyako
Morton's
Perricone's
Porcão
Provence Grill
Raja
River Oyster Bar
Rosinella

Location Index

S&S Rest.
Tobacco Rd.
Tony Chan's
Torero
Tutto Pasta
Tutto Pizza
Zuperpollo

Key Biscayne
Archie's Pizza
Aria
Bayside Seafood
La Carreta
Linda B. Steakhse.
Rusty Pelican
Stefano's
Sundays on Bay
Sushi Siam
Tango Grill
Two Dragons

Little Havana/Coral Way
Ayestaran
Casa Juancho
Casa Panza
Guayacan
Hy-Vong
Islas Canarias
La Carreta
Molina's
Mykonos
Old Lisbon
Outback Steakhouse
Romeo's Cafe
Sergio's
Teté Rest.
Versailles
Yambo

Miami Beach
(Including Bal Harbour, Bay Harbor Island, Sunny Isles Beach, Surfside, etc.)
Aquatica Beach Bar
Arnie & Richie's Deli
Benihana/Samurai
Cafe Avanti
Cafe Prima Pasta
Café Ragazzi
Caffe Da Vinci
Carpaccio
Christine Lee's
Crab House
Crystal Cafe
Elia
Forge, The
French Bakery Cafe
Las Vacas Gordas
Lemon Twist
Mama Vieja
Miami Juice
Moroccan Nights
Nina Rest.
Oasis Cafe
Oggi Caffe
Outback Steakhouse
Ouzo's Greek
Palm
Sheldon's
Shula's Steak
Tasti D-Lite
Timo
Tony Roma's
Yeung's Chinese

North Dade
(Including Aventura, North Miami and North Miami Beach)
Artichoke's
Bagels & Co.
Bamboo Club
Bamboo Garden
Bar-B-Q Barn
Bella Luna
Bellante's Pizza
Biscayne Wine
Bistro Zinc
Cheesecake Factory
Chef Allen's
Christine's Roti Shop
Fish 54
Fish Joynt
Fujihana
Hanna's Diner
Here Comes the Sun
Hiro Japanese
Houston's
Kampai
Kebab Indian

vote at zagat.com

Location Index

Kyung Ju
La Paloma
Laurenzo's Cafe
La Valentina
Little Havana
Little Saigon
Mama Jennie's
Mario the Baker
Melting Pot
Morton's
Outback Steakhouse
Paninoteca
Panya Thai
Paquito's
P.F. Chang's
Piccadilly Caf.
Pilar
Prezzo
Prime Grill
Red Thai Rm.
Roadhouse Grill
Romano's Mac. Grill
Sara's
Thai House II
Tokyo Bowl
Tuna's Waterfront
Vizio Cafe

South Beach
Abbey Dining Rm.
A Fish Called Avalon
Ago
A La Folie
AltaMar
Aura
Balans
Barton G.
B.E.D.
Big Pink
Blue Door
Blue Sea
Bond St. Lounge
Café Cardozo
Caffe Milano
Carnevale
Casa Tua
Chalán
China Grill
Dab Haus
Daily Bread
da Leo Trattoria
David's Cafe
Doraku
11th St. Diner
El Rancho Grande
Escopazzo
Front Porch Cafe
Grillfish
Hosteria Romana
Icebox Café
Il Sole
Joe Allen
Joe's Stone Crab
La Lupa di Roma
Lario's
La Sandwicherie
L'Entrecôte de Paris
Les Deux Fontaines
Lincoln Road Café
Locanda Sibilla
Macaluso's
Maiko
Mango's
Mark's South Beach
Metro Kitchen
Monty's Stone Crab
Nemo
News Cafe
Nexxt Cafe
Nikki Beach
Nobu Miami Beach
Novecento
Osteria del Teatro
Pacific Time
Paninoteca
Pao
Pearl
Pelican Café
Piola
Pizza Rustica
Puerto Sagua
Quinn's Rest.
Rosinella
Ruen Thai

Location Index

Rumi
San Loco
Señor Frog's
Shoji
Smith & Wollensky
Spiga
Sport Cafe
Spris
Sunshine & AJ's
Sushi Rock
Sushi Saigon
SushiSamba dromo
Sushi Siam
Talula
Tantra
TapTap
Taverna Opa
Texas Taco
Thai House So. Bch.
Thai Toni
Tiramesu
Tokyo Bowl
Toni's Sushi
Touch
Tuscan Steak
1220 at the Tides
Van Dyke Cafe
Wish
World Resources
Yuca

South Dade
Anacapri
Benihana/Samurai
Captain's Tavern
Daily Bread
El Toro Taco
Fancy's
Flamingo
Fleming
Grazie Cafe

Imlee
Latin American
Melting Pot
Old Cutler Oyster
Taco Rico
Tony Roma's
White Lion

West Dade
Alcazar
Bahamas Fish Mkt.
Basilico
Beverly Hills Cafe
California Pizza Kit.
Casa Larios
Chalán/El Chalán
Disco Fish
El Novillo
Graziano's
Guayacan
Islas Canarias
La Carreta
La Casita
Latin American
Lila's
Los Ranchos
Matsuri
Molina's
Mrs. Mendoza's
Old San Juan
Outback Steakhouse
Piccadilly Caf.
Pit Bar-B-Q
Romano's Mac. Grill
Sakura
Sergio's
Shorty's BBQ
Shula's Steak
Tony Roma's
Tropical Chinese

THE KEYS/MONROE COUNTY

Key West
A&B Lobster
Abbondanza
Alice's at La-te-da
Ambrosia

Antonia's
Bagatelle
Banana Cafe
Benihana
Blue Heaven

vote at zagat.com

Location Index

B.O.'s Fish Wagon
B's Rest.
Cafe Marquesa
Café Med
Café Solé
Camille's
Chico's Cantina
Commodore Waterfront
Conch Republic
Croissants de France
Deli, The
Dennis Pharmacy
Duffy's Steak
Duval Beach Club
El Siboney
Finnegan's Wake Pub
Flagler's
Grand Café Key West
Half Shell Raw Bar
Hard Rock Cafe
Hog's Breath Saloon
Hot Tin Roof
Jimmy Buffett's
Kelly's Caribbean
La Trattoria
Louie's Backyard
Mangia Mangia
Mangoes
Martha's
Martin's Cafe
Meteor Smokehse.
Michaels
Monte's Fish Mkt.
Mo's
Nicola Seafood
Old Town Mexican
One Duval
Opera Italian
Origami
Papa's
Pepe's Cafe
Pisces
PT's Late Night
Salute
Seven Fish
Shula's on the Beach
Sloppy Joe's

Square One
Thai Cuisine
Turtle Kraals
Two Friends Patio

Lower Keys
Dining Rm./Little Palm
Mangrove Mama's
No Name Pub
Rusty Anchor

Middle Keys
Barracuda Grill
Castaways
Cracked Conch Cafe
Gallagher's Gourmet
Herbie's
Hurricane Grill
Keys Fisheries
Leigh Ann's Coffee
Little Italy
Porky's Bayside
Quay, The
Seven Mile

Upper Keys
Atlantic's Edge
Bayside Grill
Bentley's
Calypso's Seafood
Crack'd Conch
Fish House
Frank Keys Cafe
Ganim's
Green Turtle Inn
Gus' Grille
Islamorada Fish
Kaiyó
Lorelei
Manny & Isa's
Marker 88
Morada Bay Beach
Mrs. Mac's Kitchen
Old Tavernier
Outback Steakhouse
Papa Joe's
Pierre's
Señor Frijoles

Location Index

Snapper's
Snook's
Squid Row
Sundowners on the Bay

Time Out BBQ
Whale Harbor Inn
Ziggie's

FT. LAUDERDALE/BROWARD COUNTY

Ft. Lauderdale
Ambry
Andre's Steakhse.
Angelo of Mulberry
Anthony's Runway 84
Big City Tavern
Bimini Boatyard
Bistro Mezzaluna
Black Orchid Cafe
Blue Moon Fish
Bongusto! Rist.
Brasserie Las Olas
Buca di Beppo
Bungalow 9
By Word of Mouth
Café La Bonne Crepe
Cafe Martorano
Cafe Seville
Cafe Vico
California Pizza Kit.
Canyon
Carlos & Pepe's
Casablanca Cafe
Casa D'Angelo
Charley's Crab
Cheeburger Cheeburger
Cheesecake Factory
Chuck's Steakhse.
Creolina's
Crepe Christina
Dan Marino's
Darrel/Oliver's Bistro
Eduardo de San Angel
Ferdo's Grill
15th St. Fisheries
Food Lover's Cafe
French Quarter
Grandma's French Cafe
Greek Island Taverna
Grill Room

Hi-Life Cafe
Himmarshee
Hops
Houston's
Il Mulino
India House
Indigo
Jackson's Steakhse.
J. Alexander's
Japanese Village Steakhse.
Las Vegas
La Tavernetta
Le Cafe de Paris
Lester's Diner
Louie Louie
Maguire's Hill 16
Mai-Kai
Mangos
Mark's Las Olas
Max's Beach Pl.
Max's Grille
Mezzanotte
Outback Steakhouse
Pizza Rustica
Rainbow Palace
Red Coral
Regalo
River House
Roadhouse Grill
Ruggero's
Rustic Inn Crabhse.
Ruth's Chris
Sage French
Samba Rm.
San Loco
Scopa
Shirttail Charlie's
Shooters
Shula's on the Beach
Solo Trattoria

vote at zagat.com

Location Index

Sublime
Swiss Chalet
Tarpon Bend
Taverna Opa
Thai Spice
3030 Ocean
Timpano Italian
Tokyo Bowl
Tokyo Sushi
Tom Jenkins BBQ
Tropical Acres
Victoria Park
Wine Cellar
Wings 'N Things
Yesterday's

Greater Ft. Lauderdale
(Including Lauderdale-by-the-Sea, Oakland Park and Wilton Manors)
Aruba Beach Cafe
Athena by the Sea
Benihana
Catfish Dewey's
Costello's
Galanga
Gibby's Steaks
La Spada's Hoagies
Old Florida
Primavera
Seawatch
Siam Cuisine

Northeast Broward County
(Including Deerfield Beach, Lighthouse Point and Pompano Beach)
Bellante's Pizza
Brooks
Cafe Claude
Calypso Rest./Raw Bar
Cap's Place Island
Charley's Crab
Darrel/Oliver's Cafe
French Place
Gianni's
Hops
Houston's
JB's on the Beach
Joe's Riverside Grille
Madras Café
Pellegrino's
Roadhouse Grill
Seafood World
Sunfish Grill
Whale's Rib

Northwest Broward County
(Including Coral Springs, Margate and Tamarac)
Anita's Mexicano
Bellante's Pizza
Beverly Hills Cafe
Bonefish Grill
Bonefish Willy's
Cheeburger Cheeburger
Dan Marino's
Hobo's Fish Joint
Hong Kong City BBQ
Hops
Jasmine Thai
La Spada's Hoagies
La Vie en Rose
Lester's Diner
Melting Pot
Outback Steakhouse
Piccadilly Caf.
Roadhouse Grill
Romano's Mac. Grill
Runyon's
Tony Roma's

Southeast Broward County
(Including Dania Beach, Hallandale and Hollywood)
Argentango Grill
Bavarian Village
Beverly Hills Cafe
Chez Andrée
Christina Wan's
Conca D'Oro
Frankie's Pier 5
Fulvio's 1900
Giorgio's Grill
Hollywood Prime

Location Index

Islamorada Fish
Martha's Supper Club
Michael's Kitchen
O'Hara's Hollywood
Padrino's
Redfish Bluefish
Sakana
Satine
Sugar Reef
Taverna Opa
Tony Roma's
Tumi
Wan's Sushi

Southwest Broward County
(Including Cooper City and Pembroke Pines)
Bahama Breeze
Bamboo Garden
Bellante's Pizza
Beverly Hills Cafe
Capriccio
Cheeburger Cheeburger
Cohiba Brasserie
Hops
Jalapeños Mexican Kitchen
La Brochette
La Carreta
Las Vegas
Nami
Outback Steakhouse
Roadhouse Grill
Roasted Pepper
Romano's Mac. Grill
Tony Roma's

West Broward County
(Including Davie and Weston)
Armadillo Cafe
Buca di Beppo
Cheeburger Cheeburger

East City Grill
Geronimos Bar & Grill
Ichiban
Il Toscano
La Spada's Hoagies
Max's Grille
Roadhouse Grill
Shorty's BBQ
Tarantella
Tarpon Bend

West Central Broward County
(Including Lauderhill, Lauderdale Lakes, Plantation and Sunrise)
Bahama Breeze
Beverly Hills Cafe
Bin 595
Caspian Persian Grill
Cheeburger Cheeburger
Cheesecake Factory
811 Bourbon St.
Hops
Jalapeños Mexican Kitchen
J. Alexander's
Joe's Crab Shack
Josef's
La Barraca
La Creperie
Las Vegas
Legal Sea Foods
Lester's Diner
Mario the Baker
Outback Steakhouse
Padrino's
Piccadilly Caf.
Romano's Mac. Grill
Silver Pond
Su Shin
Wolfgang Puck Cafe

PALM BEACH/PALM BEACH COUNTY

Central Palm Beach County
America
Amici Ristorante

Anchor Inn
Angelo & Maxie's
Bellagio
Ben's Steakhse.

vote at zagat.com

Location Index

Bice Ristorante
Big City Tavern
Bimini Twist
Bizaare Ave. Cafe
Bohemian Gardens
Brewzzi
Brogue's
Cabana
Café Boulud
Cafe Cellini
Cafe L'Europe
Café Protégé
California Pizza Kit.
Capri Blu
Charley's Crab
Cheeburger Cheeburger
Cheesecake Factory
Chez Jean-Pierre
Chuck & Harold's
City Cellar Wine
Couco Pazzo
Crazy Buffet
Cucina Dell' Arte
Dave's Last Resort
Don Ramon's
Dune Deck Cafe
Echo
E.R. Bradley's
Flagler Steakhse.
Four Seasons
Ginger Wok
Green's Pharmacy
Hamburger Heaven
Havana
Hops
I & J's Station Hse.
Il Trullo
John Bull English Pub
John G's
Lake Avenue Grill
L'Anjou
L'Avenue
Legal Sea Foods
Le Mont
Leopard Lounge
L'Escalier
Maison Carlos
Marcello's La Sirena
Mark's CityPlace
McCarty's
Melting Pot
Mississippi Sweets
Montezuma
Morton's
Nando's Beefeeder's
Okeechobee
Old Key Lime
Orchids of Siam
Outback Steakhouse
Painted Horse
Palm Beach Fish
Palm Beach Grill
Park Ave. BBQ
P.F. Chang's
Piccadilly Caf.
Pizza Girls Pizza
Raindancer Steakhouse
Renato's
Rhythm Cafe
Riggin's Crabhse.
Saigon Tokyo
Savanna's PB
Sorrento
Spoto's Oyster
Stresa
Suite 225
Sunset Grill
Sushi Rok
Ta-boo
Testa's
Too Jay's Deli
Trevini
Tsunami
264 the Grill
Vangelli's

Martin County
Benihana
Conchy Joe's Seafood
11 Maple St.
Flagler Grill
Hops
Outback Steakhouse
Park Ave. BBQ

Location Index

Rottie's
Too Jay's Deli

North Central Palm Beach County
Cafe Chardonnay
Cafe du Parc
Cardello's Pizza
Carmine's Ocean Grill
Cheeburger Cheeburger
Crab Pot
Don Ramon's
El Colonial
La Fonda Del Sol
Le Mistral
Max & Eddie's
Mondo's
Mrs. Smokey's BBQ
No Anchovies!
Off the Vine
Paddy Mac's
Park Ave. BBQ
Portofino's
Redfire Grill
River House
Ruth's Chris
Saigon Sun
Sailfish Marina
Shula's Steak House
Spoto's PGA
Too Jay's Deli
Tropical Bistro

North Palm Beach County
Bistro, The
Buonasera
Cobblestone Cafe
Courtyard Grill
Don Ramon's
Gallery Grille
Harry and the Natives
Hurricane Café
Il Trullo
Jetty's
Juno Beach Fish
Kee Grill
Lazy Loggerhead
Little Moirs Food
Marc's Chophse.
Outback Steakhouse
Park Ave. BBQ
Reef Grill
Sandbar & Grill
Schooner's Seafood
Seaside Meeting Pl.
Sinclair's
Tabica Grill
Too Bizaare
Too Jay's Deli

South Palm Beach County
Addison
Arturo's
Banana Boat
Beverly Hills Cafe
Big City Tavern
Bistro Zenith
Blue Anchor Pub
Boston's
Boulevard Grille
Brasserie Mon Ami
Brewzzi
Busch's Seafood
Cafe Bellino
Caffe Luna Rosa
Cay Da
Cheeburger Cheeburger
Cheesecake Factory
Chuck's Steakhse.
City Oyster
Cuban Cafe
DaDa
Dakotah 624
De La Tierra
Eilat Cafe
Falcon House
GiGi's Tavern
Gotham City
Grille, The
Henry's
Hops
Houston's
Ichiban
J. Alexander's
Johannes

vote at zagat.com

Location Index

Kathy's Gazebo
Kee Grill
Kyoto Sushi
La Belle Epoque
Lana's Cafe
La Petite Maison
La Trattoria
La Tre
La Vieille Maison
La Villetta
Le Vieux Paris
Linda B./Boca Raton
Louie Louie
Lucca
Luna Pazza
Maggiano's Little Italy
Mario's of Boca
Mario's Tuscan
Mark's at Park
Max's Grille
Maxwell's Chophse.
Melting Pot
Monty's Stone Crab
Morton's
Mykonos
New York Prime
Nirvana
Outback Steakhouse
Out of Denmark
Padrino's
Park Ave. BBQ
Peter's Stone Crabs

Pete's Boca Raton
P.F. Chang's
Pineapple Grille
Pranzo
Prezzo
Renzo's of Boca
Romano's Mac. Grill
Sapori
Siam Gourmet
Snappers
Sopra
Splendid Blendeds
Swiss Chalet
32 East
Tin Muffin
Tom's Place
Tony Roma's
Too Jay's Deli
Uncle Tai's
Wilt Chamberlain's
Zemi

St. Lucie County
Le Brittany
Too Jay's Deli

West Palm Beach County
Bamboo Club
Beverly Hills Cafe
California Pizza Kit.
Park Ave. BBQ
Prezzo
Too Jay's Deli

Special Feature Index

SPECIAL FEATURES

For multi-location restaurants, the availability of index features may vary by location.

Boat Docking Facilities
Baleen
Banana Boat/P
Bayside Seafood
Big Fish
Bimini Boatyard/B
Blue Moon Fish/B
Busch's Seafood/P
Castaways/K
Charley's Crab/B
Crab Pot/P
15th St. Fisheries/B
Garcia's
Giorgio's Grill/B
Gus' Grille/K
Half Shell Raw Bar/K
Islamorada Fish/K
Jetty's/P
Joe's Riverside Grille/B
Joe's Seafood
Keys Fisheries/K
La Tavernetta/B
Lorelei/K
Marker 88/K
Martha's Supper Club/B
Mezzanotte/B
Monty's Stone Crab
Morada Bay Beach/K
Old Key Lime/P
Old Tavernier/K
Pierre's/K
Quay, The/K
Red Fish Grill
River House/P
Rustic Inn Crabhse./B
Sailfish Marina/P
Shirttail Charlie's/B
Shooters/B
Snapper's/K
Snook's/K
Sundays on Bay
Sundowners on the Bay/K
Taverna Opa/B
Whale Harbor Inn/K

Breakfast
(See also Hotel Dining)
Abbey Dining Rm.
A La Folie
Alice's at La-te-da/K
Arnie & Richie's Deli
Ayestaran
Bagel Emporium
Bagels & Co.
Balans
Banana Cafe/K
Big Pink
Blue Heaven/K
Boston's/P
B's Rest./K
Café Cardozo
Cafe Demetrio
Café La Bonne Crepe/B
Caffe Luna Rosa/P
Camille's/K
Chuck & Harold's/P
Croissants de France/K
David's Cafe
Deli, The/K
Deli Lane Cafe
Dennis Pharmacy/K
Dune Deck Cafe/P
Duval Beach Club/K
11th St. Diner
El Toro Taco
E.R. Bradley's/P
Flagler's/K
Flamingo
French Place/B
Front Porch Cafe
Gables Diner
Gallery Grille/P
Ganim's/K

vote at zagat.com

Special Feature Index

Garcia's
Grandma's French Cafe/B
Granny Feelgood's
Green's Pharmacy/P
Green Street Cafe
Gus' Grille/K
Hamburger Heaven/P
Harry and the Natives/P
Hurricane Café/P
Islas Canarias
John G's/P
La Carreta
La Carreta/B
La Casita
La Sandwicherie
Latin American
Lazy Loggerhead/P
Le Bouchon du Grove
Leigh Ann's Coffee/K
Lester's Diner/B
Lincoln Road Café
Little Italy/K
Miami Juice
Mrs. Mac's Kitchen/K
News Cafe
Nexxt Cafe
Off the Vine/P
One Duval/K
Papa's/K
Pelican Café
Pepe's Cafe/K
Picnics at Allen's
Restaurant St. Michel
Sailfish Marina/P
S&S Rest.
Seaside Meeting Pl./P
Sergio's
Seven Mile/K
Sheldon's
Square One/K
Testa's/P
Texas Taco
Too Jay's Deli/P
Two Friends Patio/K
Van Dyke Cafe
Versailles
Whale Harbor Inn/K

Brunch

Alice's at La-te-da/K
Aria
Armadillo Cafe/B
Bagatelle/K
Balans
Baleen
Beverly Hills Cafe
Bimini Boatyard/B
Bizcaya Grill
Blue Heaven/K
Blue Moon Fish/B
Brasserie Las Olas/B
Café Solé/K
Camille's/K
Charley's Crab/B
Charley's Crab/P
Cheesecake Factory/P
Chuck & Harold's/P
De La Tierra/P
Dining Rm./Little Palm/K
E.R. Bradley's/P
Flagler's/K
Gallery Grille/P
Gus' Grille/K
Icebox Café
Joe Allen
La Palma
La Vie en Rose/B
Le Bouchon du Grove
Louie's Backyard/K
Mangoes/K
Mangrove Mama's/K
Martha's Supper Club/B
Max's Grille/B
McCarty's/P
Nemo
News Cafe
Nexxt Cafe
Nina Rest.
Novecento
Off the Vine/P
One Ninety
Perricone's
Pineapple Grille/P
Restaurant St. Michel
River House/B

subscribe to zagat.com

Special Feature Index

Rusty Pelican
Sage French/B
Seaside Meeting Pl./P
Sergio's
Shula's Steak
Snapper's/K
Snook's/K
Soyka
Sugar Reef/B
Sunset Tavern
SushiSamba dromo
Ta-boo/P
Testa's/P
Tropical Chinese
1200 at the Biltmore
1220 at the Tides
Two Sisters
Versailles

Buffet Served
(Check availability)
Aria
Baleen
Bellante's Pizza
Bellante's Pizza/B
Bin 595/B
Bizcaya Grill
Café Protégé/P
Charley's Crab/B
Crab House
Crazy Buffet/P
Dining Rm./Little Palm/K
Gus' Grille/K
House of India
Imlee
India House/B
La Palma
Madras Café/B
Mario's of Boca/P
Nemo
Old San Juan
One Ninety
Padrino's/B
Padrino's/P
Raja
Renaisa
Restaurant St. Michel

River House/B
Rusty Pelican
Shula's Steak
Tarpon Bend/B
Tumi/B
1200 at the Biltmore
Whale Harbor Inn/K
Yesterday's/B

Business Dining
Angelo & Maxie's/P
Aria
Arturo's/P
Atlantic's Edge/K
Balans
Baleen
Bangkok Bangkok
Bangkok Bangkok
Barracuda Grill/K
Bentley's/K
Beverly Hills Cafe
Bice Ristorante
Bice Ristorante/P
Bizcaya Grill
Black Orchid Cafe/B
Brasserie Las Olas/B
Busch's Seafood/P
Cafe L'Europe/P
Cafe Sambal
Cafe Seville/B
Caffe Abbracci
Caffe Milano
Capital Grille
Casa D'Angelo/B
Christine Lee's
Christy's
Creolina's/B
Crystal Cafe
Darrel/Oliver's Cafe/B
David's Cafe
Diego's
East City Grill/B
Echo/P
Eduardo de San Angel/B
El Novillo
Flagler's/K
Flagler Steakhse./P

vote at zagat.com 235

Special Feature Index

Forge, The
Graziano's
Grill Room/B
Havana Harry's
Himmarshee/B
Houston's
Il Trullo/P
Jackson's Steakhse./B
Joe's Stone Crab
Kathy's Gazebo /P
La Dorada
La Paloma
Le Mont/P
L'Escalier/P
Les Halles
Linda B. Steakhse.
Little Havana
Louie's Backyard/K
Mai-Kai/B
Marc's Chophse./P
Mark's Las Olas/B
Max's Grille/B
Maxwell's Chophse./P
Monty's Stone Crab
Morton's
New York Prime/P
Norman's
Okeechobee/P
Ortanique on Mile
Osteria del Teatro
Palm
Palm Beach Grill/P
Palme d'Or
Pascal's on Ponce
Pellegrino's/B
Perricone's
P.F. Chang's
Pierre's/K
Porcão
Prezzo
Provence Grill
Rainbow Palace/B
Redfish Bluefish/B
Red Lantern
Ristorante La Bussola
Rosinella
Ruth's Chris

Ruth's Chris/B
Sakura
Samba Rm./B
Shibui
Shula's on the Beach/K
Shula's Steak
Sinclair's/P
Smith & Wollensky
Spoto's Oyster/P
Spoto's PGA/P
Sunfish Grill/B
Ta-boo/P
3030 Ocean/B
32 East/P
Timpano Italian/B
Tony Chan's
Trattoria Sole
1200 at the Biltmore
Two Dragons
Two Sisters
Victoria Park/B
Yesterday's/B
Yuca
Zemi/P

Catering

Addison/P
Alcazar
Alice's at La-te-da/K
Anita's Mexicano/B
Anokha
Armadillo Cafe/B
Arnie & Richie's Deli
Arturo's/P
Athena by the Sea/B
Aura
Bagel Emporium
Bagels & Co.
Bamboo Club
Bamboo Garden
Bangkok Bangkok
Barton G.
Bentley's/K
Berries
Beverly Hills Cafe
Beverly Hills Cafe/B
Bice Ristorante

236 subscribe to zagat.com

Special Feature Index

Big Cheese
Bond St. Lounge
Bongos
Botticelli
Boulevard Grille/P
Busch's Seafood/P
By Word of Mouth/B
Café Ibiza
Café Protégé/P
Cafe Seville/B
Café Solé/K
Caffe Abbracci
Caffe Milano
Calypso Rest./Raw Bar/B
Calypso's Seafood/K
Capriccio/B
Captain's Tavern
Carmine's Ocean Grill/P
Carnevale
Casa Paco
Castaways/K
Chef Allen's
Cobblestone Cafe/P
Cohiba Brasserie/B
Crab House
Cracked Conch Cafe/K
Creolina's/B
Daily Bread
Darrel/Oliver's Cafe/B
David's Cafe
De La Tierra/P
Don Ramon's/P
Duval Beach Club/K
East City Grill/B
Echo/P
Edelweiss
Eilat Cafe/P
El Colonial/P
Elia
Flagler's/K
Flamingo
Fujihana
Ganim's/K
Globe Cafe & Bar
Grappa
Graziano's
Grillfish

Guayacan
Havana/P
Havana Harry's
Here Comes the Sun
Hi-Life Cafe/B
Hiro Japanese
House of India
Icebox Café
Il Fico
Imlee
India House/B
Islamorada Fish/K
Jake's
Joe's Seafood
Kaiyó/K
Kampai
Kelly's Caribbean/K
Khoury's
Kyoto Sushi/P
La Barraca/B
La Carreta
Lan
Lana's Cafe/P
La Palma
La Paloma
La Sandwicherie
Las Vegas/B
Le Bouchon du Grove
Little Havana
Little Italy/K
Lombardi's
Lorelei/K
Madras Café/B
Mai-Kai/B
Mangoes/K
Mario the Baker
Maroosh
Max's Grille/B
Mezzanotte/B
Michael's Kitchen/B
Miyako
Mondo's/P
Monty's Stone Crab
Mykonos
Nemo
Nicola Seafood/K
Nirvana/P

Special Feature Index

Novecento
Oasis Cafe
Off the Vine/P
Oggi Caffe
Old Cutler Oyster
Old Lisbon
Old San Juan
Old Tavernier/K
Old Town Mexican/K
One Duval/K
One Ninety
Opera Italian/K
Orchids of Siam/P
Origami/K
Original Daily Bread
Ortanique on Mile
Ouzo's Greek
Padrino's/B
Paquito's
Park Ave. BBQ/P
Pascal's on Ponce
Paulo Luigi's
Peppy's in Gables
Perricone's
Peter's Stone Crabs/P
Pino's
Pit Bar-B-Q
Pizza Rustica
Porky's Bayside/K
Prezzo
Provence Grill
Punjab Palace
Restaurant St. Michel
River House/B
Sage French/B
S&S Rest.
Sara's
Shoji
Shorty's BBQ
Shula's Steak
Siam Palace
Square One/K
Stefano's
Sugar Reef/B
Suite 225/P
Sushi Maki
Su Shin
SushiSamba dromo
Tabica Grill/P
Thai House So. Bch.
Thai House II
Thai Orchid
Thai Spice/B
Thai Toni
Timpano Italian/B
Tin Muffin/P
Tiramesu
Tobacco Rd.
Tom Jenkins BBQ/B
Tom's Place/P
Toni's Sushi
Tony Chan's
Too Bizaare/P
Too Jay's Deli/P
Trattoria Luna
Trattoria Sole
Tropical Bistro/P
Tropical Chinese
Tuscan Steak
Two Chefs
Vizio Cafe
Wish
Wolfgang Puck Cafe/B
Yasuko's

Celebrity Chefs

Alice's at La-te-da/K, *Alice Weingarten*
Azul, *Michelle Bernstein*
Bizcaya Grill, *Willis Loughead*
Blue Door, *Claude Troisgros*
Cacao 1737, *Edgar Leal*
Café Boulud/P, *Daniel Boulud*
Carmen, *Carmen Gonzalez*
Casa D'Angelo/B, *Angelo Elia*
Chef Allen's, *Allen Susser*
Chispa, *Robbin Haas*
Christina Wan's/B, *Christina Wan*
Darrel/Oliver's Cafe/B, *Darrel Broek/Oliver Saucy*
Eduardo de San Angel/B, *Eduardo Pria*
11 Maple St./P, *Mike Perrin*

Special Feature Index

Elia, *Kris Wessel*
Four Seasons/P, *Hubert Des Marais*
Kaiyó/K, *Dawn Sieber*
Mark's Las Olas/B, *Mark Militello*
Nobu Miami Beach, *Nobu Matsuhisa/T. Buckley*
Norman's, *Norman Van Aken*
Ortanique on Mile, *C. Hutson*
Pacific Time, *Jonathan Eismann*
Palme d'Or, *Philippe Ruiz*
Pao, *Kiki Anchana Praropkul*
Pascal's on Ponce, *P. Oudin*
Romeo's Cafe, *Romeo Majano*
Talula, *A. Curto/F. Randazzo*
32 East/P, *Nick Morfogen*
Timo, *Tim Andriola*
Two Dragons, *Elizabeth Barlow*
Wish, *E. Michael Reidt*
Zemi/P, *Michael Schwartz*

Child-Friendly
(Besides the normal fast-food places; * children's menu available)
A&B Lobster/K*
Alcazar*
Antonia's/K
Aquatica Beach Bar*
Archie's Pizza*
Aria*
Aruba Beach Cafe/B*
Athena by the Sea/B*
Atlantic's Edge/K*
Aura
Ayestaran
Bagatelle/K*
Bagel Emporium*
Bahama Breeze*
Bahama Breeze/B*
Bahamas Fish Mkt.*
Baja Fresh Mexican Grill*
Baleen*
Bamboo Club/P
Bamboo Garden*
Bamboo Garden/B*
Banana Boat/P*
Bangkok Bangkok
Bangkok Bangkok
Bar-B-Q Barn*
Barracuda Grill/K*
Barton G.
Bavarian Village/B*
Bayside Grill/K*
Bayside Seafood*
Bella Luna
Bellante's Pizza*
Bellante's Pizza/B*
Benihana/B*
Benihana/K*
Benihana/P*
Benihana/Samurai*
Bentley's/K*
Berries
Beverly Hills Cafe*
Beverly Hills Cafe/B*
Big Cheese*
Big Pink*
Bimini Twist/P
Bistro Zinc*
Bizcaya Grill*
Blue Heaven/K*
Blu la Pizzeria*
Bongos*
Bongusto! Rist./B
Boston's/P*
B's Rest./K*
Buca di Beppo/B
Café Cardozo*
Cafe Marquesa/K
Cafe Med*
Cafe Sambal*
Café Solé/K*
Café Tu Tu Tango*
Caffe Da Vinci*
California Pizza Kit.*
California Pizza Kit./B*
California Pizza Kit./P*
Calypso's Seafood/K*
Camille's/K*
Capital Grille
Cap's Place Island/B*
Captain's Tavern*

vote at zagat.com 239

Special Feature Index

Cardello's Pizza/P*
Carnevale*
Carpaccio
Casa Paco*
Casa Panza*
Caspian Persian Grill/B
Castaways/K*
Catfish Dewey's/B*
Cay Da/P
Chalán/El Chalán
Charley's Crab/P*
Chart House*
Cheeburger Cheeburger/B*
Cheeburger Cheeburger/P*
Cheesecake Factory
Cheesecake Factory/B
Cheesecake Factory/P
Chico's Cantina/K*
Christine Lee's
Chuck & Harold's/P*
Chuck's Steakhse./P*
Citronelle
Cobblestone Cafe/P
Conch Republic/K*
Conchy Joe's Seafood/P
Crab House*
Crab Pot/P*
Crack'd Conch/K*
Crazy Buffet/P*
Croissants de France/K
Crystal Cafe
Daily Bread
da Leo Trattoria
Dan Marino's/B*
Dave's Last Resort/P*
Deli, The/K*
Deli Lane Cafe*
Dennis Pharmacy/K*
Dogma
Duffy's Steak/K*
Dune Deck Cafe/P*
Duval Beach Club/K*
East City Grill/B*
11th St. Diner*
Elia*
El Novillo*
El Rancho Grande

El Toro Taco*
E.R. Bradley's/P*
Ferdo's Grill/B*
15th St. Fisheries/B*
Finnegan's Wake Pub/K*
Fish House/K*
Flamingo*
Frank Keys Cafe/K
Fritz & Franz Bierhaus*
Fujihana*
Gables Diner*
Gallery Grille/P*
Ganim's/K*
Garcia's
Gordon Biersch Brewery*
Grand Café Key West/K
Grandma's French Cafe/B
Greek Island Taverna/B
Green's Pharmacy/P
Green Street Cafe*
Green Turtle Inn/K*
Grille, The/P*
Guayacan*
Gus' Grille/K*
Half Shell Raw Bar/K*
Hamburger Heaven/P
Hanna's Diner*
Hard Rock Cafe*
Hard Rock Cafe/K*
Harry and the Natives/P*
Havana Harry's*
Here Comes the Sun*
Hiro Japanese
Hops/B*
Hops/P*
Hosteria Romana
Hot Tin Roof/K
House of India
Houston's
Hurricane Grill/K*
Ichiban/B*
Il Toscano/B
Imlee
Islamorada Fish/K*
Islas Canarias*
Jake's *
JB's on the Beach/B*

Special Feature Index

Joe's Crab Shack/B*
Joe's Riverside Grille/B*
Joe's Seafood*
John G's/P
John Martin's*
Jumbo's*
Juno Beach Fish/P*
Kaiyó/K*
Kampai*
Kelly's Caribbean/K*
La Barraca/B
La Carreta*
La Casita*
La Dorada*
La Gastronomia
La Loggia
La Palma
Lario's*
Las Culebrinas*
Las Vegas/B*
Latin American*
La Trattoria/K*
Laurenzo's Cafe*
La Valentina*
Le Bouchon du Grove
Le Festival*Casa *
Legal Sea Foods/B*
Les Halles*
Lester's Diner/B*
Lila's*
Lincoln Road Café
Linda B. Steakhse.
Little Havana*
Little Italy/K*
Little Moirs Food /P*
Locanda Sibilla*
Lorelei/K*
Los Ranchos*
Madras Café/B*
Maggiano's Little Italy/P
Mai-Kai/B*
Mama Jennie's*
Mama Vieja*
Mangrove Mama's/K*
Mario's of Boca/P*
Mario the Baker/B*
Mariposa*

Martha's/K*
Max's Beach Pl./B
Max's Grille/B*
Miami Juice
Michaels/K*
Michael's Kitchen/B*
Mississippi Sweets/P
Molina's*
Mondo's/P*
Monte's Fish Mkt./K*
Monty's Stone Crab*
Morada Bay Beach/K*
Mrs. Mac's Kitchen/K*
Mrs. Mendoza's*
Mykonos
Nando's Beefeeder's/P*
New Chinatown
Nicola Seafood/K*
Nina Rest.*
No Anchovies!/P*
No Name Pub/K
Novecento*
Off the Vine/P*
Oggi Caffe*
Old Cutler Inn*
Old Cutler Oyster*
Old Florida/B*
Old Tavernier/K*
Old Town Mexican/K
One Ninety
Opera Italian/K
Outback Steakhouse*
Outback Steakhouse/B*
Outback Steakhouse/P*
Ouzo's Greek*
Paddy Mac's/P*
Padrino's/B*
Palm
Palm Beach Fish/P*
Paninoteca*
Paquito's*
Park Ave. BBQ/P*
Paulo Luigi's*
Pepe's Cafe/K*
Peppy's in Gables
Piccadilly Caf.*
Picnics at Allen's*

Special Feature Index

Pineapple Grille/P*
Pino's
Pit Bar-B-Q
Pizza Rustica
Porky's Bayside/K
Portofino's/P*
Prezzo*
Prezzo/P*
PT's Late Night/K*
Puccini & Pasta*
Puerto Sagua*
Punjab Palace*
Reef Grill/P
Riggin's Crabhse./P*
River House/B*
Roadhouse Grill*
Roadhouse Grill/B*
Roasted Pepper/B*
Romano's Mac. Grill*
Romano's Mac. Grill/B*
Romano's Mac. Grill/P*
Rosinella
Rustic Inn Crabhse./B*
Rusty Pelican*
Sailfish Marina/P*
Salute/K
S&S Rest.*
San Loco
Sara's*
Schooner's Seafood/P*
Señor Frijoles/K*
Señor Frog's*
Sergio's*
Seven Mile/K
Sheldon's*
Shibui*
Shorty's BBQ*
Shula's on the Beach/K*
Shula's Steak*
Silver Pond/B
Snapper's/K*
Snappers/P*
Snook's/K*
Soyka*
Spoto's Oyster/P*
Spris*
Squid Row/K*

Stefano's*
Sundays on Bay*
Sundowners on the Bay/K*
Sunshine & AJ's
Sushi Maki*
Su Shin/B
Sushi Rock
Sushi Saigon
Sushi Siam
Swiss Chalet/B
Swiss Chalet/P*
Taco Rico*
Tambo Rest.
Tango Grill*
TapTap
Tarantella/B*
Taverna Opa
Tequila Sunrise
Testa's/P*
Texas Taco*
Thai Cuisine/K
Thai House So. Bch.
Thai Orchid
Thai Spice/B
Thai Toni
Time Out BBQ/K*
Tiramesu
Titanic Brewery*
Tobacco Rd.
Tokyo Bowl
Tokyo Bowl/B
Tokyo Sushi/B
Tom Jenkins BBQ/B
Tom's Place/P*
Toni's Sushi
Tony Chan's
Tony Roma's*
Tony Roma's/B*
Tony Roma's/P*
Too Bizaare/P
Too Jay's Deli/P*
Trattoria Luna
Trattoria Sole*
Tuna's Waterfront*
Turtle Kraals/K*
Tutto Pasta
Tutto Pizza

Special Feature Index

Two Friends Patio/K*
Two Sisters*
Vangelli's/P*
Versailles*
Wan's Sushi/B
Whale Harbor Inn/K*
Whale's Rib/B*
White Lion
Wilt Chamberlain's/P*
Wings 'N Things/B*
Wolfgang Puck Cafe/B*
Yasuko's*
Yeung's Chinese
Ziggie's/K*

Dancing
Addison/P
Banana Boat/P
Bayside Seafood
Ben's Steakhse./P
Bistro Zinc
Bongos
Boston's/P
Bungalow 9/B
Capriccio/B
Casa Panza
Chuck & Harold's/P
Dakotah 624/P
Diego's
E.R. Bradley's/P
Fish 54
Flagler's/K
GiGi's Tavern/P
Giorgio's Grill/B
Grass Lounge
Hog's Breath Saloon/K
Hurricane Grill/K
Jimmy Buffett's/K
La Paloma
La Valentina
Lorelei/K
Mama Vieja
Mangos/B
Mango's
Marc's Chophse./P
Martha's Supper Club/B
Mezzanotte

Mezzanotte/B
Molina's
Monty's Stone Crab
Morada Bay Beach/K
Nikki Beach
O'Hara's Hollywood/B
Old Cutler Oyster
One Duval/K
Pete's Boca Raton/P
Señor Frog's
Shooters/B
Sinclair's/P
Sloppy Joe's/K
Snapper's/K
Sopra/P
Stefano's
Ta-boo/P
Tantra
Tarpon Bend/B
Taverna Opa
Taverna Opa/B
Tequila Sunrise
Timpano Italian/B
Titanic Brewery
Tobacco Rd.
Touch
Vangelli's/P
Yesterday's/B

Delivery
Ambrosia/K
Andiamo! Pizza
Archie's Pizza
Arnie & Richie's Deli
Bagel Emporium
Bagels & Co.
Baja Fresh Mexican Grill
Bamboo Club/P
Bamboo Garden
Bamboo Garden/B
Big Cheese
Big Pink
Bistro, The/P
Bistro Zinc
By Word of Mouth/B
Cafe Demetrio
California Pizza Kit./P

vote at zagat.com

Special Feature Index

Camille's/K
Casa Paco
Cheeburger Cheeburger/P
Christina Wan's/B
David's Cafe
Deli Lane Cafe
Doraku
El Rancho Grande
Gables Diner
Galanga/B
Grand Café Key West/K
Granny Feelgood's
Here Comes the Sun
House of India
Hurricane Grill/K
Il Fico
La Carreta
La Gastronomia
La Loggia
La Sandwicherie
La Spada's Hoagies/B
Las Vegas/B
Little Havana
Los Ranchos
Maiko
Mama Jennie's
Mario's of Boca/P
Mario the Baker/B
Max & Eddie's/P
Max's Grille/B
Meteor Smokehse./K
Miyako
Mykonos
Off the Vine/P
Ouzo's Greek
Padrino's/P
Paninoteca
Perricone's
Pineapple Grille/P
Pizza Girls Pizza/P
Pizza Rustica
PT's Late Night/K
Punjab Palace
Red Lantern
Red Thai Rm.
Sakana/B
San Loco
Sara's
Sergio's
Seven Fish/K
Sheldon's
Shoji
Sorrento/P
Suite 225/P
Sunshine & AJ's
Sushi Maki
Sushi Saigon
Sushi Siam
Swiss Chalet/B
Swiss Chalet/P
Taco Rico
TapTap
Texas Taco
Thai Cuisine/K
Thai House So. Bch.
Thai House II
Thai Spice/B
Tokyo Bowl
Tony Chan's
Tony Roma's
Tony Roma's/P
Too Jay's Deli/P
Tumi/B
Wan's Sushi/B
Wilt Chamberlain's/P
Wings 'N Things/B
Yeung's Chinese
Zuperpollo

Dessert

A La Folie
America/P
Aria
Atlantic's Edge/K
Azul
Bagel Emporium
Baleen
Barton G.
Beverly Hills Cafe
Big Pink
Blue Heaven/K
By Word of Mouth/B
Café Ragazzi
Café Tu Tu Tango

Special Feature Index

Captain's Tavern
Chart House
Cheesecake Factory
Cheesecake Factory/B
Cheesecake Factory/P
Chispa
Conch Republic/K
Croissants de France/K
Daily Bread
Darrel/Oliver's Cafe/B
Deli, The/K
Edelweiss
Escopazzo
Forge, The
Four Seasons/P
Gallagher's Gourmet/K
Grandma's French Cafe/B
Graziano's
Hanna's Diner
Hard Rock Cafe/K
Hi-Life Cafe/B
Hot Tin Roof/K
Houston's
Icebox Café
Joe Allen
Josef's/B
La Barraca/B
Lan
Leigh Ann's Coffee/K
Mariposa
Mark's at Park/P
Mark's CityPlace/P
Mark's Las Olas/B
Mark's South Beach
Meteor Smokehse./K
Michaels/K
Morton's
Nemo
Norman's
Pacific Time
Palme d'Or
Pepe's Cafe/K
Rumi
Ruth's Chris
Seven Fish/K
Smith & Wollensky
Soyka

SushiSamba dromo
Tasti D-Lite
Teté Rest.
Timo
Tuscan Steak
1200 at the Biltmore
Wish

Dining Alone
(Other than hotels and places with counter service)
Abbey Dining Rm.
A La Folie
Anokha
Bagels & Co.
Baja Fresh Mexican Grill
Balans
Bella Luna
Ben's Steakhse./P
Big Pink
Bizaare Ave. Cafe/P
Botticelli
Café Cardozo
Cafe Cellini/P
Cafe Demetrio
Cheeburger Cheeburger/B
Chuck & Harold's/P
Cobblestone Cafe/P
Cracked Conch Cafe/K
Creolina's/B
Croissants de France/K
DaDa/P
Deli, The/K
Dennis Pharmacy/K
Dogma
Don Ramon's/P
Echo/P
11th St. Diner
Flagler's/K
Flagler Steakhse./P
French Place/B
Grandma's French Cafe/B
Green Street Cafe
Hanna's Diner
Here Comes the Sun
Houston's
Icebox Café

vote at zagat.com

Special Feature Index

India House/B
Islamorada Fish/B
Islamorada Fish/K
Joe Allen
John Bull English Pub/P
Kelly's Caribbean/K
Kyung Ju
Lan
Laurenzo's Cafe
Lemon Twist
Les Deux Fontaines
Les Halles
Little Havana
Maguire's Hill 16/B
Maiko
Mangoes/K
Mariposa
Melody Inn
Miami Juice
Morton's
Mrs. Mendoza's
Mykonos
News Cafe
Off the Vine/P
Okeechobee/P
Paddy Mac's/P
Palm Beach Grill/P
Paninoteca
Pellegrino's/B
P.F. Chang's
Picnics at Allen's
Rainbow Palace/B
Sakura
Samba Rm./B
S&S Rest.
Sinclair's/P
Smith & Wollensky
Sport Cafe
Sunfish Grill/B
Texas Taco
Thai Orchid
Toni's Sushi
Tony Chan's
Too Bizaare/P
Tropical Bistro/P
Victoria Park/B

Early-Bird Menus
Ambry/B
Balans
Benihana/K
Benihana/Samurai
Bimini Twist/P
Bohemian Gardens/P
Cafe Avanti
Café Protégé/P
Café Solé/K
Camille's/K
Cardello's Pizza/P
Frankie's Pier 5/B
Guayacan
Here Comes the Sun
Himmarshee/B
Jetty's/P
Joe's Riverside Grille/B
Juno Beach Fish/P
Kee Grill/P
La Vie en Rose/B
Maggiano's Little Italy/P
Mai-Kai/B
Mama Jennie's
Max & Eddie's/P
Max's Grille/B
Nando's Beefeeder's/P
No Anchovies!/P
Off the Vine/P
Okeechobee/P
Reef Grill/P
Riggin's Crabhse./P
Sandbar & Grill/P
Sorrento/P
Sunset Grill/P
Tabica Grill/P
Tambo Rest.
Tantra
Tequila Sunrise
Testa's/P
Tom's Place/P
Tony Roma's/B
Tony Roma's/P
Tropical Acres/B
Two Chefs
Two Friends Patio/K
Wan's Sushi/B

Special Feature Index

Whale Harbor Inn/K
Wine Cellar/B
Yesterday's/B

Entertainment
(Call for days and times of performances)
A Fish Called Avalon (varies)
Alcazar (piano)
Alice's at La-te-da/K (cabaret)
America/P (DJ)
Aruba Beach/B (gospel/jazz)
Ayestaran (piano)
Bahama Breeze (varies)
Bahama Breeze/B (varies)
Baleen (varies)
Banana Boat/P (reggae)
Banana Cafe/K (piano)
Bayside (reggae/bands)
Ben's Steakhse./P (bands)
Bice Ristorante (varies)
Bin 595/B (guitar)
Bistro Zinc (DJ)
Black Orchid Cafe/B (guitar)
Bongos (DJ/Salsa)
Boston's/P (bands)
Brasserie Las Olas/B (jazz)
Brogue's/P (Irish)
Bungalow 9/B (DJ/bands)
Cafe Demetrio (bands)
Café Ibiza (Latin/jazz)
Cafe Seville/B (flamenco)
Café Tu Tu Tango (varies)
Capriccio/B (piano/violin)
Casablanca Cafe/B (jazz/rock)
Casa Juancho (Spanish)
Casa Larios (varies)
Casa Paco (Accordion)
Casa Panza (flamenco)
Chuck & Harold's/P (band)
Cohiba Brasserie/B (flamenco)
Conca D'Oro/B (varies)
Conch Rep./K (calypso/reggae)
Conchy Joe's/P (reggae)
DaDa/P (DJ)
da Ermanno (jazz)
Dakotah 624/P (DJ)
David's Cafe (varies)
Diego's (piano/vocals)

Doraku (DJ/hip hop)
811 Bourbon St./B (bands)
El Novillo (varies)
E.R. Bradley's/P (DJ)
Finnegan's/K (karaoke)
Flagler's/K (piano)
Giorgio's Grill/B (DJ)
Gordon Biersch (bands)
Grand Café Key West/K (vocals)
Grass Lounge (DJ)
Green Turtle/K (magic shows)
Harry/Natives/P (band/vocals)
Havana/P (Cuban)
Himmarshee/B (guitar)
Hog's Breath/K (folk/rock)
Hot Tin Roof/K (jazz/piano)
Hurricane Grill/K (bands/varies)
Jackson's Steakhse./B (jazz)
Jake's (jazz)
JB's on the Beach/B (bands)
Jimmy Buffett's/K (bands)
John Martin's (bands/varies)
La Barraca/B (flam./accordion)
La Dorada (piano/guitar)
La Palma (vocals)
La Paloma (piano/vocals)
Lario's (Cuban/Latin)
Las Culebrinas (varies)
La Tavernetta/B (varies)
La Trattoria/K (Latin/jazz)
La Valentina (Mariachi band)
Le Mont/P (piano)
Leopard/P (guitar/bands)
Les Deux Fontaines (Dixieland)
Linda B. Steakhse. (piano)
Lombardi's (Latins)
Lorelei/K (varies)
Los Ranchos (varies)
Magnum (piano bar)
Maguire's Hill 16/B (Irish)
Mai-Kai/B (Polynesian)
Mangos/B (band)
Mango's (Latin/varies)
Mangrove Mama's/K (varies)
Marc's Chophse./P (piano)
Maroosh (belly dancer)
Martha's/K (piano)
Martha's Supper Club/B (varies)
Max's Beach/B (piano/vocals)

vote at zagat.com

Special Feature Index

Maxwell's/P (piano/bass/vocals)
Mezzanotte (DJ)
Mezzanotte/B (DJ)
Molina's (varies)
Monty's Stone Crab/P (varies)
Morada Bay/K (guitar/varies)
Moroccan Nights (varies)
Nina Rest. (varies)
Nirvana/P (guitar)
Off the Vine/P (jazz)
O'Hara's/B (jazz/R&B)
Old Cutler (guitar/steel drums)
Old Cutler Oyster (varies)
Old Key Lime/P (rock)
One Duval/K (piano bar)
One Ninety (DJ/bands)
Ouzo's Greek (belly dancers)
Paddy Mac's/P (Irish)
Palme d'Or (piano)
Pearl (varies)
Perricone's (jazz)
Pescado (jazz)
Pete's Boca/P (Top 40/lounge)
Piccadilly Garden (piano)
Porky's/K (guitar/bongos)
Portofino's/P (bands)
Prezzo (varies)
Regalo/B (jazz)
Restaurant St. Michel (piano)
Ristorante La Bussola (piano)
River House/B (varies)
Rottie's/P (jazz)
Rusty Pelican (piano)
Satine/B (DJ/parties)
Señor Frog's (DJ/bands)
Shirttail Charlie's/B (steel drums)
Shula's on the Beach/B (varies)
Shula's Steak (varies)
Sinclair's/P (DJ)
Sloppy Joe's/K (blues/jazz)
Snapper's/K (pop)
Snook's/K (varies)
Sopra/P (sax)
Spoto's PGA/P (jazz)
Square One/K (piano)
Stefano's (DJ/piano)
Sundays on Bay (varies)
Sundowners/K (varies)
Sunset Tav. (DJ/karaoke/band)
Ta-boo/P (DJ/piano)
Taco Rico (varies)
Tambo Rest. (varies)
Tantra (varies)
TapTap (varies)
Tarpon Bend/B (varies)
Taverna Opa (varies)
Taverna Opa/B (varies)
Tequila Sunrise (Mariachi)
Timpano Italian/B (jazz)
Titanic (blues/rock/karaoke)
Tobacco Rd. (blues/rock)
Tony Roma's (varies)
Tony Roma's/P (varies)
Too Bizaare/P (bands)
Tsunami/P (DJ)
Tumi/B (band)
1200 at the Biltmore (Latin/jazz)
Two Friends Patio/K (karaoke)
Van Dyke Cafe (jazz)
Vangelli's/P (DJ)
Whale Harbor Inn/K (guitar)
White Lion (jazz band)
Yesterday's/B (varies)
Zuperpollo (Int'l/tango)

Historic Places

(Year opened; * building)
1889 Old Key Lime/P
1890 Turtle Kraals/K*
1902 De La Tierra/P*
1909 Pepe's Cafe/K
1910 Louie's Backyard/K*
1912 Tobacco Rd.
1913 Joe's Stone Crab*
1917 Sloppy Joe's/K*
1920 Café Solé/K*
1920 Chuck & Harold's/P*
1921 Flagler's/K
1921 Old Cutler Inn
1921 Testa's/P
1922 La Palma*
1924 DaDa/P*
1925 Lake Avenue Grill/P*
1926 Cafe Demetrio*

Special Feature Index

1926 Palme d'Or*
1927 Kelly's Caribbean/K
1929 Cap's Place Island/B
1930 Boston's/P*
1931 No Name Pub/K*
1937 Papa Joe's/K
1938 Green's Pharmacy/P
1938 S&S Rest.
1940 Cafe Avanti*
1940 Ta-boo/P
1945 Hamburger Heaven/P
1946 Arnie & Richie's Deli
1946 Bar, The
1946 Fox's Sherron Inn
1947 Bohemian Gardens/P
1947 Green Turtle Inn/K
1947 Okeechobee/P
1948 Bar-B-Q Barn
1948 11th St. Diner*
1948 Picnics at Allen's
1948 Sheldon's
1949 Tropical Acres/B
1950 Blu la Pizzeria*
1950 Deli, The/K
1951 Castaways/K
1951 Hurricane Grill/K
1951 Shorty's BBQ
1951 Shorty's BBQ/B

Hotel Dining

Alexander Hotel
  Shula's Steak
Avalon Majestic
  A Fish Called Avalon
Biltmore Hotel
  1200 at the Biltmore
Boca Raton Resort
  Lucca/P
Brazilian Court Hotel
  Café Boulud/P
Breakers, The
  Flagler Steakhse./P
  L'Escalier/P
Casa Tua
  Casa Tua
Cheeca Lodge & Spa
  Atlantic's Edge/K
Chesterfield Hotel
  Leopard Lounge/P
Clinton Hotel
  Pao
David William Hotel
  Carmen
Delano Hotel
  Blue Door
  Blue Sea
Doubletree Grand
  Tony Chan's
Eden Roc Hotel
  Aquatica Beach Bar
Four Seasons
  Four Seasons/P
Grand Bay Hotel
  Bice Ristorante
Grove Isle Hotel
  Baleen
Gulf Stream Hotel
  Lake Avenue Grill/P
Holiday Inn
  Mario's of Boca/P
Hotel Astor
  Metro Kitchen
Hotel Ocean
  Les Deux Fontaines
Hotel of South Beach
  Wish
Hotel Place St. Michel
  Restaurant St. Michel
Hyatt Key West
  Nicola Seafood/K
Hyatt Regency
  Two Sisters
Jupiter Beach Resort
  Sinclair's/P
Little Palm Island Resort
  Dining Rm./Little Palm/K
Mandarin Oriental
  Azul
  Cafe Sambal
Marquesa Hotel
  Cafe Marquesa/K
Marriott Harbor Beach
  3030 Ocean/B
Marriott Key Largo
  Gus' Grille/K

vote at zagat.com

Special Feature Index

Nash Hotel
  Mark's South Beach
Ocean Key Resort
  Hot Tin Roof/K
Park Central Hotel
  Quinn's Rest.
Pelican Hotel
  Pelican Café
Penguin Hotel
  Front Porch Cafe
PGA Nat'l Resort & Spa
  Shula's Steak House/P
Renaissance Hotel
  Bin 595/B
  Darrel/Oliver's Bistro/B
Ritz-Carlton
  Aria
Ritz-Carlton Coconut Grove
  Bizcaya Grill
Riverside Hotel
  Grill Room/B
  Indigo/B
Sands Harbor Resort
  Joe's Riverside Grille/B
Seashell Beach Resort
  Gallagher's Gourmet/K
Shore Club Hotel
  Ago
Sonesta Beach Resort
  Two Dragons
South Park Ctr.
  Imlee
Sundy Inn
  De La Tierra/P
Tides Hotel
  1220 at the Tides
Townhouse Hotel
  Bond St. Lounge
Westin Diplomat
  Hollywood Prime/B
  Satine/B
Wyndham Reach Resort
  Shula's on the Beach/K
Yankee Trader Hotel
  Shula's on the Beach/B

"In" Places
Abbondanza/K
Ago
Amici Ristorante/P
Angelo & Maxie's/P
Arturo's/P
Azul
Balans
Barton G.
Big City Tavern/B
Big City Tavern/P
Big Pink
Bistro Mezzaluna/B
Blue Door
Blue Heaven/K
Blue Sea
Bond St. Lounge
Boulevard Grille/P
Cafe Martorano/B
Cafe Prima Pasta
Café Tu Tu Tango
Caffe Abbracci
Canyon/B
Carpaccio
Casa Tua
China Grill
Chispa
Chuck & Harold's/P
Creolina's/B
DaDa/P
Echo/P
E.R. Bradley's/P
Falcon House/P
Forge, The
Four Seasons/P
Globe Cafe & Bar
Gotham City/P
Grass Lounge
Himmarshee/B
Houston's
Houston's/B
Joe Allen
Joe's Stone Crab
Kaiyó/K
Lario's
Leopard Lounge/P
Lorelei/K
Mangoes/K
Mango's
Mark's CityPlace/P

Special Feature Index

Mark's Las Olas/B
Mark's South Beach
Max's Beach Pl./B
Metro Kitchen
Mezzanotte
Nemo
Nikki Beach
Oggi Caffe
Old Tavernier/K
One Ninety
Ortanique on Mile
Osteria del Teatro
Pacific Time
Palm
Pearl
Pellegrino's/B
Prezzo
Rumi
Samba Rm./B
Satine/B
Seven Fish/K
Sinclair's/P
Sopra/P
Soyka
Sport Cafe
Spoto's Oyster/P
Spoto's PGA/P
Sublime/B
Sushi Rock
Ta-boo/P
Tantra
Taverna Opa/B
Testa's/P
32 East/P
Tobacco Rd.
Toni's Sushi
Trattoria Sole
Turtle Kraals/K
Tuscan Steak
Two Chefs
Van Dyke Cafe

Late Dining
(Weekday closing hour)
Ago (12 AM)
A La Folie (12 AM)
America/P (2 AM)
Aquatica Beach Bar (1 AM)
Argentango Grill/B (12 AM)
Aura (12 AM)
Ayestaran (1 AM)
Bahama Breeze/B (12 AM)
Balans (12 AM)
Banana Boat/P (12 AM)
Bar, The (12:30 AM)
B.E.D. (12:30 AM)
Big City Tavern/B (12 AM)
Big City Tavern/P (12 AM)
Big Pink (12 AM)
Blue Door (1 AM)
Blue Sea (12 AM)
Bond St. Lounge (12 AM)
Boston's/P (2 AM)
Café Cardozo (12 AM)
Cafe Med (12 AM)
Cafe Prima Pasta (12 AM)
Café Tu Tu Tango (12 AM)
Caffe Milano (12 AM)
Casa Juancho (12 AM)
Cheesecake Factory (varies)
China Grill (12 AM)
Chuck's Steakhse./B (12 AM)
Conch Republic/K (12 AM)
Cucina Dell' Arte/P (3 AM)
DaDa/P (1:30 AM)
Dakotah 624/P (1 AM)
Dave's Last Resort/P (1 AM)
David's Cafe (24 hrs.)
Diego's (12 AM)
Doraku (12 AM)
11th St. Diner (12 AM)
E.R. Bradley's/P (3 AM)
Finnegan's Wake Pub/K (2 AM)
Fish 54 (12 AM)
Flanigans Loggerhead (4 AM)
Fox's Sherron Inn (1:30 AM)
French Place/B (2 AM)
Fritz & Franz Bierhaus (1 AM)
GiGi's Tavern/P (12 AM)
Grass Lounge (12:30 AM)
Hard Rock Cafe/K (12 AM)
Hiro Japanese (3:30 AM)
Hog's Breath Saloon/K (2 AM)
Hurricane Grill/K (2 AM)

vote at zagat.com

Special Feature Index

Il Sole (12 AM)
Islas Canarias (12 AM)
Jake's (12 AM)
Jimmy Buffett's/K (1 AM)
John Martin's (12 AM)
Kyoto Sushi/P (12 AM)
La Carreta (varies)
La Carreta/B (varies)
Lario's (12 AM)
Latin American (1 AM)
La Valentina (12 AM)
Lemon Twist (12 AM)
Les Halles (12 AM)
Lester's Diner/B (24 hrs.)
Lincoln Road Café (12 AM)
Little Saigon (1 AM)
Locanda Sibilla (12 AM)
Maiko (12 AM)
Mango's (4 AM)
Meteor Smokehse./K (2 AM)
Moroccan Nights (1 AM)
Nemo (12 AM)
News Cafe (24 hrs.)
Nobu Miami Beach (12 AM)
Novecento (12 AM)
O'Hara's Hollywood/B (2 AM)
Old Cutler Oyster (2 AM)
Papa's/K (12 AM)
Pelican Café (1 AM)
Piola (1 AM)
Pizza Rustica/B (1 AM)
Porcão (12 AM)
PT's Late Night/K (4 AM)
Puerto Sagua (2 AM)
Rosinella (12 AM)
Ruen Thai (12 AM)
San Loco/B (2 AM)
Señor Frog's (varies)
Sergio's (12 AM)
Shoji (12 AM)
Shula's Steak (12 AM)
Smith & Wollensky (2 AM)
Sport Cafe (12:30 AM)
Spris (1 AM)
Suite 225/P (2 AM)
Sunset Tavern (3 AM)
Sushi Rock (12 AM)
SushiSamba dromo (12 AM)
Tantra (12 AM)
Taverna Opa (varies)
Taverna Opa/B (varies)
Thai House So. Bch. (12 AM)
Timpano Italian/B (12 AM)
Tiramesu (12 AM)
Titanic Brewery (1AM)
Toni's Sushi (12 AM)
Touch (1 AM)
Tuna's Waterfront (2 AM)
Tuscan Steak (12am)
Two Friends Patio/K (1 AM)
Van Dyke Cafe (2 AM)
Versailles (1 AM)
Yambo (12 AM)
Zuperpollo (12 AM)

Meet for a Drink

Alice's at La-te-da/K
America/P
Amici Ristorante/P
Angelo of Mulberry/B
Aruba Beach Cafe/B
Bahama Breeze/B
Banana Boat/P
Bar, The
Barton G.
Bice Ristorante
Bice Ristorante/P
Big City Tavern/B
Big City Tavern/P
Bimini Boatyard/B
Bizaare Ave. Cafe/P
Blue Door
Bond St. Lounge
Bonefish Grill/B
Café Cardozo
Café Tu Tu Tango
Canyon/B
Carlos & Pepe's/B
Carmen
Casablanca Cafe/B
Casa Tua
Chuck & Harold's/P
City Cellar Wine/P
DaDa/P

Special Feature Index

Dave's Last Resort/P
Echo/P
E.R. Bradley's/P
Falcon House/P
Fox's Sherron Inn
GiGi's Tavern/P
Giorgio's Grill/B
Globe Cafe & Bar
Grass Lounge
Hog's Breath Saloon/K
Houston's
Houston's/B
JB's on the Beach/B
Jimmy Buffett's/K
Joe Allen
Joe's Riverside Grille/B
John Martin's
Kelly's Caribbean/K
Lake Avenue Grill/P
Lario's
Le Mont/P
Leopard Lounge/P
Lorelei/K
Magnum
Maguire's Hill 16/B
Mai-Kai/B
Mangos/B
Mango's
Mark's at Park/P
Mark's CityPlace/P
Mark's Las Olas/B
Max's Beach Pl./B
Max's Grille/B
Michaels/K
Monty's Stone Crab
Off the Vine/P
O'Hara's Hollywood/B
Old Key Lime/P
One Duval/K
Palm
Palm Beach Grill/P
Palme d'Or
Pearl
Pelican Café
Pete's Boca Raton/P
Pierre's/K
Pineapple Grille/P
Prezzo
PT's Late Night/K
Ristorante La Bussola
Rumi
Samba Rm./B
Sandbar & Grill/P
Señor Frog's
Shula's Steak
Sloppy Joe's/K
Sopra/P
Sport Cafe
Spoto's Oyster/P
Sublime/B
Sundays on Bay
Ta-boo/P
Tarpon Bend/B
Tequila Sunrise
32 East/P
Tobacco Rd.
Turtle Kraals/K
1200 at the Biltmore
Two Friends Patio/K
Van Dyke Cafe
Zemi/P

Microbreweries
Brewzzi/P
Calypso Rest./Raw Bar/B
Gordon Biersch Brewery
Hog's Breath Saloon/K
Hops/B
Hops/P
Kelly's Caribbean/K
Maguire's Hill 16/B
No Name Pub/K
PT's Late Night/K
Titanic Brewery

Noteworthy Newcomers
Ago
Andre's Steakhse./B
Anita's Mexicano/B
Argentango Grill/B
Bin 595/B
Bonefish Grill/B
Bungalow 9/B
Cacao 1737
Café Boulud/P

vote at zagat.com

Special Feature Index

Carmen
Casa Tua
Chez Andrée/B
Chispa
Citronelle
Cohiba Brasserie/B
Elia
Gallery Grille/P
Gotham City/P
Grass Lounge
JB's on the Beach/B
Josef's/B
La Barraca/B
Madras Café/B
Max & Eddie's/P
Nina Rest.
Nirvana/P
Novecento
Ouzo's Greek
Painted Horse/P
Palm Beach Fish/P
Pilar
Red Coral/B
Redfish Bluefish/B
River Oyster Bar
Splendido
Sublime/B
Sunset Grill/P
Sunshine & AJ's
Talula
Tambo Rest.
Timo

Offbeat
Abbondanza/K
Alice's at La-te-da/K
Ambrosia/K
Anokha
Ayestaran
Bahamas Fish Mkt.
Bali Café
Banana Cafe/K
Bar, The
Bayside Seafood
B.E.D.
Bentley's/K
Berries

Big Fish
Biscayne Wine
Bizaare Ave. Cafe/P
Black Orchid Cafe/B
Blue Heaven/K
B.O.'s Fish Wagon/K
B's Rest./K
Buca di Beppo/B
By Word of Mouth/B
Cafe Martorano/B
Café Pastis
Calypso's Seafood/K
Cap's Place Island/B
Casa Panza
Crack'd Conch/K
Cracked Conch Cafe/K
DaDa/P
Daily Bread
David's Cafe
Deli, The/K
Dennis Pharmacy/K
11th St. Diner
Falcon House/P
Flamingo
Fox's Sherron Inn
Gables Diner
Garcia's
Gil Capa's Bistro
Grandma's French Cafe/B
Green Turtle Inn/K
Half Shell Raw Bar/K
Hanna's Diner
Hy-Vong
Islamorada Fish/K
Joe's Seafood
Johannes/P
La Lupa di Roma
La Paloma
Lario's
L'Entrecôte de Paris
Little Saigon
Lorelei/K
Mai-Kai/B
Mama Vieja
Mango's
Melting Pot
Miami Juice

Special Feature Index

Miss Saigon
Monte's Fish Mkt./K
Monty's Stone Crab
Moroccan Nights
Mo's/K
Nikki Beach
No Name Pub/K
Old Cutler Inn
One Ninety
Ouzo's Greek
Pearl
Piccadilly Garden
Picnics at Allen's
Pineapple Grille/P
Porcão
Puerto Sagua
Red Thai Rm.
Renaisa
Rhythm Cafe/P
Romeo's Cafe
Rumi
Rusty Anchor/K
Salute/K
Samba Rm./B
S&S Rest.
San Loco
Scotty's Landing
Seven Fish/K
Shorty's BBQ
Siam Lotus
Sloppy Joe's/K
Tantra
TapTap
Taverna Opa
Taverna Opa/B
Tequila Sunrise
Titanic Brewery
Tobacco Rd.
Tropical Bistro/P
Turtle Kraals/K
Two Friends Patio/K
Versailles
White Lion
Yambo
Zuperpollo

Outdoor Dining
(See also Waterside;
G=garden; P=patio;
S=sidewalk; T=terrace;
W=waterside)
Abbey Dining Rm. (T)
Addison/P (P)
A Fish Called Avalon (S, T)
Ago (T)
A La Folie (G)
Alice's at La-te-da/K (G, P)
AltaMar (S)
Anchor Inn/P (P, W)
Andiamo! Pizza (P)
Anokha (S)
Aquatica Beach Bar (W)
Argentango Grill/B (P)
Aria (P)
Aruba Beach Cafe/B (P, W)
Athena by the Sea/B (S)
Atlantic's Edge/K (T, W)
Aura (P)
Azul (T)
Bagatelle/K (G, T)
Baja Fresh Mexican Grill (P)
Balans (S, T)
Baleen (P, T, W)
Bamboo Club (P)
Banana Boat/P (P, W)
Banana Cafe/K (P)
Barracuda Grill/K (P)
Barton G. (G)
Bayside Grill/K (W)
Bayside Seafood (P, W)
Bellagio/P (P)
Bella Luna (P)
Beverly Hills Cafe (P)
Bice Ristorante (T)
Big Cheese (P)
Big City Tavern/B (P)
Big Fish (G, W)
Bimini Boatyard/B (P, W)
Blue Door (T)
Blue Heaven/K (G, P)
Blue Moon Fish/B (T, W)
Blu la Pizzeria (S)
Bongos (T, W)

vote at zagat.com 255

Special Feature Index

B.O.'s Fish Wagon/K (P)
Boston's/P (P, W)
Brasserie Las Olas/B (P)
Busch's Seafood/P (P, W)
Café Boulud/P (T)
Café Cardozo (S, T)
Café Ibiza (P)
Café Med/K (G)
Café Pastis (S)
Cafe Sambal (P, W)
Café Solé/K (G, T)
Café Tu Tu Tango (P)
Caffe Da Vinci (S)
Caffe Luna Rosa/P (P, W)
Caffe Milano (P, W)
Calypso's Seafood/K (P)
Capri Blu/P (P)
Cap's Place Island/B (P, W)
Carnevale (T)
Carpaccio (P)
Casablanca Cafe/B (P)
Casa Larios (P)
Casa Paco (T)
Castaways/K (P, W)
Charley's Crab/B (P, T, W)
Chart House (P, W)
Chez Andrée/B (P, W)
Chico's Cantina/K (P)
China Grill (P)
Chuck & Harold's/P (G, P, S)
City Cellar Wine/P (P)
Commodore Water./K (P, W)
Conch Republic/K (P, W)
Crab House (P, W)
Crab Pot/P (P, W)
da Leo Trattoria (P, S)
De La Tierra/P (G, P, T)
Deli Lane Cafe (P, S)
Diego's (T)
Din. Rm./Little Palm/K (P, T, W)
Disco Fish (P)
Dogma (P)
Doraku (P)
Dune Deck Cafe/P (P, W)
11 Maple St./P (P)
11th St. Diner (P)
Elia (G, P, S)

El Rancho Grande (S)
El Toro Taco (P)
E.R. Bradley's/P (P, W)
15th St. Fisheries/B (P, T, W)
Finnegan's Wake Pub/K (P)
Fish 54 (T)
Flagler's/K (T, W)
Frank Keys Cafe/K (P)
French Bakery Cafe (S)
Fritz & Franz Bierhaus (P)
Front Porch Cafe (S, T, W)
Fujihana (S)
Garcia's (P, W)
Gianni's/B (G)
Giorgio's Grill/B (P, W)
Globe Cafe & Bar (S)
Gordon Biersch Brewery (P)
Gotham City/P (P)
Grand Café Key West/K (G, P)
Granny Feelgood's (S)
Grass Lounge (P)
Green Street Cafe (S)
Gus' Grille/K (T, W)
Half Shell Raw Bar/K (P, T, W)
Harry and the Natives/P (P)
Himmarshee/B (P, S)
Hog's Breath Saloon/K (P)
Hollywood Prime/B (P, W)
Hops/P (P)
Hosteria Romana (S)
Houston's/B (P)
Hurricane Café/P
Hurricane Grill/K (P)
Icebox Café (S)
Ichiban/P (G)
Il Fico (P)
Il Sole (P)
Il Toscano/B (P)
Indigo/B (P)
Islamorada Fish/B (P, W)
Islamorada Fish/K (P, W)
JB's on the Beach/B (P)
Jetty's/P (P, W)
Joe's Riverside Grille/B (T, W)
Joe's Seafood (T, W)
Johannes/P (P)
John G's/P (P, W)

256   subscribe to zagat.com

Special Feature Index

Kelly's Caribbean/K (G, P)
Keys Fisheries/K (P, W)
La Carreta (P)
Lake Avenue Grill/P (P)
La Loggia (S)
La Lupa di Roma (P)
Lana's Cafe/P (S)
La Palma (G)
Lario's (P)
Las Vacas Gordas (S)
La Tavernetta/B (P, W)
Latin American (S)
La Trattoria/K (P)
La Valentina (P)
La Vieille Maison/P (P)
Lazy Loggerhead/P (P)
Le Bouchon du Grove (P, S)
Lemon Twist (T)
L'Entrecôte de Paris (S)
Le Provençal (P, S)
Les Deux Fontaines (G, P, T, W)
Linda B. Steakhse. (T)
Locanda Sibilla (P)
Lombardi's (P, W)
Lorelei/K (P, T, W)
Los Ranchos (T, W)
Louie's Backyard/K (T, W)
Mama Jennie's (P)
Mangia Mangia/K (G)
Mangoes/K (G, P, T)
Mangos/B (P)
Mango's (P)
Mangrove Mama's/K (G)
Mariposa (T)
Marker 88/K (P)
Mark's at Park/P (P)
Mark's CityPlace/P (P)
Mark's South Beach (P)
Martin's Cafe/K (G)
Max's Beach Pl./B (P, W)
Max's Grille/B (P, W)
Max's Grille/P (P)
Meteor Smokehse./K (P)
Metro Kitchen (G)
Mezzanotte/B (P, W)
Michaels/K (G)
Monte's Fish Mkt./K (P, W)

Monty's Stone Crab (P, W)
Morada Bay Beach/K (P, T, W)
Mykonos (P)
Mykonos/P (P)
Nemo (P, T)
News Cafe (G, P, S)
Nexxt Cafe (P, S)
Nicola Seafood/K (P, W)
Nikki Beach (G, W)
Nina Rest. (T, W)
Off the Vine/P (P)
Oggi Caffe (P)
O'Hara's Hollywood/B (P, S, T)
Old Cutler Inn (P)
Old Key Lime/P (G, P, W)
Old Tavernier/K (T, W)
Old Town Mexican/K (P)
One Duval/K (T, W)
Origami/K (P)
Original Daily Bread (T)
Ortanique on Mile (P)
Ouzo's Greek (S)
Pacific Time (P)
Palm Beach Fish/P (S)
Paninoteca (P, S)
Papa Joe's/K (P)
Papa's/K
Pascal's on Ponce (S)
Paulo Luigi's (P)
Pearl (P, W)
Pelican Café (S, T)
Pepe's Cafe/K (P)
Peppy's in Gables (S, T)
Perricone's (G, P, T)
Peter's Stone Crabs/P (S)
P.F. Chang's (P)
Piccadilly Garden (G)
Pierre's/K (T, W)
Pineapple Grille/P (G, P)
Pino's (S)
Pisces/K
Pit Bar-B-Q (P, W)
Pizza Girls Pizza/P (S)
Pizza Rustica (S)
Porky's Bayside/K (P)
Portofino's/P (P, W)
Prime Grill (T, W)

vote at zagat.com

Special Feature Index

Provence Grill (P)
Puccini & Pasta (P)
Quay, The/K (P, W)
Quinn's Rest. (S, T)
Red Coral/B
Red Fish Grill (P, W)
Red Thai Rm. (P)
Renato's/P (T)
Restaurant St. Michel (S)
River House/B (P, T, W)
Rosinella (P, S)
Rottie's/P (P, T)
Rusty Pelican (T)
Sailfish Marina/P (P, W)
Salute/K (P, W)
Samba Rm./B (P, S)
San Loco/B (S)
Schooner's Seafood/P (P)
Scotty's Landing (P, W)
Seawatch/B (P, W)
Señor Frijoles/K (P)
Señor Frog's (P, S, T)
Sergio's (P, S, T)
Seven Mile/K (P, W)
Shirttail Charlie's/B (G, W)
Shoji (G, S)
Shooters/B (P)
Shula's on the Beach/B (P, W)
Shula's on the Beach/K (T, W)
Shula's Steak (P, W)
Smith & Wollensky (P, W)
Snapper's/K (P, W)
Snook's/K (P, W)
Sorrento/P (P)
Soyka (G, P)
Spiga (P)
Splendid Blendeds/P (P)
Sport Cafe (G, P, S, T)
Spoto's Oyster/P (S)
Spoto's PGA/P (P)
Spris (S)
Square One/K (T)
Stefano's (P)
Sugar Reef/B (S, W)
Suite 225/P (P)
Sundays on Bay (P)
Sundowners/K (P, W)

Sunset Grill/P (G)
Sunset Tavern (P)
Sunshine & AJ's (S)
Sushi Maki (S)
Sushi Saigon (S)
SushiSamba dromo (S)
Sushi Siam (P, S)
Talula (G, P)
Tango Grill (P)
Taverna Opa (P)
Taverna Opa/B (P, T, W)
Tequila Sunrise (P)
Testa's/P (G, S, T)
Teté Rest. (T)
Thai Cuisine/K (P)
Thai House So. Bch. (S)
Thai Orchid (P, S)
Timpano Italian/B (P, S)
Tiramesu (G, P, S)
Tobacco Rd. (P)
Tokyo Sushi/B (S)
Tony Chan's (P, W)
Torero (T)
Trattoria Sole (S)
Trevini/P (S)
Tuna's Waterfront (P, W)
Turtle Kraals/K (G, P, T, W)
Tutto Pasta (S)
Tutto Pizza (S)
1200 at the Biltmore (G)
1220 at the Tides (T)
Two Friends Patio/K (P)
Two Sisters (P)
Van Dyke Cafe (G, P, S)
Whale Harbor Inn/K (P, W)
White Lion (G)
Wish (G)
World Resources (P, S)
Yesterday's/B (T, W)
Yuca (S)
Zemi/P (P)

People-Watching
A&B Lobster/K
A Fish Called Avalon
Ago
Alice's at La-te-da/K

Special Feature Index

Amici Ristorante/P
Anthony's Runway 84/B
Aruba Beach Cafe/B
Bahamas Fish Mkt.
Balans
Barton G.
Bice Ristorante/P
Big City Tavern/B
Bimini Boatyard/B
Bistro Mezzaluna/B
Blue Door
Blue Heaven/K
Blue Sea
Brewzzi/P
Café Cardozo
Cafe L'Europe/P
Cafe Martorano/B
Cafe Med
Caffe Milano
Carnevale
Carpaccio
Casa Tua
Chart House
China Grill
Chuck & Harold's/P
Commodore Waterfront/K
da Leo Trattoria
Echo/P
E.R. Bradley's/P
Falcon House/P
Fleming
Forge, The
Front Porch Cafe
GiGi's Tavern/P
Globe Cafe & Bar
Grass Lounge
Green Street Cafe
Half Shell Raw Bar/K
Havana Harry's
Himmarshee/B
Hosteria Romana
Il Sole
JB's on the Beach/B
Joe Allen
Joe's Stone Crab
Kathy's Gazebo /P
La Lupa di Roma

Lario's
Las Vacas Gordas
La Trattoria/K
La Valentina
Le Bouchon du Grove
Leopard Lounge/P
L'Escalier/P
Les Deux Fontaines
Lester's Diner/B
Lincoln Road Café
Lombardi's
Lorelei/K
Mangoes/K
Mango's
Mark's at Park/P
Mark's CityPlace/P
Mark's Las Olas/B
Mark's South Beach
Max's Grille/P
Metro Kitchen
Mezzanotte
Monty's Stone Crab
Morton's
News Cafe
New York Prime/P
Nexxt Cafe
Nikki Beach
Nobu Miami Beach
No Name Pub/K
Pacific Time
Palm
Palm Beach Grill/P
Palme d'Or
Paninoteca
Paulo Luigi's
Pearl
Perricone's
Pete's Boca Raton/P
Prezzo
PT's Late Night/K
Rosinella
Rumi
Samba Rm./B
S&S Rest.
Satine/B
Shooters/B
Shula's Steak

vote at zagat.com

Special Feature Index

Sloppy Joe's/K
Sopra/P
Soyka
Spoto's Oyster/P
Spris
Sushi Rock
Sushi Siam
Ta-boo/P
Tantra
Taverna Opa
Taverna Opa/B
32 East/P
Tiramesu
Tobacco Rd.
Toni's Sushi
Touch
1220 at the Tides
264 the Grill/P
Van Dyke Cafe
Versailles
World Resources
Yuca

Power Scenes
Ago
Alice's at La-te-da/K
Amici Ristorante/P
Antonia's/K
Aria
Azul
Baleen
Big City Tavern/B
Big City Tavern/P
Bistro Mezzaluna/B
Black Orchid Cafe/B
Blue Door
Cacao 1737
Caffe Abbracci
Caffe Da Vinci
Capital Grille
Carpaccio
Casa D'Angelo/B
Casa Juancho
Casa Tua
Chef Allen's
Diego's
Fish Joynt

Flagler Steakhse./P
Forge, The
Four Seasons/P
Gordon Biersch Brewery
Graziano's
Grill Room/B
Havana Harry's
Himmarshee/B
Jackson's Steakhse./B
Joe Allen
Joe's Stone Crab
La Carreta
La Palma
Le Mont/P
Le Provençal
Mark's Las Olas/B
Max's Beach Pl./B
Metro Kitchen
Morton's
New York Prime/P
Nobu Miami Beach
Norman's
Oggi Caffe
Ortanique on Mile
Pacific Time
Palm
Palme d'Or
Pascal's on Ponce
Perricone's
Restaurant St. Michel
Ristorante La Bussola
Ruth's Chris
Samba Rm./B
Seven Fish/K
Shibui
Shula's Steak
Sinclair's/P
Smith & Wollensky
Stefano's
Ta-boo/P
Tantra
32 East/P
Toni's Sushi
Tuscan Steak
Versailles

Special Feature Index

Private Rooms
(Restaurants charge less at off times; call for capacity)
Abbondanza/K
Addison/P
Amalfi
Amici Ristorante/P
Anchor Inn/P
Andre's Steakhse./B
Angelo & Maxie's/P
Angelo of Mulberry/B
Anita's Mexicano/B
Antonia's/K
Aquatica Beach Bar
Aria
Armadillo Cafe/B
Atlantic's Edge/K
Ayestaran
Benihana/K
Benihana/Samurai
Bentley's/K
Beverly Hills Cafe
Bice Ristorante
Big Cheese
Bimini Boatyard/B
Bin 595/B
Bistro Zinc
Bizcaya Grill
Blue Moon Fish/B
Bohemian Gardens/P
Bongos
Bongusto! Rist./B
Brooks/B
Bungalow 9/B
Cabana/P
Cacao 1737
Café Boulud/P
Cafe L'Europe/P
Cafe Med
Cafe Prima Pasta
Café Protégé/P
Cafe Vico/B
Caffe Da Vinci
Camille's/K
Capital Grille
Capriccio/B
Carmen

Casablanca Cafe/B
Casa D'Angelo/B
Casa Juancho
Casa Paco
Charley's Crab/B
Charley's Crab/P
China Grill
Christine Lee's
Christy's
Commodore Waterfront/K
Crack'd Conch/K
Darrel/Oliver's Cafe/B
De La Tierra/P
Diego's
Echo/P
Eduardo de San Angel/B
El Novillo
Escopazzo
15th St. Fisheries/B
Flagler's/K
Fleming
Forge, The
French Quarter/B
Gotham City/P
Grand Café Key West/K
Graziano's
Green Street Cafe
Grille, The/P
Guayacan
Gus' Grille/K
Havana Harry's
Hosteria Romana
House of India
Islamorada Fish/K
Jackson's Steakhse./B
Joe's Stone Crab
John Martin's
Kathy's Gazebo /P
Kelly's Caribbean/K
La Brochette /B
La Carreta
La Casita
La Creperie/B
La Dorada
La Loggia
La Palma
La Paloma

vote at zagat.com

Special Feature Index

Lario's
Las Culebrinas
Las Vegas/B
Latin American
La Vieille Maison/P
Le Cafe de Paris/B
Le Festival*Casa
Le Provençal
Les Deux Fontaines
Les Halles
Linda B. Steakhse.
Little Havana
Lorelei/K
Los Ranchos
Louie's Backyard/K
Maggiano's Little Italy/P
Mai-Kai/B
Mariposa
Mark's South Beach
Maroosh
Martin's Cafe/K
Michaels/K
Monty's Stone Crab
Morton's
Nemo
No Name Pub/K
Norman's
Oggi Caffe
Old Cutler Inn
Old Lisbon
Paddy Mac's/P
Palm
Palme d'Or
Pelican Café
Pete's Boca Raton/P
P.F. Chang's
Piccadilly Caf.
Pierre's/K
Pisces/K
Porcão
Portofino's/P
Quay, The/K
Quinn's Rest.
Rainbow Palace/B
Raindancer Steakhouse/P
Red Fish Grill
Restaurant St. Michel

Ristorante La Bussola
River House/B
River House/P
Rumi
Rusty Pelican
Ruth's Chris
Ruth's Chris/B
Sailfish Marina/P
Samba Rm./B
Seawatch/B
Seven Mile/K
Shooters/B
Shorty's BBQ
Shula's Steak
Sinclair's/P
Smith & Wollensky
Snappers/P
Sopra/P
Square One/K
Stefano's
Sunset Tavern
Sushi Saigon
Taco Rico
Tantra
TapTap
Testa's/P
3030 Ocean/B
32 East/P
Timpano Italian/B
Titanic Brewery
Tobacco Rd.
Tony Chan's
Tony Roma's/P
Torero
Tropical Acres/B
Tropical Chinese
Tsunami/P
Tumi/B
Turtle Kraals/K
1220 at the Tides
Two Chefs
Two Sisters
Whale Harbor Inn/K
Wilt Chamberlain's/P
Wine Cellar/B

Special Feature Index

Wolfgang Puck Cafe/B
Yesterday's/B
Yuca

Prix Fixe Menus
(Call for prices and times)
Angelo & Maxie's/P
Arturo's/P
Benihana/Samurai
Blue Door
Blue Moon Fish/B
Bonefish Willy's/B
Brasserie Las Olas/B
Brooks/B
Cacao 1737
Cafe Chardonnay/P
Cafe Claude/B
Cafe du Parc/P
Cafe Marquesa/K
Café Med/K
Carmine's Ocean Grill/P
Chef Allen's
China Grill
Cobblestone Cafe/P
Couco Pazzo/P
Creolina's/B
Crystal Cafe
Doraku
Echo/P
Food Lover's Cafe/B
Francesco
Hanna's Diner
Hi-Life Cafe/B
Hot Tin Roof/K
Islas Canarias
Johannes/P
La Loggia
L'Anjou/P
La Petite Maison/P
Las Vegas/B
La Trattoria/P
La Vieille Maison/P
Le Brittany/P
Le Mistral/P
Leopard Lounge/P
L'Escalier/P
Le Vieux Paris/P

Linda B./Boca Raton/P
Little Havana
Lorelei/K
Maggiano's Little Italy/P
Mai-Kai/B
Marc's Chophse./P
Mario's Tuscan/P
Mark's at Park/P
Mark's South Beach
Maroosh
Martha's Supper Club/B
Melody Inn
Melting Pot
Melting Pot/P
New Chinatown
No Anchovies!/P
Nobu Miami Beach
Norman's
Novecento
Orchids of Siam/P
Outback Steakhouse
Porcão
Romeo's Cafe
Shooters/B
Siam Gourmet/P
Square One/K
Stefano's
Tony Chan's
Tumi/B
Vangelli's/P
Wine Cellar/B

Quiet Conversation
Abbey Dining Rm.
AltaMar
Amalfi
Anokha
Antonia's/K
Bagatelle/K
Balans
Baleen
Bangkok Bangkok
Bangkok Bangkok
Barracuda Grill/K
Ben's Steakhse./P
Bizaare Ave. Cafe/P
Black Orchid Cafe/B

vote at zagat.com 263

Special Feature Index

Boulevard Grille/P
Busch's Seafood/P
Cafe Avanti
Cafe Cellini/P
Café Ibiza
Cafe Marquesa/K
Cafe Seville/B
Caffe Da Vinci
Chef Allen's
Chez Jean-Pierre/P
Cobblestone Cafe/P
Creolina's/B
Crystal Cafe
De La Tierra/P
Eduardo de San Angel/B
Escopazzo
15th St. Fisheries/B
Francesco
Grandma's French Cafe/B
Green Street Cafe
Grillfish
Hi-Life Cafe/B
Icebox Café
India House/B
Johannes/P
Josef's/B
Kelly's Caribbean/K
La Dorada
Lake Avenue Grill/P
L'Anjou/P
Las Vegas/B
La Tavernetta/B
La Vie en Rose/B
La Vieille Maison/P
Le Brittany/P
Le Cafe de Paris/B
Le Mistral/P
Le Mont/P
L'Escalier/P
Martin's Cafe/K
Max's Beach Pl./B
Morada Bay Beach/K
Oasis Cafe
Out of Denmark/P
Palme d'Or
Pascal's on Ponce
Pellegrino's/B
Peppy's in Gables
Provence Grill
Rainbow Palace/B
Renato's/P
Ristorante La Bussola
Romeo's Cafe
Ruen Thai
Ruth's Chris
Sage French/B
Seven Fish/K
Sheldon's
Shula's on the Beach/K
Siam Lotus
Stresa/P
Sunfish Grill/B
Thai House So. Bch.
Thai Toni
Toni's Sushi
Trattoria Luna
264 the Grill/P
Victoria Park/B
Yasuko's
Yesterday's/B
Zemi/P

Raw Bars

A&B Lobster/K
Aruba Beach Cafe/B
Azul
Baleen
Bentley's/K
Blue Moon Fish/B
Bonefish Willy's/B
Brasserie Mon Ami/P
Calypso Rest./Raw Bar/B
Cap's Place Island/B
China Grill
City Oyster/P
Conch Republic/K
Conchy Joe's Seafood/P
Crab House
Crazy Buffet/P
Dave's Last Resort/P
Duval Beach Club/K
Echo/P
Elia
Fish House/K

Special Feature Index

GiGi's Tavern/P
Half Shell Raw Bar/K
Hog's Breath Saloon/K
Hurricane Grill/K
Islamorada Fish/B
Joe's Seafood
La Dorada
Legal Sea Foods/B
Legal Sea Foods/P
Les Deux Fontaines
Monte's Fish Mkt./K
Monty's Stone Crab
Monty's Stone Crab/P
Nemo
Nicola Seafood/K
Old Cutler Oyster
Old Key Lime/P
Papa Joe's/K
Papa's/K
Pepe's Cafe/K
Pescado
Quay, The/K
Quinn's Rest.
River Oyster Bar
Rustic Inn Crabhse./B
Snapper's/K
Spoto's Oyster/P
Spoto's PGA/P
Tarpon Bend/B
3030 Ocean/B
Tokyo Bowl
Turtle Kraals/K
Two Dragons
Two Friends Patio/K
Whale Harbor Inn/K
Whale's Rib/B

Reserve Ahead

A&B Lobster/K
Alcazar
Alice's at La-te-da/K
Ambrosia/K
Anacapri
Angelo of Mulberry/B
Anokha
Anthony's Runway 84/B
Antonia's/K
Atlantic's Edge/K
B.E.D.
Bice Ristorante/P
Bizcaya Grill
Brooks/B
Cafe Avanti
Cafe Chardonnay/P
Cafe Seville/B
Café Solé/K
Caffe Abbracci
Casa D'Angelo/B
Casa Tua
Charley's Crab/B
Chef Allen's
Chez Jean-Pierre/P
Dakotah 624/P
Dining Rm./Little Palm/K
Eduardo de San Angel/B
Escopazzo
Finnegan's Wake Pub/K
Fleming
Forge, The
Four Seasons/P
Francesco
Gianni's/B
Grass Lounge
Graziano's
Grazie Cafe
Grill Room/B
Il Trullo/P
Johannes/P
Kathy's Gazebo /P
La Belle Epoque/P
La Petite Maison/P
La Vieille Maison/P
La Villetta/P
Le Bouchon du Grove
Le Brittany/P
Le Mistral/P
Leopard Lounge/P
Le Provençal
Les Deux Fontaines
Linda B. Steakhse.
Mai-Kai/B
Mangrove Mama's/K
Marcello's La Sirena/P
Mario's Tuscan/P

vote at zagat.com

Special Feature Index

Mark's South Beach
Maroosh
Martha's Supper Club/B
Martin's Cafe/K
Morton's/P
One Duval/K
Opera Italian/K
Out of Denmark/P
Palm
Palme d'Or
Pascal's on Ponce
Pellegrino's/B
Pisces/K
Prezzo
Prime Grill
Rainbow Palace/B
Randazzo's
Red Fish Grill
Red Thai Rm.
Renato's/P
Ristorante La Bussola
Romeo's Cafe
Samba Rm./B
Sapori/P
Sergio's
Sopra/P
Spiga
Splendid Blendeds/P
Square One/K
Tambo Rest.
Tantra
32 East/P
Tropical Bistro/P
1200 at the Biltmore
Two Dragons
Uncle Tai's/P

Romantic Places

Addison/P
A La Folie
Alice's at La-te-da/K
Amalfi
Angelo of Mulberry/B
Antonia's/K
Aria
Arturo's/P
Atlantic's Edge/K
Azul
Bagatelle/K
Baleen
Barracuda Grill/K
Bice Ristorante
Biscayne Wine
Black Orchid Cafe/B
Blue Moon Fish/B
Brooks/B
Cacao 1737
Café Boulud/P
Cafe Chardonnay/P
Cafe L'Europe/P
Cafe Marquesa/K
Cafe Seville/B
Caffe Vialetto
Calypso's Seafood/K
Capri Blu/P
Casablanca Cafe/B
Casa Tua
Chez Jean-Pierre/P
Creolina's/B
Crystal Cafe
De La Tierra/P
Dining Rm./Little Palm/K
Eduardo de San Angel/B
Escopazzo
Flagler's/K
Forge, The
Four Seasons/P
Francesco
Grillfish
Hi-Life Cafe/B
Hot Tin Roof/K
Il Trullo/P
Joe's Seafood
Josef's/B
Kathy's Gazebo /P
Kelly's Caribbean/K
La Belle Epoque/P
La Palma
La Paloma
La Petite Maison/P
La Tavernetta/B
La Vie en Rose/B
La Vieille Maison/P
Le Brittany/P

Special Feature Index

Le Mistral/P
Le Mont/P
Leopard Lounge/P
Le Provençal
L'Escalier/P
Louie's Backyard/K
Marker 88/K
Martin's Cafe/K
Max's Beach Pl./B
Melody Inn
Metro Kitchen
Michaels/K
Morada Bay Beach/K
Moroccan Nights
Morton's
Nina Rest.
Norman's
Novecento
Old Lisbon
One Duval/K
Out of Denmark/P
Palme d'Or
Pearl
Peppy's in Gables
Perricone's
Piccadilly Garden
Pierre's/K
Primavera/B
Rainbow Palace/B
Red Fish Grill
Renato's/P
Restaurant St. Michel
Ristorante La Bussola
River House/B
Romeo's Cafe
Ruggero's/B
Samba Rm./B
Satine/B
Seven Fish/K
Shirttail Charlie's/B
Shula's on the Beach/K
Sinclair's/P
Smith & Wollensky
Spiga
Sugar Reef/B
Sundowners on the Bay/K
Thai Toni

Toni's Sushi
Trattoria Luna
Trattoria Sole
Trevini/P
1200 at the Biltmore
1220 at the Tides
Two Dragons
Two Sisters
Victoria Park/B
Wish
Yesterday's/B

Singles Scenes
Ago
Aruba Beach Cafe/B
Banana Boat/P
Big City Tavern/B
Big City Tavern/P
Bimini Boatyard/B
Blue Door
Blue Heaven/K
Boston's/P
Cabana/P
Cafe Martorano/B
Café Tu Tu Tango
Caffe Milano
Calypso's Seafood/K
China Grill
DaDa/P
Dave's Last Resort/P
Duval Beach Club/K
East City Grill/B
11th St. Diner
E.R. Bradley's/P
Falcon House/P
Fish 54
Forge, The
Front Porch Cafe
GiGi's Tavern/P
Giorgio's Grill/B
Globe Cafe & Bar
Gotham City/P
Grass Lounge
Half Shell Raw Bar/K
Himmarshee/B
Houston's
Jake's

vote at zagat.com

Special Feature Index

JB's on the Beach/B
Jimmy Buffett's/K
John Martin's
Kelly's Caribbean/K
Lario's
Mango's
Mark's Las Olas/B
Martha's/K
Mezzanotte
Mezzanotte/B
Monty's Stone Crab
Nemo
Nikki Beach
O'Hara's Hollywood/B
Old Cutler Oyster
Pearl
Pete's Boca Raton/P
Prezzo
Rhythm Cafe/P
Rumi
Samba Rm./B
Señor Frog's
Shooters/B
Sopra/P
Soyka
Sushi Rock
Tantra
Tarpon Bend/B
Taverna Opa
Taverna Opa/B
Thai House So. Bch.
Thai Toni
32 East/P
Titanic Brewery
Tobacco Rd.
Tuna's Waterfront
Turtle Kraals/K
Tuscan Steak
Van Dyke Cafe
Yasuko's

Sleepers
(Good to excellent food, but little known)
Anita's Mexicano/B
Bayside Grill/K
Bin 595/B
Bongusto! Rist./B
Bungalow 9/B
Café Med/K
Calypso's Seafood/K
Casa Paco
Casa Panza
Cay Da/P
Citronelle
Courtyard Grill/P
Crack'd Conch/K
Crepe Christina/B
Elia
Flagler's/K
Flamingo
Frank Keys Cafe/K
Gallery Grille/P
Gil Capa's Bistro
Hanna's Diner
Herbie's/K
Hong Kong City BBQ/B
Hosteria Romana
India House/B
Johannes/P
Kaiyó/K
Keys Fisheries/K
L'Avenue/P
Lemon Twist
Lila's
Lombardi's
Mangrove Mama's/K
Miyako
Mo's/K
Old Tavernier/K
One Ninety
Opera Italian/K
Pisces/K
Prime Grill
Renaisa
Seafood World/B
Siam Cuisine/B
Sinclair's/P
Squid Row/K
Stefano's
Su Shin/B
Sushi Rok/P
Time Out BBQ/K
Tokyo Sushi/B

Special Feature Index

Tutto Pizza
Vangelli's/P
Yasuko's
Zuperpollo

Teen Appeal
Abbondanza/K
Archie's Pizza
Aruba Beach Cafe/B
Baja Fresh Mexican Grill
Benihana/K
Benihana/Samurai
Berries
Big Pink
Blue Heaven/K
Café Tu Tu Tango
Cheeburger Cheeburger/B
Cheesecake Factory/B
Dave's Last Resort/P
Deli, The/K
Dennis Pharmacy/K
Duval Beach Club/K
11th St. Diner
Front Porch Cafe
Hard Rock Cafe
Hard Rock Cafe/K
Il Mulino/B
Kelly's Caribbean/K
Kyoto Sushi/P
La Carreta
La Gastronomia
La Sandwicherie
La Spada's Hoagies/B
Latin American
Mangoes/K
Mario the Baker
Mario the Baker/B
Melting Pot
Melting Pot/P
Miami Juice
Mississippi Sweets/P
Mrs. Mendoza's
News Cafe
Outback Steakhouse
Paquito's
Paulo Luigi's
P.F. Chang's

Picnics at Allen's
Piola
Pit Bar-B-Q
Pizza Rustica
Prezzo/P
Randazzo's
Spris
Sushi Maki
Taco Rico
Tarpon Bend/B
Tequila Sunrise
Texas Taco
Versailles
Wilt Chamberlain's/P

Theme Restaurants
Bahama Breeze
Benihana/B
Benihana/P
Brogue's/P
Buca di Beppo/B
Bungalow 9/B
Cap's Place Island/B
Eduardo de San Angel/B
Green Turtle Inn/K
Hard Rock Cafe
Hard Rock Cafe/K
Jimmy Buffett's/K
Joe's Crab Shack/B
Kelly's Caribbean/K
Maguire's Hill 16/B
Mai-Kai/B
Melting Pot
Melting Pot/P
Montezuma/P
Moroccan Nights
Outback Steakhouse
Outback Steakhouse/B
Out of Denmark/P
Paddy Mac's/P
Palm Beach Grill/P
Roadhouse Grill
Roadhouse Grill/B
Shula's on the Beach/B
Sloppy Joe's/K
Spoto's Oyster/P
Sublime/B

vote at zagat.com

Special Feature Index

Taverna Opa/B
Wilt Chamberlain's/P

Views
A&B Lobster/K
A Fish Called Avalon
Anchor Inn/P
Aquatica Beach Bar
Aruba Beach Cafe/B
Atlantic's Edge/K
Bagatelle/K
Baleen
Banana Boat/P
Bayside Grill/K
Bayside Seafood
Bellagio/P
Benihana/B
Benihana/K
Benihana/P
Benihana/Samurai
Bentley's/K
Big Fish
Blue Moon Fish/B
Boston's/P
Busch's Seafood/P
Cafe Sambal
Caffe Luna Rosa/P
Castaways/K
Charley's Crab/B
Charley's Crab/P
Chart House
Commodore Waterfront/K
Crab House
Crab Pot/P
De La Tierra/P
Dining Rm./Little Palm/K
Duval Beach Club/K
E.R. Bradley's/P
15th St. Fisheries/B
Four Seasons/P
Front Porch Cafe
Giorgio's Grill/B
Half Shell Raw Bar/K
Houston's
Islamorada Fish/K
JB's on the Beach/B
Jetty's/P

Joe's Seafood
John G's/P
Keys Fisheries/K
Lario's
La Tavernetta/B
Lazy Loggerhead/P
Le Mont/P
Les Deux Fontaines
Lombardi's
Lorelei/K
Los Ranchos
Louie's Backyard/K
Lucca/P
Mariposa
Marker 88/K
Martha's/K
Martha's Supper Club/B
Martin's Cafe/K
Max & Eddie's/P
Max's Beach Pl./B
Max's Grille/P
Monte's Fish Mkt./K
Monty's Stone Crab
Morada Bay Beach/K
Nicola Seafood/K
Nikki Beach
Nina Rest.
Old Key Lime/P
One Duval/K
Palme d'Or
Papa Joe's/K
Pierre's/K
Portofino's/P
Prime Grill
Quay, The/K
Red Fish Grill
River House/B
River House/P
Rottie's/P
Rusty Pelican
Sailfish Marina/P
Scotty's Landing
Seawatch/B
Shooters/B
Shula's on the Beach/K
Shula's Steak
Sinclair's/P

Special Feature Index

Smith & Wollensky
Snapper's/K
Sugar Reef/B
Sundays on Bay
Sundowners on the Bay/K
3030 Ocean/B
Tony Chan's
Torero
Tuna's Waterfront
Turtle Kraals/K
1220 at the Tides
Two Dragons
Whale Harbor Inn/K
World Resources
Yesterday's/B

Visitors on Expense Account

Alice's at La-te-da/K
Angelo & Maxie's/P
Antonia's/K
Aria
Armadillo Cafe/B
Arturo's/P
Atlantic's Edge/K
Azul
Baleen
Barracuda Grill/K
B.E.D.
Bice Ristorante
Bice Ristorante/P
Black Orchid Cafe/B
Cafe Chardonnay/P
Cafe L'Europe/P
Cafe Martorano/B
Caffe Abbracci
Caffe Milano
Carpaccio
Casa D'Angelo/B
Casa Tua
Chef Allen's
Chez Jean-Pierre/P
China Grill
Christine Lee's
Christy's
Crystal Cafe
Darrel/Oliver's Bistro/B
Darrel/Oliver's Cafe/B
Echo/P
Eduardo de San Angel/B
Escopazzo
Flagler Grill/P
Forge, The
Four Seasons/P
Himmarshee/B
Hollywood Prime/B
Jackson's Steakhse./B
Joe's Stone Crab
Johannes/P
Kathy's Gazebo /P
La Belle Epoque/P
La Vieille Maison/P
Le Brittany/P
Le Mistral/P
Le Mont/P
Leopard Lounge/P
Le Provençal
L'Escalier/P
Louie's Backyard/K
Lucca/P
Mai-Kai/B
Marc's Chophse./P
Mark's Las Olas/B
Mark's South Beach
Maxwell's Chophse./P
Monty's Stone Crab
Morton's
New York Prime/P
Norman's
One Duval/K
Ortanique on Mile
Osteria del Teatro
Pacific Time
Palm
Palme d'Or
Pascal's on Ponce
Pearl
Pete's Boca Raton/P
Pierre's/K
Rumi
Ruth's Chris
Ruth's Chris/B
Samba Rm./B
Satine/B

Special Feature Index

Shula's on the Beach/B
Shula's Steak
Shula's Steak House/P
Smith & Wollensky
Square One/K
SushiSamba dromo
Ta-boo/P
Tantra
Thai Toni
3030 Ocean/B
Timpano Italian/B
Tony Chan's
Touch
Tuscan Steak
1200 at the Biltmore
1220 at the Tides
Zemi/P

Waterside

Anchor Inn/P
Aquatica Beach Bar
Aruba Beach Cafe/B
Atlantic's Edge/K
Baleen
Bayside Grill/K
Bayside Seafood
Benihana/B
Benihana/K
Benihana/Samurai
Big Fish
Blue Moon Fish/B
Bongos
Boston's/P
Busch's Seafood/P
Cafe Sambal
Caffe Luna Rosa/P
Caffe Milano
Castaways/K
Charley's Crab/B
Charley's Crab/P
Chart House
Commodore Waterfront/K
Conch Republic/K
Conchy Joe's Seafood/P
Crab House
Crab Pot/P
Dining Rm./Little Palm/K
Dune Deck Cafe/P
Duval Beach Club/K
East City Grill/B
E.R. Bradley's/P
15th St. Fisheries/B
Flagler's/K
Gallagher's Gourmet/K
Garcia's
Giorgio's Grill/B
Gus' Grille/K
Half Shell Raw Bar/K
Hard Rock Cafe
Islamorada Fish/K
Jetty's/P
Joe's Riverside Grille/B
Joe's Seafood
John G's/P
Keys Fisheries/K
La Tavernetta/B
Les Deux Fontaines
Lombardi's
Lorelei/K
Los Ranchos
Louie's Backyard/K
Martha's/K
Martha's Supper Club/B
Max's Beach Pl./B
Miami Juice
Monte's Fish Mkt./K
Monty's Stone Crab
Morada Bay Beach/K
Nicola Seafood/K
Nikki Beach
Nina Rest.
Old Key Lime/P
Old Tavernier/K
One Duval/K
Pierre's/K
Pit Bar-B-Q
Portofino's/P
Quay, The/K
Red Fish Grill
River House/B
River House/P
Sailfish Marina/P
Salute/K
Scotty's Landing

Special Feature Index

Seawatch/B
Seven Mile/K
Shirttail Charlie's/B
Shula's on the Beach/B
Shula's on the Beach/K
Shula's Steak
Sinclair's/P
Smith & Wollensky
Snapper's/K
Snook's/K
Sugar Reef/B
Sundowners on the Bay/K
Taverna Opa/B
Tony Chan's
Tuna's Waterfront
Turtle Kraals/K
Whale Harbor Inn/K
Yesterday's/B

Winning Wine Lists

Alice's at La-te-da/K
AltaMar
Anacapri
Aria
Atlantic's Edge/K
Azul
Baleen
Bentley's/K
Bice Ristorante
Big City Tavern/P
Biscayne Wine
Blue Heaven/K
Blu la Pizzeria
Bugatti, Art of Pasta
Cacao 1737
Cafe Chardonnay/P
Café Ibiza
Cafe L'Europe/P
Cafe Marquesa/K
Cafe Sambal
Cafe Seville/B
Caffe Abbracci
Caffe Da Vinci
Caffe Milano
Captain's Tavern
Carnevale
Carpaccio

Casa Juancho
Chef Allen's
Crystal Cafe
Darrel/Oliver's Cafe/B
Dining Rm./Little Palm/K
Doraku
East City Grill/B
Escopazzo
Flagler Grill/P
Forge, The
Globe Cafe & Bar
Grappa
Graziano's
Grazie Cafe
Hanna's Diner
Henry's/P
Himmarshee/B
Hobo's Fish Joint/B
Hot Tin Roof/K
Il Sole
Jackson's Steakhse./B
Joe's Stone Crab
Johannes/P
Kelly's Caribbean/K
La Barraca/B
La Belle Epoque/P
La Lupa di Roma
La Trattoria/K
La Vieille Maison/P
L'Escalier/P
Les Halles
Louie's Backyard/K
Mangia Mangia/K
Marker 88/K
Mark's CityPlace/P
Max & Eddie's/P
Melting Pot/P
Mezzanotte
Michaels/K
Morada Bay Beach/K
Morton's
Nemo
Norman's
One Duval/K
Ortanique on Mile
Pacific Time
Palm

Special Feature Index

Palme d'Or
Pascal's on Ponce
Pierre's/K
Pineapple Grille/P
Reef Grill/P
Restaurant St. Michel
Salute/K
Shula's on the Beach/K
Shula's Steak
Smith & Wollensky
Snappers/P
Snook's/K
Square One/K
Stefano's
3030 Ocean/B
32 East/P
Timo
Tropical Bistro/P
Tuscan Steak
1200 at the Biltmore
Zemi/P

Alphabetical Page Index

All restaurants are in Miami/Dade County unless otherwise noted (B=Broward County; K=Keys/Monroe County; P=Palm Beach County).

Alphabetical Page Index

A&B Lobster House/K	90
Abbey Dining Room	18
Abbondanza/K	90
Addison, The/P	164
A Fish Called Avalon	18
Ago	18
A La Folie	18
Alcazar	18
Alice's at La-te-da/K	90
AltaMar	18
Amalfi	19
Ambrosia/K	90
Ambry, The/B	120
America/P	164
Amici Ristorante/P	164
Anacapri	19
Anchor Inn/P	164
Andiamo! Pizza	19
Andre's Steakhouse/B	120
Angelo & Maxie's /P	164
Angelo of Mulberry St./B	120
Anita's/B	120
Anokha	19
Anthony's Runway 84/B	120
Antonia's/K	91
Aquatica Beach Bar	19
Archie's Gourmet Pizza	20
Argentango Grill/B	121
Aria	20
Armadillo Cafe/B	121
Arnie & Richie's Deli	20
Arturo's Ristorante/P	165
Aruba Beach Cafe/B	121
Artichoke's	20
Athena by the Sea/B	121
Atlantic's Edge/K	91
Aura	20
Ayestaran	21
Azul	21
Bagatelle/K	91
Bagel Emporium	21
Bagels & Co.	21
Bahama Breeze	21
Bahama Breeze/B	121
Bahamas Fish Market	22
Baja Fresh	22
Balans	22
Baleen	22
Bali Café	22
Bamboo Club, The	23
Bamboo Club, The/P	165
Bamboo Garden	23
Bamboo Garden/B	122
Banana Boat/P	165
Banana Cafe/K	91
Bangkok Bangkok	23
Bangkok Bangkok	23
Bar, The	23
Bar-B-Q Barn	23
Barracuda Grill/K	91
Barton G.	24
Basilico	24
Bavarian Village/B	122
Bayside Grill/K	92
Bayside Seafood	24
B.e.d.	24
Bellagio/P	165
Bella Luna	24
Bellante's Pizza	24
Bellante's Pizza/B	122
Ben's Steakhouse/P	166
Benihana/B	122
Benihana/K	92
Benihana/P	165
Benihana/Samurai	25
Bentley's/K	92
Berries	25
Beverly Hills Cafe	25
Beverly Hills Cafe/B	122
Beverly Hills Cafe/P	166
Bice Ristorante	25
Bice Ristorante/P	166
Big Cheese	25
Big City Tavern/B	122
Big City Tavern/P	166
Big Fish	26
Big Pink	26
Bimini Boatyard/B	122
Bimini Twist/P	166
Bin 595/B	123
Biscayne Wine	26
Bistro, The/P	167
Bistro Mezzaluna/B	123
Bistro Zenith/P	167
Bistro Zinc	26
Bizaare Avenue Cafe/P	167
Bizcaya Grill	26
Black Orchid Cafe/B	123
Blue Anchor Pub/P	167
Blue Door	27
Blue Heaven/K	92
Blue Moon Fish Co./B	123
Blue Sea	27
Blu la Pizzeria del Sole	27
Bohemian Gardens/P	167
Bond St. Lounge	27
Bonefish Grill/B	123
Bonefish Willy's/B	124
Bongos Cuban Café	27
Bongusto! Ristorante/B	124
B.O.'s Fish Wagon/K	92
Boston's/P	167
Botticelli	28
Boulevard Grille/P	168

276   subscribe to zagat.com

Alphabetical Page Index

Brasserie Las Olas/B	124	Carlos & Pepe's/B	127
Brasserie Mon Ami/P	168	Carmen	31
Brewzzi/P	168	Carmine's Ocean Grill/P	171
Brogue's/P	168	Carnevale	32
Brooks/B	124	Carpaccio	32
B's Restaurant/K	92	Casablanca Cafe/B	127
Buca di Beppo/B	124	Casa D'Angelo/B	127
Bugatti, Art of Pasta	28	Casa Juancho	32
Bungalow 9/B	125	Casa Larios	32
Buonasera/P	169	Casa Paco	32
Busch's Seafood/P	169	Casa Panza	33
By Word of Mouth/B	125	Casa Tua	33
Cabana/P	169	Caspian Persian Grill/B	128
Cacao 1737	28	Castaways/K	94
Cafe Avanti	28	Catfish Dewey's/B	128
Cafe Bellino/P	169	Cay Da/P	172
Café Boulud/P	169	Chalán/El Chalán	33
Café Cardozo	28	Charley's Crab/B	128
Cafe Cellini/P	170	Charley's Crab/P	172
Cafe Chardonnay/P	170	Chart House	33
Cafe Claude/B	125	Cheeburger Cheeburger/B	128
Cafe Demetrio	29	Cheeburger Cheeburger/P	172
Cafe du Parc/P	170	Cheesecake Factory	33
Café Ibiza	29	Cheesecake Factory/B	129
Café La Bonne Crepe/B	125	Cheesecake Factory/P	172
Cafe L'Europe/P	170	Chef Allen's	34
Cafe Marquesa/K	93	Chez Andrée/B	129
Cafe Martorano/B	125	Chez Jean-Pierre Bistro/P	172
Cafe Med	29	Chico's Cantina/K	94
Café Med/K	93	China Grill	34
Café Pastis	29	Chispa	34
Cafe Prima Pasta	29	Christina Wan's/B	129
Café Protégé/P	170	Christine Lee's	34
Café Ragazzi	30	Christine's Roti Shop	34
Cafe Sambal	30	Christy's	35
Cafe Seville/B	126	Chuck & Harold's/P	172
Café Solé/K	93	Chuck's Steakhouse/B	129
Café Tu Tu Tango	30	Chuck's Steakhouse/P	173
Cafe Vico/Vico's Down./B	126	Citronelle	35
Caffe Abbracci	30	City Cellar Wine Bar/P	173
Caffe Da Vinci	30	City Oyster/P	173
Caffe Luna Rosa/P	171	Cobblestone Cafe/P	173
Caffe Milano	31	Cohiba Brasserie/B	129
Caffe Vialetto	31	Commodore Waterfront/K	94
California Pizza Kitchen	31	Conca D'Oro/B	130
California Pizza Kitchen/B	126	Conch Republic/K	94
California Pizza Kitchen/P	171	Conchy Joe's Seafood/P	173
Calypso Rest./Raw Bar/B	126	Costello's/B	130
Calypso's Seafood Grille/K	93	Couco Pazzo/P	174
Camille's/K	93	Courtyard Grill/P	174
Canyon/B	126	Crab House	35
Capital Grille	31	Crab Pot/P	174
Capri Blu/P	171	Crack'd Conch Key Largo/K	94
Capriccio/B	127	Cracked Conch Cafe/K	95
Cap's Place Island/B	127	Crazy Buffet/P	174
Captain's Tavern	31	Creolina's/B	130
Cardello's Pizza/P	171	Crepe Christina/B	130

vote at zagat.com

Alphabetical Page Index

Croissants de France/K	95	Flanigans	39
Crystal Cafe	35	Fleming – Taste of Denmark	40
Cuban Cafe/P	174	Food Lover's Cafe/B	132
Cucina Dell' Arte/P	174	Forge, The	40
Dab Haus	35	Four Seasons/P	178
DaDa/P	175	Fox's Sherron Inn	40
da Ermanno	36	Francesco	40
Daily Bread	36	Frankie's Pier 5/B	132
Dakotah 624/P	175	Frank Keys Cafe/K	97
da Leo Trattoria	36	French Bakery Cafe	40
Dan Marino's	36	French Place/B	133
Dan Marino's/B	130	French Quarter/B	133
Darrel & Oliver's Bistro 17/B	131	Fritz & Franz Bierhaus	41
Darrel & Oliver's Cafe/B	131	Front Porch Cafe	41
Dave's Last Resort/P	175	Fujihana	41
David's Cafe	36	Fulvio's 1900/B	133
De La Tierra/P	175	Gables Diner	41
Deli, The/K	95	Galanga/B	133
Deli Lane Cafe	36	Gallagher's/K	97
Dennis Pharmacy/K	95	Gallery Grille/P	178
Diego's	37	Ganim's/K	97
Dining Room at Little Palm/K	95	Garcia's	41
Disco Fish	37	Geronimos/B	133
Dogma	37	Gianni's/B	133
Don Ramon's/P	175	Gibby's Steaks/B	134
Doraku	37	GiGi's Tavern/P	178
Duffy's Steak & Lobster/K	96	Gil Capa's Bistro	42
Dune Deck Cafe/P	176	Ginger Wok/P	178
Duval Beach Club/K	96	Giorgio's Grill/B	134
East City Grill/B	131	Globe Cafe & Bar	42
Echo/P	176	Gordon Biersch Brewery	42
Edelweiss	37	Gotham City/P	178
Eduardo de San Angel/B	131	Grand Café Key West/K	98
811 Bourbon Street/B	132	Grandma's French Cafe/B	134
Eilat Cafe/P	176	Granny Feelgood's	42
El Colonial/P	176	Grappa	42
11 Maple Street/P	177	Grass Lounge	43
11th St. Diner	38	Graziano's	43
Elia	38	Grazie Cafe	43
El Novillo	38	Greek Island Taverna/B	134
El Rancho Grande	38	Green Street Cafe	43
El Siboney/K	96	Green Turtle Inn/K	98
El Toro Taco	38	Green's Pharmacy/P	179
E.R. Bradley's Saloon/P	177	Grille, The/P	179
Escopazzo	38	Grillfish	43
Falcon House/P	177	Grill Room/B	134
Fancy's	39	Guayacan	44
Ferdo's Grill/B	132	Gus' Grille/K	98
15th St. Fisheries/B	132	Half Shell Raw Bar/K	98
Finnegan's Wake Irish Pub/K	96	Hamburger Heaven/P	179
Fish 54	39	Hanna's Gourmet Diner	44
Fish House/K	96	Hard Rock Cafe	44
Fish Joynt	39	Hard Rock Cafe/K	98
Flagler Grill/P	177	Harry and the Natives/P	179
Flagler's/K	97	Havana/P	179
Flagler Steakhouse/P	177	Havana Harry's	44
Flamingo	39	Henry's/P	180

Alphabetical Page Index

Herbie's/K	98	Kaiyó/K	100
Here Comes the Sun	44	Kampai	48
Hi-Life Cafe/B	135	Kathy's Gazebo Cafe/P	182
Himmarshee/B	135	Kebab Indian	48
Hiro Japanese	45	Kee Grill/P	182
Hobo's Fish Joint/B	135	Kelly's Caribbean/K	100
Hog's Breath Saloon/K	99	Keys Fisheries/K	100
Hollywood Prime/B	135	Khoury's	48
Hong Kong City BBQ/B	136	Kyoto Sushi/P	182
Hops/B	136	Kyung Ju	48
Hops/P	180	La Barraca/B	139
Hosteria Romana	45	La Belle Epoque/P	183
Hot Tin Roof/K	99	La Brochette Bistro/B	139
House of India	45	La Carreta	48
Houston's	45	La Carreta/B	139
Houston's/B	136	La Casita	49
Houston's/P	180	La Creperie/B	140
Hurricane Café/P	180	La Dorada	49
Hurricane Grill/K	99	La Fonda Del Sol/P	183
Hy-Vong	45	La Gastronomia	49
I & J's Station House/P	180	Lake Avenue Grill/P	183
Icebox Café	45	La Loggia	49
Ichiban/B	136	La Lupa di Roma	50
Ichiban/P	181	Lan	50
Il Fico	46	Lana's Cafe/P	183
Il Mulino/B	136	L'Anjou/P	183
Il Sole	46	La Palma	50
Il Toscano/B	137	La Paloma	50
Il Trullo/P	181	La Petite Maison/P	184
Imlee	46	Lario's on the Beach	50
India House/B	137	La Sandwicherie	51
Indigo/B	137	Las Culebrinas	51
Islamorada Fish/B	137	La Spada's Hoagies/B	140
Islamorada Fish/K	99	Las Vacas Gordas	51
Islas Canarias	46	Las Vegas/B	140
Jackson's Steakhouse/B	137	La Tavernetta/B	140
Jake's Bar and Grill	46	Latin American	51
Jalapeños/B	137	La Trattoria/K	100
J. Alexander's/B	138	La Trattoria/P	184
J. Alexander's/P	181	La Tre/P	184
Japanese Village/B	138	Laurenzo's Cafe	51
Jasmine Thai/B	138	La Valentina	52
JB's on the Beach/B	138	L'Avenue/P	184
Jetty's/P	181	La Vie en Rose Cafe/B	140
Jimmy Buffett's/K	99	La Vieille Maison/P	184
Joe Allen	47	La Villetta/P	185
Joe's Crab Shack/B	138	Lazy Loggerhead Café/P	185
Joe's Riverside Grille/B	139	Le Bouchon du Grove	52
Joe's Seafood	47	Le Brittany/P	185
Joe's Stone Crab	47	Le Cafe de Paris/B	141
Johannes/P	181	Le Festival*Casa Vecchia	52
John Bull English Pub/P	181	Legal Sea Foods/B	141
John G's/P	182	Legal Sea Foods/P	185
John Martin's	47	Leigh Ann's Coffee/K	100
Josef's/B	139	Le Mistral/P	185
Jumbo's	47	Le Mont/P	185
Juno Beach Fish/P	182	Lemon Twist	52

vote at zagat.com

Alphabetical Page Index

L'Entrecôte de Paris	52	Matsuri	57
Leopard Lounge/P	186	Max & Eddie's Cucina/P	189
Le Provençal	53	Max's Beach Place/B	143
L'Escalier/P	186	Max's Grille/B	143
Les Deux Fontaines	53	Max's Grille/P	189
Les Halles	53	Maxwell's Chophouse/P	189
Lester's Diner/B	141	McCarty's/P	189
Le Vieux Paris/P	186	Melody Inn	57
Lila's	53	Melting Pot	57
Lincoln Road Café	53	Melting Pot/B	143
Linda B. of Boca Raton/P	186	Melting Pot/P	190
Linda B. Steakhouse	53	Meteor Smokehouse/K	102
Little Havana	54	Metro Kitchen + Bar	57
Little Italy/K	101	Mezzanotte	57
Little Moirs Food Shack/P	186	Mezzanotte/B	143
Little Saigon	54	Miami Juice	57
Locanda Sibilla	54	Michaels/K	103
Lombardi's	54	Michael's Kitchen/B	143
Lorelei/K	101	Mississippi Sweets BBQ/P	190
Los Ranchos	54	Miss Saigon Bistro	58
Louie Louie/B	141	Miyako	58
Louie Louie/P	187	Molina's	58
Louie's Backyard/K	101	Mondo's/P	190
Lucca/P	187	Monte's Fish Market/K	103
Luna Pazza/P	187	Montezuma/P	190
Macaluso's	55	Monty's Stone Crab	58
Madras Café/B	141	Monty's Stone Crab/P	190
Maggiano's Little Italy/P	187	Morada Bay Beach/K	103
Magnum	55	Moroccan Nights	58
Maguire's Hill 16/B	142	Morton's	59
Mai-Kai/B	142	Morton's/P	191
Maiko	55	Mo's/K	103
Maison Carlos/P	187	Mrs. Mac's Kitchen/K	103
Mama Jennie's	55	Mrs. Mendoza's	59
Mama Vieja	55	Mrs. Smokey's BBQ/P	191
Mangia Mangia/K	101	Mykonos	59
Mangoes/K	101	Mykonos/P	191
Mangos/B	142	Nami/B	143
Mango's Tropical Cafe	56	Nando's Beefeeder's/P	191
Mangrove Mama's/K	102	Nemo	59
Manny & Isa's/K	102	New Chinatown	59
Marcello's La Sirena/P	187	News Cafe	59
Marc's Chophouse/P	188	New York Prime/P	191
Mario's of Boca/P	188	Nexxt Cafe	60
Mario's Tuscan Grill/P	188	Nicola Seafood/K	104
Mario the Baker	56	Nikki Beach	60
Mario the Baker/B	142	Nina	60
Mariposa	56	Nirvana/P	192
Marker 88/K	102	No Anchovies!/P	192
Mark's at the Park/P	188	Nobu Miami Beach	60
Mark's CityPlace/P	189	No Name Pub/K	104
Mark's Las Olas/B	142	Norman's	60
Mark's South Beach	56	Novecento	61
Maroosh	56	Oasis Cafe	61
Martha's/K	102	Off the Vine/P	192
Martha's Supper Club/B	142	Oggi Caffe	61
Martin's Cafe/K	102	O'Hara's Hollywood/B	144

280 subscribe to zagat.com

Alphabetical Page Index

Okeechobee Steak/P 192	Pierre's/K 106
Old Cutler Inn 61	Pilar 67
Old Cutler Oyster Co. 61	Pineapple Grille/P 195
Old Florida Seafood/B 144	Pino's 67
Old Key Lime House/P 192	Piola 67
Old Lisbon 62	Pisces/K 106
Old San Juan 62	Pit Bar-B-Q 68
Old Tavernier/K 104	Pizza Girls Pizza/P 195
Old Town Mexican/K 104	Pizza Rustica 68
One Duval/K 104	Pizza Rustica/B 145
One Ninety 62	Porção 68
Opera Italian/K 104	Porky's Bayside/K 106
Orchids of Siam/P 193	Portofino's/P 195
Origami/K 105	Pranzo/P 196
Original Daily Bread 62	Prezzo 68
Ortanique on the Mile 62	Prezzo/P 196
Osteria del Teatro 63	Primavera/B 145
Out of Denmark/P 193	Prime Grill 68
Outback Steakhouse 63	Provence Grill 69
Outback Steakhouse/B 144	PT's Late Night/K 106
Outback Steakhouse/K 105	Puccini & Pasta 69
Outback Steakhouse/P 193	Puerto Sagua 69
Ouzo's Greek Taverna & Bar . . 63	Punjab Palace 69
Pacific Time 63	Quay, The/K 106
Paddy Mac's/P 193	Quinn's 69
Padrino's/B 144	Rainbow Palace/B 145
Padrino's/P 193	Raindancer Steakhouse/P . 196
Painted Horse Café/P 193	Raja 70
Palm 63	Randazzo's Little Italy 70
Palm Beach Fish/P 194	Redfire Grill/P 196
Palm Beach Grill/P 194	Redfish Bluefish/B 145
Palme d'Or 64	Red Coral/B 145
Paninoteca 64	Red Fish Grill 70
Panya Thai 64	Red Lantern 70
Pao 64	Red Thai Room 70
Papa Joe's Landmark/K 105	Reef Grill/P 196
Papa's/K 105	Regalo/B 145
Paquito's 64	Renaisa 70
Park Ave. BBQ/P 194	Renato's/P 197
Pascal's on Ponce 65	Renzo's of Boca/P 197
Paulo Luigi's 65	Restaurant St. Michel 71
Pearl 65	Rhythm Cafe/P 197
Pelican Café 65	Riggin's Crabhouse/P 197
Pellegrino's/B 144	Ristorante La Bussola 71
Pepe's Cafe & Steak/K 105	River House/B 146
Peppy's in the Gables 65	River House/P 197
Perricone's 66	River Oyster Bar 71
Pescado 66	Roadhouse Grill 71
Peter's Stone Crabs/P 194	Roadhouse Grill/B 146
Pete's Boca Raton/P 195	Roasted Pepper/B 146
P.F. Chang's 66	Romano's Mac. Grill 71
P.F. Chang's/P 195	Romano's Mac. Grill/B 146
Piccadilly Cafeteria 66	Romano's Mac. Grill/P 198
Piccadilly Cafeteria/B 144	Romeo's Cafe 72
Piccadilly Cafeteria/P 195	Rosinella 72
Piccadilly Garden 67	Rottie's/P 198
Picnics at Allen's Drugs 67	Ruen Thai 72

vote at zagat.com

Alphabetical Page Index

Ruggero's/B 146	Snook's Bayside/K. 108
Rumi. .72	Solo Trattoria/B 149
Runyon's/B 147	Sopra/P 200
Rustic Inn Crabhouse/B 147	Sorrento/P 200
Rusty Anchor/K 107	Soyka 76
Rusty Pelican 72	Spiga 76
Ruth's Chris. 73	Splendid Blendeds/P 201
Ruth's Chris/B. 147	Splendido 76
Ruth's Chris/P. 198	Sport Cafe. 76
Sage French Cafe/B 147	Spoto's Oyster Bar/P. 201
Saigon Sun/P 198	Spoto's PGA/P 201
Saigon Tokyo/P 198	Spris .77
Sailfish Marina/P. 198	Square One/K. 108
Sakana/B 147	Squid Row/K. 108
Sakura. 73	Stefano's. 77
Salute/K. 107	Stresa/P 201
Samba Room/B 147	Sublime/B 150
Sandbar & Grill/P. 199	Sugar Reef/B 150
S&S Restaurant. 73	Suite 225/P 201
San Loco. 73	Sundays on the Bay 77
San Loco/B 148	Sundowners on the Bay/K. . .109
Sapori/P 199	Sunfish Grill/B 150
Sara's. 73	Sunset Grill/P. 202
Satine/B 148	Sunset Tavern 77
Savanna's PB/P 199	Sunshine & AJ's 77
Schooner's Seafood/P 199	Sushi Maki 78
Scopa/B 148	Su Shin 78
Scotty's Landing. 73	Su Shin/B 150
Seafood World/B 148	Sushi Rock Cafe 78
Seaside Meeting Place/P. . . .199	Sushi Rok/P 202
Seawatch/B 148	Sushi Saigon 78
Señor Frijoles/K 107	SushiSamba dromo. 78
Señor Frog's 74	Sushi Siam 79
Sergio's 74	Swiss Chalet/B 150
Seven Fish/K. 107	Swiss Chalet/P. 202
Seven Mile Grill/K 107	Tabica Grill/P 202
Sheldon's 74	Ta-boo/P 202
Shibui. 74	Taco Rico Tex-Mex 79
Shirttail Charlie's/B 149	Talula. 79
Shoji. .74	Tambo Restaurant. 79
Shooters Waterfront Cafe/B . .149	Tango Grill 79
Shorty's Barbecue. 75	Tantra 80
Shorty's Barbecue/B. 149	TapTap Haitian. 80
Shula's on the Beach/B 149	Tarantella/B 151
Shula's on the Beach/K 108	Tarpon Bend/B. 151
Shula's Steak 75	Tasti D-Lite 80
Shula's Steak House/P 199	Taverna Opa. 80
Siam Cuisine/B. 149	Taverna Opa/B. 151
Siam Gourmet/P. 200	Tequila Sunrise 80
Siam Lotus Room. 75	Testa's/P 203
Siam Palace 75	Teté Restaurant. 80
Silver Pond/B 149	Texas Taco Factory. 81
Sinclair's Ocean Grill/P. 200	Thai Cuisine/K 109
Sloppy Joe's Bar/K 108	Thai House South Beach. . . .81
Smith & Wollensky 76	Thai House II 81
Snapper's/K 108	Thai Orchid. 81
Snappers/P. 200	Thai Spice/B. 151

Alphabetical Page Index

Thai Toni	81
3030 Ocean/B	151
32 East/P	203
Time Out Barbecue/K	109
Timo	82
Timpano/B	152
Tin Muffin Café/P	203
Tiramesu	82
Titanic Brewery	82
Tobacco Road	82
Tokyo Bowl	82
Tokyo Bowl/B	152
Tokyo Sushi/B	152
Tom Jenkins BBQ/B	152
Tom's Place/P	203
Toni's Sushi Bar	82
Tony Chan's	83
Tony Roma's	83
Tony Roma's/B	152
Tony Roma's/P	203
Too Bizaare/P	204
Too Jay's Deli/P	204
Torero	83
Touch	83
Trattoria Luna	84
Trattoria Sole	84
Trevini/P	204
Tropical Acres/B	153
Tropical Bistro/P	204
Tropical Chinese	84
Tsunami/P	205
Tumi/B	153
Tuna's Waterfront	84
Turtle Kraals/K	109
Tuscan Steak	84
Tutto Pasta	85
Tutto Pizza	85
1200 at the Biltmore	85
1220 at the Tides	85
Two Chefs	85
Two Dragons	86
Two Friends Patio/K	109
Two Sisters	86
264 the Grill/P	205
Uncle Tai's/P	205
Van Dyke Cafe	86
Vangelli's Taverna/P	205
Versailles	86
Victoria Park/B	153
Vizio Cafe	86
Wan's Sushi/B	153
Whale Harbor Inn/K	110
Whale's Rib/B	153
White Lion Cafe	87
Wilt Chamberlain's/P	205
Wine Cellar/B	153
Wings 'N Things/B	154
Wish	87
Wolfgang Puck/B	154
World Resources	87
Yambo	87
Yasuko's	87
Yesterday's/B	154
Yeung's Chinese	88
Yuca	88
Zemi/P	206
Ziggie's/K	110
Zuperpollo	88

Wine Vintage Chart

This chart is designed to help you select wine to go with your meal. It is based on the same 0 to 30 scale used throughout this *Survey*. The ratings (prepared by our friend **Howard Stravitz**, a law professor at the University of South Carolina) reflect both the quality of the vintage and the wine's readiness for present consumption. Thus, if a wine is not fully mature or is over the hill, its rating has been reduced. We do not include 1987, 1991–1993 vintages because they are not especially recommended for most areas. A dash indicates that a wine is either past its peak or too young to rate.

	'85	'86	'88	'89	'90	'94	'95	'96	'97	'98	'99	'00	'01	'02
WHITES														
French:														
Alsace	24	18	22	28	28	26	25	24	24	26	24	26	27	–
Burgundy	26	25	–	24	22	–	29	28	24	23	25	24	21	–
Loire Valley	–	–	–	–	24	–	20	23	22	–	24	25	23	–
Champagne	28	25	24	26	29	–	26	27	24	24	25	25	26	–
Sauternes	21	28	29	25	27	–	21	23	26	24	24	24	28	–
California (Napa, Sonoma, Mendocino):														
Chardonnay	–	–	–	–	–	–	25	21	25	24	24	22	26	–
Sauvignon Blanc/Semillon	–	–	–	–	–	–	–	–	–	25	25	23	27	–
REDS														
French:														
Bordeaux	24	25	24	26	29	22	26	25	23	25	24	27	24	–
Burgundy	23	–	21	24	27	–	26	28	25	22	28	22	20	24
Rhône	25	19	27	29	29	24	25	23	24	28	27	26	25	–
Beaujolais	–	–	–	–	–	–	–	–	–	22	21	24	25	18	20
California (Napa, Sonoma, Mendocino):														
Cab./Merlot	26	26	–	21	28	29	27	25	28	23	26	23	26	–
Pinot Noir	–	–	–	–	–	26	23	23	25	24	26	25	27	–
Zinfandel	–	–	–	–	–	25	22	23	21	22	24	–	25	–
Italian:														
Tuscany	26	–	24	–	26	22	25	20	29	24	28	26	25	–
Piedmont	26	–	26	28	29	–	23	27	27	25	25	26	23	–

Ready for your next course?

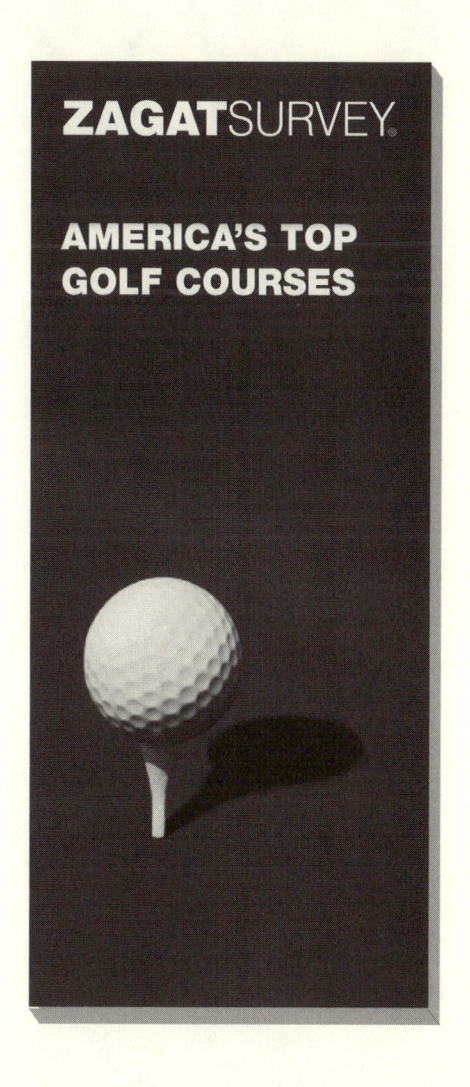

ZAGATSURVEY®

AMERICA'S TOP GOLF COURSES

America's Top Golf Courses includes ratings and reviews by avid golfers. Besides telling you what the courses and facilities are like, we'll tell you how much you'll pay and even how well you'll eat.

Available wherever books are sold, at zagat.com or by calling 888-371-5440.